Norton Commando

☆ ☆ ☆ ☆ ☆

Ultimate Portfolio

Compiled by R M Clarke

ISBN 9781855205703

BROOKLANDS BOOKS LTD.
P.O. BOX 146, COBHAM,
SURREY, KT11 1LG. UK
sales@brooklands-books.com

Brooklands Books

MOTORING

B.B. ROAD TEST SERIES

Abarth Gold Portfolio 1950-1971
AC Ace & Aceca 1953-1983
Alfa Romeo Giulietta Gold Portfolio 1954-1965
Alfa Romeo Giulia Coupés 1963-1976
Alfa Romeo Giulia Coupés Gold Port. 1963-1976
Alfa Romeo Spider 1966-1990
Alfa Romeo Spider Gold Portfolio 1966-1991
Alfa Romeo Alfasud 1972-1984
Alfa Romeo Alfetta Gold Portfolio 1972-1987
Alfa Romeo Alfetta GTV6 1980-1986
Alvis Gold Portfolio 1919-1967
AMX & Javelin Muscle Portfolio 1968-1974
Armstrong Siddeley Gold Portfolio 1945-1960
Aston Martin Gold Portfolio 1948-1971
Aston Martin Gold Portfolio 1972-1985
Aston Martin Gold Portfolio 1985-1995
Audi Quattro Gold Portfolio 1980-1991
Audi Quattro Takes On The Competition
Austin A30 & A35 1951-1962
Austin-Healey 100 & 100/6 Gold Port. 1952-1959
Austin-Healey 3000 Ultimate Portfolio 1959-1967
Austin-Healey Sprite Gold Portfolio 1958-1971
Berkeley Sportscars Limited Edition
BMW 6 & 8 Cyl. Cars Limited Edition 1935-1960
BMW 1600 Collection No. 1 1966-1981
BMW 2002 Gold Portfolio 1968-1976
BMW 6 Cylinder Coupés & Saloons Gold P. 1969-1976
BMW 316, 318, 320 (4 cyl.) Gold Port. 1975-1990
BMW 320, 323, 325 (6 cyl.) Gold Port. 1977-1990
BMW 3 Series Gold Portfolio 1991-1997
BMW 5 Series Gold Portfolio 1981-1987
BMW 5 Series Gold Portfolio 1988-1995
BMW 6 Series Gold Portfolio 1976-1989
BMW 7 Series Performance Portfolio 1977-1986
BMW 8 Series Limited Edition
BMW Alpina Performance Portfolio 1967-1987
BMW Alpina Performance Portfolio 1988-1998
BMW M Series Gold Portfolio 1976-1997
BMW Z3 & Z3M Limited Edition
Borgward Isabella Limited Edition
Bricklin Gold Portfolio 1974-1975
Bristol Cars Portfolio
Buick Performance Portfolio 1947-1962
Buick Muscle Portfolio 1963-1973
Buick Riviera Performance Portfolio 1963-1978
Cadillac Allanté 1986-1993
Cadillac Automobiles 1949-1959
Cadillac Automobiles 1960-1969
Cadillac Eldorado Performance Portfolio 1967-1978
Checker Limited Edition
Chevrolet 1955-1957
Impala & SS Muscle Portfolio 1958-1972
Corvair Performance Portfolio 1959-1969
El Camino & SS Muscle Portfolio 1959-1987
Chevy II & Nova SS Muscle Portfolio 1962-1974
Chevelle & SS Muscle Portfolio 1964-1972
Caprice Limited Edition 1965-1976
Chevrolet Muscle Cars 1966-1971
Chevy Blazer 1969-1981
Camaro Muscle Portfolio 1967-1973
High Performance Camaros 1982-1988
Camaro Performance Portfolio 1993-2000
Chevrolet Corvette Gold Portfolio 1953-1962
Chevrolet Corvette Sting Ray Gold Port. 1963-1967
Chevrolet Corvette Gold Portfolio 1968-1977
High Performance Corvettes 1983-1989
Chrysler 300 Gold Portfolio 1955-1970
Valiant 1960-1962
Citroen Traction Avant Gold Portfolio 1934-1957
Citroen 2CV Ultimate Portfolio 1948-1990
Citroen DS & ID 1955-1975
Citroen DS & ID Gold Portfolio 1955-1975
Shelby Cobra Gold Portfolio 1962-1969
Cobras & Cobra Replicas Gold Portfolio 1962-1989
Crosley & Crosley Specials Limited Edition
Cunningham Automobiles 1951-1955
Datsun Roadsters Performance Portfolio 1960-71
Datsun 240Z & 260Z Gold Portfolio 1970-1978
Datsun 280Z & ZX 1975-1983
DeLorean Gold Portfolio 1977-1995
De Soto Limited Edition 1952-1960
Charger Muscle Portfolio 1966-1974
Dodge Viper Performance Portfolio 1990-1998
ERA Gold Portfolio 1934-1994
Facel Vega 1954-1964
Ferrari Limited Edition 1947-1957
Ferrari Limited Edition 1958-1963
Ferrari Dino 308 & Mondial Gold Portfolio 1974-1985
Ferrari 328 348 Mondial Ultimate Portfolio 1986-94
Fiat 500 Gold Portfolio 1936-1972
Fiat 600 & 850 Gold Portfolio 1955-1972
Fiat Pininfarina 124 & 2000 Spider 1968-1985
Fiat X1/9 Gold Portfolio 1973-1989
Fiat Abarth Performance Portfolio 1972-1987
Ford Consul, Zephyr, Zodiac Mk. I & II 1950-1962
Ford Zephyr, Zodiac, Executive Mk. III & IV 1962-1971
Ford Cortina 1600E & GT 1967-1970
High Performance Capris Gold Portfolio 1969-1987
Capri Muscle Portfolio 1974-1987
High Performance Fiestas 1979-1991
Ford Escort RS & Mexico Limited Edition 1970-1979
High Performance Escorts Mk. I 1968-1974
High Performance Escorts Mk. II 1975-1980
High Performance Escorts 1980-1985
High Performance Escorts 1985-1990
High Perf. Sierras & Merkurs Gold Port. 1983-1990
Ford Thunderbird Performance Portfolio 1955-1957
Ford Thunderbird Performance Portfolio 1958-1963
Ford Thunderbird Performance Portfolio 1964-1976
Ford Automobiles 1949-1959
Ford Fairlane Performance Portfolio 1955-1970
Ford Ranchero Muscle Portfolio 1957-1979
Edsel Limited Edition 1957-1960
Falcon Performance Portfolio 1960-1970
Ford Galaxie & LTD Limited Edition 1960-1973
Ford GT40 Gold Portfolio 1964-1987
Ford Torino Limited Edition 1968-1974
Ford Bronco 4x4 Performance Portfolio 1966-1977
Ford Bronco 1978-1988
Goggomobil Limited Edition
Holden 1948-1962
Honda S500 • S600 • S800 Limited Edition 1962-1970
Honda CRX 1983-1987
International Scout Gold Portfolio 1961-1980
Isetta Gold Portfolio 1953-1964
ISO & Bizzarrini Gold Portfolio 1962-1974
Jaguar and SS Gold Portfolio 1931-1951
Jaguar C-Type & D-Type Gold Portfolio 1951-1960
Jaguar XK120, 140, 150 Gold Portfolio 1948-1960
Jaguar Mk. VII, VIII, IX, X, 420 Gold Port. 1950-1970
Jaguar Mk. 1 & Mk. 2 Gold Portfolio 1959-1969
Jaguar E-Type Gold Portfolio 1961-1971
Jaguar E-Type V-12 1971-1975
Jaguar S-Type & 420 Limited Edition 1963-1968
Jaguar XJ12, XJ5.3, V12 Gold Portfolio 1972-1990
Jaguar XJ6 Series I & II Gold Portfolio 1968-1979
Jaguar XJ6 Series III Perf. Portfolio 1979-1986
Jaguar XJ6 Gold Portfolio 1986-1994
Jaguar XJS Gold Portfolio 1975-1988
Jaguar XJ-S V12 Ultimate Portfolio 1988-1996
Jaguar XK8 Limited Edition
Jeep CJ-5 & CJ-6 1960-1976
Jeep CJ-5 & CJ-7 4x4 Perf. Portfolio 1976-1986
Jeep Wagoneer Performance Portfolio 1963-1991
Jeep J-Series Pickups 1970-1982
Jeepster & Commando Limited Edition 1967-1973
Jeep Cherokee & Comanche Pickups P. P. 1984-91
Jeep Wrangler 4x4 Performance Portfolio 1987-99
Jeep Cherokee & Grand Cherokee 4x4 P. P. 1992-98
Jensen Interceptor Gold Portfolio 1966-1986
Jensen - Healey Limited Edition 1972-1976
Kaiser - Frazer Limited Edition 1946-1955
Lagonda Gold Portfolio 1919-1964
Lancia Aurelia & Flaminia Gold Portfolio 1950-1970
Lancia Fulvia Gold Portfolio 1963-1976
Lancia Beta Gold Portfolio 1972-1984
Lancia Stratos 1972-1985
Lancia Delta & integrale Ultimate Portfolio
Land Rover Series I 1948-1958
Land Rover Series II & IIa 1958-1971
Land Rover Series III 4x4 Perf. Portfolio 1971-1985
Land Rover 90 110 Defender Gold Portfolio 1983-1994
Land Rover Discovery Perf. Port. 1989-2000
Land Rover Story Part One 1948-1971
Fifty Years of Selling Land Rover
Lincoln Gold Portfolio 1949-1960
Lincoln Continental Performance Portfolio 1961-1969
Lincoln Continental 1969-1976
Lotus Sports Racers Portfolio - covering 1951-1965
Lotus Seven Gold Portfolio 1957-1973
Lotus Elite Limited Edition 1957-1964
Lotus Elan Ultimate Portfolio 1962-1974
Lotus Elan & SE 1989-1992
Lotus Europa Gold Portfolio 1966-1975
Lotus Elite & Eclat 1974-1982
Lotus Elise Limited Edition
Marcos Coupés & Spyders Gold Portfolio 1960-1997
Matra Limited Edition 1965-1983
Mazda Miata MX-5 Performance Portfolio 1989-1997
Mazda Miata MX-5 Takes On The Competition
Mazda RX-7 Gold Portfolio 1978-1991
McLaren F1 Sportscar Limited Edition
Mercedes 190 & 300 SL 1954-1963
Mercedes G-Wagen 1981-1994
Mercedes S & 600 1965-1972
Mercedes S Class 1972-1979
Mercedes 230 • 250 • 280SL Gold Portfolio 1963-1971
Mercedes SLs & SLCs Gold Portfolio 1971-1989
Mercedes SLs Performance Portfolio 1989-1994
Mercedes 190 Limited Edition Extra 1983-1993
Mercedes CLK & SLK Limited Edition
Mercury Limited Edition 1947-1959
Mercury Comet & Cyclone Limited Edition 1960-1970
Cougar Limited Edition 1967-1973
Messerschmitt Gold Portfolio 1954-1964
MG Gold Portfolio 1929-1939
MG TA & TC Gold Portfolio 1936-1949
MG TD & TF Gold Portfolio 1949-1955
MGA & Twin Cam Gold Portfolio 1955-1962
MG Midget Gold Portfolio 1961-1979
MGB Roadsters 1962-1980
MGB MGC & V8 Gold Portfolio 1962-1980
MGB GT 1965-1980
MGC & MGB GT V8 Limited Edition
MG Y-Type & Magnette ZA/ZB Limited Edition
MGF Limited Edition
Mini Gold Portfolio 1959-1969
Mini Gold Portfolio 1969-1980
Mini Gold Portfolio 1981-1997
High Performance Minis Gold Portfolio 1960-1973
Mini Cooper Gold Portfolio 1961-1971
Mini Moke Gold Portfolio 1964-1994
Morgan Three-Wheeler Gold Portfolio 1910-1952
Morgan Plus 4 & Four 4 Gold Portfolio 1936-1967
Morris Minor Collection No. 1 1948-1980
Shelby Mustang Muscle Portfolio 1965-1970
Mustang Muscle Portfolio 1967-1973
High Performance Mustang IIs 1974-1978
Mustang 5.0L Muscle Portfolio 1982-1993
Mustang 5.0L Takes On The Competition
Nash & Nash-Healey Limited Edition 1949-1957
Nash-Austin Metropolitan Gold Portfolio 1954-1962
NSU Ro80 Limited Edition
NSX Performance Portfolio 1989-1999
Oldsmobile Automobiles 1955-1963
Oldsmobile Muscle Portfolio 1964-1971
Cutlass & 4-4-2 Muscle Portfolio 1964-1974
Oldsmobile Toronado 1966-1978
Opel GT Gold Portfolio 1968-1973
Opel Manta Limited Edition 1970-1975
Packard Gold Portfolio 1946-1958
Pantera Gold Portfolio 1970-1989
Panther Gold Portfolio 1972-1990
Barracuda Muscle Portfolio 1964-1974
Pontiac Limited Edition 1949-1960
Pontiac Tempest & GTO 1961-1965
GTO Muscle Portfolio 1964-1974
Firebird & Trans-Am Muscle Portfolio 1967-1972
Firebird & Trans-Am Muscle Portfolio 1973-1981
High Performance Firebirds 1982-1988
Firebird & Trans Am Performance Portfolio 1993-2000
Pontiac Fiero Performance Portfolio 1984-1988
Porsche 356 Gold Portfolio 1953-1965
Porsche 912 Limited Edition
Porsche 911 1965-1969
Porsche 911 1970-1972
Porsche 911 1973-1977
Porsche 911 SC & Turbo Gold Portfolio 1978-1983
Porsche 911 Carrera & Turbo Gold Port. 1984-1989
Porsche 911 Gold Portfolio 1990-1997
Porsche 911 Takes On The Competition 1990-1997
Porsche 914 Ultimate Portfolio
Porsche 924 Gold Portfolio 1975-1988
Porsche 928 Performance Portfolio 1977-1994
Porsche 928 Takes On The Competition
Porsche 944 Ultimate Portfolio
Porsche 968 Limited Edition
Porsche Boxster Limited Edition
Railton & Brough Superior Gold Portfolio 1933-1950
Range Rover Gold Portfolio 1970-1985
Range Rover Gold Portfolio 1985-1995
Range Rover Takes on the Competition
Reliant Scimitar 1964-1986
Renault Alpine Gold Portfolio 1958-1994
Riley Gold Portfolio 1924-1939
R. R. Silver Cloud & Bentley 'S' Series Gold P. 1955-65
Rolls Royce Silver Shadow Ultimate Portfolio 1965-80
Rolls Royce & Bentley Gold Portfolio 1980-1989
Rolls Royce & Bentley Limited Edition 1990-1997
Rover P4 1949-1959
Rover 3 & 3.5 Litre Gold Portfolio 1958-1973
Rover 2000 & 2200 1963-1977
Rover 3500 & Vitesse 1976-1986
Saab Sonett Collection No.1 1966-1974
Saab Turbo 1976-1983
Studebaker Gold Portfolio 1947-1966
Studebaker Hawks & Larks 1956-1963
Avanti 1962-1990
Starion & Conquest Performance Portfolio 1982-90
Suzuki SJ Gold Portfolio 1971-1997
Vitara, Sidekick & Geo Tracker Perf. Port. 1988-1997
Sunbeam Tiger & Alpine Gold Portfolio 1959-1967
Toyota Land Cruiser Gold Portfolio 1956-1987
Toyota Land Cruiser 1988-1997
Toyota MR2 Gold Portfolio 1984-1997
Toyota MR2 Takes On The Competition
Triumph TR2 & TR3 Gold Portfolio 1952-1961
Triumph TR4, TR5, TR250 1961-1968
Triumph TR6 Gold Portfolio 1969-1976
Triumph Herald 1959-1971
Triumph Vitesse 1962-1971
Triumph Spitfire Gold Portfolio 1962-1980
Triumph 2000, 2.5, 2500 1963-1977
Triumph GT6 Gold Portfolio 1966-1974
Triumph Stag Gold Portfolio 1970-1977
Triumph Dolomite Sprint Limited Edition
TVR Gold Portfolio 1959-1986
TVR Performance Portfolio 1986-1994
TVR Performance Portfolio 1995- 2000
VW Beetle Gold Portfolio 1935-1967
VW Beetle Gold Portfolio 1968-1991
VW Beetle Collection No.1 1970-1982
VW Karmann Ghia 1955-1982
VW Bus, Camper, Van 1954-1967
VW Bus, Camper, Van Perf. Portfolio 1968-1979
VW Bus, Camper, Van 1979-1989
VW Scirocco 1974-1981
Volvo PV444 & PV544 1945-1965
Volvo 120 Amazon Ultimate Portfolio
Volvo 1800 Gold Portfolio 1960-1973
Volvo 140 & 160 Series Gold Portfolio 1966-1975
Forty Years of Selling Volvo
Westfield Limited Edition

B.B. ROAD & TRACK SERIES

Road & Track on Alfa Romeo 1964-1970
Road & Track on Alfa Romeo 1971-1976
Road & Track on Aston Martin 1962-1990
Road & Track on Audi & Auto Union 1952-1980
Road & Track on Audi & Auto Union 1980-1986
Road & Track on Austin Healey 1953-1970
Road & Track on BMW Cars 1966-1974
Road & Track on BMW Cars 1975-1978
Road & Track on BMW Cars 1979-1983
R & T on Cobra, Shelby & Ford GT40 1962-1992
Road & Track on Corvette 1953-1967
Road & Track on Corvette 1968-1982
Road & Track on Corvette 1982-1986
Road & Track on Corvette 1986-1990
Road & Track on Ferrari 1975-1981
Road & Track on Ferrari 1981-1984
Road & Track on Ferrari 1984-1988
Road & Track on Fiat Sports Cars 1968-1987
Road & Track on Jaguar 1950-1960
Road & Track on Jaguar 1961-1968
Road & Track on Jaguar 1968-1974
Road & Track on Jaguar 1974-1982
Road & Track on Jaguar 1983-1989
Road & Track on Lamborghini 1964-1985
Road & Track on Lotus 1972-1983
R & T on Mazda RX-7 & MX-5 Miata 1986-1991
Road & Track on Mercedes 1952-1962
Road & Track on Mercedes 1963-1970
Road & Track on Mercedes 1971-1979
Road & Track on Mercedes 1980-1987
Road & Track on MG Sports Cars 1949-1961
Road & Track on MG Sports Cars 1962-1980
R & T on Nissan 300-ZX & Turbo 1984-1989
Road & Track on Pontiac 1960-1983
Road & Track on Porsche 1951-1967
Road & Track on Porsche 1968-1971
Road & Track on Porsche 1972-1975
Road & Track on Porsche 1975-1978
Road & Track on Porsche 1979-1982
Road & Track on Porsche 1985-1988
R & T on Rolls Royce & Bentley 1950-1965
R & T on Rolls Royce & Bentley 1966-1984
Road & Track on Saab 1972-1992
R & T on Toyota Sports & GT Cars 1966-1984
R & T on Triumph Sports Cars 1953-1967
R & T on Triumph Sports Cars 1967-1974
R & T on Triumph Sports Cars 1974-1982
Road & Track on Volkswagen 1951-1968
Road & Track on Volkswagen 1968-1978
Road & Track on Volkswagen 1978-1985
Road & Track on Volvo 1957-1974
Road & Track on Volvo 1977-1994
Road & Track - Henry Manney at Large & Abroad
Road & Track - Best of PS
Road & Track - Peter Egan "At Large"
Road & Track - Peter Egan Side Glances 1983-92
Road & Track - Peter Egan Side Glances 1992-97

B.B. CAR AND DRIVER SERIES

Car and Driver on BMW 1955-1977
Car and Driver on Corvette 1978-1982
Car and Driver on Corvette 1983-1988
C and D on Datsun Z 1600 & 2000 1966-1984
Car and Driver on Ferrari 1955-1962
Car and Driver on Ferrari 1963-1975
Car and Driver on Ferrari 1976-1983
Car and Driver on Mopar 1956-1967
Car and Driver on Mustang 1964-1972
Car and Driver on Pontiac 1961-1975
Car and Driver on Porsche 1955-1962
Car and Driver on Porsche 1963-1970
Car and Driver on Porsche 1970-1976
Car and Driver on Porsche 1977-1981
Car and Driver on Porsche 1982-1986
Car and Driver on Volvo 1955-1986

RACING & THE LAND SPEED RECORD

The Land Speed Record 1898-1919
The Land Speed Record 1920-1929
The Land Speed Record 1930-1939
The Land Speed Record 1940-1962
The Land Speed Record 1963-1999
The Land Speed Record 1898-1999 - Hard Bound
Can-Am Racing 1966-1969
Can-Am Racing 1970-1974
Can-Am Racing Cars 1966-1974
The Carrera Panamericana Mexico - 1950-1954
Le Mans - The Bentley & Alfa Years - 1923-1939
Le Mans - The Jaguar Years - 1949-1957
Le Mans - The Ferrari Years - 1958-1965
Le Mans - The Ford & Matra Years - 1966-1974
Le Mans - The Porsche Years - 1975-1982
Le Mans - The Porsche & Jaguar Years - 1983-91
Le Mans - The Porsche & Peugeot Years - 1992-99
Le Mans - 1923-1999 - Hard Bound
Mille Miglia - The Alfa & Ferrari Years - 1927-1951
Mille Miglia - The Ferrari & Mercedes Years - 1952-57
Targa Florio - The Post War Years - 1948-1973 - H.B.
Targa Florio - The Porsche & Ferrari Years - 1955-1964
Targa Florio - The Porsche Years - 1965-1973

B.B. PRACTICAL CLASSICS SERIES

PC on Austin A40 Restoration
PC on Land Rover Restoration
PC on Midget/Sprite Restoration
PC on MGB Restoration
PC on Sunbeam Rapier Restoration
PC on Triumph Herald/Vitesse

B.B. HOT ROD 'ENGINE' SERIES

Chevy 265 & 283
Chevy 302 & 327
Chevy 348 & 409
Chevy 350 & 400
Chevy 396 & 427
Chevy 454 thru 512
Chrysler Hemi
Chrysler 273, 318, 340 & 360
Chrysler 361, 383, 400, 413, 426 & 440
Ford 289, 302, Boss 302 & 351W
Ford 351C & Boss 351
Ford Big Block

B.B. RESTORATION & GUIDE SERIES

BMW 2002 - A Comprehensive Guide
BMW '02 Restoration Guide
Classic Camaro Restoration
Chevrolet High Performance Tips & Techniques
Chevy Engine Swapping Tips & Techniques
Chevy-GMC Pickup Repair
Engine Swapping Tips & Techniques
Land Rover Restoration Portfolio
MG 'T' Series Restoration Guide
MGA Restoration Guide
Mustang Restoration Tips & Techniques
The Great Classic Muscle Cars Compared

MOTORCYCLING

B.B. ROAD TEST SERIES

AJS & Matchless Gold Portfolio 1945-1966
BMW Motorcycles Gold Portfolio 1950-1971
BMW Motorcycles Gold Portfolio 1971-1976
BSA Singles Gold Portfolio 1945-1963
BSA Singles Gold Portfolio 1964-1974
BSA Twins A7 & A10 Gold Portfolio 1946-1962
BSA Twins A50 & A65 Gold Portfolio 1962-1973
BSA & Triumph Triples Gold Portfolio 1968-1976
Ducati Gold Portfolio 1974-1978
Ducati Gold Portfolio 1978-1982
Harley-Davidson Sportsters Pref. Port. 1965-1976
Harley-Davidson Super Glide Perf. Port. 1971-1981
Harley-Davidson FXR Series Perf. Port. 1982-1992
Honda CB750 Gold Portfolio 1969-1978
Honda CB500 & 550 Fours Perf. Port. 1971-1977
Honda CB350 & 400 Fours Perf. Port. 1972-1978
Honda Gold Wing Gold Portfolio 1975-1995
Honda CBX 1000 Gold Portfolio 1978-1982
Honda RC30 Performance Portfolio 1988-1992
Kawasaki Z1 900 Performance Portfolio 1972-1977
Kawasaki 500 & 750 Triples Perf. Port. 1969-1976
Kawasaki GPZ 900R Ninja Perf. Port. 1984-1996
Laverda Gold Portfolio 1967-1977
Laverda Performance Portfolio 1978-1988
Laverda Jota Performance Portfolio 1976-1985
Moto Guzzi Gold Portfolio 1949-1973
Moto Guzzi Le Mans Performance Portfoio 1976-89
Moto Morini 3½ & 500 Performance Port. 1974-84
Norton Dominators Performance Portfolio 1949-68
Norton Commando Ultimate Portfolio 1968-1977
Norton Rotary's Performance Portfolio 1984-1992
Suzuki GT750 Performance Portfolio 1971-1977
Suzuki GS1000 Performance Portfolio 1978-1981
Triumph Bonneville Gold Portfolio 1959-1983
Vincent Gold Portfolio 1945-1980
Yamaha RD350/400 Performance Portfolio 1972-79
Yamaha XS650 Performance Portfolio 1969-1985

B.B. CYCLE WORLD SERIES

Cycle World on BMW 1974-1980
Cycle World on BMW 1981-1986
Cycle World on Ducati 1982-1991
Cycle World on Harley-Davidson 1978-1983
Cycle World on Harley-Davidson 1983-1987
Cycle World on Harley-Davidson 1987-1990
Cycle World on Harley-Davidson 1990-1992
Cycle World on Honda 1962-1967
Cycle World on Honda 1968-1971
Cycle World on Honda 1971-1974
Cycle World on Husqvarna 1966-1976
Cycle World on Husqvarna 1977-1984
Cycle World on Kawasaki 1966-1971
Cycle World on Kawasaki Off-Road Bikes 1972-1979
Cycle World on Kawasaki Street Bikes 1972-1976
Cycle World on Norton 1962-1971
Cycle World on Suzuki 1962-1970
Cycle World on Suzuki Off-Road Bikes 1971-1976
Cycle World on Suzuki Street Bikes 1971-1976
Cycle World on Triumph 1967-1972
Cycle World on Yamaha 1962-1969
Cycle World on Yamaha Off-Road Bikes 1970-1974
Cycle World on Yamaha Street Bikes 1970-1974

MILITARY

VEHICLES & AEROPLANES

Complete WW2 Military Jeep Manual
Dodge WW2 Military Portfolio 1940-1945
German Military Equipment WW2
Hail To The Jeep
Land Rover Military Portfolio
Military & Civilian Amphibians 1940-1990
Off Road Jeeps Civilian & Military 1944-1971
Silhouette Handbook of US Army Air Forces Aeroplanes
US Military Vehicles 1941-1945
US Army Military Vehicles WW2-TM9-2800
VW Kubelwagen Military Portfolio 1940-1990
WW2 Allied Vehicles Military Portfolio 1939-1945
WW2 Jeep Military Portfolio 1941-1945

20/3Z1

CONTENTS

ACKNOWLEDGEMENTS

Five years ago we started our motorcycle Portfolio series and amongst the first subjects chosen was the Norton Commando. It has turned out to be the most popular title in our motorcycle series so far and recently went out of print. We have decided to upgrade it from a Gold Portfolio to one of our more prestigious Ultimate Portfolios which means that it is now printed on matt art paper and contains a further 36 pages with some in colour. We are currently working on extending our Norton coverage to include books on their rotary models and the Dominator.

To bring some perspective to these books we have invited Jeff Clew to provide an introduction to the motorcycle titles. Jeff with his 'in depth' knowledge of on and off road biking, is a leading authority and has written many books, workshop manuals and magazine features on the subject.

Brooklands Books with more than 400 titles in print owe a tremendous debt to the world's leading motoring journals, as without their help and support this reference series could never have come about. Our thanks are now extended to the owners of the motorcycling magazines listed below who have generously agreed to allow us to include their interesting and copyright stories in this ever expanding series. *Bike, Classic Bike, Classic Bike Guide, Classic Mechanics, Cycle, Cycle Australia, Cycle Guide, Cycle World, Modern Cycle, MotoRetro, Motorcycle Mechanics, Motorcycle Sport, Motorcycling Monthly, Motorcyclist, Motorcyclist Illustrated* and *Two Wheels*.

R.M. Clarke

The engine of the Norton Commando was based on Bert Hopwood's original 497cc design which provided the motive power in the company's first vertical twin. Hopwood had joined Norton Motors in the late 1940s after serving for many years as Edward Turner's assistant when he was employed by Triumph. Aware of what he considered to be several weaknesses inherent in the Triumph twin engine, his own design incorporated means by which he believed they could be overcome successfully.

The mechanical balance of a vertical twin engine in which the pistons rise and fall together is similar to that of a single cylinder engine. However, as the power impulses occur once each revolution they are only half that of a single cylinder engine of similar capacity and the engine runs more smoothly. As Norton Motors would find out, as the capacity of the engine was increased to 600cc, 650cc and then 750cc, vibration became more of a problem. As a result much of the advantage in making a high performance model, such as the 745cc Atlas, is lost and it becomes a less pleasant machine to ride.

The opportunity for a complete rethink occurred after the AMC Group, Norton's owner at the time, collapsed during 1966. The take-over by Manganese Bronze Holdings that followed, resulted in a new Norton development team who utilised the old Atlas engine in a new model. Their approach to overcome the vibration problem was unique. They isolated the engine, gearbox and bearing of the swinging arm rear fork from the frame by mounting the assembly in rubber bushes. Their patented Isolastic suspension really worked too, even if its adjustment was critical. As a direct result the new Norton Commando made its debut at the 1967 Motor Cycle Show, to win *Motor Cycle News* 'Machine of the Year' for five successive years and become Britain's first Superbike.

The Commando continued in production until late 1977, by which time the engine had been increased in capacity to 828cc and an electric starter fitted. Hopwood's engine had stood the test of time for almost 30 years.

Jeff Clew

Commando: The Smoothest big parallel twin I've ridden.

New British machines are such a novelty these days that one grabs the opportunity to "try it round the block" with both hands. One tries to make a clean, smart getaway with no muffing of unaccustomed clutch action before the apprehensive owner can change his mind. Easy on the throttle until out of sight and earshot—and then comes the problem of how long one can decently prolong the ride without causing the owner undue worry. Too short a ride and you can hardly be fair to the reader or the machine, which is why "impressions" are usually unadulterated praise . . . it's safer that way. Too long a ride and the best friendships can be strained. It's usually pouring with rain and you've got no proper kit, either.

In the case of the Norton Commando the circumstances were happier. It was warm and sunny so kit did not matter. This Commando belonged to Freddie Frith, the Grimsby Norton agent (need we add "the first world road-race champion, 350 c.c. class"), and over the years of a long friendship a certain rapport has been established. I have "borrowed" his machines and he has "borrowed" mine and all have been returned in a comfortingly short space of time and in one piece. And from the "impression" point of view the task was not going to be difficult, as it can be with something completely new and 'way out", because many of the essentials of the Commando are familiar. It's just that they are put together in a rather different way .

The overriding question was: "How effective is the rubber mounting of the basically Atlas engine?" The quick answer, arrived at in a few minutes, is "Beyond expectation." Now I do not know what they have done to the engine . . . they must have done quite a bit because it is now very quiet mechanically, inaudible to the rider when in motion and very nearly so when you get down alongside it . . . but the total result is the smoothest, most vibration free big parallel twin I have ever straddled. Not the "remote" electric-motor sensation of the old in-line Sunbeam (nor that machine's slow-speed engine "rock and roll" either), for you can still feel the engine at low speeds. You feel it mostly through your sit upon, not the foot rests or the handlebars, and it is difficult to decide whether it is engine vibration or torque pulsation's in the transmission. For my taste this feel of what is going on, an indication that the engine is not being run at sufficient revolutions to be altogether happy, is preferable to a completely "remote" feel. As the revs rise the "feel" decreases: progressively, not in the sudden way of climbing in and out of engine periods. In simple words the engine gets smoother and smoother as the revs build up. Whether or not there is a period at peak revs I know not. This was a new machine and only a moron would have ill-treated it. But the feeling was that no vibration would intrude no matter how it was "screwed". Nor was there any engine "shudder" from the rubber mountings in slow running or take off. How much this blessed release from the curse of all parallel twins since the very first Speed Twin of 1937 is due to engine balance, the sloping engine, or the rubber mounting, I know not and we may never know. I cannot help feeling a little smug about it for I distinctly remember writing a small piece in these pages a year or two ago suggesting that someone try the effect of (a) mounting a twin on rubber bushes and (b) sloping it considerably in the frame to try and rid us of the dreaded vibration.

Without doing a comparison test alongside a conventional Atlas I would not like to pass too much of an opinion about the power output of the Commando. "Go" is a very difficult thing to evaluate by feel. Roughness suggests brute power, and noise adds to the sensation of performance. The Commando is very quiet mechanically, as I have said, and the exhaust very low toned and inoffensive. Power output and transmission are exceptionally smooth with a "rubber cushioned" feel.

There are, therefore, no side effects to give an impression of speed and power but the Commando does unquestionably "get up and go" and, what is important these days, it can be used without causing offence. I would think, though this is merely impression with no basis of fact, that there is a much wider spread of power with this engine than with its forebears. If there is anything missing from the top end it is surely of purely academic interest, and presumably replaceable by the optional tuning kit.

I suppose the next question is: "How does it handle?" "And what about that pivoted fork anchored to the rubber-mounted engine gearbox sub-unit?" Well, the answer as far as I can say without a track test of severity beyond my humble capabilities is that it handles like a thoroughbred racer. So well that one has no hesitation whatsoever in putting it through a fast left right swerve after but a few moments' acquaintance. The ride is firm for a rider of moderate weight (10 st. 7 Ib.) but quite comfortable and the steering as taut as a bow string. It reminded me of the Dominator 88 of 1954-ish, which I always thought set a new standard in handling. Regrettably I never found later Dominators came up to that standard. I do not consider myself qualified to evaluate steering in the higher reaches of cornering, but a short circuit Manx exponent who has put a Commando through Cadwell's swervery told me he would dearly like to race one, and that's fair enough for me.

The brakes, I thought, were superb. Experience has taught me to try out strange front brakes with one finger, and one finger alone will pin the Commando down. With firm application of the front brake there were no untoward effects, no exaggerated plunging and no fork twist.

The remaining unknown was the diaphragm clutch. It is the first of the breed I have encountered, though I have no doubt that they will eventually become commonplace. On longer acquaintance I would be prepared to say that here we have the perfect clutch. It is feather light yet frees perfectly, it engages smoothly without grab and grips finally with the certainty of a dog clutch. In all those ways it is the perfect clutch, yet because it is so perfect it demands some slight new skill in operation. It has not quite the same feel as the clutches we are used to, the spring pressure seems constant instead of becoming progressively stronger as the lever is pulled, and it is therefore more difficult to judge the point at which it will begin to engage. But using a long acquired technique I have found invaluable with strange clutches . . . the technique of "burning away" with enough revs to make the clutch slip on first engagement instead of clutching hold, with danger of a stall . . . I was able to make satisfactory starts without becoming acclimatized. I cannot express an opinion about ease of starting, slow running and tickover because one plug was "on the blink" and kept cutting out at low revs, but the loss of a cylinder from time to time did not upset the equilibrium of the rubber mounts or cause the unpleasantness it does with a conventional engine mounting .

What of the rest of the machine? Well, that is venturing on tricky ground. The question of personal taste comes into it. I personally think the seat is too high and too wide . . . I had a job to touch the ground, but is it fair to hold Norton Villiers to blame for nature's failure to supply me with long enough legs?

The non adjustable footrests suited my stature, but will not necessarily suit everyone, I fear, and for me the straightest bars were just right for the "Centaur" poise so beloved of road-testers of years gone by . . . a touch of the Vincent safety-fast position. As for the styling of grass-green tank innocent of lining and the tapering tail end of seat and embryo mudguard they're just not me. I can't help trying to visualize it with a Manx style tank in traditional Norton black and silver with a fine red line. Surely the tradition behind the Norton name and styling still means something to motorcyclists? No matter, the customizers will soon produce the necessary styling aids if enthusiasts want the Commando to look like a Norton instead of a slightly space age green monster.

But personal taste apart, Norton Villiers have certainly beaten the vibration bogey and that is one of the most significant break throughs we have had for many a year.

C.E.A

Handlebar layout was quite neat. The rev counter and speedometer placed on either side of headlamp give a well-balanced effect and do not obstruct lighting switch

Tucked away under the tank on finned manifolds, the twin Amals breathe through a large air filter. Rev counter drive is taken from camshaft through timing case

Primary chaincase is designed for easy removal—just undo centre nut and clutch is exposed. Large inspection caps make maintenance simple. Above case is Zener-diode

The twin-leading-shoe front bra has a blanked off air scoop, the blanking plate can be remov for racing conditions. No bra fade under normal conditi

TOUGH BY NAME—& NATURE! CHARLES DEANE TESTS THE NORTON

COMMANDO

▶ **Wide, open roads . . . fast sweeping bends and no speed restrictions! What a marvellous place the Isle of Man is for riding the latest, hottest product from the Norton-Villiers group—the Commando.**

Wherever I stopped on the island during TT week, there was a plague of enthusiasts waiting to ask what seemed a million endless questions. How does it go? Is it as good as they say? What's the top speed? How does it compare with the featherbed?

There's no doubt that the Commando has aroused more interest among the majority of motorcyclists than any other British machine that has come on to the market for some considerable time.

The new frame, the unique engine and transmission mounting system, the diaphragm clutch—all are points which have been developed and used, not because they are different, but because they are better.

Agreed, the motor and gearbox are still basically Atlas components and the front forks are the good, old "Roadholder" type. But there ends all similarity between new and old.

Anybody who has owned or ridden the Norton 650SS or Atlas must agree that one of the most disenchanting qualities is the vibration transmitted from the engine to all corners of the frame.

But what of the Commando? Is there any vibration? Is it as smooth as the Norton men say? Well, after covering close

on a thousand road test miles, I must admit that it is the smoothest, big vertical twin I have yet ridden.

The only way of telling how fast the engine is spinning is to keep an eagle eye on the rev counter. No longer does one change gear by the amount of vibration being transmitted to the frame.

Once the engine has reached 3000 rpm on the rev counter, it becomes turbine-like in operation. Although below 3000 and especially at tick-over, there is low frequency vibration which causes the engine, gearbox *and swinging arm* unit to wobble in the rubber mounting units, which connect the assembly to the frame.

Insulated

Why the swinging arm? The reason is that the swinging arm fork is actually mounted on the engine/gearbox plates, so that the entire engine/transmission components are all isolated from the frame. This, of course, means that the rider is insulated by rubber from all normal engine/transmission vibrations.

However, this doesn't mean to say that the factory have ignored the engine vibration bogey. To help overcome the problem, they have also improved the engine balance factor to 45 per cent.

Power-wise the engine is superb, fab, marvellous, etc. In fact, I could run out of superlatives just talking about the 58 horses which are churned out by the 750 cc Norton. From 2000 rpm upwards

the bike starts to surge forward at an amazing rate and you have to think rapidly about changing gear at 6000 rpm as the rev counter is almost registering 8000 by the time you've turned off the taps and stabbed the machine into the next gear.

The performance figures speak for themselves. Top speed just over 120 mph. A standing 0 to 60 mph in 4.8 sec. isn't exactly hanging about and with a standing quarter of 12.8 sec., you're approaching drag-strip times.

To transmit all this power, the bike must have a pretty robust clutch and with the introduction of the diaphragm unit, they have picked a winner. There is no sign of slip, or drag and this is not really surprising as the diaphragm plate exerts approximately twice the pressure of the normal coil spring pressure plate. And this is without any extra exertion by the rider's left hand.

The clutch frees easily, but is a little fierce on take-up: however, one quickly becomes used to its short, smooth action.

Another of the advantages of the clutch is that it has transformed the Norton gearbox. It is now smooth, and positive in action with barely a click as the gears are swopped.

With so much performance available, it is essential that roadholding and braking are up to scratch. It has been said that the new frame is as rigid and as good as the featherbed.

But, although the handling is good, I personally don't think it quite matches

❝ The engine is superb, fab... ❞

nging arm is adjustable for 1 and gave a comfortable but ride at all times. The Avon tyre gave excellent on wet roads

The footrests were the type that would bend rather than break, but seemed strong enough for the heaviest rider. The stop-light switch is on brake arm

The side panel must be removed to check battery level or capacitor connections. In front of the battery is chain oiler. Capacitor enables running without battery

With the dualseat removed access is gained to the oil tank and toolkit, which tucks neatly away in a hollowed-out rear seat unit. Toolkit supplied was quite good

MM SUPER TEST

the featherbed. At average speeds, the steering is perfect through any bend. But unlike the featherbed, if you really push the Commando hard through a long, fast bend at 90 plus and have cause to shut the throttle, there is a certain amount of whipping. Not serious twitching, but enough to make you open the throttle to regain complete stability.

Braking, with the twin-leading-shoe front brake, is progressive and can only be described as first-class. Whether it was from 90 or 30 miles-an-hour, there was always the feeling that you are in complete control of the machine.

The riding position of the Commando, using the almost straight, British-style bars, was comfortable and there was adequate room for a fair-sized pillion passenger.

But, for high-speed motorcycling, the footrests are too far forward and too low. Above 80 mph, I found that my knees and thigh muscles were aching through constantly gripping the tank to stop myself sliding backwards.

Another complaint, also discovered while using the Commando performance, was lack of ground clearance, especially with two people on board. Quite often I found myself scratching round a bend with the centre stand scraping the ground. And this was in spite of the fact that it was tucked well up beneath the gearbox and quite difficult to hook down for parking.

Once on the ground, the centre stand remained there, and lifting the hefty bike on its rest proved no problem.

On returning from the island, I made use of the Commando as a ride-to-work mount. I found that the engine was very tractable in all gears, although it wasn't really possible to use top gear at less than the legal 30 miles-an-hour without the low frequency vibration being felt on the handlebars and footrests.

In fact, while standing at traffic lights, I discovered that petrol was overflowing from the float chambers due to the whisking that the floats were receiving in their vibrating bowls.

Handling in traffic was reasonable once you were above 10 mph, with the light glass-fibre tank and seat playing their part in keeping the bulk of the weight low down. This provided quicker response to changes of direction on the bike.

My only and constant problem on all but the lightweights is saddle height. With my short legs and the broad, 31 inch high Commando dualseat, I had difficulty in balancing on tip-toe, especially when starting the mighty engine from cold.

I don't believe in straining the centre stand by starting the engine with the bike on the stand. And believe me, when you're five foot nothing, you have to perform marvellous balancing acts to get any big bike started off the stand!

The one advantage with the Commando is its new 12-volt alternator, capacitor ignition system, which provides sparks in plenty—

COMMANDO FRAME DESIGN

DIAPHRAGM MAKE

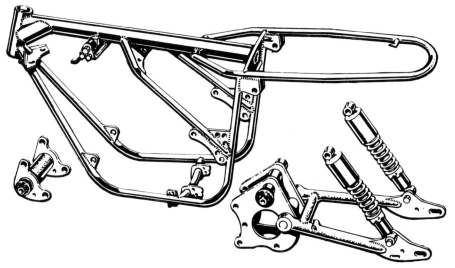

The secret of the ''no vibration'' Norton Commando is in the frame. The engine is mounted in large, rubber couplings at the front of the engine plates, at the rear above the gearbox and at the cylinder headsteady point.

To tame and transmit 58 bhp you need a very strong clutch. Norton-Villiers have overcome the problem with this

have ridden '

even without the battery—to give third kick starting when cold, first time when hot.

The remainder of the electrical system is basically the same as any other big twin on the market. The 12-volt headlamp houses an ammeter and main beam warning light, together with the easily reached pilot and headlight switch. There is also a headlight flasher combined with the windtone horn button and dipswitch on the left-hand handlebar.

Lighting can only be described as good as the majority of 12-volt systems on the road, although with lack of vibration, I think the Commando could well be fitted with the car-type quartz-halogen headlight. This would really improve light power for fast night riding.

Norton-Villiers seem to have spent some considerable time on the detail points of the Commando and although the machine is the most expensive yet to come from a British manufacturer, you get a lot for your money.

The toolkit alone can tackle almost any job except a major stripdown on the bike, while there are other little extras such as the built-in ignition timing disc in the primary chaincase and the rear chain oiler.

Unfortunately, on our particular test model, the chain oiler was a little too liberal and we managed to use just over a pint and a half on the run from Liverpool to London.

But, in spite of the few criticisms, to me it has been one of the most exciting bikes I have ridden for some considerable time.

LIGHT CLUTCH

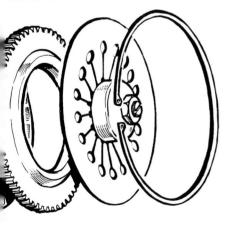

unique diaphragm unit, which exerts double the usual pressure on the plates, but requires no extra effort to operate.

COMMANDO 750
MM SUPER TEST

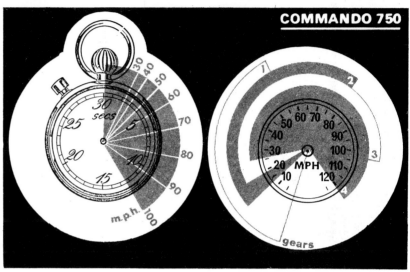

COMMANDO 750

Performance

Speeds in gears

	Minimum	Maximum
1st	—	55
2nd	12	80
3rd	18	105
4th	25	122

Acceleration

0–30	2.0 sec.	0–40	2.8 sec.
0–50	3.6 sec.	0–60	4.8 sec.

0–70	6.4 sec.	0–80	8.2 sec.
0–90	10.1 sec.	0–100	12.2 sec.

Standing quarter-mile: 12.8 sec., terminal speed 104 mph.

Fuel consumption: overall 55 mpg, varying between 40 mpg and 62 mpg, depending on use.

Braking: from 30 mph, using both brakes on a dry tarmac surface: 28 ft.

Specification

Engine: Twin-cylinder four-stroke, ohv. Bore 73 mm. (2.875 in.) × stroke 89 mm. (3.503 in.), giving capacity of 745 cc (45 cu. in.). Compression ratio 8.9:1. Developing 58 bhp at 6500 rpm.

Transmission: Four-speed gearbox, driven by triple row primary chain running in oil bath, through a four-plate clutch. Clutch spring is diaphragm type.
Gear ratios (overall, with standard 19-tooth gearbox sprocket):

1st—12.4:1	2nd—8.25:1
3rd— 5.9:1	4th—4.84:1

Electrical equipment: A 10 amp./hr. 12-volt battery with positive earth is supplied by a Lucas RM21 alternator via a rectifier and Zener-diode. Ignition is by twin contact breakers and coils and is the capacitor type.

Carburettors: Twin Amal 930 concentric models are used, with 220 main jets, 25 pilot jet, No. 3 throttle valve, and 0.107 needle jet.

Dimensions: Overall length 87½ in., overall width 26 in., ground clearance 6 in., weight 415 lb., wheelbase 56¾ in., seat height (rider seated) 31 in.

Capacities: Fuel tank 3.25 gallons, oil tank 5 pints, gearbox 1 pint, primary chaincase 200 cc (7 fl.oz.), front forks 150 cc (5½ fl.oz.) each leg.

Wheels: Front wheel is WM 2 rim with 3.00 × 19 ribbed tyre, and has a twin-leading-shoe 8 in. brake. Rear wheel is GP WM 2 rim with 3.50 × 19 tyre, using single-leading-shoe 8 in. brake.

Price: £456 19s. 4d., manufactured by Norton-Villiers Ltd, Plumstead Road, Woolwich, London, S.E.18.

NORTON COMMANDO

Is this the instant classic?

OUT OF the crate, the first Norton Commando in America reeled off a series of low 13-sec. blasts up the quarter-mile, with terminal speeds close to, and occasionally touching, 100 mph. Later, a man who previously never had competed in a road race entered the same 745-cc Commando in a race meeting, won his heat of the production event, placed 2nd in the Grand Prix heat, then won the Grand Prix main. He also set fast lap time of the day, beating times recorded by all the grand prix machinery, and was leading the production final when a loose spark plug blew out.

What does this make the Commando? Is it a racer with a wild cam, and a rumpity-rump idle that hates delays at traffic lights? No! The Commando is simply a sports roadster that offers a sensational blend of shattering performance, well mannered tractability, racebred handling, and fierce, sure stopping power. Its achievements on drag strip and race circuit in no way mar its ability to trundle quietly to the neighborhood drug store. The Commando, manufactured by the Nor-

Villiers group, really is anything its owner wishes it to be.

Perhaps even more exciting than the performance figures is the fact that the factory has tamed the vibration problem. Anyone who has experience of large displacement British parallel Twins will know that the majority of them, including Nortons, vibrate. The rider feels the sensation through handlebar grips, footpegs, and seat. In the worst instances, vibration can spoil the fun of a long journey. Vibration also can cause nuts and bolts to fall off, light bulbs to shatter, and tachometer and speedometer to break. Instruments often shake so much that they are difficult to read.

At rest, with engine idling, the Commando also is a vibrator. The front wheel jogs up and down, and fuel tank and exhaust pipes judder. But, when the engine rpm rise above 3800, the roughness disappears, and in its place is an uncanny smoothness. This turbine-like sensation remains right up to peak rpm of 7000. Hard acceleration gives an impression akin to turning up the rheostat on a giant electric motor. The bike breaks forward at a phenomenal rate, but only the exhaust note and rapidly moving instrument needles tell the rider that the engine is working hard.

The first few miles on a Commando actually are misleading. Acceleration seems brisk, but not fierce. Suddenly, the reason for this sensation becomes obvious—there is no rattling or thrashing to give a false illusion of speed. The Commando possesses enough savage power to blow off virtually anything on the road. And, all the time, the rider is freed of the distractions of vibrating controls and components, and is thus able to concentrate 100 percent on reading the road.

Norton Villiers' mastery of the vibration problem obviously did not occur by accident. The task was accomplished by design of an entirely new frame, and by rubber-mounting the engine and gearbox.

Vital parts of the frame are a 2.25-in. diameter backbone which extends from the steering head to the area of the upper rear suspension mounts, and two struts which pass from the

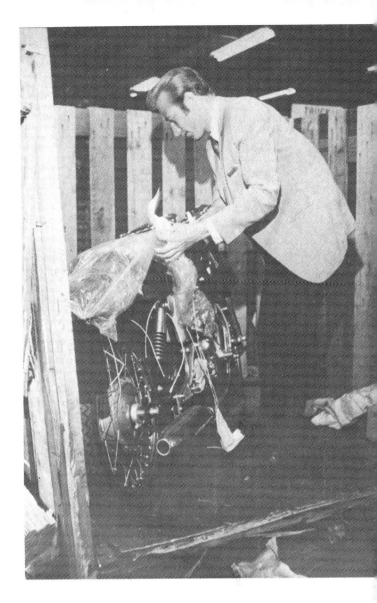

center of the backbone to the rear legs of the engine loops. This section forms a triangulated structure, and provides the greater part of the frame's resistance to torsional stresses. The remaining frame tubes—the duplex engine loops, and the rear mudguard support—are not stressed, and serve only to locate components. Because so few of the frame tubes are stressed, Norton Villiers has been able to hold total frame weight to 24 lb. The factory says this is approximately 30 percent lighter and stronger than anything it previously has made.

Frame configuration is fairly orthodox. However, the method used to mount the swinging arm pivot on the plates which link the separate engine and gearbox—rather than directly to the frame—shows a completely new line of engineering thought. Engine and transmission are supported in the frame by large rubber bushes at the front of the crankcase, behind the gearbox, and at the cylinder head. Thus the entire unit, including the rear fork pivot, is suspended in the frame. Vibration which emanates from the crankshaft is absorbed before it can affect rider or machine. Detroit engineers long have employed rubber engine-to-chassis-to-body-mountings to produce the sought-after boulevard ride of Lincoln and Cadillac. Norton Villiers has joined the club.

The factory also has taken a look at every other feature a high performance sports bike should possess. The engine behind those quick quarter-mile figures is the ohv Atlas unit, already used on Atlas roadster and Ranger street scrambler machines, and noted for reliability and power. For the Commando, several modifications have been made. Compression ratio has been raised to 8.9:1, and primary drive has been strengthened by adopting a triplex chain, in place of the single-row chain previously employed. A cast alloy primary casing replaces the stamped steel unit found on Atlases. Service has been simplified by the use of only one fixing bolt for the casing. Previous engines employed about a dozen bolts around the casing perimeter. A plug in the casing covers an inspection hole that permits ignition timing to be checked with a strobe light.

The engine also features parallel induction ports, and widely spaced exhaust ports, to provide maximum breathing efficiency. A built-up forged steel crankshaft, with central iron flywheel, is supported on plain bearings. Two-piece connecting rods and alloy pistons operate inside a cast iron cylinder block. Valve operation is by forged steel rockers, large diameter

tappets, alloy pushrods, and a chain driven camshaft.

Laycock de Normanville, a firm which specializes in automobile transmissions, designed the new four-plate, diaphragm spring type clutch—one of the smoothest, lightest units ever fitted to a large displacement motorcycle. Two-finger pressure is sufficient for gear changes, even though the clutch exerts nearly double the pressure of the conventional unit it replaces.

Carburetion also has been subject to change. Amal Concentrics supersede the Monoblocs used on Atlases. They are fed by a large air cleaner. Because of the engine's forward tilt, downward curving induction stubs are employed, to avoid an excessively high carburetor location.

A crankshaft driven alternator, and 12-V battery supply power for ignition. The bike also is fitted with a capacitor, a little device that stores energy and enables the engine to be started with or without the battery—that means no problems should the battery be exhausted. Lights also can be operated without the battery, provided the engine is running.

Performance and flexibility are the Commando's specialties. Usable power begins at 2000 rpm, and frantic gear changing is not necessary in order to get places fast. Only one fault marred the Commando's roadability. Center and sidestands are set so low that the left side—where the sidestand is attached—continually scrapes the ground on all corners where little more than average lean is required. With the pillion seat occupied, the stands hit the pavement so quickly that any attempt at fast cornering is downright dangerous. Even the right side, where only the center stand projects, easily can be made to scrape the ground.

In view of the care which has been taken with the remainder of the machine, it seems odd that Norton Villiers has allowed this very obvious and potentially dangerous fault to go farther than prototype Commandos. Anyone who intends to make full use of the bike's considerable cornering abilities, may wish to remove, or find a new location for, the sidestand, and perhaps the center stand.

Handling itself is superbly stable in all kinds of conditions. The front fork is the famous Norton Roadholder pattern, with two-way damping and single-rate springs. This fork has earned what is virtually a worldwide reputation for its excellent handling qualities. Rear suspension is by Girling hydraulic spring/damper units, with springs adjustable to three different positions. Cornering is not light, yet the Commando is one of the best handling heavyweights available. Its charm lies in its absolute steadiness, and refusal to veer from the chosen line. This breeds a relationship of total confidence between rider and machine.

Gear change action is typically Norton—crisp, satisfyingly "solid," with swift and short pedal movements. There are no false neutrals, and first gear is engaged from rest with no clunks or grating.

In the quest for greater speed, the factory has not forgotten to provide adequate brakes. On the front wheel is a new twin leading shoe unit of 8-in. diameter, that works quietly and powerfully, with light lever pressures. The rear brake is a standard Norton component, effective and strong. The front unit has a scoop to draw in cooling air, but the scoop is intended mainly for racing. For road use, it is blanked off by an easily removable metal cover plate.

A fairly short, straight handlebar was fitted to the test machine, and proved ideal for fast riding. However, a high rise American pattern bar also is available, and will be fitted to a great number of Commandos sold in the U.S. Rider comfort is provided for by a generous, well padded seat, which is roomy enough for two people who spend long hours in the saddle. Footpegs are located by large alloy castings attached to the

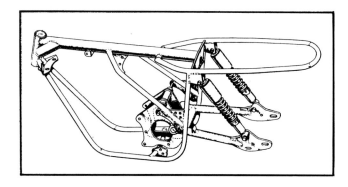

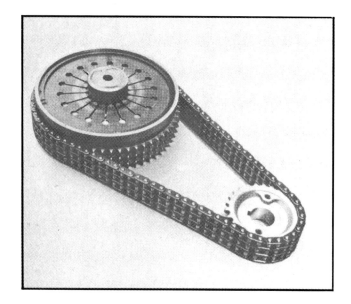

frame, a method that helps prevent vibration from reaching the feet.

In appearance, the Commando is truly a stunning motorcycle. A fiberglass fuel tank, with quick action flip-up filler cap, and rear mudguard unit, also formed of fiberglass, take much of the credit for the smart looks. During the test period, the Commando attracted considerable attention from other motorcyclists, and the most frequent question was: "Where did the fiberglass come from?" They were impressed when told that it was standard factory equipment!

The front mudguard is of alloy. Large 19-in. wheels carry a 3-in. section tire in front, and a 3.50-in. Avon Grand Prix at the rear. This cover is formed in the same mold as Avon racing tires, though its rubber content is less "sticky," and therefore longer wearing, than the racing versions. Oil tank filler cap and battery are housed beneath the seat, which is quickly detached by undoing two retaining knobs—one at each side. An exterior plastic window enables instant oil level checks to be made.

Not content with offering power, smoothness, handling, brakes and good looks all in one machine, Norton Villiers has decided to offer enthusiasts a true mindblower in the form of three high performance conversion kits, the "wildest" of which provides a claimed top speed of 137 mph! The factory says this kit, the Stage III, powers the bike to 100 mph in a mere 11.5 sec. This stage puts the engine into full racing tune, and is not intended for street use. Stages I and II are for brave road riders who like to show drivers of 400-cu. in. engined automobiles what acceleration is *really* about. The first kit offers a claimed 10 percent power boost, 120 mph top speed, and a 0 to 100 time of 13.75 sec. Stage II, says the factory, gives 16 percent additional power, 130 mph, and acceleration to the "ton" in just 12.75 sec. A fourth kit, which customizes appearance only, includes clip-on handlebars and rearset footpegs (to make the rider feel like Mike Hailwood!), alloy wheel rims, colored fork and rear suspension gaiters, and other items.

Opposition during the bike's road racing debut was not exactly championship material. Its achievements there were still magnificent, considering that it remained in as-you-buy-it street trim, apart from removal of side and center stands, a change of plugs, and the addition of number plates. To prove that these results were not obtained by luck, the bike was given a second road race outing, among much stiffer opposition. It easily won the production event, and placed 3rd in the Grand Prix event, behind two genuine racing machines equipped with fairings.

During drag strip tests a staff member of the West Coast distributor actually recorded a staggering quarter-mile time of 13.13 sec., with a terminal speed of 100.44 mph. The best time set on the CYCLE WORLD test day was 13.47 sec., and the bike proved capable of setting a whole series of times in the low 13s, with no sign of distress from the sorely punished clutch. The Commando's performances actually make it the second fastest machine CYCLE WORLD ever has tested. Only the Dunstall Norton, produced by racing specialist and customizer Paul Dunstall, has bettered the Commando's times in the quarter mile. And, even the Dunstall machine employed a modified version of the Norton 750 engine.

Even in basic form, the Commando embodies an extravaganza of delectable qualities that leave riders talking in a lengthy series of superlatives. Undoubtedly, never before has a motorcycle offered such smoothness combined with such power. Certain fabled machines, such as the Vincent and the Ariel Square Four, have earned places high in the list of all-time great motorcycles. No one should be surprised if the Commando acquires a reputation that will allow it to join that select band.

NORTON COMMANDO

SPECIFICATIONS

List price	$1457
Suspension, front	telescopic fork
Suspension, rear	swinging arm
Tire, front	3.00-19
Tire, rear	3.50-19
Brake, front, diameter x width, in.	8.0 x 1.25
Brake, rear, diameter x width, in.	7.0 x 1.25
Total brake swept area, sq. in.	58.9
Brake loading (test weight/swept area) lb./sq. in.	9.83
Engine type	ohv parallel Twin
Bore x stroke, in., mm	2.875 x 3.503, 73 x 89
Displacement, cu. in., cc	45, 745
Compression ratio	8.9:1
Carburetion	(2) 30-mm Amal concentric
Ignition	battery, coils
Claimed bhp @ rpm	n.a.
Oil system	dry sump
Oil capacity, pt.	6
Fuel capacity, gal.	3.9
Starting system	kick, folding crank
Lighting system	battery, alternator
Air filtration	paper element
Clutch	multi-plate, diaphragm spring
Primary drive	triplex chain
Final drive	single-row chain
Gear ratios, overall:1	
5th	none
4th	4.84
3rd	5.90
2nd	8.25
1st	12.40
Wheelbase, in.	57.1
Seat height, in.	31.3
Seat width, in.	11.8
Footpeg height, in.	11.4
Ground clearance, in.	5.3
Curb weight (w/half-tank fuel), lb.	431
Test weight (fuel and rider), lb.	601

PERFORMANCE

Top speed, actual, (@ 7250 rpm), mph	114.5
Calculated top speed in gears (@7000 rpm), mph	
5th	none
4th	110.4
3rd	90.6
2nd	64.8
1st	43.2
Mph per 1000 rpm, top gear	15.77
Speedometer error:	
50 mph indicated, actually	48.54
60 mph indicated, actually	58.01
70 mph indicated, actually	69.07
Acceleration, zero to:	
30 mph, sec.	3.2
40	3.8
50	4.6
60	5.5
70	6.6
80	7.6
90	9.8
100	14.9
Standing 1/8th mile, sec.	8.21
terminal speed, mph	83.40
Standing 1/4th mile, sec.	13.47
terminal speed, mph	96.35

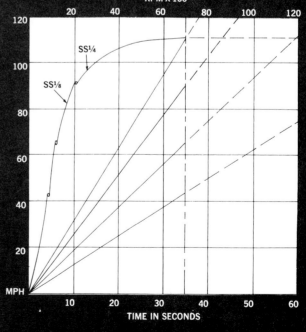

ACCELERATION AND ENGINE / ROAD SPEED
RPM X 100

The best old-fashioned Big British Twin on the market

NORTON 745 COMMANDO

IN the 18 months or whatever it is since the Commando was introduced we had ridden perhaps five miles on one. And finally when we ran one to earth at the old Woolwich factory we could only have it for a week because of a long-standing arrangement to loan it to the men at *Motorcyclist Illustrated*, who had the idea of riding it from Lands End to John O'Groats in a day, dawn to dusk. (This is not meant to be a "trailer" for the next issue of *MCI*, but we mention it because it seems an entertaining idea.)

Test outing on the Commando at Brands Hatch. This model has covered 12,000 miles at home and abroad

So we had TYV 40F for seven days, though by the time these words appear we should have it back for an extended test and more thorough evaluation. Perhaps you will take this as a progress report.

The fact is, it is a very nice bike. With the B.S.A./Triumph three, the Honda CB 750 (read M. R. W.'s comments elsewhere in this issue), and now the Commando there are three big bikes we should be very happy to own. Any one of them, or all three. There is no question of putting the Commando last in this short list because it is the cheapest or possibly the most conventional, engine mounting aside. Its engine was designed years back— in 1947, probably a year or two before that, if you count the all-iron 497 Dominator as its direct forebear. That accounts for the unfashionably long stroke, 89 mm. to 73 mm. bore, which pushes

piston speed a shade high and keep maximum r.p.m. down to a moderat 6,000, which is rather tame compare with the designed-yesterday, high-revvin engines of the other 750s. But the powe response of the big twin has a lot to b said for it. Instant, hard, always there whatever the gear. No need to get th tacho. needle past 5 thou before the powe comes along. So you can say that it i simpler to drive than the others, and w should estimate it is as fast, perhap faster, over a 100 miles of mixed roads . . though its top speed is short of the othe by maybe 10 m.p.h. That is, 115 to 125 No question of needing five or six speed with this sort of power ; there is tremen dous torque from 3,000 r.p.m.

And the rubber mounting of the engine Well, it's done the job. The old-tim Atlas, which had the same engine more o less, and was not much slower, woul swell your wrists and melt the gristle i your joints. A monster to take you fron 0 to 60 in seven seconds and make life a purgatory. Now, in the Commando, tha old 745 engine seems r-e-f-i-n-e-d. A littl shake at tickover but nothing unpleasant a sort of insulated shake like you have in a B.M.W. at tickover, and even some vibra tion above that, but diminishing, up to 2,500–3,000 r.p.m.—and from then on there is no vibration. (Well, to be coo and precise, detached or pedantic, there' probably a little—there must be—but it's so slight, the sort of feel you get through a car's steering wheel, something working away at the far end of rubber joints.) Yet paradoxically the bike feels solid and taut, has an all-of-one-piece feeling—more so than the Norton twins in pre-rubber-mounted times.

You can see we like the Commando.

The riding position is first class. High seat, low flat handlebar, high footrests : it all goes with the good looks of the bike which make the threes and the Honda seem staid, impressive mainly through sheer weight and size rather than fine line.

Third gear whistled us well past 90, top (in favourable conditions) to 110-112, all to a muted *whoom* from the exhausts. The gearbox was superb (we have never ridden a Norton with a bad gearbox), the diaphragm-spring clutch light and positive. No oil appeared outside the engine, not more than a pint was used in 300 miles.

But wait till we've covered a thousand or two miles on it and we'll give all the facts. As we said, this is a "progress report".

Norton COMMANDO

MOTORCYCLE
SCOOTER & THREE-WHEELER
MECHANICS
THE ILLUSTRATED HOW-TO-DO-IT MAGAZINE

ENGINE ANALYSIS No. 3

A close-up of Norton's latest, most powerful twin

▶ Latest in a long line of famous machines, Norton introduced their Commando in 1967 at the last Earls Court show.

They first built the 750 cc twin for the American market where there was a demand for a big, comfortable bike that could pull top gear from 15 to 100 mph.

To do this they increased the 68 mm bore of their 650 to 73 mm, modified the crankcase to take the bigger pistons and put the 750 on the export market.

In order to keep the motor flexible and give good acceleration, the compression ratio was a low 7.3:1 and the machine used the same gearing as the 650.

Since then though, the de-sign has been developed, and with the current trend towards big bikes in this country making the 750s popular on the home market, the performance has been considerably increased.

The early 750 produced 47 bhp at 6,500 rpm; now, with compression ratios of 10:1, the works PR Commandos are giving around 66 bhp at 7000 rpm. In any terms that's a lot of power!

MAIN SPECIFICATION

Lubrication

Gear-type pump driven from timing side of crankshaft.

Normal running pressure	45–55 psi

Engine

Bore	2.875 in.
	73.025 mm
stroke	3.503 in.
	73.045 mm
capacity	45.5 cu. in.
	745 cc
compression ratio	8.9:1
power output	60 bhp at 6800 rpm
spark plug	N6Y
spark plug gap	.023–.028 in.
contact breaker gap	.014–.016 in.
ignition timing (full advance)	28° btdc

tappet clearance, cold:

inlet	.006 in.
exhaust	.008 in.

valve spring free length:

inner	1.531 in.
outer	1.700 in.
inlet valve length	4.069 in.
stem diameter	.3095–.3105 in.
exhaust valve length	4.020 in.
stem diameter	.3095–.3105 in.
valve seat angle	45°

valve timing:

check with tappet clearance of .016 in.

inlet opens	50° btdc
inlet closes	74° abdc
exhaust opens	82° bbdc
exhaust closes	42° atdc
piston ring gap (compression)	.013 in.

crankshaft journal diameter:

drive side	1.1815–1.1812 in.
timing side	1.1807–1.1812 in.
max permissible ovality	.001 in.
max permissible regrind	−.030 in.

main bearings:

drive side	single dot roller 30 × 72 × 19 mm
timing side	single dot ball 30 × 72 × 19 mm

carburettor:

type	Amal
model	930 (2 off)
choke diameter	1.180 in.
main jet	220
needle jet	.106
needle location	central notch
throttle slide	3
pilot jet (early models)	25

Transmission

engine sprocket	26 t
clutch	57 t
gearbox	21 or 19 t

wheel	42 t

internal ratios:	
1st	2.56
2nd	1.7
3rd	1.22
4th	1.0

overall ratios:

gearbox sprocket	21 t	19 t
4th	4.38	4.84
3rd	5.35	5.9
2nd	7.45	8.25
1st	11.2	12.4

primary chain	triplex, endless
	3/8 × .225 in. (92 pitches)
rear chain	single row
(21 t)	5/8 × .380 in. (99 pitches)
(19 t)	—(98 pitches)
camshaft chain	single row
	3/8 × .225 in. (38 pitches)
ignition chain (early models)	single row
	3/8 × .155 in. (42 rollers)
clutch	four driving plates
	four driven (bonded) plates
	cable operated
	diaphragm spring

Dimensions

oil tank	5 pints (2.8 litres)
gearbox	1 pint (2.8 litres)
chaincase	7 fl. oz. (200 cc)
engine/gearbox weight dry	144 lb.

Electrics

12-volt ac/dc lighting from Lucas RM 21 alternator and battery, with positive earth.

Battery charging is from full alternator output through bridge rectifier controlled by Zener diode.

Ignition is by twin coils and Lucas 2 MC capacitor, using Lucas 6CA contact breaker.

Torque wrench settings

Cylinder head nuts, bolts (3/8 in.)	360 lb. in.
„ „ „ „ (5/16 in.)	240 lb. in.
cylinder base nuts	240 lb. in.
big-end cap nuts	300 lb. in.
rocker shaft cover plate bolt	100 lb. in.
cam chain tensioner nuts	180 lb. in.
oil pump stud nuts	180 lb. in.
banjo bolts	180 lb. in.
engine mounting bolts	300 lb. in.
alternator studs	120 lb. in.

RACE SPECIFICATION

Norton Villiers can supply conversion kits giving three stages of tune for fast road work up to full production-racing trim. The kits are the results of extensive testing.

STAGE 1 parts:

Gasket set (top overhaul)	*Competition spark plugs*
10:1 compression ratio pistons	*Timing disc*
Special exhaust valves	*Patent silencers*
3 pairs carburettor main jets	*Tank decals*

The second stage kit gives a good bit more power, mainly in the middle rev range and needs workshop facilities to fit. To give an idea of the increased performance, the top speed is raised to 130 mph with a 0–80 mph time of 7.5 sec.

STAGE 2 parts:

Gasket set	*3 pairs carburettor jets*
10:1 compression ratio pistons	*Tank decals*
Special exhaust valves	*Competition spark plugs*
Special inlet valves	*Timing disc*
Special valve springs	*Sports camshaft*
Induction manifolds	*Exhaust pipes*
	Patent silencers

Finally, the full-blown race kit gives still more power, a top speed of 137 mph and acceleration 0–80 mph in 6.9 sec.

STAGE 3 parts:

Gasket set	*Competition spark plugs*
10:1 compression ratio pistons	*Timing disc*
Special exhaust valves	*Domiracer camshaft*
Special inlet valves	*Special cam followers*
Special valve springs	*Racing exhaust pipes*
Flexible induction manifolds	*Racing megaphones*
1¼ in. bore carburettors	*Tank decals*

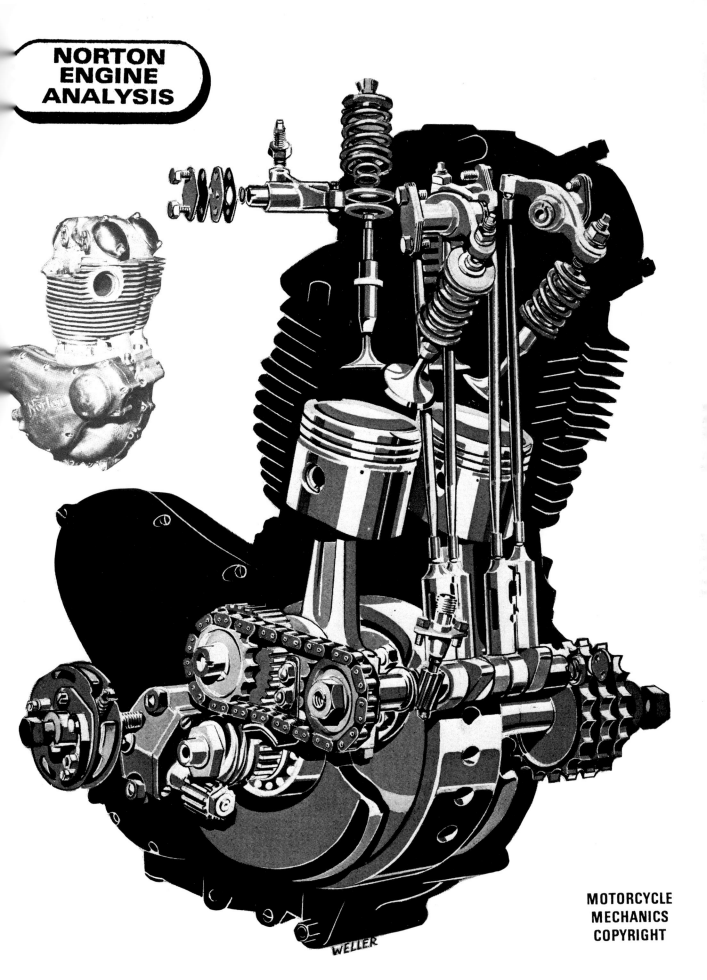

WELLER

ENGINE ANALYSIS NORTON COMMANDO

DEVELOPMENT

▶ **The ancestor of the big Norton twin was the 500 cc Dominator model 7 designed by Herbert Hopwood and first built in 1949.**

This machine gained popularity and was produced until the end of 1952 without change. Meanwhile, the famous featherbed frame had been introduced on the racing machines, and in 1953 the first twin appeared in one. This was again a 500, the Dominator 88, but until 1954 it was only available on the export market.

For 1953 the Model 7 had another frame, also all-brazed but with a pivoted rear fork instead of the plunger design so far used.

At this stage the basic engine had remained almost unchanged and still used a cast iron cylinder head.

Aluminium alloy was first used for the head in 1955, on both the model 7 and 88, and this year saw the testing of a new high-lift camshaft and an experimental 600 cc twin.

Both proved successful and for 1956

the 88 and the new model, designated Dominator 99, were fitted with the new cam.

Also during 1956, Doug Hele and Herbert Hopwood returned to Norton and continued the development work on the twins.

Right up to 1958, all these machines were equipped with magneto ignition and a dc dynamo mounted in front of the cylinder block, driven from the camshaft.

In '58 this was changed for coil and battery ignition, fed by a crankshaft-mounted alternator.

The development work continued and the 1961 Dominator 88 SS had small bore siamesed exhausts with a special silencer and twin $1\frac{1}{16}$ in. Monoblocs. This gave a top speed of 110 mph with about 115 mph from the 99 SS.

When the first 650 appeared late in 1961, the external appearance of the motor was almost the same as the 99, but there were several major changes.

The extra capacity was obtained by lengthening the stroke of the 99 from 82 to 89 mm and shortening the con-rod and piston skirt slightly so that the long stroke bottom half would fit into the 99 block and head.

An improved head was in fact used, but this was not available on the home market until 1962. The main difference was in the downdraught intakes and wider splayed exhausts which gave better cooling.

Around this time the big Norton twins were becoming very popular in production racing, doing well in the Thruxton 500-miler and the Silverstone 1000 kilometre races. Also a 500 cc works "Domiracer" was entered in the 1962 TT, ridden by Tom Phillis into third place and clocked up a lap at over 100 mph.

However, this was not to be a racing comeback for Norton, and as the work on the 650 and 750 models progressed the 88 and 99 Dominators were dropped from the range.

WORKSHOP INFORMATION

SPECIAL TOOLS

▶ **While the Commando engine remains similar to earlier Norton twins in appearance, many of the parts are different and are not interchangeable.**

For instance, the valves and push-rods look very much like those used on earlier engines, but have different lengths.

On the cylinder head, note that there are heat-insulating washers between the valve springs and the head to reduce heat transfer to the springs.

When checking the free length of the springs, compare with the length given in the specification and if any spring is more than $\frac{3}{16}$ in. shorter than the given length it should be replaced.

The springs are rated and should be fitted with the two close coils against the bottom spring seat.

The valve guides, which are all identical, are a force fit in the head, and may be drifted out after the head has been heated (in an oven) to 200 deg. C. (392 deg. F.) but no more. A suitable drift for removing/replacing the guides is shown in the diagram, or there is a special tool available.

the silencing ramp. To do this, check the right-hand inlet valve with the left-hand inlet valve fully open, repeating the process for the other valves.

When splitting the crankcase, the drive side case comes away from the shaft, leaving the inner member of the roller bearing on the shaft. After removing the camshaft and crankcase breather, the shaft can then be driven out of the timing side case using a suitable sleeve drift to protect the shaft.

The big-end caps are machined in place on the connecting rods and are not interchangeable. To identify them there is an oblique mark which lines up with a similar mark on the rod.

Timing

On the rebuild, if the timing chain has been removed from the sprockets, the timing must be reset. Turn the engine until the mark on the small pinion is at 12 o'clock. Fit the sprockets and chain so that the mark on the intermediate pinion lines up with that on the small one and so that

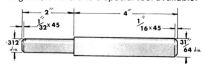

Dimensions for valve guide drift

The tappets are machined in pairs and must be refitted in the same order as they were removed, with the bevelled edges facing the front of the engine.

When the tappet clearance is being checked, it is essential that the tappet is on the base circle of the cam and not on

When removing the timing sprockets keep the timing by wiring the chain up

there are six outer plates on the chain separating the timing marks on the two sprockets.

The Commando uses capacitor ignition which allows the engine to be started without the battery. When running with the battery disconnected, the terminals and leads must be insulated to prevent a possible short circuit.

The 2MC capacitor is a polarised unit and must be fitted the right way round. First the capacitor must be positioned with the terminals facing downwards. Second, there are two Lucar terminals, the smaller, $\frac{3}{16}$ in. one is the positive (earth) terminal and is identified by a red spot. The other is a double $\frac{1}{4}$ in. terminal and is the negative connection.

Late engines do away with the ignition chain and have a 6CA contact breaker mounted on the offside of the camshaft. The rev-counter drive is taken from a worm on the camshaft via a vertical spindle set in the front of the crankcase.

Norton 750cc Commando S

For the high-performance street-sport rider, here's a slenderized, stylized, high-pipe version of Norton's famous 58 bhp Commando—complete with "floating drive."

PHOTOGRAPHY: HERMANN BACHMANN

● Last season Norton's Commando was just about the only interesting new bike in the big bore, snort, grunt and sprint category. It was a real intimidator, with a 750cc engine and a performance capability that included quarter-mile times in the 13-second bracket. It was big and it was fast, and those things alone would have made it interesting.

But the Commando had more than speed and size: it offered, in addition, an ingenious frame and engine-mounting package conceived around the sensible but often ignored notion that big-bike riders don't want to pay for big performance with big amounts of vibration. No matter how sweet it is to have a bike with lots of lunge, sooner or later you have to settle down to a nice, steady cruise, and nobody wants to find that this cruising speed brings on the familiar, hated buzzing of handlebar grips, foot pegs, etc..

Norton found an answer, and applied it in the Commando, their new fiberglass-paneled successor to the famous Atlas. In the Commando, they have suspended the engine and gearbox in large-diameter rubber bushings. It was revolutionary, and it worked. The bushings stopped the transmitting of engine vibration to the motorcycle (and its rider) and made the Commando not only fast, but smoother than smooth.

That was last year, the last season before the arrival of the BSA, Triumph, Kawasaki and Honda multis. These bikes solved the vibration problem by adding cylinders (which reduces the shaking at its source—the engine) and have completely transformed the big bike scene. And Norton's Commando couldn't care less. In an almost arrogant assertion that it had won the game before the other players arrived, the Commando made its appearance

this year in very near original form. There is a high-pipe version Norton has named the "Commando S", but they must feel that the basic machine, which was the first modern Superbike, is adequate to meet the multi's challenge. They are probably right, for if a bike gives you performance and smoothness, it matters little how it is acquired.

No one at Norton has said what the significance of "S" in the designation Commando S might be, but it probably stands for Sport. Not that you can fault the standard Commando for sportiness in how it behaves, but it is somewhat low key in its looks, what with conservative dark green paint and all. The S, by contrast, is all polished aluminum alloy, glittering chrome, and brilliant metal-flake-red paint. It's a dazzler.

Besides flashier paint and upswept pipes, the Commando S (as compared to the straight

21

If you have doubts about handling from a cush mounted swingarm, forget them. The Commando S feels light, tracks superbly, and corners with precision.

Commando) has a smaller fuel tank, more slender fenders, less paneling and ungaitered fork tubes in the naked-leg Real Racer tradition. Its engine, in "stage one" tune, is identical to those in other Commandos except for a few detail improvements that are to be incorporated in all models.

Most of the improvements only a longtime rider of Nortons would notice. Like the tachometer drive, which has for years been mounted outside the timing case cover, and always got knocked off when you dropped the bike. This item has been moved around to the inboard side of the timing chest and is safely out of harm's way. Now, in the same space at the end of the camshaft, you will find the ignition's contact points, which are in a recess covered by a stout metal plate. These points were previously around behind the cylinders in a small canister. They are much more accessible in their new location.

None of the changes have affected power output. They do make the engine a bit cleaner (albeit left with a superfluous bulge on the timing chest) and easier to service. The styling revisions won't make the bike go any faster either, but they add a kind of *pizzaz* we found appealing. They remind us of the old red and black Atlas, which was once the fastest thing on the road and was, in addition, always a mean-looking motorcycle.

But don't let anyone tell you that the Atlas was a better motorcycle than the Commando. It was a lot heavier, and not nearly as smooth because it didn't have Norton's new, patented engine-isolation system. We'll give you the details, because they are interesting, but the most important thing to be said about the system is that it works, and works very well. At any engine speed above 2000 rpm, we didn't get *any* engine-induced shaking through the frame. You would think from rid-

ing the bike that the engine didn't vibrate— and in so thinking you would be wrong. The Commando's engine began life as a long-stroke 500, and a series of slight increases in bore (and considerable increases in stroke) have brought it to its present 73mm x 89mm dimensions. As in all British vertical twins, the Norton's crankpins fly around in formation and the pistons whiz up and down together, which provides for evenly spaced firing impulses, but leaves the engine in a bad state for primary balance. And in the Norton, friends, those pistons are making three and a half inches at every pass through their cylinders. The engine shakes; it would require repealing a few physical laws to make it otherwise.

The shaking is there, but it is stopped before it can get very far, and what is used to stop the vibration is so simple it is hard to imagine why someone has not done it before. As you may know, the Norton has its transmission separate from the engine, and the two are tied together by a pair of plates in the old Atlas. In the Commando, the transmission is bolted into an encircling cradle, and the cradle is bolted very solidly against the back of the engine's crankcase. Another smaller cradle is bolted to the front of the engine, and this one carries only a short, large-diameter tube. Look carefully, and you will see a similar tube at the upper, rearmost corner of the gearbox cradle. These two tubes provide the only connection between the engine and the frame, and they are stuffed full of rubber bushings, spacers and shim washers. Before vibration can get to the frame, it must travel across those rubber bushings—and it can't.

There is another big crosstube in the back of the gearbox cradle, and this contains the rear-suspension's swing-arm pivot. That's right, the rear suspension in hinged on the engine/gearbox assembly so that it, too, is isolated from the frame.

Give any experienced road racer just that much information, and he'll either turn ghastly pale or fall to the ground, howling and cackling with laughter. In the bad old days there were several bikes around that had swing-arms more or less flexibly mounted not by intent. It was just faulty understanding of structure. Handling, in such cases, was abominable.

To get good handling, you must have wheels that remain in alignment; a swing-arm wiggling back and forth did terrible things to the way a bike tracked around corners. Like we have said, this was a matter of bad design, and was done inadvertently; Norton provided the flexibility by intent, and were careful that all of the flexing occurred in a plane that would not upset handling. Those rubber bushings we talked about have a great deal of "give" in a fore and aft, or vertical plane. Shim washers are used to hold the sideplay to no more than .010 of an inch. The engine and swing-arm,

The Commando's long-stroke twin engine descends directly from the Atlas: it is and always was a real torquer. Now a twin-leading-shoe brake adds stopping power.

can move—but only in a plane that can't influence handling.

While on this subject, we should mention that there have been conflicting reports about the Commando's handling. Some have found it delightful; others have compared it with the old Atlas' handling in most unfavorable terms. Those who have been critical of the Commando have attributed it to the rubber engine/gearbox/swing-arm mounting. No doubt they are right, for if the mounts have any perceptible sideplay, the handling suffers. Excessive side clearance in some machines would account for the adverse opinions. We just want everyone to know that this point is critical, and the Commando owner who notes any instability in his machine should check the clearance. No mention of this is made in the owners' manual; details are to be found in the workshop manual.

With or without the "floating drive", the Commando's frame would rate special discussion. It is a very simple design layout, with a large-diameter "backbone" tube extending back from the steering head to a point under the seat, where it ends in a crosstube to which the rear shocks are connected. A pair of support tubes sweep down from the steering head, level off under the engine/gearbox assembly, and then sweep back up and terminate at the upper shock-mounting points. The structure is completed by a pair of diagonal tubes that extend down from the middle of the backbone to a point just above the gearbox, where loads from the rearmost engine/gearbox/swingarm mounting are fed into the frame. It all looks too simple to be effective, but it isn't. In fact, it is a far more rational structure than the old "Manx" frame that

gave Norton a reputation for fine handling: at least as rigid—and much, much lighter. To be exact, the Commando's frame is 28 pounds lighter than the "featherbed" frame that held the Atlas together.

Even though the basic powerplant and gearbox haven't been changed much from Norton's Atlas, the system used for getting the drive from one to the other is vastly better. With the previous single-row primary chain, fairly frequent adjustments and replacements were required, and the old clutch inclined to slip when you wanted it to hold and drag when it should have been disengaged. All that has been changed. The drive now travels down a triple chain and into a clutch that is the best we have seen in many moons. This clutch is conventional to the extent that it has multiple, alternate plain and friction material faced plates. It is unconventional in having fewer, thicker plates and a diaphragm spring to provide the pressure. The thick plates do not have that slight warp one always finds in their thinner counterparts, and that gives the clutch a very "solid" feel. The diaphragm spring, like all of its kind, has an "overcenter" action that provides a lot of pressure on the plates when the clutch is engaged, but becomes weaker as you squeeze in the clutch lever. The total result is a clutch that is wonderfully light yet positive, and not likely to slip once fully engaged. We aren't alone in thinking that it is an especially good clutch: Helmut Fath chose to use the same clutch in his 78 bhp URS four.

This new clutch and primary drive are housed in a new cast aluminum case, which is a big improvement over the old pressed steel one. The gear change mechanism has changed

for the better (perhaps we should say, redesigned for there wasn't much wrong with how the Norton's gearbox worked before).

The Commando's engine, more than somewhat long of stroke, does not rev as freely as it might if its bore/stroke dimensions were reversed. However, it does deliver the power—about 58 bhp—and that is really all that matters. The power peak is a 6500 rpm, and the bike we had for testing began to feel strained above 7000. But then, that gives you almost 100 mph in third gear, so you need not feel shortchanged.

If the Commando's rev range does not extend very far, it at least allows you to use what it has without shaking your fillings loose. The engine sits down there, joggling quietly by itself, while you perch above it, largely unaware of its trembling unless you look around the tank to see what it is doing. Idling at perhaps 1000-1200 rpm, the engine is below the frequency range at which the rubber cushions are absolutely effective, so you can feel a few tremors coming up through the frame. Take your hands off the bars and they will quiver slightly, as do the forks—but you only notice this because of the contrasting utter smoothness above 1800 rpm.

But idling and watching the handlebars move are just not where it's at. Pull in the clutch, snick the gearbox into first cog, ease the lever forward and wind on throttle. Right then you will discover where the Commando *lives*. You could get pitcher's elbow from the way it snaps your arms straight, but the only thing you get from the engine besides that mad surge forward is a slight tremble from the right footpeg. The Commando loves to sprint—and it is as polite about the whole thing as an Edwardian butler. (And as appealing, to those with a taste for the luxurious.)

A big luxury, in a curious way, is the necessity for riding by the tach. You don't have to do that with any other big twin: when the vibration begins to make your ribs rub together, it's time to change up a notch. Not a big problem out on the open road, but in traffic you find yourself running up and down through the gears just to keep the engine out of its resonant phases. And to give you the thrust you need for openings in traffic.

None of this applies to the Commando. You just leave the thing in second or third and do everything with the throttle. You have to keep an eye on the tach to make sure the revs don't go completely out of sight, but at anything between 2500 and 6500 rpm you get all the acceleration you can comfortably use, and you can hold a steady speed anywhere between without giving yourself a vibromassage.

If one applies racing standards to the Commando, it must be said that the handling falls just short of perfect. There's a touch of fuzziness in the way it tracks around turns when

Massive alloy casting mounts footpegs to backbone type frame, also serves as heat-sink for diode.

**A big motorcycle is often fast but not quick.
Watch the Commando S rap out a quarter-mile in 13.1 sec
with 102 mph at the traps—a real sprinter!**

you are working it hard. As compared to the best racing bikes it has this one flaw, but the Commando stands well above all other touring or road-sport motorcycles in every other regard. The others have at least as much flexing at the swing-arm, and they lack the Commando's rigid handlebar mounting. Rubber handlebar mounts and big, squishy grips may be necessary to keep vibration away from your hands; they don't do a thing for precision in handling. The Commando bars are solid; its grips are firm; the connection between hand and fork is precise and direct.

Those forks, incidentally, despite the clean, all-metallic look, are basically the same "roadholder" forks of yore. These acquired their considerable good-handling reputation largely on the basis of Norton's racing successes, but even the forks on production street bikes were superior to most of those on

Norton's competitors. The metering principle is somewhat complicated in execution, but damping has been sorted out very well for hard street use. Damping on compression is uniform and light, although the spring rate is progressive. On extension, the Commando's forks provide stiffer as well as fully progressive damping. As the forks extend, an internal piston squeezes oil through a series of orifices. The greater the extension, the fewer are the orifices that remain above the piston, and hence the stiffer action. The result is a very durable fork that will track beautifully over the most corrugated pavement you'll ever find. To slow you down when needed, the Commando has a new twin-leading-shoe brake at the bottom of those forks. It is as good as most competitors of similar design, but it *will* fade if worked hard enough.

In all other things, the Commando scores

well. It carries two-up quite well, with reasonable comfort for both rider and passenger, and without a drastic decrease in performance. With the present ignition system, starting is much easier than back in the Norton's magneto era. It still takes a good, healthy swing of the kickstart lever to make it all happen—but it will start. It is, with the new double-leading-shoe front brake and improved performance, a much better sprint and stop machine than the old Atlas—and it is a vastly improved tourer. The S model's small tank is a tourer's embarrassment, however, as it offers a cruising range of scarcely more than a hundred miles. If long hauls are your style, get the "pure" road version with the bigger tank. Maybe you should get the bigger tank—whatever you plan to do. That Commando is so much fun to ride you won't want to stop even for fuel. ◉

NORTON 750 COMMANDO S

Price suggested retail	East Coast, POE $1479
Tire, front	3.00 in x 9 in.
rear	3.50 in. x 19 in.
Brakes, front	Twin leading shoe 8.0 in. x 1.25 in.
rear	Single leading shoe 7.0 in. x 1.25 in.
Brake swept area	59.6 sq. in.
Specific brake loading	9.89 lb/sq. in.
Engine type	Four-stroke push rod, vertical twin
Bore and stroke .	2.875 in. x 3.503 in., 73mm x 89mm
Piston displacement	45 cu. in., 745cc
Compression ratio	8.9 : 1
Carburetion	(2) 30mm, Amal Concentric
Air filtration	Paper element
Ignition	Battery and coil
Bhp @ rpm	About 58 @ 6,500
Mph/1000 rpm, top gear	16.1
Fuel capacity	20pt.
Lighting	Alternator, 120 watts
Battery	12 v, 9 ah
Gear ratios, overall	(1) 12.4 (2) 8.25
	(3) 5.9 (4) 4.84
Wheelbase	56.75 in.
Seat height	31 in.
Ground clearance	6 in.
Curb weight	415 lb.
Test weight	590 lb.
Instruments	Speedometer, tachometer
0–60 mph	5.6 seconds
Standing start ¼ mile	13.18 seconds—101.69 mph
Top speed	110 mph

It's the ruggeᵈ

The 58 bhp power house! Note repositioned rev counter drive and cb unit. The motor remained clean and oil tight on test

Give the Commando S a fistful of throttle and your arms feel as though they're being pulled out of their sockets! The sheer power of 58 horses being unleashed at the turn of a wrist gives a sense of freedom, exhilaration and the feeling that you just want to ride, ride, and keep on riding.

The S-type was obviously designed for the American market with its abundance of chomium plating and metal-flake finish paintwork on fuel tank and battery and toolbox covers.

The upswept handlebars give

a very comfortable riding position for speeds up to the 70 mph limit, but when we tried the bike on a race circuit, wind pressure above this speed meant that we were having to hang on hard to keep our seat. It was quite tiring on both legs and arms over any distance and it proved that for long distance, high-speed motorcycling it is necessary to have either drop or straight handlebars to give a comfortable leaning position into the wind.

The other modifications to produce the S-type from the standard fastback Commando, include upswept exhausts, both

of which sweep to the left of the motor, a different dual-seat, a ridiculously small fuel tank and front forks which have the upper stanchion covers removed.

Frame- and engine-wise, the S-type is the same as the fastback, with the unique engine/gearbox/swinging arm unit all isolated from the main frame by large Metalastik bushes.

We received the Commando direct from the new Norton factory at Andover and it had just completed its running-in mileage.

Everything was correctly adjusted and running sweetly ready for a 120-mile run up the M1 and back.

Starting was a second or third kick affair providing you gave a hefty, long swing on the kick-start. It was no good giving a gentle prod as it needed brute force to turn the heavy motor.

We had filled the fuel tank from empty to completely full with just over 2.2 gallons of five-star. Weaving our way through the busy London traffic, it was pleasant to discover that the bike responded instantly to rider's directional control at any speed.

Only when stopping was difficulty encountered as the height of the saddle, combined with width of the machine with upswept exhaust pipes, makes it hard to touch a steadying toe on the ground. Also, it became quite hot on the inside left leg in spite of the two protection shields around the pipes. Taller riders probably wouldn't experience either of these problems.

Acceleration in traffic was of course superb and without using more than a quarter throttle it was possible to head most cars away from traffic lights. But if more was used and the revs were allowed to build up in first gear, the exhaust note became crisp and too noisy for comfort.

In fact, the note was reminiscent of a racing Domi with the reverse cone meggas and on the over-run, the crackle made quite

a few heads turn in disapproval.

Before starting out on the run to Warwickshire, a check was made on tyres, pressures and oil level as one can't afford to take chances on the motorway. The oil level was a pint below full mark and it was topped up to maximum level.

And so out of London on to the M1 slip road at Hendon, where at last we could give the Commando its head. By using peak revs in each gear, the 70 limit could be exceeded in second gear, but not wishing to offend other road users or break any laws, a wise compromise of

Underside of chaincase. Note timing hole on alternator cap

5000 rpm in the gears was settled for. This gave fair performance without a trace of vibration from the rubber-mounted power unit.

Loping along at a very gentle 70 mph on barely half throttle, the Commando almost laughed at the Marples limit. Then, just short of the Watford Gap fuel and coffee point, the bike cut out and then quickly burst back into life as reserve fuel was switched on.

Just on 70 miles had been covered from full tank to reserve and with 1.4 gallons to full tank again, it meant the reserve was 0.8 of a gallon and the bike was achieving approximately

(left) Rear brake pedal is adjustable for height as shown.
(right) Seat lifts off although oil filler is hard to reach.

one!

Commando "S": 750 cc of Norton brute power produces explosive acceleration . . . breath-taking speed and delight

MM SUPER TEST

Upswept meggas are smart but can be a little too noisy

50 miles per gallon.

After leaving the bike standing in the car park for ten minutes while the rider had a quick cuppa, he returned to find the ground beneath the rear half of the machine soaked with oil. This was apparently dripping from the rear chain and the extra pint added before the run had obviously either been pumped out of the breather on the tank or from the rear chain oiler.

Either way, the bike was fairly well lubricated on the outside at the rear. Also, that old Norton bogey of unscrewing exhaust pipe rings had struck and the nearside pipe was hanging loose. After wiping oil from the tyre

Rear chain oiler lubricates too much when oil is very hot

COMMANDO 'S'

the rugged one!

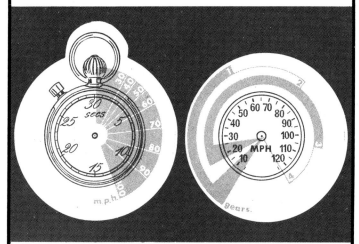

The really effective stopper!

and tightening the exhaust, we proceeded on our journey.

Needless to say, the exhaust ring came loose again, but as the oil had found its own "correct" level, it stopped lubricating the rear tyre. The exhaust needs wiring.

We returned to London later that evening in the dark and on the unlit A5 approach to the motorway, the lights proved their worth. They were well up to the 70 mph limit with a long, powerful 12-volt beam.

One other small fault was discovered on the run back to London and that was a sticking gearchange pawl. Although the change was light and positive, due to the excellent clutch operation, at the top end of the rev band, it seemed as if high frequency vibration made the upwards change gear pawl stick in its housing and it didn't allow gears to be swapped until the engine revs slowed down.

Later, we encountered a similar fault with a sticking cb advance/retard unit, which gave a rapid tickover until the motor was slowed by dragging the clutch to assist the bobweight springs to return the unit to retard.

However, both these minor faults applied to this particular machine and obviously would not be encountered on all the Commando S bikes!

Handling on the Commando up to 70 mph was precise and like being on rails, the suspension was firm and on bumpy roads seemed a little too solid.

However, it isn't until you start to use all the performance

of a machine that you discover any shortcomings in roadholding.

On the track the Commando S was a beauty and could be made to follow any line one wished without really trying. Only once did the bike show signs of wavering from the straight and narrow. That was when the throttle had to be shut off at about 95 mph in a long right-hand bend. For three or four seconds, until the throttle was opened again, the rear end twitched violently. As soon as the power was turned back on it stopped . . . thank goodness!

Braking from any speed was excellent. All other controls are well placed and smooth to operate.

One final criticism . . . the centre stand. A course with Charles Atlas is needed to lift this machine on to the stand!

Our final conclusions are that the Commando S is a fun, fun, fun bike! Two up it's terrific, one up it's fantastic and well worthy of the title—Motorcycle of the Year. We're all looking forward to our next test of the Commando!

PERFORMANCE

Speeds in Gear

	Minimum	Maximum
1st	6	55
2nd	12	80
3rd	18	104
4th	26	124

Acceleration

0–30 2.2 sec. 0–40 3.0 sec.
0–50 4.0 sec. 0–60 5.2 sec.
0–70 7.0 sec. 0–80 8.8 sec.

0–90 10.8 sec. 0–100 13.2 sec.
Standing quarter-mile: 13.4 sec.
Terminal speed 102 mph.

Fuel consumption: Overall 54 mpg; varying between 38 and 66 mpg, depending upon use of machine.

Braking: From 30 mph using both brakes on dry tarmac: 28 ft. 6 in.

SPECIFICATION

Engine: Twin-cylinder, four-stroke, ohv. Bore 73 mm x stroke 89 mm, giving 745 cc capacity. Compression ratio 8.9:1. Developing 58 bhp at 6500 rpm.

Transmission: Four-speed gearbox, driven by triple row chain running in oil bath, through a diaphragm spring four-plate clutch. Gear ratios (overall, with 19-tooth gearbox sprocket):
1st—12.4   2nd—8.25
3rd— 5.9   4th—4.84

Electrical equipment: A 10 amp/hr. 12-volt battery with positive earth is supplied with current by a Lucas RM21 alternator via a rectifier and Zener-diode. Ignition is by twin contact breakers and coils and has a 12-volt capacitor in system.

Carburettors: Twin Amal 930

concentrics with 220 main jets, 25 pilot jet, No. 3 throttle valve and 0.107 needle jet.

Dimensions: Length 87½ in., width 26 in., ground clearance 6 in., weight 415 lb., wheelbase 56¾ in., seat height with rider seated 31 in.

Capacities: Fuel tank 2.2 gal., oil tank 5 pints, gearbox 1 pint, primary chaincase 200 cc (7 fl. oz.), front forks 150 cc (5½ fl. oz.).

Wheels: Front—WM2 rim with 3.00 × 19 ribbed tyre. Twin-leading-shoe 8 in. front brake. Rear—WM2 rim with 3.50 × 19 GP tyre and 8 in. single-leading-shoe brake.

Price: £499 12s. 2d., manufactured by Norton-Villiers Ltd, North Way, Walworth Industrial Estate, Andover, Hants.

Twin carbs with air filter breathe in, upswept pipes breathe out!

NORTON COMMANDO PRODUCTION RACER

We Sample A 130-mph Speedster, Try Ourselves, And Track-Test Two Tracks.

CYCLE WORLD
R O A D   T E S T

RARE IS THE ROAD RIDER who has not, regardless of what he is riding, twisted the throttle just a little harder than is necessary to get from Point A to Point B. In every rider, there's a little bit of a racer. The road, fraught with perils real and imaginary, public and private, becomes a temptress at every curve.

That's what riding is all about. Not the fact that you get there, but how you get there. Some guys get quite good at it. Those that aren't, think they are. Even the squid who has been on a motorcycle for only three days of his entire life just *knows* he is the fastest thing that ever came 'round a bend.

Only the race track can give a man proper perspective, with a good dose of exhilaration thrown in. It's unique—the reason why the CYCLE WORLD staff jumps at the chance to rent a track and go play racing with a properly fitted machine. It's an absolute ball, all of it tax deductible.

Take away the roadside grit, the greasy, traveled surface, the imagined cop in every dark cranny, the family sedan coming at you, straddling the center line.

Take away the speed limit, which is always in the back of your mind even when you exceed it. Take away the yellow line. Both sides of the road are yours, not just the one lane. Blind corners are free for the shooting. Going fast is all up to you, the laws of physics, and how well your *"huevos"* are wired to the throttle hand. With nothing extraneous to impede your progress, about 98 percent of the action will be above 60 mph, not below it. The world goes by much faster now, as the physical penalties for sloppiness go up by the square of the speed, rather than in direct proportion...

Cool morning fog was just beginning to clear at Orange County International Raceway. A 745-cc Norton Commando sat on its stand in the middle of the tower bend. Click, crank. The photographer was using lots of film, very carefully. We were getting impatient. Brian Slark of Norton-Villiers quipped, "He must have shares in Eastman-Kodak."

CYCLE WORLD has already tested the original Commando (Sept. 1968), but this one is a bit different. It is an FIM-style production racer. The engine, frame and rolling gear must be over-the-counter items, although certain engine components will usually be hotter than standard fare. It must be more or less legal for the street, so it has silencers and lights. For safety, and comfortable operation at high speeds, the machine may have rear-set pegs and seat, large capacity gas tank, racing tires and a partial fairing. The gearing, internal and overall, may be changed to suit the circuit. A typical race for this machine would be the 750-cc production TT at the Isle of Man.

It is a Commando, but it is not a Commando. It could be ridden on the street, but to do so would be a waste. The engine varies little from standard, but has been assembled with "tlc"—tender loving care. Good old tlc, and a few appropriate parts. That's all it takes to introduce the rider to a demanding and competitive sport.

Norton's production racer is ideally suited to learning this pastime, because of its flexible nature. The long-stroke (73 by 89 mm) vertical Twin delivers its torque in a broad power band, with a claimed peak of 66 bhp at a modest 7000 rpm, up 6 bhp at 6800 rpm. There is no embarrassment if you forget to downshift. Turn on the gas and the bike levers itself away at anything above 3000 rpm.

Surprisingly little has to be done to a machine to make it run fast. In the case of the production racer, all the parts necessary are on Norton's shelf. According to the Norton-Villiers distributors on the West Coast, they will be made available to U.S. buyers in early 1970. Alterations to the standard Commando engine consist of: raising the compression ratio from 8.9:1 to 10.4:1 with a pair of new pistons, the flat tops of which protrude into a head with recessed squish area; larger valves; heavy duty valve springs; lightened and polished rocker arms; and a sports cam.

Cam timing is moderate. Inlet opens 44.5 (precise fellows, those British!) degrees btc, closes 63.4 degrees abc. Duration is 288 degrees. Exhaust opens at 63 degrees bbc, closes at 28 degrees atc; resulting duration, 271 degrees. The duration figures are comparable with the run-of-the-mill big bore sports roadsters, such as the Triumph 650 or the BSA Three. In practical terms, this cam is perfectly adaptable to street operation and doesn't even make the engine go "rump-rump."

The rest of engine and transmission remains unchanged. This includes pushrods and tappets. The exhaust system is the same one on the street bike, complete with effective silencers. The eight-plate (four drive, four driven) diaphragm clutch is unmodified and takes the extra "pressure" without a whimper. Carburetion is also standard—two 30-mm Amal Concentrics fitted with 240 main jets for OCIR, which is near sea level.

The racer fired immediately on a run-and-bump start. In the first few tuning laps, it became quite evident that Orange County was much too small a course to the Norton Commando. We had on our hands a machine that wanted to do more than 125 mph, but lacked enough straightaway to find out just how *much* more.

Drag racing plays the major role at OCIR, and the AFM people who run there from time to time must make do with a layout none too conducive to good road racing. Running the Commando counterclockwise from the tower, you negotiate a half-mile straightaway at about 120 mph, then haul down in hurried fashion for a 40-mph hairpin.

It was at this point that some of the stock running gear components began to complain. The standard 8-in. double leading shoe front brake had racing linings installed, but grabbed mercilessly and then proceeded to fade in the next few laps, reducing stopping power to an uncompetitive level. Careful installation could cure some of this problem. The rear

brake was not so grabby, but indiscreet foot pressure, combined with soft rear suspension (and damper travel inhibited by the forward cant of the units), could produce rear wheel patter. Handily, if you overshoot the turn, which we did once, Orange County has a nice, long sandbox for you to play in.

If you make it through the turn, entering wide to avoid running across a false apex with resultant wide and sloppy exit, the best part of the course follows. Accelerating all the while, you bear to the left side of the pavement and set up for a gradual 30-degree right-hander, feeding to a short straight and an identical 30-degree left-hander. This is a classic Keppel Gate, Isle of Man, situation. Use the whole road through the right-hander and you are on the wrong line to get the best speed exiting from the left-hander—an important point as higher speed on the following straightaway will net you better lap times.

The basically good Commando handling, the compliment of a road racing layout and an excellent, rigid double cradle frame and wide swinging arm mounting, showed itself well here. It is a heavy machine and has to be cranked hard, but it tracked true through this S-bend, held to line well, and showed no sign of front end wobble, in spite of speed through the latter bend ranging from 100 to 105 mph.

The rest of the course is straightforward and dull. A brief straight, a quick jog left and then right moving the rider about 20 feet over from his original path down the back straight. Then a sweeping left-hand turn through an oil-impregnated

parking lot back to the tower and the front straight. Basically, this adds up to a horsepower course, with only two turns requiring braking, and one S-Bend requiring impeccable handling. A mere hors d' oeuvre. But our appetites were whetted, so we moved to the entree...

Riverside yawns at you. Turns disappear into the yellow haze. They are sweeping and wide. The back straight seems endless, the high speeds insignificant. Rider and machine—a germ swimming trancelike across an uncaring set of tonsils. A true International Raceway.

First on the agenda was a top speed run, utilizing the entire back straight. It runs for almost a mile, adding impetus with a downward dip onto a certified flat where the times are measured. After a switch to 230 main jets to compensate for the 1500-foot altitude, the racer ran through at 131.02 mph at 6500 rpm, pulling a 3.83 top gear. The Commando is thus the fastest "production" machine ever tested by CYCLE WORLD. At this speed, surging in the carburetor float chambers became evident, probably induced by a sympathetic engine vibration working the floats up and down, alternately causing too much or too little fuel to enter the float chamber. Isolating the carburetors from vibration on rubber extensions would probably correct the surge and result in a few mph increase.

A 130-mph machine is an excellent match for the Riverside circuit, as it reaches speeds that require the rider to make full use of the wide paving. The entire course had just undergone complete renovation at the time of our visit, with new paving, a redesigned Turn 9, and new stands for 10,000 people at the starting straight and in the famous Riverside S-bends. The only racers to run on it so far were Dan Gurney, in a Trans-Am sedan, and a gaggle of Formula III drivers, so the pavement was fresh and clean. Track manager Dave Berg alerted the land-mover jockeys to keep an eye out for our little red speedster and graciously told us to let her rip.

Gathering speed through the right-hand 450-foot radius Turn 9, which was widened and enlarged by adding a dogleg to the left off the back straight, the Norton is rock steady, leaned well over and beginning to drift at about 80 mph. The triangular section K81s were just getting scrubbed in and seemed to offer much more feel at Riverside than they did at Orange County.

After Turn 9, a thousand-foot straight slings the machine at well over 100 mph in fourth gear towards Turn 1, a scary, slightly uphill left-hander—scary because you can't see where it goes. Naturally, it is approached from the right-hand side of the straight. You peel off late, but at full throttle. There's a bump near the apex of this turn that lightens the bike at about 110 mph and gives a good reading of the suspension.

The front end of the Commando tracked perfectly over the rise, and the rear, with the spongy springing, reported back in fairly good shape, yeilding only a small oscillation that ceased quickly.

Then on to a short straight, brake to about 80 for a 30-degree right, the first turn in the Esses. The lack of sure braking was a deterrent here, as the turn may be banzaied much faster than first appears possible. The best riders go through fast enough to create an extra turn requiring a leftward flick of the machine before going right for a quickly following Turn 3.

The 420-lb. weight of the production racer is somewhat of a disadvantage in the Esses, as it resists the nine, deft flicking back-and-forth movements required from the entry of Turn 2 to the entry of the slow 180-degree Turn 6. That last turn is the one most likely to cause trouble to bikes with marginal ground clearance as it slams the decelerating machine sharply uphill, compressing suspension just about the time you must shove the bike over hard to the right at 60 mph. With no centerstand, the Commando passed this test well, the ground working against the rider's toe like a belt sander, foot pointed down on the pegs.

Then follows another third gear straight to Turn 7, the hairiest spot on the 2.55-mile "short" course used for motorcycle racing. The world gets very large and the rider very insignificant here, as the machine swoops downward and then back upward to a distant turn, invisible behind the crest of a hill. The rider must calculate his shut-off points precisely from the 4-3-2-1 markers on the shoulder. Just before the crest, a set of violent squiggles painted on the pavement reminds late-brakers that "it's all over, jack." Behind the crest awaits a steep drop and a slow first-gear left-hander, which becomes an adverse camber, because the line cuts across from the extreme right at the crest to an apex at the bottom of the hill.

Approaching Turn 7 requires two neat downshifts and hairline full-force braking. Not having the latter, we would have preferred backshifts on the Commando to be made with a positive downward jab of the foot, rather than the old-style upward toe pull. Apparently, someone who was used to the old pattern installed a reversed cam plate in the gearbox. Fortunately, reversing the lever to reach a rear-set peg on a stock Commando gearbox (which shifts one-up-three-down in normal position), makes it shift in the more preferable one-down-three-up pattern.

After a wide approach to Turn 7-A (Turn 8 is part of the long 3.3-mile big car course), you enter the back straight halfway in the middle, with a 2170-ft. run to Turn 9. Approaching peak revs in fourth gear, the rider has time to listen to the engine. The feeling on the Commando is fantastically smooth for a big Twin, as the rubber engine mounting isolates the engine, preventing vibration from getting through to the frame, bars, seat and pegs. Hence the name "isolastic." Displacement of 750 cc is the present practice maximum for a vertical Twin, and it is nearly impossible to balance it to run smoothly at all speeds. Norton found the answer: if you can't stop it from shaking, put it in quarantine.

Finally comes the rapid right-hand Turn 9, entered by bearing left through a dogleg at about 115 to 120 mph. Easy stuff on the Commando. The dogleg is hardly a turn as it is extremely wide and allows plenty of room for error. Then another 1000 feet to Turn 9, shift down to third and get ready to peel off at the "Good Grief!" sign following the distance markers.

Then, confidence inspired by the machine's stability, you are ready to go around again, and again. Only next time, maybe, you'll try the Esses just a little bit harder...

NORTON PRODUCTION RACER

SPECIFICATIONS

List price	n.a.
Suspension, front	telescopic fork
Suspension, rear	swinging arm
Tire, front	Dunlop K81 3.60-19
Tire, rear	Dunlop K81 4.10-19
Engine, type	ohv vertical Twin
Bore x stroke, in., mm	2.87 x 3.50, 73 x 89
Piston displacement, cu. in., cc	45.5, 745
Carburetion	(2) Amal Concentric 30 mm
Ignition	12V battery-coil
Claimed bhp @ rpm	66 @ 7000
Oil system	gear pump, dry sump
Oil capacity, pt.	6.0
Fuel capacity, U.S. gal.	4.5
Recommended fuel	premium
Starting system	kick, folding crank

POWER TRANSMISSION

Clutch	multi-plate, wet
Primary drive	triplex chain
Final drive	3/8-in. x 5/8-in. chain
Gear ratios, overall:1	
5th	none
4th	3.83
3rd	4.21
2nd	5.10
1st	8.35

DIMENSIONS

Wheelbase, in.	56.7
Seat height, in.	29.5
Seat width, in.	11.0
Handlebar width, in.	23.0
Footpeg height, in.	12.0
Ground clearance, in.	5.0
Curb weight (w/half-tank fuel), lb.	420
Weight bias, front/rear, percent	46/54

PERFORMANCE

Top speed, mph	131.02 @ 6500 rpm
Piston speed (@7000 rpm), ft./min.	4080

TEST CONDITIONS

Air temperature, degrees F	78
Humidity, percent	60
Wind velocity, mph	none
Strip alignment, relative wind:	

WIND

S ———————————————→ F

Norton Commando

Above 40 m.p.h. the Commando and the Honda 4 feel much the same

NORTON Villiers were the early birds among the bigger and better machines that have now garnered the arresting classification of "Superbike". With a fine balance between the aim to produce something really new, and the need to use as much of the older components as possible, the now famous rubber-isolated layout was designed.

The engine unit from the Atlas was carefully improved to give better reliability, and the weaker points eliminated or changed. The introduction of a single plate diaphragm clutch solved the problems associated with 58 b.h.p.—and appropriate torque—in a dramatic manner: having just dismounted from a ride on the Norton, I think it's incredible that this delightfully light and positive control could have been overlooked for so long before the Commando appeared.

The awful primary chain case of the older Nortons was redesigned as a single alloy casting, which certainly cured the oil leaks but was too wide for the hard-riding owners who bought the first Commandos. The handling and road-holding encouraged cornering that ground away mainstands, silencers, and even the new and shiny alloy primary chaincases. The final touch was a complete overhaul of the appearance. The new spine frame was shrouded by a smoothly styled fibreglass tank which merged smoothly with the wide seat, and flowed onward to a rear protrusion tipped with the rear light. This great swathe of fibreglass transformed the appearance, and reduced the weight by a considerable amount.

The final result is now familiar on the roads of Europe and America : a long sleek shape picked out with shining alloy, and with little of the fussy, bitty effect of the traditional British twin.

All this is well known to most of our readers, and the Commando must now compete for attention with a motley array of the large and powerful multi-cylindered machines. We thought that it was time that we took another look at the British side of this market, and indulged in a little comparative comment, to boot.

I have ridden the Triumph Trident, the Kawasaki 3, the Honda 4, the Munch Mammoth since last I rode a Commando, and the overall conclusion is that Norton Villiers' aim was excellent—the Commando still lies right up there with the best of the new breed. The almost venerable antiquity of the basic Norton engine is the only feature of the Commando that does not compare well with all the others. However it hardly matters how the power is produced as

long as the unit is reliable, sturdy, long-lived and not unduly temperamental—or so I was thinking while travelling down to Andover by train to collect the machine on one bitingly cold Saturday morning.

The new factory is really in the country : only a few yards from the station the houses ended, and green fields began. The factory lies on an attenuated industrial estate that still has a predominently green appearance, and it is only a brief spin from the Andover bypass to Thruxton circuit.

The actual collection of the machine was somewhat amusing. When the formalities had been concluded, I noticed that there was no key for the machine. It turned out that the key was in the possession of the managing director, who came in to hand it over. Obviously there is no danger of the staff of Norton Villiers getting out of touch with the machines that they sell !

In the course of conversation several broad hints were dropped as to the next round of refinements to the Commando, and as the first batch of Fastbacks to be assembled at Andover has not yet been started, who knows how soon improvements might appear?

The first question must be on disc brakes : the works production racers have worn several varieties, and their success must make their fitting a question only of economics. A hard-driven Commando can test the standard twin-leading-shoe front brake quite severely—although the damp and snowy

weather has not allowed me to press the machine to this extent on this occasion—and a good disc brake will provide all the braking power that one could ever require—except at very low speeds. At very low speeds the action of a disc brake is a little slow, and many people will be perfectly happy with the standard brake now fitted.

Electric starting would be my own choice as a first improvement to the Commando. I would hardly describe the machine as hard to start, but the compression ratio is definitely high, and the heft required for a good swing requires a sturdy right leg. This is rather embarrassing when, with a pillion passenger aboard, it is necessary to start the engine with the bike on an off-camber : it weighs a hearty 415 lb, remember. These are the times when an electric starter is a real boon. Unfortunately the small and powerful starter motors used by the Japanese, which weigh only 10-15 lb with all the associated gubbins, have no immediately obvious English equivalent —but from the confident comments from the MD it is highly likely that a solution has been or will be found.

Although the styling of the Commando in its Fastback form has received design awards, the tank is rather on the small side : it is likely that a larger tank will be forthcoming.

Even after the first hundred yards it was obvious that the Commando should be classed with the Honda 4 for sheer spread of torque, completely eclipsing the somewhat pallid bottom end power

Sedate cornering style shown on one of the earlier Commando Fastbacks

of the Kawasaki and BSA/Triumph threes. Unfortunately the rubber suspension does not come into effect until about 3,000 r.p.m., and the gargantuan shaking of the engine unit is distinctly evident. These movements are not vibrations in the usual sense: more akin to the sensation of riding over very rippled surfaces on an unsprung machine. This kind of sensation can be completely ignored after a while, and never causes the discomfort produced by high-frequency vibrations.

The actual machine that I was riding was about a year old, and had been fitted with an S-type engine (note the neater positioning of the tachometer drive) but evidently had not been blessed with the softer rubber suspension bushes used on later models. The softer rubber isolates the rider from vibrations right down to about 1,500 r.p.m., a point that I have not had the opportunity to check as yet.

The factory is so close to the open road that only a few minutes later I was speeding down the main road to Basingstoke and London, and as the engine warmed up the rain eased. The feel of the Commando is slightly leaden. There are no illusions possible about the weight beneath you, and on corners this mass makes itself felt. This does not imply any heaviness in the handling, it is simply necessary to press lightly

against the tank for the Commando to track round with excellent stability; one is merely made to feel that there is a lot of machine going round the corner underneath you.

The main curb on cornering was hardly the handling, or even the ground clearance—the considerable power of the engine was simply enough to spin the wheel merrily on the wet surface, and until I had refamiliarized myself with the response to the throttle in each gear I was in no hurry to scratch round corners.

As this familiarity returned the other features of the Commando became more obvious. Strong cross winds were easily ignored, and the steering showed little signs of wandering at high speed in spite of the absence of any damper.

The easy gait of 65-75 m.p.h. required very little effort on the rider's behalf, the only vibration that was noticed came through the footrests, and was occasionally annoying, but the eager response to the throttle smoothed out hills, swept away cars, and destroyed the miles without any very high speeds becoming necessary.

The Commando is an open road machine: the acceleration and ill-defined cruising speed allow one to set a speed and then maintain an average very close to that speed without bursts of flat-out running. There is no specific speed at

which the Commando feels particularly happy, the only provision being that one never seems to travel much slower than 55. The lack of noise and vibration to let one know how fast either engine or machine is travelling means that a sharp eye must be kept on both tachometer and speedometer.

In town one needs to look at neither: in either third or top the vibrations are quite unmistakable, and were it not for the anger of wheelspin in second gear I would have used second for most town work. It is unfortunate that this most commonly used area of performance is so uncomfortable to use, though with more familiarity the shaking would fade into the background and be no longer felt. The softer rubbers I've mentioned might help here.

Above 40 m.p.h. the Honda 4 and the Commando feel much the same. There is no need to use excessive revs, or to play tunes on the gearbox with either machine: simply open the throttle and watch the needles rotate. The acceleration feels lazy, and it is with a distinct sense of shock that one appreciates that the speedometer is *already* reading in three figures: strangely, this sensation is not apparent on the Kawasaki 3—the faint tingle from the smooth three-cylinder engine is just sufficient to "sense" the speed for you; the Triumph Trident, a four-stroke, is more like the

Commando in this respect. The wide torque band of Honda and Commando means that the dramatics of the Kawasaki 3 are not apparent. There is no sudden jolt in the back, more a feel of a high-speed lift getting under way.

A two-up load the Norton hardly notices at all, only at low speeds in high gear, and by the fact that ground clearance on cornering is affected. The addition of panniers and carrier, plus touring gear for two people, would cut the ground clearance to a positively alarming minimum. The mainstand and silencer positioning have been altered since the machine's introduction, but there is still a problem in this direction.

The seat has plenty of room for two people, and the passenger footrests allow the kickstarter to be used without requiring the passenger to remove foot and close up the rest. Unfortunately the driver's footrests are not adjustable, and certainly with my own length of leg I would have very much appreciated the provision of some form of adjustment. The scheme that Honda use on the CB 72/77, (sadly) abandoned since, would be ideal. My British Standard Passenger had no adverse comments on the passenger accommodation, the biting cold distracting her attention from matters of critical judgement to the attractions of a hot drink and a warm home.

Accessories are up to a good standard.

The headlamp flasher is really valuable in giving advance warning of one's rapid approach, and produces far more effect than a blast from the horn. On this particular Commando the horn was very anaemic: this is not typical of the breed, and normally the Commando horn produces a far healthier cry than most other makes of motorcycle can boast. The speedometer and tachometer are well calibrated, and the aluminium containers are a nice touch, especially when compared with the plastic cans used for the Honda 4 at a far higher price.

The electric fittings are typical of modern Lucas equipment: 12-volt battery, capacitor ignition, and an alternator . . . and perhaps an electric starter in future?

The consumption of fuel is always judged on a double standard: all two-strokes seem to have their own private standard, and four-strokes theirs. The Commando comes in the class of thirsty four-strokes, and "normal" two-strokes —albeit of half the capacity. My typical petrol consumption has been 55 m.p.g., in mixed going.

The finish of the Norton Commando has been attacked on several counts, but most of these could be traced to the use of painted fibreglass on the original series models. The paint wore off rather quickly, and led to some dissatisfaction. finish is good, and few blemishes were

Current Commandos use colour impregnated materials, and should be completely free of any such criticism.

An overall assessment of the Commando is that the machine as a whole is admirably suited to the demands of both touring and sporting riders, and the antiquity of the engine is obtrusive only at low speeds. Flexibility suffers a little, but not enough to matter: for some more traditional motorcyclists lower compression pistons would make the Commando far more attractive, but the average buyer will probably be quite happy.

The machine does not feel very refined: rather it is solid, all of a piece, and with an integrity all of its own. The natural competitor is the Honda 4, and the Commando retails at over £150 less, in addition to being actually available!

The mooted refinements of starter motor and better brakes and tank will go a long way towards closing the apparent gap in specifications between these two, and with flashing indicators, would meet the opposition head on.

The only thing that makes *me* hesitate is the engine. It is so complex to deal with when compared with the luxuries of horizontally split crankcases, and almost trivial simplicity of Italian and Japanese overhead camshafts. To

Continued on page 203

NORTON 750 COMMANDO
A MUSCLE MACHINE FROM ACROSS THE POND

MOTORCYCLIST TEST REPORT

WELL-STYLED 750cc Norton Commando features gas tank/seat combination in fiberglass. Saddle slips under rear of tank and is held in place by two knurled knobs mounted above rear shocks.

MUFFLERS, as on many other models, are set at angle to allow clearance for vertical wheel travel.

COMPRESSION ratio on the Commando is 8.9-to-1. Bore and stroke are 73 x 89mm. Gearbox is 4-speed, constant mesh. Top speed is claimed to be 111 mph.

PARK A NORTON COMMANDO on a street anywhere in the United States, go into a store, come out five minutes later, and there's a crowd of people gathered around the bike debating if they like or don't like the looks of the machine. What is there about a motorcycle like this one that makes people do this? Read on and let's find out!

What is a Norton Commando? As far as we can see it's a blend of many things, but above all, some of the most radical and unusual styling changes that have bombed down the pike in many a moon. Look at the photos with this test. How about that wild looking fiberglass body? How about the space-age styling? This is only part of what a Norton Commando is.

How about that gigantic looking twin-cylinder engine? Does it look familiar? It certainly ought to, as basically it's the same Atlas engine as used in the milder street and street scrambler machines manufactured by Norton. Some changes have been made, but really not that many. The 8-to-1 compression has been raised slightly to 8.9-to-1, and a beefier primary chain has been utilized, but other than a few outward modifications to the engine, everything remains the same. What does this mean to you? It means that one of the new Commandos will bomb thru the quarter mile in close to a flat 13 seconds, which is really hauling. It means that if you owned our test bike, you could crank it up to an effortless 111 miles an hour. Chances are that those of you who are Norton fans have heard of the Englishman, Paul Dunstall. This man turns out a modified Norton, using the basic Atlas engine with very few modifications. His latest machine cranks out a hairy 72 brake horsepower at roughly seven grand, and clocks a straightaway speed of right around 150 miles an hour.

As far as engines go, the Atlas is nothing special. It's not desmodromic, doesn't have four valves per cylinder, but yet it is horribly reliable, extremely powerful and definitely well made. Connecting rods are composed of a rod and cap assembly, the cylinder is cast iron, the head aluminum, and the somewhat crude looking forged iron crank rides on plain steel bearings. Sounds kind of like the family car, doesn't it? As you look closer you begin to notice some things that take it out of the ordinary classification. The engine is capable of doing some

BRAKES on the Commando would do justice to a locomotive. Front unit is of double leading shoe variety.

deep breathing, as it has a gigantic set of valves, exhaust ports sticking out at almost right angles to the cylinder, and parallel intake ports almost wide enough to cram your fist down without hitting the walls. Two big 30mm Amal (improved Amal) Concentrics feed the gas and air mixture into the large, hungry cylinders. Engine capacity is about 745cc. Bore and stroke is 73 by 89 millimeters. The material we received with our test bike didn't claim any specific horsepower at any specific rpm, and it's kind of silly to try and guess something like this, but still we'd be willing to eat our hats if this thing didn't crank out at least 40 large horses at somewhere around 6500 rpm. If any of you out there have done any dyno testing of this engine, we'd like to hear from you.

Look over the bore and stroke dimensions with the stroke so much bigger than the bore. Add to that the long intake tracts leading to the carburetors, the somewhat nominal compression ratio and the 30mm carbs. What does this tell you? You're right, gobs and gobs of torque. In fact, you really don't know what torque is until you clamber aboard a big machine like this one. Power is there in usable amounts at right around 2500 rpm, and as you go higher in the rpm range, there's more and more of it on tap. Once you've shifted into 4th gear you can drop your speed down to right around fifteen miles an hour, and then without doing anything other than smoothly rolling on your throttle, dial it up to way over 100 miles an hour. This is torque with a capital T. Here is where the only real problem we encountered with our test bike came into being. The monster has so much usable horsepower that it gobbled up a chain every time we turned up the wick to full blow. We've got to admit that this was probably our fault, as we noticed that every time a chain did give up the ghost, the rear tire was smoking and spinning like nothing we had ever seen before. Oh well! One other thing — the automotive-type diaphragm clutch is completely slip-proof. It grabs and holds hard, but the effort needed to pull it in at the handlebar is negligible.

The beefy looking dual downtube cradle type frame is fairly standard as far as frames go. Taken into consideration with some of the other components, the frame becomes unusual. The entire engine and transmission is slung from soft rubber bushes, just like an aircraft engine is supported in rubber Lord Mounts. The swing arm assembly for the rear shocks hangs on separate plates on each side instead of being bolted directly to the rear base of the frame, as in most other motorcycles. Because of this somewhat novel setup, road shocks and engine vibration is just about nil. No one has yet found a way to keep a large vertical twin from shaking the insides out of your watch and the fillings from your teeth, so Norton went in another direction and ended up by producing a bike almost completely devoid of vibration.

Norton suspension has always been some of the best around, and the Commando follows that tradition. The large double damped telescopic forks smooth out anything short of whacking a curb, and no matter what you do, they won't clunk or bang on rebound. The 3 position rear shocks are set in their mounts at an accute angle that looks strange, but works fine.

The Commando has a set of brakes on it that would do justice to a locomotive. It stands to reason if you're going to ride one of the fastest production motorcycles in the world, you might as well have some brakes to bring it to a rapid halt. They're both large internal expanding units, with the front being of the double leading shoe variety, and the rear single leading shoe.

Let's get back to how the bike looks. If you haven't seen

NORTON 750 COMMANDO TEST

one yet, you're missing a real treat. The entire top section of the machine is a fiberglass seat and tank combination that boasts some of the best glass work that we've run across. Color is maroon and silver with accents of black. The large soft seat slips in under the rear of the gastank and then is held in place by two knurled knobs mounted above the rear shock absorbers. The oiltank and battery access box are silver with the words "Commando 750" imprinted on them. The rest of the bike is all glistening chrome and polished aluminum.

We couldn't come up with too many complaints on our test bike. We've already mentioned that it munched chains, but we haven't heard anything from any owners, so it's possible we acquired a dud in that respect. The headlight refused to work until we did a little sleuthing and came up with a disconnected wire. After we hooked this up, all was well. We've heard quite a few complaints about the center stand dragging under hard cornering conditions, but as our machine wasn't equipped with one, we can't vouch for this fact. The sidestand on our test bike would scrape a little, but we were really honking on when it happened, and we don't think it will do this under ordinary conditions.

The new Norton Commando is one heck of a wild machine. It goes fast, stops fast and looks better than most bikes on the road today. Try one and see what we mean!

SPECIFICATIONS: NORTON COMMANDO 750

Displacement	745cc
Bore and Stroke	73 x 89mm
Compression	8.9-to-1
Engine Type	OHV vertical twin
Clutch	Diaphragm type
Gearbox	Separate, 4-speed constant·mesh
Gear Ratios	1st: 12.40, 2nd: 8.25, 3rd: 5.90, 4th: 4.84
Lubrication	Dry sump
Ignition	Battery, coil
Suspension	Front: Tubular telescopic Rear: Swing arm
Tires	Front: 3.00 x 19 Rear: 3.50 x 19
Gastank Capacity	3.9 gallons
Oiltank Capacity	6 pints
Wheelbase	57.2 inches
Ground Clearance	5.3 inches
Top Speed	111 mph
Price	$1449 L. A.

ENGINE	Excellent	Good	Fair	Poor	Unsatisfactory
Starting		•			
Throttle Response	•				
Vibration		•			
Noise		•			
TRANSMISSION					
Gear Spacing	•				
Clutch Smoothness	•				
Shifting speed	•				
CONTROLS					
Handlebar position	•				
Ease of operation	•				
Location	•				
BRAKES					
Lever pressure	•				
Pedal pressure	•				
Fade resistance	•				
Directional stability	•				
Stopping distance	•				
SUSPENSION					
Front	•				
Rear	•				
Ride control	•				
Dampening	•				
APPEARANCE					
Paint	•				
Construction and welds	•				
Chrome and trim	•				
ELECTRICAL					
Wiring	•				
Headlight		•			
Taillight	•				
Horn	•				
GENERAL					
Spark plug accessibility	•				
Instrumentation	•				
Side stand		•			
Center stand					
Seat comfort	•				
Muffling	•				
Tool storage space	•				

COMMENTS: An instant classic. One of the fastest production motorcycles in the world. Extremely reliable. Excellent braking. Fine bike for touring use.

THE NORTON COMMANDO

In this, the age of the super multi-cylinder motorcycle, it's extremely easy to forget just how strong a good running twin can be. After riding the three and four cylinder machines you tend to dismiss the commonplace two potter as passe. No way, baby! One ride on a machine like the Norton Commando S and you begin to realize that a strong good handling twin is as much motorcycle as most people will ever be able to use.

The Norton Commando, successor to the Atlas, was introduced late in 1968 and to say that it created quite a stir is a gross understatement. The Commando bristled with innovations. In styling alone the new Norton was head and shoulders above most of the competition. A new frame configuration and method of mounting the engine added to the appeal of the new machine. The Norton

Commando might well be called the first of the super bikes.

The S model of the Commando is little more than a scrambler type version with high pipes and an appearance designed to appeal to the off-road enthusiast. The Commando S has in its own way all the good looks of its older brother. The high pipes are fitted with reverse cone megaphones and perforated heat shields. Pipe placement is good and even the passenger can reach the footpeg without developing an odd curve in the left leg. Red metalflake paint is used on the tank and side panels and silver metalflake covers the taillight bracket. With the exception of the frame those are the only painted surfaces you'll find on the Commando S, everything is polished alloy or chrome plated. Fuel capacity is slightly more than 2.5 gallons, not the best setup for a machine that

Two cylinders are more than sufficient.

qualifies as an excellent tourer. Tank shape is good with knee knotches that really work molded into the side panels.

Both fenders are chrome plated with the aft mudguard carried in the high position. The seat, easily detached by means of knurled knobs, is long, wide and well padded and comfortable. Removing the seat gives access to the oil tank and tool-kit. Norton has updated the appearance of their forks by giving them a Ceriani look. Huge alloy plates bolted to the frame serve as mounting points for the footpegs. Instrumentation on the Commando S is good and more important the speedometer and tach are placed in such a way that they are not obscured by the control cables. The face of the speedo is fitted with a high beam warning light and an ammeter is mounted in the headlight shell.

One of the most impressive features of the Norton is the ease of starting. Little effort, considering the size of the engine, is required to bring the big twin to life. Both float bowls should be tickled until they flood at which point one or two kicks will fire the thing off. (Granted, the kicks must be on the firm side.)

The Commando series of machines replaces the old Atlas which, in its day, was one of the fiercest bikes on the road. The Featherbed frame which supported the Atlas was something of a legend and before replacing it Norton made damn certain they had something better. The Commando frame is twenty odd pounds lighter and every bit as rigid as the tubing used in the Atlas. The new frame consists mainly of a large diameter backbone tube that runs from the steering head to a cross plate back in the sub-frame loop. The smaller diameter down tubes descend from the steering head, pass under the engine and curve sharply upward to terminate at the sub-frame loop. The only additional support comes from a pair of diagonal stringers that run from the center of the backbone to the area where the gearbox is mounted.

The Commando S really gets tricky in the way in which the engine/transmission/swinging arm and the cylinder head are supported by large rubber bushings. This rather unique form of mounting accounts in large part for the smoothness of the Commando S. At low revs, below 1700, at a stop light the bike vibrates like a champ. Once you pull out and the rev counter passes two grand the Norton smooths out to a degree that is hard to imagine. The Commando S is as smooth as any of the three and four cylinder machines that now grace the highways. Isolastic is the term Norton-Villiers uses to describe their method of mounting the engine/gearbox in the frame, it's apparently a combination of the words isolate and elastic. If such is the case the word is well chosen.

Powering the Norton Commando is an engine developed from the Atlas series of machines. At 89mm stroke is definitely on the long side. Bore is 73mm and total capacity of the engine is 745 cubic centimeters. Maximum horsepower (approximately 60bhp) develops at 6,500 rpm. Real power starts to build at about 2,000 revs and the bike pulls strong right on up to maximum. The intake ports are parallel and rather close together; on the other hand, the exhaust ports are widely spaced and aim outwards. This configuration gives a swirl effect which aids breathing. A light alloy head is fitted atop the cast iron barrels. The connecting rods are cap fastened to the build-up forged crankshaft and the alloy pistons rise and fall at the same time.

Drive to the camshaft is by chain and the valve train components consist of: forged rockers, light alloy pushrods and large diameter tappets. Primary drive has been improved considerably with a triplex chain replacing the single row device found in the earlier Atlas power units. The clutch is a four plate, diaphragm spring type device. The diaphragm spring gives an "overcenter" action that exerts a tremendous amount of pressure when the clutch is engaged. As the clutch is disengaged the pressure becomes weaker giving an action that is very light.

The four speed transmission is carried in a separate case which is bolted firmly to the rear of the crankcase. The ratios are well chosen and the Commando S will reach close to 100 while still in third. Action of the box is precise and changes are made with short pedal movement and no distressing noise. Even the shift into low is accomplished without a clunk.

A pair of concentric bowl Amal carburetors pass the fuel into the engine. Aside from a tendency to drain quickly when the engine is turned off the blenders gave us no cause for complaint. The pipes are among the sportiest looking we've yet to see. The tone given off by the exhaust system is kind of a bass/baritone growl. Nothing ill mannered, just authoritative!

The power of the Commando S and the way in which it is delivered is very impressive. The machine has great gobs of torque which means that it's not necessary to continually change gears when threading your way through traffic. Accelerating, the machine comes off the line with a great surge of power that doesn't diminish until the bike is well past the 100 mph mark. Because of the wide power band it's not necessary to get anywhere near max revs in a lower gear before changing up.

Text continued on page 147

Make	NORTON
Model	COMMANDO S
Price as Tested	$1,450.00 (Approx.)
Engine Type	4 CYCLE, TWIN CYLINDER
Bore	73mm
Stroke	89mm
Displacement	745cc
Compression Ratio	8.9:1
B.H.P. at R.P.M.	55 (approx.) at 6,500
Carburetor	AMAL CONCENTRIC BOWL (2)
Ignition	BATTERY & COIL
Fuel Capacity	2.7 GALLONS
Lubricating System	DRY SUMP
Clutch Type	WET, MULTI-DISC
Final Drive	CHAIN
Starting System	KICK, FOLDING LEVER
Gear Ratios	1st, 11.18:1; 2nd, 7.42:1; 3rd, 5.35:1; 4th, 4.35:1
Top Speed	112 MPH
Tire Size	FRONT, 3.00x19; REAR, 3.50x19
Suspension	FRONT, TELESCOPIC FORK REAR, SWINGING ARM
Frame Type	TUBULAR STEEL
Weight	410 POUNDS
Wheelbase	56 INCHES
Ground Clearance	6 INCHES
Peg Height	10 INCHES
Seat Height	32 INCHES

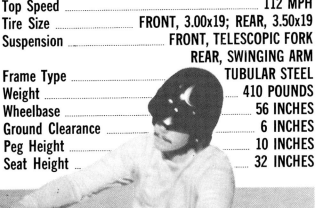
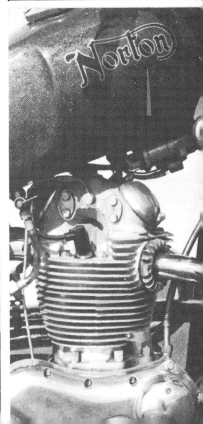

THE COMMANDO,

In the final months of the year 1968 Norton introduced a radical new high performance machine called the Commando. While the engine in the Commando was based on the already proven Atlas power plant, almost everything else on the machine was new. The generous use of fiberglass in the construction of the gas tank, seat base, and rear fender gave the machine a sleek road racing appearance. Performance was every bit as impressive as the appearance of the new bike; the Commando handled like a dream and it was one of the fastest machines then on the market. Thinking back, it becomes obvious that the Norton Commando introduced in 1968 was the first of a breed of machines that we have come to call "Super Bikes."

After spending considerable time with the latest edition of the Norton Commando, we are pleased to find that our initial impressions were correct. The Norton Commando is still capable of running with the best of them!

Perhaps the most revolutionary feature on the new machine, once you peer beneath the fiberglass work, is a totally new frame. The main member of the frame is a 2.25 inch tube which extends from the top of the steering head to a point well within the subframe loop. This backbone tube terminates at a substantial cross brace which serves several strengthening purposes. A pair of cradle tubes descend from the steering head, pass beneath the engine and then curve upwards to terminate at the aforementioned cross brace. An additional pair of small diameter diagonal stringers run between the center of the backbone tube and the cradling members.

While the swinging arm offers nothing out of the ordinary in the way in which it is constructed, the manner in which it is mounted to the bike is unique. The engine, transmission, and swinging arm are mounted in what Norton chooses to call an Isolastic system. The engine, trans, and swinging arm are bolted to two extremely robust plates which are mounted in the frame by means of large rubber bushings. The Isolastic system of mounting the engine and other components is an effort on the part of the Norton designers to do away with vibration. The effort is successful to a surprising degree, and the Commando is indeed one of the smoothest motorcycles we have ever ridden. We must admit that when we first heard that the swinging arm was mounted on rubber bushed plates, we were taken a-back. We had visions of the Norton

ONE OF THE FIRST SUPER BIKES, REMAINS ONE OF THE BEST

Commando being akin to an earlier Norton that was commonly referred to as the "Garden Gate" model. The Garden Gate Norton gained its name from the way in which the rear end would swing when the bike was forced into a corner. Much to our surprise, the Commando proved to be one of the best handling big roadsters we have ever ridden. The bike does feel a bit strange at first; the front end has a very precise feel about it, while the rear end does feel a bit mushy. However, only a few miles of twisting mountain road are required to prove that the Commando is indeed a super handler. At 430 pounds the bike is not light, yet when forced into a turn it will hold any line the rider chooses to take.

Remarkably free of excessive gusseting, the Norton Commando frame weighs but 25 pounds and the overall quality of finish is quite high. Welds are nicely dressed, and the glossy black enamel paint is nicely applied.

Excellent suspension is another feature which accounts for the way in which the Norton Commando handles. Many years ago the Norton Roadholder forks established themselves as one of the finest front suspension components to be found. Road surfaces have, if anything, improved as the years have passed, and the Roadholder forks remain among the best to be found. Cosmetic changes (removal of metal covers and rubber gaiters) have improved the appearance of the Norton forks. Suspension at the rear of the Commando is provided by Girling hy-

draulic shock absorbers which are fitted with three-way adjustable springs. The springs used on the shock absorbers are chrome plated and of the constant rate variety. Only the lower half of the spring is exposed, the upper half is protected by a chromed metal cover.

The front forks are fitted with constant rate springs, and damping is of the two-way variety. Aft of the forks might be considered a bit on the firm side; however, information fed back to the rider with this sort of arrangement is extremely precise. Mushy front ends tend to soak up almost all road shocks and leave the rider with little knowledge of what is going on down below. We much prefer a slightly firmer ride which lets the rider know the state of his contact with the pavement.

Powering the Norton Commando is an engine which has been around for a number of years. The Atlas power plant is an overhead valve parallel twin with a bore of 73 mm and a stroke of 89 mm. Total capacity of the engine is 745 cubic centimeters and the compression ratio is 8.9:1. Cast of light alloy, the cylinder head is formed with parallel induction ports which direct the incoming charge toward one side of the combustion chamber. The exhaust ports are widely spaced; the spacing of the intake and exhaust ports is intended to provide maximum breathing efficiency. Valve train components consist of a chain driven cam shaft, light alloy pushrods, large diameter tappets, and steel rockers.

Plain bearings are provided to support the forged steel built-up crank-

shaft. The cylinders are of cast iron, pistons are of alloy, and the two-piece connecting rods are "H" in section.

Ignition is supplied by a 12 volt battery, and a crankshaft driven alternator. A capacitor in the electrical system stores energy and makes it possible to start the machine without benefit of the battery. The primary case cover on earlier Atlas' were of stamped steel and were held in position by a handful of bolts. The Norton Commando uses a cast alloy cover which is held in place by means of a single locating bolt. Three screw-in plugs in the cover (one for strobe light timing, one to check tension of the primary drive chain, and one provided for clutch adjustment) ease maintenance chores.

Clutch operation is surprisingly light for a machine of the Norton's capacity. The Commando is fitted with a four-plate, diaphragm spring type clutch which applies almost double the pressure of the normal units found in motorbikes. The non-unit gearbox on the Norton is operated from the right side of the machine, and the shift pattern is: up for low, then down for the remaining speeds. The transmission, even when brand new, shows no sign of stiffness, and gear changes are made with a satisfying lack of bother.

Six pints of lubricating oil are carried in a tank secured to the right side of the machine. Two filters are built into the lubricating system; a mesh metal filter is incorporated into the nut which secures the speed line in position. An additional filter is built into the crankcase drain plug. The filter element here is held in position by a

750 COMMANDO

MODERN CYCLE ROAD TEST

Norton
COMMANDO TEST

circlip. Both filters can be dismantled for purposes of cleaning. One of the things that really impressed us about the Norton power plant was the way in which it remained oil tight. Some machines of English manufacture have a tendency to ooze their lubricant; the Commando remains pleasantly free of oil scum.

Paired 30 mm Amal concentric bowl carburetors feed the gas/air mixture to the combustion chambers. Both carburetors draw clean air through a paper element filter which should be replaced periodically, depending on the amount of dust common to the owner's particular riding area. The exhaust system on the Commando offers nothing really out of the ordinary, yet it proves to be quite attractive. While appearing to be reverse taper megaphones, the devices on the ends of the exhaust systems are in point of fact very efficient mufflers. The mufflers are kicked-up at a slight angle which is not only visually attractive, but practical in that it keeps them from grounding during hard cornering.

The Norton is a fast touring machine, and the designers at the factory have taken care to insure that the braking system is capable of coping with the bike's power output. The double leading shoe front binder is housed in a full width finned alloy hub. A more common single leading shoe stopper, also mounted in a full width alloy hub, is used to brake the rear of the machine. Both brakes are operated by cables. Naturally, due to the nature of the Commando, we indulged in considerable enthusiastic mountain riding. We are pleased to report that the brakes on the Norton are in keeping with the nature of the machine and they are surprisingly free of fade.

Nineteen inch chrome steel rims are laced to the alloy hubs. The front rim is fitted with a 300 ribbed tire, and at the rear of the machine is a 3.50 x 19 inch semi-triangulated cover. The

tires supplied on the Commando a quite similar to those used on out-an out road racing bikes, and they a count in good part for the precis manner in which the bike handles.

It is somewhat surprising, conside ing the size of the machine, but th Norton Commando seems to "fit" wide variety of riders. The relationshi between the footrests, saddle, an handlebars is such that even extende high speed touring is not overly f tiguing. Much of the lack of rider f tigue can be traced to the almost t tally vibrationless performance of th bike. The aforementioned Isolastic su pension system effectively damps ou almost all vibration at anything abov idle. (It's actually something of a sur prise to look in the rear view mirro on a motorcycle and be able to mak out something other than a blurre image!) The saddle is long, well pad ded, and just a hair on the wide sid at its forward end. A couple of ou shorter test riders did complain abou the width of the seat.

No one complained about the wa in which the Norton Commando per forms. Flexibility is the word that mos quickly comes to mind when tryin to describe the performance of th Commando. Good, usable powe comes in just a shade under 200 rpms and from there on up the bike pull like a freight train. The width of th power band makes it possible to ride through a twisty section without constantly rowing on the shift lever to keep the bike on the bubble.

In its stock form the Norton is a motorcycle that will reach speeds in excess of 110 mph, it's a bike that will handle on a par with any production machine on the road, it's a machine with shattering acceleration, and it's a damn good looking bike. When the bike was introduced in 1968, it was the first of the Super Bikes. In 1971 it remains one of the best of the Super Bikes.

Make	NORTON	Final Drive	CHAIN
Model	COMMANDO ROADSTER	Starting System	KICK-FOLDING LEVER
Price as Tested	$1,460.00	Gear Ratios	1st, 12.4:1; 2nd, 8.25:1;
Engine Type	4-CYCLE, VERTICAL TWIN		3rd, 5.9:1; 4th, 4.84:1
Bore	73mm	Top Speed	112.7 MPH
Stroke	89mm	Tire Size	FRONT: 3.00 x 19: REAR: 3.50 x 19
Displacement	745cc	Suspension	FRONT: TELESCOPIC FORK;
Compression Ratio	8.9:1		REAR: SWINGING ARM
B.H.P. at R.P.M.	N.A.	Frame Type	DOUBLE CRADLE
Carburetor	AMAL (2-30mm)	Weight	429 POUNDS
Ignition	BATTERY AND COIL	Wheelbase	57 INCHES
Fuel Capacity	2.7 GALLONS	Ground Clearance	6 INCHES
Lubricating System	DRY SUMP	Peg Height	11.2 INCHES
Clutch Type	DIAPHRAGM	Seat Height	32 INCHES

Styling on the Norton Commando has stood the test of time, and the bike remains one of the most attractive roadsters to be found. The saddle is well padded though a bit on the wide side.

Non-unit construction remains the order of the day on the Norton product. The 750cc engine is one of the most potent twins around.

Famed Norton Roadholder forks have been modernized to improve appearance. Their action remains as good as ever.

Exhaust system on the Commando is tucked well up out of the way where it will have no effect on cornering angles.

NORTON 750 COMMANDO FASTBACK

Something Old. Something New.
Something Borrowed . . .
An Assemblage Of Purist Traits
Which Make It The Best Of
The British Big Twins.

THOSE OF THE HONDA generation who don't know what it is like to ride a "purist" road machine would do well to examine the Norton Commando. If English roadsters can be said to have a feeling, a way of behaving, a way of looking that no other motorcycles in the world can quite duplicate, then the Commando can be said to epitomize that feeling at its best.

If you look at the Commando as a source of revelatory new ideas in motorcycle engineering, you'll find few. It's the way in which the old ideas are assembled that makes this Norton more than just another ancient Big Twin.

For instance, what is new about a long-stroke vertical Twin with separate crankcase and gearbox units? Nothing. With the demise of Velocette and Royal Enfield, Norton-Villiers is the only British manufacturer to retain the practice. The others abandoned the separate gearbox for the easier to manufacture, and more oil-tight, unit construction concept. Norton's faithful adherence to the separate gearbox scheme is probably not out of any positive conviction that it is "better," but rather that it exists and works well.

ISOLATING THE ENGINE

The one bit of technical novelty in the Commando is the use of rubber mounting blocks to isolate the engine from the frame. It is an automotive idea of long standing that has proven effective in preventing the transmission of engine vibrations to the frame and therefore to the rider.

The first Commando, which incorporated this innovation, appeared in 1968, after a long succession of Norton big Twins, from 500 to 600 to 650 to 750cc, dubbed Dominators and Atlases. These earlier bikes had a frame resembling that of the Norton Manx racing 500, one which was so conducive to good handling that in England it became a depository for other engines—the Triumph, to make the Triton, and the Vincent, to make the Vinton.

The new frame for the Commando is fairly conventional, incorporating a double cradle and large single backbone. An unusual twist, aside from the "Isolastic" engine mounting bushes, is the mounting of the swinging arm pivot on the plates supporting the engine and gearbox, rather than on the frame itself. The engine is canted forward in the frame, to allow room for the addition of two triangulating members, which link and rigidify the rear part of the cradle with the backbone.

FRAME MODIFICATIONS

Two modifications differentiate the 1971 Commando from the first one. The cross-member underneath the engine has been moved forward slightly to facilitate quick removal of the sump cap. And the trail has been reduced by half an inch, to correspond with Norton's successful 750-cc production racers. This has been done with new fork crowns. An improved stem with sealed thrust ball races is part of the redesign here.

Trail, the distance measured between points on the ground intersected by a line drawn through the steering head and a vertical line from axle center, is the factor that most affects the "quickness" of a bike's handling. Shortening the trail should drastically quicken the Commando's handling, but there is another factor which counteracts the geometry change. As with the production racers, Norton has adopted the use of a big 4.10-19 road racing tire at the front (the standard one was a 3.00-19). Fat front tires for road racing big bikes have come into vogue in recent years, as they have on racing cars, because the contact patch is bigger. With more rubber on the ground, traction is improved. But, trail is increased by increasing the circumference of the front wheel.

ROBUST AND TRADITIONAL

Engine construction is robust throughout, and surprisingly oil-tight, considering the extra seams and joints created by vertically split crankcases and separate gearbox unit. Quality control has become a standard part of the manufacturing operation in the last few years, and cylinder head and crankcase castings are all pressure checked. The aluminum primary chaincase, which one expects to drip oil first off, proved quite oil-tight, also.

The engine resembles the original 750 Atlas. A built-up forged steel crankshaft, with central iron flywheel, is supported on ball and roller bearings. Two-piece, plain-bushed connecting rods and alloy three-ring pistons operate inside a cast-iron cylinder barrel. The valves are actuated by a chain-driven camshaft through alloy pushrods, large tappets and forged steel rockers.

You would expect that a clutch capable of handling the brutish power produced by a 750 Twin would be a handful, but only a normal, firm squeeze is required on the clutch lever. The four-plate diaphragm spring clutch was specially designed for the Commando by Laycock de Normanville, a firm which specializes in automobile transmissions. The virtue of this particular design is that it allows almost double the plate pressure without noticeably increasing the hand pressure required to operate it.

Power is taken from the engine to the transmission by means of a triplex chain. It is a four-speed gearbox, shifting on the right side in the "Olde English" pattern, which requires an upward pull for first gear from neutral, then downward pushes for the higher gears. This used to be the accepted pattern for British motorcycles, most of which have since gone to the up-for-higher, down-for-lower gear configuration. In spite of its present rareness, it is not a hard pattern to learn, and even has something to recommend it, as any stoplight drag freak will soon find out.

So use of the bigger 4.10-in. tire on the Commando in part reduces the effect of shortening trail by means of steering geometry changes. Thus, the steering is not noticeably quicker than in previous models. As the bigger front tire is heavier and tends therefore to resist deflection to a greater degree, the "quickening" effect of any trail reduction will also be diminished.

If you are used to the self-aligning effect of a smaller front tire in cornering, the new one, which leaves more up to the rider, takes some getting used to. Once you do, you'll find that the Commando sticks well, corners beautifully, and, like its predecessors, should establish among the purists that eyeball-rolling reverence so common to passionate Manx and Dommie fans. Aiding the rider who indulges in daring angles of inclination, the mellow-sounding and legal 88 db straight-through glasspack mufflers have been tilted up slightly from the horizontal. This will obviate grounding in turns, although a somewhat loosely sprung center stand will flop down and make alarming sounds before you get the mufflers even close to the ground. Having reported this to the distributor, we were informed that a stronger spring is being fitted to keep the stand "up tight."

MADE FOR THE HIGHWAY

If you are primarily an around-town, under 50-mph sort of rider, you will not derive the fullest possible appreciation of this motorcycle, although it maneuvers through traffic with a fair amount of ease for its size. It is a high-speed sporting machine, and needs lots of open winding road and freeway to unfold its true nature. It accelerates to 80 or 100 mph in great, smooth, animal-like rushes, and you may ignore the gearbox entirely in most passing situations above 55 mph.

As such is the case, it is hardly fair to call the Norton's powerplant old-fashioned. If it does the job, it does the job, and that should be the criterion for most people. The Commando can stay with any of the other so-called Super-bikes, even speaking only in terms of sheer acceleration. The sole objection to making a 750-cc engine in parallel Twin configuration is that it can be quite a shaker, due to primary imbalances produced at the crankshaft by the reciprocation of large pistons and beefy connecting rods.

By isolating the engine in those rubber bushes, it can jiggle to its heart's content, yet leave the rider unshaken enough to

enjoy the engine's virtues—torque and flexibility.

The Commando's engine is a long-stroked wonder (bore 73mm, stroke 89mm) in this day of square and oversquare bore/stroke configurations. Fortunately, it reaches its power peak at about 7000 rpm, which converts to a piston speed of 4100 feet per minute. Piston speed is a rather loose factor upon which engineers try to predict the stress to which an engine is being subjected, and how long it will wear. A figure of 4000 fpm has been considered, in the past, the upper limit of reliability. Lately, this old rule of thumb has risen, due to the improved quality of modern engine materials. Beyond that, one must consider the normal operating range of the Commando, which is far lower than 4100 fpm.

As the engine has a broad powerband and achieves most of its horsepower before the rpm limit is reached, it will be operated at lower rpm and therefore be subjected to less stress than the peak piston speed would first lead you to believe.

REFINING THE GEARBOX

Some improvements have been made in the gearbox this year in the interest of greater reliability. First, second and third gears are now made of a slightly harder grade of steel, "EN 39" instead of "EN 34." All the shoulders of the mainshaft and layshaft are radiused for increased strength. Due to the machine's newness, the selection of second gear offered light resistance but soon began working itself out. The internal ratios are ideal, with no large jumps between gears.

It is an interesting curiosity to note that the Commando, when delivered in Europe, has a countershaft sprocket two teeth higher than the American models. All this has to do with national character, we Yanks being oriented to blinding acceleration while the purists overseas think that top speed is

where it's at. As a result, the Commando for the U.S. will easily red-line in top gear, and has the power needed to pull a higher gear at a faster top speed.

DETAIL CHANGES, AND LUCAS . . .

Several detail changes make the new Commando much easier to live with, notably the rear wheel, which now incorporates a vaned rubber cushioned hub. It smooths the bike's progress at slow speeds and counteracts chain snatch, as well as insures that the drive train will not suffer the ill effects of sudden stresses imposed by rider malfeasances.

The center stand is much easier to use, having been modified with a longer locating lip and mounted on the engine plates in such a position that even a 98-lb. weakling can cope with it. The sidestand is longer, and is more secure on soft surfaces, as it has more support area. Another minor change, a straight-ended chain guard, makes it possible to remove the rear wheel without having to dismantle the chain guard at the same time. The oil tank, located under the snap-off seat, is larger, with an increase in capacity from 3 to 4 quarts; the filler cap comes with a dip stick for easy checking.

The Commando has new controls for the electrical accessories, which it will have in common with most of the other British brands, as they are made by Lucas. They are rather curious, if the intent of Lucas was to rationalize and modernize the system. The "wingtip" thumb switches are annoying to operate, because of the pointed tips, and the auxiliary buttons that are placed above and below them are too small and indefinite in feel. For this, you cannot blame Norton, as the Lucas company is somewhat of a monopoly in England. The Smith tachometer and speedometer faces are simpler and easier to read for the average rider. The odometer counter was a clinker and quickly went awry, trying to make us believe that it had been around the world three times and back. Too bad that Norton-Villiers has to bear up under these outside annoyances, for which they have no direct responsibility. Otherwise, the machine is a beautifully executed whole.

A SLEEK, LUSH TOURER

The people at Norton-Villiers like to call the Commando their "European" version, their "fastback." It does have some of the character of a sleek, lush grand touring car. The striking red slash of the integrated fuel tank and fender is nicely offset by the supple black leather saddle, the front of which is lipped to provide knee pads at the rear of the tank. If you are too long-legged, or short-legged, however, they don't provide a perfect match for the position of your knees, leaving you with some indecision about where to sit in the saddle. Or you may find that they make your legs stick out into the airstream.

But this idiosyncrasy is soon forgotten when you fire up that throbbing big Twin. It requires a heavy kick when the engine is cold to overcome the oil drag, but the starting procedure is easy. Use the choke lever and flood the carburetor float bowls generously with the tickler and a few prods will bring it to life. Once warm, the Commando is a first-kick starter.

Ease into first, and there's no clunking. Away into traffic, out onto the highway, and turn it on. There are absolutely no flat spots in the power curve. Dial it on and you accelerate, with no hesitation.

As you gain rpm, the rubber mounting does its job. The handlebars don't shake or make your hands tingle.

Happiness is the first fast bend. The Commando is solid, secure, and as easy handling as some 500s. There may be something to "purism" after all. Updated. Commando-style. ◙

NORTON 750 COMMANDO FASTBACK

SPECIFICATIONS

List price	$1595 West Coast
Suspension, front	telescopic fork
Suspension, rear	swinging arm
Tire, front	4.10 x 19
Tire, rear	4.10 x 19
Brake, front, diameter x width, in.	80 x 1.25
Brake, rear, diameter x width, in.	7.0 x 1.25
Total brake swept area, sq. in.	58.9
Brake loading, lb./sq. in.	9.45
Engine, type	ohv parallel Twin
Bore x stroke, in., mm	2.875 x 3.503, 73 x 89
Piston displacement, cu. in., cc	45, 745
Compression ratio	9.9:1
Claimed bhp @ rpm	60 @ 6800
Claimed torque @ rpm, lb.-ft.	54 @ 4600
Carburetion	(2) 30-mm Amal Concentric
Ignition	battery and coil
Oil system	dry sump
Oil capacity, pt.	8
Fuel capacity, U.S. gal.	3.9
Recommended fuel	premium
Starting system	kick, folding crank
Lighting system	12-V alternator
Air filtration	paper element
Clutch	multi-plate, diaphragm spring
Primary drive	triplex chain
Gear ratios, overall:1	
5th	none
4th	4.84
3rd	5.90
2nd	8.25
1st	12.40
Wheelbase, in.	57
Seat height, in.	32
Seat width, in.	11.7
Handlebar width, in.	32
Footpeg height, in.	11.6
Ground clearance, in.	5.5
Curb weight (w/half-tank fuel), lb.	426
Weight bias, front/rear, percent	46/54
Test weight (fuel and rider), lb.	556

TEST CONDITIONS

Air temperature, degrees F	52
Humidity, percent	91
Barometric pressure, in. hg.	28.72
Altitude above mean sea level, ft.	50
Wind velocity, mph	6-9
Strip alignment, relative wind:	

PERFORMANCE

Top speed (actual @ 7380 rpm), mph	116.40
Computed top speed in gears (@ 7000 rpm), mph:	
5th	none
4th	110.5
3rd	90.3
2nd	64.6
1st	43.0
Mph/1000 rpm, top gear	15.75
Engine revolutions/mile, top gear	3820
Piston speed (@ 7000 rpm), ft./min.	4100
Lb./hp (test wt.)	9.26
Fuel consumption, mpg	43
Speedometer error:	
50 mph indicated, actually	47.67
60 mph indicated, actually	56.98
70 mph indicated, actually	66.27
Braking distance:	
from 30 mph, ft.	36.7
from 60 mph, ft.	141.6
Acceleration, zero to:	
30 mph, sec.	3.3
40 mph, sec.	4.0
50 mph, sec.	4.8
60 mph, sec.	5.4
70 mph, sec.	6.2
80 mph, sec.	7.0
90 mph, sec.	9.3
100 mph, sec.	13.0
Standing one-eighth mile, sec.	8.14
terminal speed, mph	84.60
Standing one-quarter mile, sec.	13.11
terminal speed, mph	101.67

ACCELERATION / ENGINE AND ROAD SPEEDS / RPM X 100

Norton 750cc Commando Street Racer

PHOTOGRAPHY: DAVID GOOLEY

Many were the Norton *aficionados* who shed a tear at the demise of the fabled Manx, its tractor-like pulling ability and rock steady handling pushed aside by the demands of commercialism. Seeking to console its customers for the loss of the Manx, the Norton people revamped a production OHV Twin and introduced their 500cc "Domiracer," its title derived from the Dominator Twins, forerunners of the Atlas 750.

The Domiracer's grave was dug before its introduction. Completely outclassed by the

Your mind blurs. You're Nixon and Rayborn, Agostini and Hailwood. Anyone can be a racer—all you need is the machine to inspire the right frame of mind.

onslaught of Italian and Japanese multis, Norton shelved the project and concentrated all their engineering efforts on the ultimate road burner: the Norton 750 Commando.

The innovative rubber mounting of the Atlas 750 engine in the new Commando alloy steel frame proved an instant sales success for Norton. Heaps of vibration-free power coupled with nimble handling were just the incentives needed to start juices flowing within the competition-starved Norton racing department. At last the return of

The Production Racer feels even better than it looks– kind of a cross between a Commando and a Manx. The stout 750cc engine gives a power spread of 3000 rpm, suspension and damping are nearly perfect for the weight of the machine, and the brakes— to say that the Commando Racer's brakes are excellent is a bit of an understatement. For this kind of performance, the price you pay is hardly worth mentioning.

Highly modified 750 engine produces 68 hp.

Shock angle contributed to slight wheel hop.

Smith instrumentation is simple, accurate.

the invincible Manx in modern twin-cylinder form seemed possible.

Rule changes within the F. I. M. formed a class for Open Production Road Racing: just the Commando's cup of tea. What better way to prove the product (and boost sales) than to engage in the gentlemanly art of pavement scuffling?

To support their competition effort Norton-Villiers built a performance facility near the new plant in Andover. The shop borders right on the Thruxton Race Circuit. In less than a minute they can check out a handling change by popping out the back door and gassing it around the race course; a great help in shortening development time between prototype and final production version of any hot machine.

Handling the reins for this operation is Performance Shop Director Peter Inchley. Peter gets his engineering advice from Bob Trigg, designer of the Commando frame, and seat-of-the-pants impressions from the racer-engineer Peter Williams. The team is well qualified to carry out performance development on the Commando, having served their respective apprenticeships in the ranks of motorcycle racing and design.

Besides building and testing Commando road racers and AJS Motocross machines, the shop also manufactures speed accessories for Norton and AJS marketed under the trade name "Norvil." These goodies consist of engine hop-up parts, disc front brakes, fiberglass parts, aluminum replacement pieces and items for increasing the performance of the Commando and the AJS motocross machines.

The Norton Villiers Performance Shop builds a limited number of Commando Production Racers each year. Some they keep for factory supported events, and the rest are sold to their dealers. This gives the private owner a chance to buy a new factory-built racer which is street-legal.

A considerable amount of effort goes into putting a Commando Racer together. It's not just a standard model with a tire change and new fiberglass. The frame is checked closely for flaws and measured to conform exactly to Commando specifications. Brackets are fabricated to mount the fairing and instruments. Special fork yokes are fitted that increase the fork rake for better high-speed stability. Matched progressive fork springs, slightly shorter than standard to lower the overall height of the machine, are installed in the otherwise standard fork legs. Girlings take care of the rear.

Dunlop dural aluminum WM2 x 19 rims are spoked to both wheels. The front brake is a 11.5 diameter disc using a Lockheed caliper and hand lever/master cylinder unit. The rest of the components (hub, disc, etc.) are made by Norton. The caliper bolts to a special alloy fork leg that has a cast-on mounting lug. The rear hub is standard, trued to a perfect seven-inch diameter, with a ventilated back plate. The linings are Ferodo Racing.

Each engine component is carefully inspected and hand-assembled. All castings (head, cylinder and crankcases) are individually selected from standard molds. The head is cleaned up and has .125-inch oversize intakes with standard size exhaust valves. The guides are aluminum-bronze. Rocker arms, push rods and tappets are stock except for a little polishing and careful fitting. The standard aluminum intake manifolds are replaced by fabricated steel ones that enter the head at a straighter angle. Carburetors are standard 30mm Amal Concentrics (carb size and type must remain the same as the production model under FIM rules), using 280 main jets.

The racing valve springs are matched for tension. The sports camshaft rides in the standard bronze bushings and gives a wide power band. Valve timing inlet opens 44.5 degrees BTC and closes 63.4 degrees ABC with a duration of 288 degrees. Exhaust opens 63 degrees BBC and closes 28 degrees ATC for 271 degrees of duration.

Ten-and-a-half to one Hepolite pistons use two compression rings and one oil ring.

The aluminum connecting rods are checked and matched. The standard-weight flywheel, balanced to 52%, is carried by roller bearings on both sides. The drive train is strengthened by substituting Renolds racing chain for the standard primary and final drive units. The clutch assembly is stock, but the gearbox has closer ratio gears and a 21-tooth countershaft sprocket. Sprockets from 19t through 24t are available to suit any circuit. Or to gear properly for gunning down other pretenders on the street.

The engine-to-frame mounting bushings are shimmed to zero clearance, keeping the wiggles to a minimum. The bright yellow gas tank, fairing, seat, and front fender are fiberglass. The rear fender is standard, as is the taillight and headlight. The mufflers are straight-through with enough baffling to make them respectable. The exhaust pipes are tucked in for ground clearance when cornering and the mufflers are rubber mounted to prevent vibration cracking.

Norton was proud of their new Commando Production Racer and wanted to show the world it could run: they entered the 1970 Thruxton 500 Production race. Thruxton had been traditionally Triumph Bonneville country until Peter Williams showed them his taillight on the Commando. Next was the Isle of Man. Hopefully Norton could follow Thruxton with a *coup de grace* at the Island, winning the two most prestigious production motorcycle races in Great Britain, and regaining the once familiar taste of victory. Unfortunately, this was not to be. Williams looked like a sure winner until the final lap. Almost, but not quite. They had sipped the ambrosia of success and would be back next year, possibly to widen their scope of competition and compete in America on the super-bowls of Daytona and Talladega. They are well equipped to do so. A properly set-up Commando, modified to the limit of the existing AMA Class "C" rules, could feasibly run 150 mph and stay together for 200 miles.

Mounting the Norton Racer to get an in-motion impression makes the picture complete. It feels even better than it looks—kind of a cross between a Commando and a Manx. The gear shift is typical Commando: crisp, positive and smooth. The clutch action is on the stiff side—stiffer than the stock Commando, and does engage without a trace of slip, even after repeated dragstrip starts. The throttle action is also first rate.

Unlike most factory Production Racers, the Norton can be bought, and it won't cost the Privateer an arm and a leg, either. Another plus: it's streetable.

Idle to W.O.T. consumes a little over quarter turn, with the slides snapping back without a bit of hesitation. The Smiths speedo and tach are likewise excellent.

Starting off the performance phase of the test was the quarter-mile. This is where the tall gearing proved to be a drawback. Getting off the line was hardly inspirational and winding the engine past 7000 and feeding in the clutch didn't help either. Even at the end of the strip the Racer was just beginning to wind out in third at about 6000 with more to go. Still, it cranked off five consecutive runs, a 30-minute break, and five more at between 99 and 101 mph. Elapsed times ranged from the mid 14s down to a consistent batch in the high 13s. The best run of the day was a 101.36 at 13.84—not bad for a 125 mph bike with a skinny rear tire.

Whatever the Commando Racer lacked in getting off the line it more than made up for in stopping. What a difference the front disc makes over the standard paltry drum. If the standard Commando were to come equipped with this excellent stopping device, the machine would be the best available touring motorcycle in the areas of brakes, handling and acceleration. Bar none. You just flat can't beat it with the existing machinery available today.

To say that the Commando Racer's brakes are excellent is an understatement. They are fantastic. The feel between locking the wheel and stopping the forward motion of the machine is broad enough to accommodate all but the most insensitive of lever squeezers. It is almost as if the rider had his own fingers directly on the caliper. The rear is good, but no match for the front— it would lock up if a little too much toe were applied. Fade didn't set in, although the front chattered a slight bit after several 100 mph hard stops. Stopping distances of around 100 feet at 60 mph were child's play. Even a panic stop at an indicated 100 mph on the speedo was accomplished after a few gulps and a minor skid in less than 160 feet.

Naturally the handling portion of the evaluation took the longest, but was certainly the most enjoyable. The front suspension spring rate and damping is nearly perfect for the weight of the machine: just stiff enough to control front end dive under hard braking, but not so harsh that the wheel loses ground contact over ripples.

The rear suspension is satisfactory; it's not equal to the front. The forward cant of the damper units causes them to lose some of

their efficiency. The mounting angle is necessary to keep the top lug as close as possible to an area of frame strength. The Reynolds 531 frame tubes are under compression or tension forces only. There is a minimum of bending and twisting taking place to weaken them. To mount the top of the rear shocks farther back on the subframe would defeat this sound engineering practice and possibly cause frame tube failure. The shock angle and the solid-mounted rear brake backing plate contributed to the slight rear wheel hop when braking hard: the only flaw in an otherwise near-perfect combination.

The engine's power range is another area of commendation. Thanks to smallish carburetors and a slight back pressure in the mufflers, the engine pulled like a freight train from 4000 all the way past 7000. With a 3000 rpm power band, even city traffic is bearable—although the Racer is a bit sluggish in tight corners due to minimal steering lock, tall gearing and 400-pound bulk.

But it's a small price to pay for being able to ride beyond the stoplights into the rolling hills of the country. This is where the Commando is at home. Shooting hard into bends, downshifting, braking and clutching. Right wrist thrust hard into the wind as you pull out of the turns, upshifting at full bore. Your mind blurs. You're Nixon and Rayborn, Agostini and Hailwood. Anyone can be a racer. All you need is the machine to inspire the right frame of mind. And the Norton Commando Production Racer is just the machine for the trip, mental or physical. ◉

NORTON COMMANDO 750 PRODUCTION RACER

Price, suggested retail .... P.O.R. (Price on Request)	Mph/1000 rpm, top gear 17.8
Tire, front .... 3.60 in. x 19 in.	Fuel capacity .... 4.5 gal.
rear .... 4.10 in. x 19 in.	Oil capacity .... 6.0 pints
Brake, front ...... 11.5 in. x 1.5 in.	Lighting .... 12v, 120 watts
rear ...... 7.0 in. x 1.125 in.	Battery 12v, 8ah
Brake swept area ..... 133.07 sq. in.	Gear ratios, overall .... (1) 11.18
Specific brake loading .... 4.23 lb/sq. in., at test weight	(2) 7.42 (3) 5.35 (4) 4.35 (5) None
Engine type ..... OHV Vertical Twin	Wheelbase .... 57.0 in.
Bore and stroke ... 2.87 in. x 3.50 in., 73mm x 89mm	Seat height .... 29 in., with rider
Piston displacement ... 45.46 cu. in., 745cc	Ground clearance . 5.5 in., with rider
	Curb weight ... 406 lbs., with ½-tank of gas
Compression ratio 10.25:1	Test weight ..... 566 lbs., with rider
Carburetion(2) 30mm Amal Concentric	Instruments .Tachometer-Speedometer
Air filtration .... None	0-60 mph .... 6.4 seconds
Ignition .... Battery-Coil w/Capacitor	Standing start ¼ mile . 13.84 seconds 101.36 mph
Bhp @ rpm .... 68 @ 7,000 rpm	Top speed ....Approx. 125+ mph

NORTON
COMMANDO

WHEN SOMEONE USES THE EXPRESSION "MUSCLE MACHINE", YOU KNOW THEY MUST BE TALKING ABOUT THE NORTON 750 COMMANDO

motor CYCLIST MAGAZINE ROAD TEST

YOU CAN ALWAYS TELL if you're riding an honest-to-goodness musclebike, by just looking at the kid in the car next to you at a stoplight. For some reason the kids that have cars with jacked-up rear ends and engines that make funny "rump-rump-rump" noises can smell a musclebike from a quarter-mile away. If the kid's grinning at you, you can be sure that you're sitting astride a toad, and when the green-for-go light comes on he's going to gobble you up. But, if you look over at him and he's scratching an adolescent bump and staring up at his headlining, you know automatically you're riding a musclebike and he doesn't care to go.

During the two weeks we had our Commando for a test we couldn't get the car jockies to stop scratching and look our way even when we honked that fine Lucas horn.

The Norton engine stuffed in our test model is the same one that's been around a long time. It's a vertical twin unit having overhead valves and breathing thru two 33 millimeter Amal Concentric carburetors. The carburetors, in turn, inhale thru what might very well be the world's biggest Filtron air cleaner.

From the time this engine was introduced, to the present, there just haven't been any major problems that anyone could gripe about, other than a little bit of oil seeping past some of the gaskets, which seems to be a characteristic of all English motorcycles, both good and bad.

The cam and contact breaker assembly which rides at the end of it, are driven by a single-roller chain. The crank, of the bolt-together variety, rides on roller bearings on the driven side and ball bearings on the timing side. Bearings for the rods, both top and bottom, are of the bushed variety, and since they worked so well for so many years, there's certainly no reason to change them now.

The distributor claims a dynomometer tested 49.5 horsepower at 6,500 revolutions per minute, which we have

NORTON COMMANDO ROAD TEST

bsolutely no problem believing. The dynotested torque, ranked out at 5,500 rpm, was 44.2 foot pounds. Check the orque rating on your bike against this, and you'll get some ort of an idea what real torque is. Without making any changes to the motorcycle after we got it, it turned an honest-to-goodness 113 miles an hour on our favorite flat spot. Quarter-mile time seemed to run between 14 seconds, or a rifle less, with terminal speeds in the 103-104 mile-an-hour category.

Vertical twin engines have always had vibration problems, and Norton was no exception. To keep riders from having the fillings shaken out of their teeth, Norton developed what they call Isolastic Suspension, which is basically nothing more than mounting the engine and gearbox on rubber mounts. This has been done for years by the aircraft industry in the mounting of their engines. A tiny bit of vibration will sneak thru at low rpm's, but once you reach cruising speeds, vibration disappears completely.

One of the first things you'll notice when you see the Commando is that the 4-speed gearbox is not an integral part of the engine. For years and years manufacturers bolted their gearboxes behind the engine with robust mounts and they seemed to work quite well. It still does today, even if it doesn't look quite as pretty. It sure makes it easy to adjust that primary chain. We understand that a five-speed gearbox listed as an option is available on the racing version of the Norton. Since everything is basically the same, there doesn't seem to be any reason you couldn't get one for your street Commando. Gear ratios of the standard box are 1st: 12.4-to-1, 2nd: 8.2-to-1, 3rd: 5.9-to-1, and 4th: 4.8-to-1. The big Norton engine has so much torque, that there is no drop at all in between gears. Would you believe that a fast shift from second to third will get a squeak of protest from the rear tire?

Down thru the years, Norton has always been known for the superb handling characteristics of their motorcycles, and the Commando is no exception. The combination of the beautifully built frame and better-than-average suspension has got to be the answer. There are a lot of big bikes on the market today that are downright hairy to take thru a series of fast bends on a winding mountain road. They're just not designed for riding like this. Most of them are strictly for touring and nothing more. Not so for the Commando. If you so desire, you can go out on a Saturday and play roadracer on winding mountain roads, and on Sunday, take a quick trip from Los Angeles to Phoenix and back without even feeling tired. The pleated and heavily padded seat adds to the pleasure of riding the big Norton. You don't slip and slide on it, and no matter how hard the jolt (if it can somehow sneak past the suspension) it certainly won't make it past the seat.

Helping the spot-on handling are those very fine Avon GP street tires. No matter how hard you push them, they stick, and then seem to stick even more. We found that we could lean the Commando over, to such an acute angle that we could actually get the left footpeg (which is up quite high) to drag on the pavement. At no time do the tires feel squirrely, and what's even nicer, when they do get ready to make a move, you know about it in advance.

The Commando has more than ample braking power to stop its fairly light 423 pounds. The front unit is internal expanding single leading shoe, and if you've got enough muscle to grip the lever on the handlebar, you've got more brake than you could use on a motorcycle twice this size. The rear unit is also internal expanding, and it seems to work just as well as the one up front.

The Commando certainly is not a motorcycle for the novice rider, as you'd better know what you're doing when you light the fuse on this bomb. Without a doubt, the Commando is one of the hottest motorcycles we have ever flung a leg over. When you drop the clutch make sure your knees are tight around the seat and gas tank, or you'll find yourself sliding over the rear fender. The tachometer begins to redline at 7 grand, and that 150-mile-an-hour speedometer really isn't that optimistic. As we mentioned earlier, if you crank up the wick all the way you can even get the tires to chirp in the higher gears. Along with being a go-fast, the Commando is also a good-looker. The tank and side panels are finished in a yellowish orange, very similar to the color found on the new Porsche. Both fenders are chrome, as is the headlight. The frame and other miscellaneous parts are painted in glossy black. Lending a nice contrast to this is the chrome, dull alloy, and polished aluminum of the rest of the bike. A very sporty look is produced by the rubber-mounted, radically-upswept mufflers. Two things are nice about the mfuflers; one is that they're very quiet, and two, any moisture produced by condensation drains into the exhaust pipe where it rapidly turns to steam, instead of turning into rusted mufflers (as is the case in many other motorcycles).

Here are some of the comments, both good and bad, that the members of the *motorCYCLIST* staff came up with: Neat seat . . . Chain oiler good, but not adjustable . . . Clutch pull better

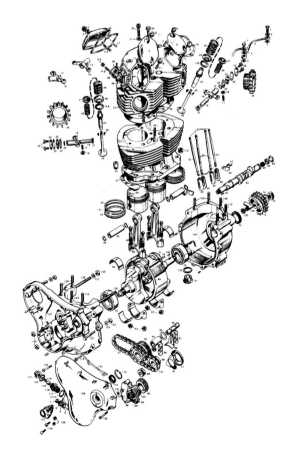

55

COMMANDO Norton, aimed at experienced rider, is one of the most muscular of all muscle bikes.

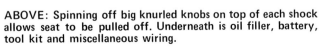

ABOVE: Spinning off big knurled knobs on top of each shock allows seat to be pulled off. Underneath is oil filler, battery, tool kit and miscellaneous wiring.

RIGHT: You're looking at one of most powerful front brakes on market today. Big Norton not only goes, it also stops!

than average for Norton, but clutch as good as ever for Norton . . . Need a pet gorilla for putting Commando on centerstand. Didn't even know there was a sidestand until bike was laid over on side for photographs . . . Speaking of laying bike over on side, footpegs drag when cornering hard . . . Adjustable Girlings' exceptional rear shocks, but better yet, adjusting tool included along with better-than-average tool kit . . . Air filter gigantic, but almost impossible to get to . . . Rubber mounts on everything.— engine, rear of bike, mufflers — excellent . . . Gas tank held on by two bolts up front and rubber band in rear, also excellent . . . Trouble light socket mounted on aircleaner

could be used for electric vest . . . Norton engine functional, but far from pretty. Head on test model better than average, but barrel fins crudely cast and finished . . . Unbelievable horsepower with (thank goodness) brakes to match . . . Compare the power-to-weight ratio with all the other musclebikes on the market. You'll be pleasurably surprised . . . The forklock actually works, and is located where it can be used. We can't say the same for the ignition switch . . . Engine not oil tight, but much better than before . . . Go look for Corvettes and GTO's. They can't bother you.

If you're an experienced rider and you're ready to move up to a big bike, you might just consider one of the most muscular of all the musclebikes. The Norton Commando is a most unusual motorcycle in many respects.

SPECIFICATIONS: NORTON 750 COMMANDO

Make	Norton
Model	Commando
Displacement	745cc
Engine	Overhead valve twin cylinder
Bore and Stroke	73 x 89mm (2.875 x 3.503 inches)
Compression	9-to-1
Horsepower	49.5 at 6,500 rpm
Torque	44.2 foot pounds at 5,500 rpm
Carburetors	two 30 millimeter Amal Concentric
Ignition	12 volt battery and coils
Starting	Kick
Clutch	Wet, multi-plate
Gearbox	4 speed
Gear ratios	1st: 12.4-to-1, 2nd: 8.2-to-1, 3rd: 5.9-to-1, 4th: 4.8-to-1
Tire Size	Front: 3.00 x 19 Rear: 4.10 x 19
Brakes	Front: Internal expanding, dual leading shoe
Brakes	Rear: Internal expanding, single leading shoe
Suspension	Front: Telescopic fork Rear: Swing arm
Frame	Dual downtube, cradle type
Weight	423 pounds
Ground Clearance	6 inches
Wheelbase	57 inches
Top Speed	113 miles per hour
Price	$1,495.00 (Los Angeles)

ENGINE	Excellent	Good	Fair	Poor	Unsatisfactory
Starting	●				
Throttle Response	●				
Vibration		●			
Noise	●				
TRANSMISSION					
Gear Spacing	●				
Clutch Smoothness	●				
Shifting speed	●				
CONTROLS					
Handlebar position	●				
Ease of operation	●				
Location	●				
BRAKES					
Lever pressure			●		
Pedal pressure	●				
Fade resistance	●				
Directional stability	●				
Stopping distance	●				
SUSPENSION					
Front	●				
Rear	●				
Ride control	●				
Dampening	●				
APPEARANCE					
Paint	●				
Construction and welds	●				
Chrome and trim	●				
ELECTRICAL					
Wiring	●				
Headlight	●				
Taillight	●				
Horn	●				
GENERAL					
Spark plug accessibility	●				
Instrumentation	●				
Side stand	●				
Center stand			●		
Seat comfort	●				
Muffling	●				
Tool storage space	●				

COMMENTS: We said it all above. The Command has to be one of the wildest motorcycles we've ever ridden.

THUNDER TWIN

CYCLE GUIDE
TEST REPORT
NORTON
COMMANDO SS

Norton is one of the legendary marques among motorcycles. A ride on the Commando will tell you why.

For more than two generations the name Norton' has been synonymous with racing and high performance machinery. Few existent motorcycle manufacturers have the history of racing machines and victories that Norton does. But in the past couple of years the high performance motorcycle has seen some drastic changes. The era of the multis and big-inch two-strokers from the Orient seemed destined as a death blow to the British twins. And for some of them it has been.

Norton is now the only British motorcycle manufacturer now producing a 45-inch vertical twin. Beyond that, the Commando is one of the few machines made today recognized as a true superbike. Somehow, the Norton/Villiers factory has managed to completely re-design a new motorcycle around an engine that, by all modern standards, should have been obsolete a few years ago. But as sporting machines (or superbikes) go, the Commando is one of the best performing machines available today.

None of the success the Commando is now having is due to any fluke of fate. Unlike some of their compatriots, Norton realized the Japanese would try to dominate the big bike market. They decided to stick with their 750cc OHV vertical twin engine and the AMC four-speed gear box. But without going into extensive engine fabrication and assembly work to eliminate the vibration they were infamous for, they had to come up with another solution to the problem.

The method Norton uses to eliminate the vibration, or rather to keep it from getting to the frame and the rider, they call 'Isolastic.' In layman's jargon it's simply rubber mounting, the same principle automobiles use. The engine, gear box and drive line are insulated from the chassis in three points. This allows the engine and drive system to vibrate without getting to the chassis, and therefore the rider.

Actually, this Isolastic system is quite simple, yet unique to motorcycle use. Once this was perfected Norton proceeded to design a new chassis around the rubber mounted engine and driveline components. The machine still closely resembles some of the old mounts in many respects. The engine and gear box are identical in

appearance to the units they've been using for years. The only outward difference is that the engine has been tilted at more of a forward angle than when mounted in the older machines. This apparently is an effort to lower the center of gravity and make the new chassis more compact.

Our main criticism of this engine is that the cam and ignition are chain driven. After the chain stretches, as all chains do, it is difficult to maintain accurate ignition and valve timing without replacing the chain with a new one. This deterioration of the ignition timing probably contributes to the engine vibration, which is considerable. A gear driven cam and ignition system would be a considerable improvement.

Replacing the four-speed transmission with a five-speed unit would be a most desirable modification. The improvement in performance would be quite noticeable, because with the present gear ratios, the engine is required to operate over an RPM range that is wider than its best power band. The lag in acceleration, after changing gears, was especially apparent during quarter-mile drag strip runs. A close ratio, five-speed gear box would enable the engine to stay ''on the pipe''

The front forks work quite well. They are very stable and provide good damping. The Avon tires, front and rear, provide excellent traction. The front brake is adequate.

The instruments are attractive and easily read, excepting the odometer that was stuck between numbers. The handlebars are comfortable and completely absent of vibration.

The kick arm is easily reached, though a good deal of muscle is required to kick the engine through. The good old AMC gear box operated without complaint.

more of the time, with quicker acceleration.

The machine we tested was the new Commando SS model, which is made primarily for the American market. The differences from the other Commando models are the pipes, gas tank, high front fender and handlebars. The rest of the machine is identical to the entire Commando line. Appearance wise, it is a handsome machine. The fiberglass gas tank (2.3 gallons), plastic side panels and fenders are all nicely finished. The saddle contours well with the lines of the SS, though it leaves something to be desired in the comfort department for long tours. Overall, the Commando SS is a well finished machine with a masculine appearance.

In the mornings we never could quite find the right combination to get the fire burning in one or two kicks. It seemed to always take at least a half dozen hefty swipes on the kick arm. Later, we found that the engine needs to be virtually flooded by tickling the twin Amal concentrics, and a wide open throttle did the trick when

The "SS" high pipes were designed for the American market. We didn't particularly care for them. The rear brake leaves something to be desired. The solid foot pegs should be made to fold.

The saddle is easily removed by loosening the two thumb screws. The oil tank, battery and tool kit are shown. The tool kit is very complete.

cold. Once warmed, just one kick would do the deed.

There is one thing about the Norton that every motorcyclist likes: the sound of the exhaust. There is nothing that has that muscular sound of power that is music to so many ears as a sharp, well-tuned Commando. Once fired, the engine requires a minimal amount of warm up time before she's ready to go. The wet, multi-disc diaphragm, spring-pressured clutch dis-

engages and engages without any drag or slippage, hot or cold.

The gear shift pattern is one up, then three down, on the right side. The stock Commando engine produces an enormous amount of muscle over a broad RPM range. Accelerating away from a stop, passing, and pulling a large load are effortless tasks for the engine. Because of its wide power range, the Commando is an easy machine to ride.

The muscle the undersquare (bore 73mm, stroke 89mm) Commando engine produces is surprising. The relatively high compression ratio of 9:1 would indicate a lack of low speed power. The answer is that the cam-

The twin Amal Monoblocs seemed to be well matched to the engine. Air filtration is good and the ignition switch is conveniently located.

shaft has the same configuration as the old Atlas, and the long extinct Matchless twins. This choice of cam is perfect for all around use.

The machine we tested had many miles already on the engine and chassis. Only the SS components had been added. This machine was loose enough to run at its best. The only thing we had to check regularly was the oil level. With the engine as loose as this one, it would consume some oil when being pushed hard for long periods. We prefer to have a machine that has been well run in to do our tests, as it is a more accurate indication of what the machine is like after being in an owner's hands for some time. Also, it permits us to flog a machine with little fear of seizing or galling new parts.

Even with this engine being loose,

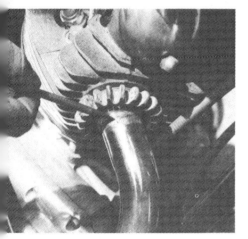

The exhaust head pipes, right and left side, fractured several times, even after being welded. We have been told the factory has corrected this problem.

it performed with consistency and strength. Our quarter-mile speeds and times are not indicative of what this machine will really do. It happened that the only day we had availability to the drag strip, it was damp from a day long mist. But even with the damp surface, the SS put in a surprisingly good time and respectable speed. There's no doubt that we lost more than a half second's time and a few mph due to the wet surface.

To match the strong performance of the engine, the Norton people have developed an excellent handling chassis and suspension units. The British have long excelled in producing fine handling road machines, and the Commando is no exception. Compared with other production machinery in its class, the Commando ranks as high as any in the handling department. Over both winding mountain roads and open highway, we found it absolutely predictable in turns and stable on the road.

Up front the Commando uses forks

With two riders aboard, the Commando will still run at a hundred miles an hour without straining the engine.

The Norton is a superb handling road machine. It's fast and stable and can be bent over a long way before the undercarriage grounds.

of its own design that appear identical to the AJS motocrossers. These units are a bit on the stiff side when cold and for some lighter riders. But they perform fairly well. At the rear Norton uses the Girling units that perform quite well.

The chassis is a conventional appearing tubular double cradle frame. The big difference is that the swing arm is mounted in rubber (polymer), directly to the engine and gear box assemblies, rather than to the chassis. The intent here was to eliminate the chain vibration from the chassis,

which it does. The bad side effect is that the swing arm and rear wheel will move slightly from side to side. Under normal operation, this rear wheel movement is not very noticeable, but once you start putting the machine through its paces, the rider can feel this movement. In turns this causes the rear end to flex. It can be especially noticed when crossing rippled surfaces at an angle.

The Commando will cruise effortlessly at ninety per with the rider sitting up and still have throttle on tap. The braking is adequate for a large machine, although we found they would fade some in downhill mountainous type riding. They did not fade to the point of disappearing, but the stopping power was definitely reduced. It would be nice to see a hydraulic disc up front.

One item that really insures fine handling qualities are the Avon GP tires. They track straight as an arrow on the open road and provide superb traction and stability in the corners, even when damp.

The high pipes proved to be a real annoyance to us. First, they aren't tucked in close enough, making the inside of the rider's legs rest against them. Also, we had the pipes fracture three times just at the outlet of the exhaust port, requiring welding. This was due to the metal being paper thin where it comes out of the exhaust port. Combined with the pressure of the rider's legs and the vibration of the engine, a crack would appear on the thin surface. We have been informed that our findings have been forwarded to the factory, and the flaw will be corrected before mass production starts.

Another thing we didn't care for was the rigid foot pegs.

The overall comfort of the machine is good, except for the saddle hardness on long rides. The engine vibration is not transmitted to the rider or chassis. The Commando is one of the few machines that has no blurring problem of the rear view mirror, due to vibration. The handlebars are comfortable, as are the hand grips. But the switches and buttons are difficult to operate while riding. A little redesigning is in order here.

The speedometer and tachometer are pretty accurate. The only trouble we had was that the odometer, while still working, was hung up between numbers all the way across the digits. This made it difficult to tell exactly how many miles we travelled.

We found the Commando would consistently average 38 miles per gallon, regardless of how hard or easy it was ridden. This is about what we expected. With the SS model tank, you have to keep an eye on the mileage, as the bike's not good for a hundred-mile, non-stop jaunt.

One of the nice conveniences that is standard with the Commando is the electrical plug (that odd looking item on the front side of the air box). Through this the battery can be charged from an outside source. The most convenient factor is being able to get electricity from this outlet to power additional lights, glove warmers, and even an electric shaver, if you have a 12-volt model.

One item the factory might think about changing is the mounting of the front fender. It is bolted to a flexible mount that allows the fender to move about. At higher speeds the fender wobbles, shakes and moves with great freedom, to the distress of the rider.

Overall, we found the new Norton Commando SS to be just about all the machine a man might want in the way of a high performance vertical twin. In the sporting and super bike classes, it excels in performance and handling. As far as the Americanized SS Commando goes, we hope to see the factory correct the few areas of trouble we encountered. If you're in the market for a high performance, big-bore machine, the Commando would be worth looking at.

—Dave Holeman **CG**

NORTON COMMANDO SS

ENGINE

Type	verticle twin cylinder four cycle
Bore and stroke	73x89mm
Displacement	745cc
Compression Ratio	8.9:1
Rated Max. Horsepower	60 @ 6,800 rpm
Ignition	alternator/battery
Carburetion	twin 30 mm Amal concentrics
Lubrication	pressure fed dry sump

DIMENSIONS

Length	87.5 in.
Seat height	31.5 in.
Wheelbase	56.8 in.
Ground Clearance	6 in.
Dry weight	389 lbs.

WHEELS AND BRAKES

Front tire size	4.10x19 in.
Front brake type	double leading shoe
Rear tire size	4.10x19 in.
Rear brake type	internal expanding

TRANSMISSION

Type	constant mesh 4-speed
Clutch	wet, multi plate
Internal gear ratios	1st, 2.56:1; 2nd, 1.7:1; 3rd, 1.22:1; 4th, 1:1

PERFORMANCE

Indicated highest one-way speed	110
Quarter-mile acceleration:	
Top speed	95.54 (Damp surface)
Elapsed time	13.597 (Damp surface)

GENERAL

Air filtration	dry paper
Battery type	12V 5AH

CAPACITIES

Fuel tank	2.3 gal.
Oil tank & sump	6.9 pts.
Gear box	9 pts.
Fuel consumption	38 mpg

FRAME AND SUSPENSION

Front suspension	telescopic, oil dampened
Rear suspension	adjustable spring over shock
Frame type	tubular, double cradle

OPTIONAL EXTRAS

F.I.M. racing kit

COLORS

Orange, Yellow & Blue

PRICE AS TESTED

$1,595.00 FOB Los Angeles

DISTRIBUTOR(S)

WEST: Norton/Villiers Corp., 6765 Paramount, North Long Beach, 90805

EAST: Berliner Motors, Plant Road, Hasbrouck Hts., N.J. 07604

Norton 750cc Commando Roadster

Four years of development
have refined Norton Villiers'
superbike into a vastly satisfying
and quick personal
bike for the knowledgeable and
experienced cyclist.

Norton carries on in its own way, with an engine wedded to tradition and a running gear drawn from contemporary design. Had this blend of past and present remained unchanged for 1971, our renewed acquaintance with Norton would still have been a welcome experience. The test model was a Commando Roadster, virtually the same as the Commando S in our Superbike Comparison Test a year ago [see *Cycle*, March '70]. The only immediately apparent change was the use of downswept exhaust pipes on the new model. But, as we were to realize during the test, several detailed changes have made an excellent bike even better.

The Commando shouldn't be as good a bike as it is. The basic engine was first introduced in the Dominator 500cc models of the late 1950s. From there, the powerplant was stretched to 600ccs in the Nomad Scrambler, and then boosted 650ccs in the Manxman, and finally inflated to 750 in the Atlas. In its day the Atlas was a fairly nice machine. A frame and suspension package descended from the fabled Manx roadracer, endowed the Atlas with good handling. And the big 750 was awfully fast. But at just about that same point in time, the cycle-buying public began getting persnickity. The Atlas shook all over with a serious case of Bad Vibes, and the engine leaked more oil than it burned.

Coincidentally, Associated Motors, who owned Norton at the time, was entering its death throes. A British holding company, a corporate hyphenate called Manganese-Bronze, stepped in and collected Norton along with several other foundering old-line companies. A new company, Norton-Villiers, emerged from all these high-office dealings, and a bright young engineer named Bob Trigg was given the task of creating a marketable big machine for Norton. His first impulse was probably to scrap the old twin and start out with a fresh three-or-four cyl-

inder design. But the management must have decided to wing along on the old engine for awhile until the company got back on its feet.

What Trigg devised was a first-rate motorcycle which has won the "Machine of the Year" award in the British motorcycle press for three consecutive years.

Starting the bike is no job for the inexperienced and weak-kneed, since it takes a healthy thrust on the kickstart lever to turn the engine over. First operation in the stoking-up routine is to open one of the two fuel valves. Both valves feed both carburetors, so leaving one of them off holds part of one side of the tank in reserve. The Amal Concentric carbs have flood buttons for cold engine starts. Choke slides are also provided, but they were never needed in the mild Southern California December. The Commando's ignition switch has been mercifully moved off the left side-panel. Before, the rider was forever hitting the key with his calf and, at times, actually switching off the sparks. The new four-position switch is shock-mounted in a black rubber sheath, slightly inboard and forward of its previous

location. The switch stops are arranged Japanese-style, beginning in the most counter-clockwise position and operating thus: parking lights, off, ignition, and running lights. The key can only be removed in the parking light and off positions. A lunge on the pedal of the kickstart lever usually brings the long-stroke powerplant to life on first try.

There's all kinds of commotion going on down between your legs as the engine warms to an uneven, loping idle. The Commando's unique rubber engine-mounting system allows the engine to move around somewhat. The handlebars and forks dance and shake too. Another thing that strikes the rider right away is the sound. The mufflers are even quieter for 1971, but that throaty sound remains. Just the sharp crack is gone.

Pulling the clutch lever revealed one area in which Norton has gone backwards. Last year's machines had an amazingly easy pull, but this test bike required a herculean effort to operate. The clutch throwout mechanism contains a steel ball that rides against the end of the pushrod and is actuated by a cam lever. Apparently there is some sort of trick, which all Norton tuners know, whereby a modification of the cam lift rate makes for an easier draw on the clutch lever. If this is so, the factory hasn't heard about it. The new Lucas handlebar levers don't help the situation any. Made of die-cast aluminum alloy, the levers have sharply radiused corners that bite into fingers. Apart from the awfully hard draw, the clutch action is otherwise progressive and positive; the clutch doesn't slip or grab.

As the engine revs pass the 2000 mark, all of the engine's bobbing and shaking disappears. The smoothness is uncanny. Most bikes go through a series of vibration stages as the revs build, with the engine alternating fitfully between primary and secondary unbalance. But once above 2000 rpm, everything is calm. This complete lack of the

Fat 4.10 x 19 Avon GP tire was adopted from production racer, forks are Roadholders internally.

shakes is due to Bob Trigg's marvelous "iso-lastic" suspension-type engine-mounting system. The name is derived from the fact that the engine is isolated from the bike parts which touch the rider by means of a system of elastic (rubber) cushions. In this arrangement the engine, gearbox, and swingarm are all bolted together *via* a series of joining plates. The plates are then elastic-mounted to the frame, with very carefully spaced limiting washers to prevent the engine unit from deflecting from the frame in anything but a vertical plane. Anything more than a very slight cocking of the rear wheel would make for miserable handling.

Riding the Commando in slow traffic brought out another subtle change in this year's model. The steering trail has been shortened by a half-inch to make low-speed handling a little lighter. Actually, the change was made in the first place to get rid of a bit of high-speed oversteer in the Commando Production Racers, and the low-speed lightness is a by product. Much of this steering ease is offset by the use of a much bigger front tire than on previous models. In 1970 the S model was fitted with a 3.00 x 19 Avon ribbed tire. The new rubber is a 4.10 x 19 Avon GP, patterned after Avon's famous racing tire. So the Commando now wears GPs front and back. The new front tire has a much greater sectional radius, a fact which requires more rider muscle to make the bike turn. The big tire performs better out on the

freeway. Earlier models with the smaller tire tended to follow pavement seams; and those round, raised discs that separate the lanes on freeways would cause the bike to turn too abruptly. On iron bridge gratings the old combination proved positively scarey.

The bigger front tire would allow more stopping power if the front brake were any better. As it is, the brakes begin to fade before the limit of tire adhesion is reached. We had hoped that the standard Commandos would come with the Lockheed disc brake which the Norton Production Racers carry up front. Such was not to be. On our first ride, we thought that something was drastically wrong with the front brake, but it was only the internal friction in a dry cable. The only lubricant on hand was a can of Dri-Slide, a very nonviscous solution of molybdenumdisulfide in a volatile solvent. Our first notion was that the stuff would be only marginally effective on the highly loaded cable and lever fitting. The lubricant ran down the inner cable like gasoline, taking about a minute to run out the bottom. The improvement was amazing. The brake would still fade after hard use, but at least you could feel it coming. Another problem that compounded the braking deficiency was the amount of compression in the outer cable. The harder the lever was pulled, the more the cable compressed. The result was a very disconcerting feel in any emergency situation.

Despite the distraction and aggravation caused by the front brake and stiff clutch, the big Norton really comes into its own up in the switchback mountain roads. The effect of crowding the Commando to the limit of its brakes is akin to riding a roller coaster with brakes, steering, and gearshift. You go harder and harder until the scenery starts to blur, and suddenly you are acting out a conscious escape dream. The big stroker's extremely flat torque curve combines with the silky smooth gearbox to make the acceleration seem effortless. The machine gives off no feel or sound that jar your brain

Commandos differ from the other superbikes by offering simple, uncluttered good looks combined with lightweight, easy handling and an engine that delivers lots of torque over a wide range of engine speeds. The others are lacking in at least one of the critical areas.

back to reality. Once you adjust your rhythm to the power of the front brake, the dream lasts until you come to a stop sign or run out of gas.

Complementing the engine isolation is a new shock absorber in the rear wheel hub that is new this year. In the Norton gearbox there is about 60 degrees of free shaft rotation between the engaging dogs of the lower gears. The resulting slack would cause a noticeable snap in the rear wheel when you opened and closed the throttle under load on the older Commandos. On their production racers, the snap caused failure of some gears. The new shock absorber and heavier gears eliminate the problem.

Normal maintenance on the Roadster is straightforward and rather easily carried out. There are some 10 pounds of crude black-painted tools stored behind the left side-panel. With these assorted stone axes, you can perform all the tasks outlined in the owner's manual. Only the screwdriver needs a little dressing on a grinding wheel before it will fit the breaker points screws.

The Roadster can be quickly stripped in the field for troubleshooting and adjusting. A couple of knurled knobs fasten the seat brackets to the ends of the upper shock absorber mounting bolts. After loosening the knobs, the seat can be pulled up and back for removal. Both side-panels come off after twisting a Dzus fastener on the front of each panel. Removing the two $^9/_{16}$-inch nuts from the front of the fuel tank and detaching the feed lines from the valves lets you lift off the tank. With the tank and side-panels off, the rocker covers are exposed for setting the valve lash, and all the electrical components are accessible.

The ignition timing reference marks can be viewed by taking out the smaller plug on the primary drive case. By removing the cap on the right side timing case, the ignition points are bared for inspection and adjustment. There's even a power supply receptacle mounted on the air filter box so that you can plug in a timing or trouble light. Rumor

An immensely strong backbone tube prevents flexing between loads from steering head and rear wheel.

New 40/50 watt headlight is much improved.

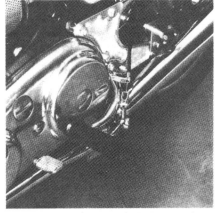

Footrest and brake unit are best-looking in industry.

New mufflers are quieter without restricting.

Coils look cobby but run cool in air blast.

has it that English Commando riders plug in their electric boots at this handy outlet.

The other two large plugs on the primary cover allow you to inspect the primary chain tension and to adjust the end play in the clutch throw-out pushrod. For some obscure reason Norton still uses leather washers under these primary case plugs. If neoprene O-rings were employed, the plugs would be a little more difficult to remove, but then again, they wouldn't fall off in the street. Or even steadily weep oil. There's a huge fat O-ring that fits all the way around the primary case cover. Using an O-ring in one place but not in others is a mystery to us.

Primary chain tension (or, more correctly, lack of it) is adjusted by loosening the separate gearbox and changing its position relative to the engine with positioning bolts.

Oil is changed on the Roadster by first draining the oil tank under the right side-panel, and then removing the sump strainer

under the engine. Last year the sump strainer plug was hidden under a frame tube, but on the new models the plug is easily taken out. A new shock-mounted oil tank holds a full gallon of oil.

Grease fittings are provided at the swing-arm pivot, brake pedal pivot, and the front brake cam pivots. The fittings are not designed for any readily available grease gun. There are no fittings on the control cables or wheel bearings or steering head bearings.

The rear chain oiler proved overactive. The oiler is fed off the oil pressure relief valve return line. A T fitting leads to a three-inch length of transparent plastic tubing which is half filled with felt. The theory is that the felt will saturate with oil and slowly meter it through a smaller hose, thus lubing the chain. Unfortunately, the length of tubing which holds the metering felt is mounted vertically and continues to drip until the felt is dry. The oil falls from the chain onto

whatever is under the parked bike. Moreover, the fiber washers, used on feed and return lines between the oil tank and engine tend to age fairly quickly, and the slightest jar or overtightening will disintegrate them. Soft aluminum washers would work better.

Riding the Roadster around in the dead of night demonstrated that the Lucas headlights have been much improved. A new 40/50 watt headlight bulb shoots a blazing beam of light out to illuminate the road, and the new fiberglass taillight keeps trailing car drivers alert. A lever switch on the headlight body turns on the lights, and the dip switch is on the left handlebar. The right handlebar throttle housing holds a button which momentarily flashes the high beam; the feature may be useful when crossing street intersections without traffic controls, or when signaling other drivers of your approach. Both the front and rear brakes trigger the stop-light.

NORTON 750 COMMAND ROADSTER

Price, suggested retail	East and West Coast, POE $1590
Tire, front	4.10 in. x 19 in. Avon "GP"
rear	4.10 in. x 19 in. Universal
Brake, front	8 in. x 1.25 in.
rear	7 in. x 1.25 in.
Brake swept area	59.6 sq. in.
Specific brake loading	9.5 lb/sq. in., at test weight
Engine type	Pushrod OHV twin
Bore and stroke	2.875 in. x 3.503 in., 73mm x 89mm
Piston displacement	45 cu. in., 745 cc
Compression ratio	8.9:1
Carburetion	(2) 30mm Amal
Air filtration	Dry paper element
Ignition	Battery-coil
Bhp @ rpm	58 @ 6500 rpm
Fuel capacity	3.9 gal.
Oil capacity	8 pints
Lighting	12v, 68 watts
Battery	12v, 8ah
Gear ratios, overall	(1) 12.4 (2) 8.25 (3) 5.9 (4) 4.84
Wheelbase	58 in.
Seat height	32 in., with rider
Ground clearance	7 in., with rider
Curb weight	419 lbs., with ½-tank of gas
Test weight	569 lbs., with rider
Instruments	150 mph Speedometer, 9000 rpm tach
0-60 mph	5.5 seconds
Standing start ¼ mile	13.03 seconds 102.16 mph
Top speed	110 mph

Standing ¼-Mile 102.16 at 13.03

The regular Lucas electrolytic capacitor system allows the alternator to supply a normal amount of current to the coils even if the battery is completely dead. In fact, if the negative battery lead wire is carefully insulated, you can run the bike with the battery completely removed and all the electrical components will function.

Another lighting improvement this year is in the instruments. Both tach and speedo are extremely easy to read at night, yet there is no irritating glare. Similar to aircraft instruments, the light is soft and green, from what appears to be luminous paint.

No matter where we rode the Roadster during the test, the inevitable comment from people was: "Oh, wow, what a good-looking bike." Not charming, or beautiful, or bitchin', or even ballsy. Always a simple "good-looking." There is nothing managed or contrived or ornate about the Commando's appearance. What little gingerbread that remained on last year's model has been pared away. The little chromed halo on the headlight rim and those gaudy up-swept exhaust pipes with their perforated leg shields are both gone. Everything that's left is clean and simple. The visual appeal of the Roadster rests with the attractive shapes and locations of the major components, and the finishes selected for them. Cleaner engine case castings would, however, improve the machine's looks. The race-bred placement of the ignition coils down under the gas tank looks somewhat peculiar, but dropping them into a blast of cool air is more important than discreetly tucking the coils up under the tank.

The Commando tends to make an expert drag racer out of all but the most spastic riders. Winding on the rightside handle-grip and dumping the velvet-smooth clutch produces no-wheelie, dead straight starts every time. For a comparison of the Commando's drag strip manners, relative to the other superbikes, refer to the Big Seven Showdown in the March '70 issue. Most Commandos seem to run in the low 13s or high 12s, at just over the ton. Our Roadster clicked off several effortless and almost identical runs, the fastest of which was 13.03 seconds at 102.16 mph.

The Norton Commando Roadster is a very excellent example of what we at *Cycle* have come to call superbikes. It is the lightest, most maneuverable one of the bunch. As such, the bike is a genuine pleasure for the knowledgeable and experienced cyclist to own and ride. Since Norton Villiers has shown no hesitation in the past toward improving the Commando, they will probably not dally in correcting weaknesses. Next year we hope to see a better stopping and more oil-tight machine which will be easier to lube and maintain. Then the Commando will be as much of a joy for the newcomers to cycling as it is for the old hands. ◉

The Roadster is most at home out beyond the pale, after the scenery has turned to a blur.

PHOTOGRAPHY: LARRY WILLETT

BOLT-ON SPEED!

Fitting the Dunstall 810 conversion is simply a matter of changing barrels, pistons and studs as Roy Gilbert demonstrates here

First disconnect all the trimmings on the standard motor—exhaust pipes, carbs, cables, head steady, etc, and move coils to clear the exhaust rocker boxes

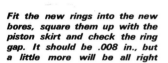

Fit the new rings into the new bores, square them up with the piston skirt and check the ring gap. It should be .008 in., but a little more will be all right

Warm the new pistons and fit to the connecting rods. The pistons are stamped "L" and "R" on the intake valve cutaways—be sure to fit them the right way round

Support the pistons on wooden blocks and fit the barrels. Unless you have someone to help it is advisable to use ring clamps on the pistons

Fit the heads, making sure the intake side stud locates. Note that the longer pushrods go to the inside—they can be held with an elastic band until fitted

John Robinson rides the converted Commando

The 810 conversion bolted on to a bog standard Commando will obviously give more power. To be precise, an extra 60 cc's worth of torque from tickover all the way up to maximum.

Apparently the larger pistons don't affect the engine's top revs and don't upset the balance of the engine either.

However, as the Dunstall men were quick to point out, to get the *full* benefit you really need a Dunstall head and camshaft. Then you'll have so much power that the gearing will need altering—why not fit a Quaife five-speeder?—and it will go so fast that you really ought to have a disc brake as well.

Just to prove the point they then wheeled out the latest Dunstall Norton—1972 style. This is fitted with Dunstall equipment from the disc brake to the new siamesed exhaust including, of course, the big-bore barrels.

Incidentally, camshaft is stan-

dard on this particular machine.

When it runs it makes low rumbling noises and emits a lower than standard exhaust note. It's difficult to say whether this is due to the exhaust system or the bigger engine, or maybe both.

Under way it feels just like the Norvil production racer, even to the light feeling at the steering head which changes to a tremor if you roll it off in a turn.

I suspect that it is a shade quicker than the Norvil version, but we weren't able to take full performance figures mainly because the motor had only done about four miles and we didn't have time to run it in. In fact, we were threatened with all sorts of nasty things including the bill for damages if we took it over 5000.

The Dunstall Commando pulls nicely from tickover upwards, even with high gearing. In fact it could be run in a higher gear and would take it with no effort at all—that was just about the most pleasant facet of the bike.

Occasionally I crossed my fingers and gave it a big handful—well not a really big handful, Mr. Dunstall—just to hear the engine thunder up to, er, 5000. Even when changing up at this speed it wouldn't lose any steam in the next gear and carried on happily to 5000 in top without even thinking about it. It's nice not to have to cane a machine through the gears in order to get any top gear performance.

full stop

The twin discs on the front were initially a bit disappointing —they are heavy to use and don't bite very hard until they get hot. After three or four crash stops they *do* get hot and then they come on hard enough to lock up the front wheel, if you feel like trying.

On reflection, I'm probably doing them a bit of an injustice because although at 5000 in top the engine hasn't really started to work, it's still whistling along at a fair old rate. A very deceptive rate, actually,

  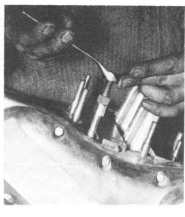 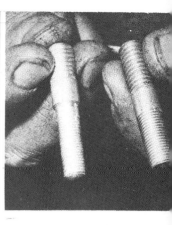

Slacken off the head nuts, set the pistons at bdc, undo the nuts at the base of the barrels and lift off the head and barrels together, remove head on bench

New studs are provided with the conversion kit and as they are different from the originals, they have to be swapped over. Leave new intake side stud loose until . . .

. . . barrel is fitted. Remove the old pistons after warming them and replace studs in crankcase. A pair of pliers is usually enough, or you can lock two nuts together

As you can see, the new studs are of a different size to the old ones. When refitting head and barrel, tighten them down evenly in a diagonal sequence

For £65 plus 50p post and packing, all this can be yours. There's no exchange system but new standard parts would cost something in the region of £58

QUICKER COMMANDO!

on normal gearing it runs out at 89 mph, meaning that at its maximum of 7000 rpm the Commando should be clocking 125 mph.

Paul Dunstall says that it will pull a higher gear and will go faster, but loses out on acceleration, so this seems to be the best compromise.

On the subject of facts and figures, Dunstall claims 70 bhp at 6800 rpm, just with the 810 conversion. The rev limit is 7000—"we have gone over that, but don't recommend it."

So that's the latest of the British bigsters—a basic capacity conversion to make high speed touring a cinch on a standard Commando, with extras to build up a really potent machine.

Buying any sort of performance is expensive and that's how it is with Dunstall's parts. On the other hand it's interesting to note that should you need to buy new barrels, pistons and gaskets, you'd end up paying nearly as much.

If you're into rear-set footpegs for the street, Dunstall's are as nice as any. And his Blair-designed exhaust system is clearly superior to anything on the market in terms of performance and silence.

CYCLE ROAD TEST:

DUNSTALL NORTON 810

• What it is not: relaxed, or relaxing; comfortable, cushy, or soft; mass-market-oriented; prosaic; sensible; easy to get used to; or in any way gentle in premise.

What it is: remarkably smooth of engine (bless the genius of Bob Trigg, who designed the Commando); rewarding once familiar; a fantastic stopper; oil-thirsty; fast, within the limits imposed by tractability; visually startling; intensely personal; reliable; and a remarkably successful and well thought-out hot-rod.

Sunset Boulevard, heading west from Brentwood towards Pacific Palisades in moderate traffic. The road, a non-divided four-laner, lots of off-camber, smooth corners, no smog, temperature about 75 degrees. You watch the traffic around you, and you can see the cars slow but struggling with the turns, bodies shifting on their undercarriages, front tires curled under and groping, people moving around within swaying towards the outside of the turns, the cars' rear bumpers jerking up when the brakelights come on; you can visualize the car passengers clutching door-handles and dashboards and waiting anxiously for the road to straighten out.

And you're carving, out there on Sunset, precisely, playing Calvin Rayborn loose

among the radishes, red jacket, red helmet, a fire-engine-red motorcycle, hands down low, feet up high, knees working on the gas tank, notching a succession of perfect shifts, steering the motorcycle rather than merely leaning it over, tinkering with the precision that the motorcycle demands and responds to, fooling with the enormous torque that Paul Dunstall has given an already torquey engine, trailing behind you the most beautiful, rich, deep, smooth exhaust note this side of Milwaukee, listening to the hiss of the centerstand as it kisses the pavement going around right-handers, feeling solid resistance as the sidestand grounds on turns to the left. Dunstall's 810 Norton Sprint: this is where it belongs, this is where it belongs: out where *other* people can see it.

For a hot-rod (American terminology, or close enough, for England's Cafe Racer), the mighty 810 is surprising in its restraint. One

gets the impression that, had he wanted to do so, Dunstall could have built the 810 to be quite a bit faster. But then it would have lost reliability, it would have become hard to start (which it isn't), it would have been a handful to ride, and it would have been lots noisier. As it is, it is well-integrated for a semi-custom, conservative mechanically, and not as punishing as you would expect.

But you can't buy one. Not complete, not in this country. You could go to England, have Paul do one up to your specifications, and bring it back with you under the Personal Export provisions. Or you could buy all the parts from Dunstall and do one up yourself.

Here's how Paul goes about it. He buys a complete Norton Commando, strips off all the standard parts that he plans to replace, and sells them back to Norton-Villiers: parts like the gas tank, seat, handlebars, sliders,

cylinder assembly, pistons, front brake, exhaust system, valves, cam followers, foot controls, and front fender. He then installs $\frac{1}{8}''$ larger intake valves, his own guides and springs, reshapes the combustion chamber to accommodate a cylinder assembly with 3mm more bore and about 10 pounds less weight, decreases the intake valve angle from 28 degrees to $26\frac{1}{2}$ degrees from the vertical, polishes and re-contours the ports, hogs out the intake manifolds, sticks in his own lightweight cam-followers, and adds a high-pressure oil feed to the rocker assemblies; the engine uses, of course, Paul's own lightweight 10-1 cast pistons (the crank assembly doesn't have to be rebalanced), and a pair of 32mm Amal Concentric carburetors. Which just about does it for the engine.

The tank and seat, both beautifully rendered in color-impregnated fiberglass, replace the stock Norton items. The seat is se-

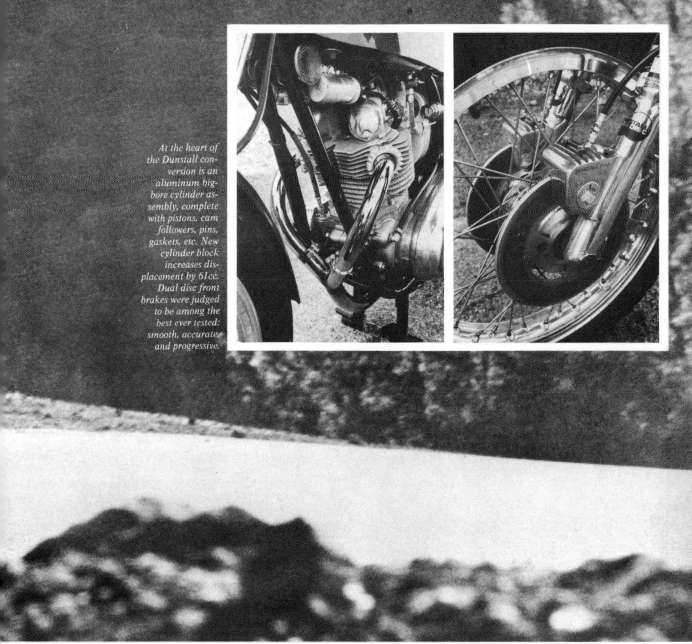

At the heart of the Dunstall conversion is an aluminum big-bore cylinder assembly, complete with pistons, cam followers, pins, gaskets, etc. New cylinder block increases displacement by 61cc. Dual disc front brakes were judged to be among the best ever tested: smooth, accurate and progressive.

PHOTOGRAPHER: BILL DELANEY

cured only by a pair of tabs which a pair of large knurled aluminum hand knobs attach to the upper shock mounts, and an additional tab which rests on the frame loop used on the stocker to support the rear fender and the taillight assembly. The tank is held by rubber-doughnut-bushed bolts in front and a rubber band looping under the backbone tube behind.

Semi-clip-ons are used instead of standard handlebars, the front fender is Dunstall's own lightweight fiberglass item, and the slick dual disc front brakes come from Dunstall as well.

Farther back, aluminum mounting plates locate the rear-set brake and shift mechanisms—plates which are less attractive but more competition-looking than the stock polished Norton forgings. The plates also support (in rubber bushings) Dr. Gordon Blair's patented two-into-one-back-into-two

exhaust system, one of the bike's more pleasing aspects.

What's left? Norton's fabled Commando frame, Roadholder forks, the engine's shortblock, Norton-Girling rear shock absorbers with slightly heavier springs, and the stock rear brake assembly, reduced in effectiveness by a variation in leverage at the foot pedal.

The bike takes a lot of getting used to. An historic imprecision in low-speed metering accuracy by the Amal carburetors means, simply, that the bike stalls a lot before you get used to it. But the bike starts easily, even if it is rough to kick over—that is, it starts easily if you know what you're doing: just the right amount of throttle, and just the right amount of choke. (The choke lever is mounted on a stub of capped handlebar tubing clamped in the stock handlebar position on the top triple-clamp. A good way to use the handlebar bosses, but a bit heavier than

necessary.) The right footpeg has to be folded up before you can try to start the engine; and when it's finally running, you have to be careful returning the kickstarter lever to its normal position. If you aren't, your toe will contact the underside of the shift lever, and before you know it, the transmission has been bumped into first and you've stalled again. Don't worry about it; the first time it happens, you'll be so damned mad that it'll never happen again.

Once underway, you can't help feeling like a gen-you-wine roadracer. It's a neat feeling, within limits. The bike, face it, is a bit of a handful in town, what with its reluctance to idle and the fact that the seat gets you pretty high up in the air, which makes footing around difficult for a six-footer and nearly impossible for somebody five-feet-eight. Additionally, the seat offers minimal padding, and what padding it does have tends to slide around under its covering and ultimately migrate towards the rear, where the passenger sits (who has an enormous amount of room, but nothing except the operator to hang onto).

But what makes the 810 most awkward in the city is the seating position. The footpegs are a solid 6—8 inches behind their stock location, and the handlebars are lower, farther to the front, and closer together than on a production Commando. So you support most of your upper-body weight on your hands, which becomes tiring, unless you call into play a bunch of little muscles in your back and pelvis, which is even more tiring.

The punishment meted out to your hands and forearms is worsened by the character of the Dunstall handgrips. They are relatively small in diameter, faintly barrel-shaped, and tightly patterned. Without gloves, after a hundred miles or so they begin to feel like wood rasps. With gloves, you're simply left with a pair of very stiff wrists. Stiff, and

tired, because the clutch is rather heavy, and the throttle springs are remarkably stout, which an extremely slow throttle does little to alleviate.

Around town, the engine makes up for as much of it as it can. The 810 is a revelation. Bob Trigg's Isolastics have seen to *all* of the engine vibration. (To find out how much there is, simply prop your foot up on the chaincase at about 35 mph and keep it there. If you can.) Once the carburetors come off idle, metering is accurate enough, and the Dunstall chuffs along quiet, smooth, and sedate as a BMW. Blair's exhaust system for the 810 is a marvel. Two short header pipes converge just in front of the forward engine mount, a single larger tube carries the exhaust below the engine, and it splits back into two mufflers right under the transmission. The mufflers themselves are quite simple; a perforated disc is located up front, perforated tubing lined with fiberglass along the muffler's main body, and a nest of seven

short, small-diameter lengths of tubing at the big end. According to Dunstall, the system is worth five mph in the quarter and five mph on top. It may well be. But performance improvements aside, the pipes are worth their weight in gold in terms of exhaust note and solid noise reduction. In *Cycle*'s decibel test, the 810 registered 88.9 dB(A), or about two decibels more than the two 100cc street machines tested in the March issue, and four decibels *less* than the Suzuki 380 tested in the same issue. At last! A high-performance exhaust system that honest-to-God *muffles*!

Enough of city traffic—the 810 can tolerate it, but barely. The bike is noticeably more relaxed romping through mountain roads, banked turns, switchbacks, long straightaways with tight corners at the end where it can show off its superb front brakes. Both nine-inch discs are rigidly mounted—they don't float. Neither do the

Continued on next page

DUNSTALL NORTON 810

Price, suggested retail	N/A
Tire, front	4.10 in. x 19 in.
rear	4.10 in. x 19 in.
Brake, front	9.0 (O.D.) in. x 1.25 in. (2)
rear	7.0 in. x 1.25 in.
Engine type	OHV 360° vertical twin
Bore and stroke	2.996 in. x 3.503 in., 76mm x 89mm
Piston displacement	49.2 cu. in., 806cc
Compression ratio	10:1
Carburetion	2; 32mm; Amal concentrics
Air filtration	Paper element
Ignition	Battery and coil
Bhp @ rpm (claimed)	70 @ 7000 rpm
Fuel capacity	5 gal.
Oil capacity	8 pints
Lighting	12v, Alternator
Gear ratios, overall	(1) 11.2 (2) 7.45 (3) 5.35 (4) 4.38
Curb weight	400 lbs., with ½-tank of gas
Wheelbase	57 in.
Test weight	565 lbs., with rider
Weight distribution	183 Front, 217 Rear
Gas mileage	41-45 MPG
Sound level, California standard	88.9 dB(A)
Standing start ¼ mile	12.70 seconds 102.65 mph

DUNSTALL

calipers. But they don't have to, since each caliper assembly has two live pucks. (Which makes Dunstall's installation different from the single disc found on the front of the Honda Fours and the 450 and on the Kawasaki 750 and 500. On the Japanese bikes, the caliper assembly has to pivot, since only one live puck is used.) Both caliper slave cylinders are governed by a single master cylinder with two brake lines. One runs directly to the right caliper; the other incorporates a pressure switch (similar to that on the Hondas) that controls the stop light. Lever pressure is lighter than any of the Hondas or the Kawasakis (or, for that matter, either of the two new Norton Commandos), and braking force was judged to be superior to all. The front tire, a massive 4.10—19 Dunlop Roadmaster K81, is a necessity. The brake demands it. But the tire imposes a penalty of its own: while the 810 steers accurately, it cannot be flicked left-right-left in the manner of some of the more nimble middleweights.

Giganto front tire or no, a quite peculiar front-end imprecision was noticed at high speed on the drag strip. Static weight distribution is 183 lbs. front and 217 lbs rear. Under hard acceleration midway through third gear, with the rider towards the rear of the seat and down out of the wind, the front end would begin a low frequency, hunting oscillation; the forks were swinging slowly a few degrees to the left and right of dead center, and felt temporarily as if the bike's front-end geometry could have used a little more trail.

It wasn't noticeable in the switchbacks—the 810 is solid as a rock, predictable, forgiving, its engine comfortably free of any soft spots above 3000 rpm, its shift linkage, bellcranks and all, positive and accurate. Only a few nickel-dime disturbances keep it from perfection: throttle action is stiff enough to make accurate downshift/front brake unison a bit of a bother, the rear brake could use some help, and the sidestand and centerstand are abominations. The left-mounted sidestand is useless—it's weak, and it won't get out of the way when fast lefthanders are attempted, grounding well before the tires' limits are approached. The centerstand is not as lethal in a cornering situation; it doesn't drag badly, but its spring isn't strong enough to keep it flat against the motorcycle's belly. In its defense, the bike can be pulled up on its centerstand a lot easier than can a production Norton. *Not* in its defense, you can't pull it down with your foot, and it looks to be two or three pounds heavier than it has to be.

Out of the mountains and onto the freeways; the tautness of the 810's suspension and the minimal padding of its seat afford slightly less than Moto Guzzi touring pleasure, but at 70 mph, the chest-full of wind you catch is just enough to finally lift the load off your hands and arms. Standard

Lucas blade-type switches for turn-indicators and high-low beam selection are a bit punishing to the touch and over-positive, but the indicators (once you get used to up for right and down for left) and the lights work more than passably well. Here the torque of the big Norton is most noticeable. Four thousand rpm corresponds to 70 mph in top, and the Dunstall pulls as hard from 70 mph in fourth as normal 650s and 750s pull from 40 mph in third gear. The 810 kit feels like it really works, and the mufflers will guarantee that you won't blast some blue-haired lady out of her air-conditioned, Thunderbird revery. Again, the engine transmits *no* vibration through the frame to your fanny, hands, or feet, which more than compensates for the Dunstall's taut suspension on the freeway.

Dunstall equipment is handled in this country by several distributors, one of whom is Barney Tillman in East Los Angeles. Barney set up *Cycle*'s 810, and made a fine job of it, too; just before attacking Orange County International Raceway we returned the Dunstall for a little sharpening, and asked him about the smoke pouring out of the mufflers. He explained that, when Dunstall modifies the cylinder head, he discards the valve seals; as a result, oil runs into the combustion chambers through the intake valve guides. The problem could also have been caused by the oil-control rings. It's not really a major problem, but our 810 needed a quart of 30-Weight about every 90 miles ("Check the gas, and fill up the oil."), and the bike had a tendency to detonate slightly at low speeds under intermediate loading.

The 810 was acceleration-tested in the company of a brand new 750 Kawasaki Three, brought along by the Big K's new American R&D honcho, Bryon Farnsworth, former *Cycle* staffer and renowned Baja Man of Steel. Like every Norton product tested since 1969, the 810 is a cinch to ride at the drags. Its torque can be called upon to generate just exactly the right amount of wheelspin, its 57-inch wheelbase reduces the possibility of bothersome wheelstands, and Dunstall's rear-set shift apparatus (up for first) just plain makes the 810 easier to ride. The bike also proved to be remarkably consistent: 12.93-101.12, 13.02-100.00, 12.97-101.01, and 12.95-100.67. With the air cleaner removed and larger jets installed, the 810 went 12.77-101.58, 12.84-102.15, 12.84-102.62, 12.85-102.62, and a final 12.70-102.04. Its best trap speeds were attained by leaving the transmission in third all the way through the lights, the engine flattening out right at the ET beam at 7100 rpm. And the bike's freedom from vibration was all the more apparent after a few shots on the Kawasaki, which tends to buzz uncomfortably under full throttle (but which did generate slightly more trap speed than the 810: 103.44 mph).

So much of what's nice about the Dunstall 810 comes from Norton: its snick-snick transmission, its wondrously strong

clutch, its absolute freedom from the punishment of vibration, its precise handling characteristics. But Dunstall has improved it markedly in certain areas: his Dunstall front disc brake is vastly superior to the old Norton drum (and significantly better than even the new Norton disc); his Blair-computer-designed exhaust system is so rich of note and so mellow of decibel that every big four-stroke ought to have one, save possibly the already constrained BMW and Moto Guzzi; his fiberglass tank and seat/fender is of a quality seldom seen in the United States, rich, lustrous, light, and strong; and the 810 kit does provide noticeably more torque than a stock 750.

But what of that fabled Dunstall quarter-mile performance? The 810's best numbers were 12.70-102.62, certainly more than presentable insofar as ET is concerned—the 810 is fully three-tenths quicker (with no air-cleaner) than the stock Commando *Cycle* tested back in March of 1971, an indication of more low-and mid-range grunt—but Dunstall claims an ET of 11.9 for the 810, a time which could only be the product of that Good Dense English Air (the same peculiar atmospheric condition also surrounds certain Japanese test facilities at certain times of the year). The bike may indeed run subtwelve-second quarters but not in the United States, and not at Orange County (one of the very fastest strips in North America), and not in 1972, and not on pump gasoline.

The $295 front brakes? Certainly. The exhaust system? Absolutely. The $260 810 kit? Well, it's worth three-tenths, and it knocks 10 pounds off engine weight, and it's made of aluminum, all of which are worth something.

The rest of it? If you like a street machine that looks like a roadracer, and feels like one, bad aspects as well as good; if you like a big gas tank that you can lock between your knees; then, sure. ◉

SYLVAIN MICHAELIS

NORTON COMMANDO 850 INTERSTATE

A Reserved English Gentleman?
Not A Chance.

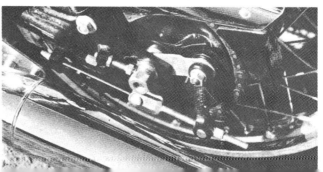

Photography: Fernando Belair, Jody Nicholas, D. Randy Riggs

■ THE TERM superbike means a lot of different things to different people. Americans seem to think the prime criterion is quarter-mile acceleration, although a few cafe racing types desire handling in direct proportion to speed potential.

In Europe, the scene is entirely different. To Europeans, a true superbike is a machine capable of handling somewhat irregular and varied road conditions at speeds upwards of 80—sometimes upwards of 100 mph. You see, the European likes to hop countries, and he likes to do it on a responsive machine in a helluva hurry.

To be honest, both methods of ascertaining whether or not a bike deserves the title superbike are fun. But to be equally honest, we must point out that machines capable of filling the bill in both areas...machines like Norton's 850 Interstate...are extremely rare.

What the 850 Interstate is, precisely, is a performance-oriented Commando with a gargantuan 6.5 gal. gas tank and different mufflers. The mufflers on the Interstate are not upswept much, and while cornering clearance suffers slightly,

room is provided for saddlebags. Really, it would be difficult to come up with a simpler approach, but in Norton's case, the end result is most effective.

Walk up to an Interstate. Take a good, long look. The immense black tank with the gold pinstriping and tasteful use of chrome, spells out class in any one of a hundred languages.

Swing a leg over. The seat and tank are wide, but not uncomfortably so. Purists will find the bars too wide, but the stock units are comfortable in the American tradition. The

shift is on the right, with low at the top of the pattern; just the opposite of today's norm.

Electric starting is not present, and the big Norton must be in neutral before the kickstart lever will engage. As has always been the case with British engines, starting is not particularly enjoyable when it's cold out. First, you have to turn on the ignition switch, located awkwardly by the aircleaner on the left-hand side of the machine. Next, flood both carburetor float bowls by depressing the tickler buttons until gas runs all over the engine cases. Messy. After ignoring the choke device altogether, swing the kickstart lever out and really stand on it. You have to use every ounce of body weight in a determined effort, and even then, engine turn over is slow, almost casual.

Sometimes the Twin will fire on the first or second kick, but if it doesn't, figure on 10 or 15 prods with the kickstarter. When it does light up, it rumbles with authority and soon settles to a throaty, although somewhat irregular idle, which it will maintain almost indefinitely. (Starting, thankfully, is a one or two kick affair when warm).

With a sigh of relief, you tug up on the shift lever to engage low gear. There is no clunk, like on Japanese bikes. The clutch takes hold with the lever very close to the handlebars, but engagement is smooth, just like the gearbox.

Ease out of the driveway and into traffic. Low speed handling is surprisingly good. Steering is light and there is absolutely no tendency to wallow or fall over in slow turns. The isolastic engine mounts, however, are not capable of absorbing the 850s throbbing pulsations below 2700 rpm or so, and this will detract some from an otherwise pleasant trip through traffic.

To really appreciate an Interstate, you've got to head out for the open road, preferably one with a lot of turns in it. Nortons, you see, are absolutely superb handlers; superb enough, in fact, to make a fast trip through the mountains seem casual.

You can flick the bike from side to side through S-bends without any protest at all from the chassis. It's more like riding a good 500, than an 850. The Dunlop TT 100 tires stick like glue, and unless you're really pushing, unwanted drifts simply do not occur.

Aside from scenery rushing past, there is little feeling of speed, either. This is mostly due to the engine, which is usually well below redline, and which doesn't require constant shifting. The bike is almost vibrationless from mid-rpm on up. Just punch fourth and regulate your speed with the throttle. It's as simple as that.

Brakes can handle the speed potential, too. There's a disc up front, manufactured by Norton under license from Lockheed. The double-acting caliper presses the two 1.5-in. wide brake pucks against the 10.7-in. diameter disc for an effective swept area of 84 sq. in.

The disc has the stopping power all right, but unfortunately, the master cylinder is mounted to the handlebar as on the Japanese systems, with the front brake lever pressing directly on the master cylinder piston. This means that the brake begins working as soon as the lever is pulled, making it difficult for people with small hands to get a good grip on the lever. It would be very simple to put an adjusting screw in the lever to allow the rider to adjust the point of lever engagement with the master cylinder piston, but it has been overlooked for the second year in a row.

The rear brake is a conventional drum unit, which works well enough, but isn't particularly impressive, especially after a fast ride through the hills. Naturally, most of the braking force is provided by the front brake, but the rear unit on the Interstate could stand some improvement.

Performance-wise, all Nortons, the Interstate included, must be considered innovative, because they've occupied the top rung on the ladder several times. But they haven't accomplished this with futuristic design, especially where the engine is concerned!

Basic design for the Norton Twin is decades old; and changes, with the exception of displacement increases, have been subtle. Even after all the years, and the generally accepted superiority of horizontally-split crankcases, Norton still retains the vertically-split crankcase configuration. This makes the incorporation of a central main bearing difficult, although not impossible: AJS and Matchless vertical Twins used a central main bearing right up until they stopped being manufactured in the early 1960's.

One of the main complaints that riders have about verically-split crankcases is that they are prone to leaking small amounts of oil. This is not the case on the Interstate, however, due to the large area of the mating surfaces and the obvious

care which Norton uses in the machining of these areas.

In spite of the engine displacement increase from 745 to 828cc, which comes about by the use of 77mm pistons instead of smaller 73mm ones, the crankcase is identical to the 750, except for more metal being removed from the crankcase lips to accommodate the larger cylinder barrel. Strength to support the crankshaft in its roller main bearings is assured by generous cast-in webbing around the bearing bosses. The

inevitable crankshaft "whip" such an engine design produces at ultra-high rpm, is also lessened by this webbing.

The connecting rods are still two-piece units featuring plain, thin-shell big-end bearings, with the pistons being supported by plain, brass bushings. Conventional three-ring flat-top pistons yield a compression ratio of 8.5:1.

Also new on the Commando 850 is the cast-iron cylinder

A triple-row primary chain transmits power to a diaphragm-type eight-plate clutch.

barrel. Besides being slightly larger physically, and having a 4mm larger bore, there are four holes running vertically on the outside edges to allow through-bolts to be employed. Earlier Nortons had the cylinder barrel attached to the crankcase by nine studs and nuts, and the cylinder head attached to the barrel by ten bolts and studs. Only in extreme situations did this arrangement give any trouble, but a cylinder would occasionally break loose from its cast-in lip if a piston seized. The four through-bolts eliminate this possibility.

Concentric 32mm carburetors feed the cylinders through

NORTON COMMANDO 850

SPECIFICATIONS

List price	$2055
Suspension, front	telescopic fork
Suspension, rear	swinging arm
Tire, front	4.10-19
Tire, rear	4.10-19
Brake, front, diameter x width, in.	(2) 10.5 x 1.5
Brake, rear, diameter x width, in.	7.0 x 1.25
Total brake swept area, sq. in.	112
Brake loading, lb./sq. in. (160-lb. rider)	5.41
Engine, type	OHV vertical Twin
Bore x stroke, in., mm	3.03 x 3.50, 77 x 89
Piston displacement, cu. in., cc	50, 828
Compression ratio	8.5:1
Claimed bhp @ rpm	60 @ 5900
Claimed torque @ rpm, lb.-ft.	49 @ 5000
Carburetion	(2) 32mm Amal concentric
Ignition	coil and battery
Oil system	gear pump, dry sump
Oil capacity, pt.	6
Fuel capacity, U.S. gal.	6.56
Recommended fuel	premium
Starting system	kick, folding crank
Lighting system	12V alternator
Air filtration	dry treated paper
Clutch	multi-plate, wet; diaphragm spring
Primary drive	triplex chain (3/8 x .225)
Final drive	single-row chain (5/8 x 3/8)
Gear ratios, overall:1	
5th	none
4th	4.60
3rd	5.61
2nd	7.53
1st	11.78
Wheelbase, in.	57.2
Seat height, in.	31.5
Seat width, in.	10
Handlebar width, in.	32
Footpeg height, in.	12.4
Ground clearance, in.	5.9
Front fork rake angle, degrees	28
Trail, in.	4.36
Curb weight (w/half-tank fuel), lb.	446
Weight bias, front/rear, percent	47/53
Test weight (fuel and rider), lb.	581
Mileage at completion of test	1197

TEST CONDITIONS

Air temperature, degrees F	61
Humidity, percent	29
Barometric pressure, in. hg.	30.23
Altitude above mean sea level, ft.	468
Wind velocity, mph	1-3
Strip alignment, relative wind:	

PERFORMANCE

Top speed (actual @ 7000 rpm), mph	116
Computed top speed in gears (@ 7000 rpm), mph	
5th	none
4th	116
3rd	95
2nd	71
1st	45
Mph/1000 rpm, top gear	16.58
Engine revolutions/mile, top gear	3648
Piston speed (@ 7000 rpm), ft./min.	4083
Lb./hp (160-lb. rider)	10.10
Fuel consumption, mpg	43-47
Speedometer error:	
50 mph indicated, actually	49
60 mph indicated, actually	57
70 mph indicated, actually	68
Braking distance	
from 30 mph, ft.	31
from 60 mph, ft.	119
Acceleration, zero to:	
30 mph, sec.	2.8
40 mph, sec	3.2
50 mph, sec.	4.1
60 mph, sec.	5.0
70 mph, sec.	5.9
80 mph, sec.	7.4
90 mph, sec.	9.0
100 mph, sec.	12.2
Standing one-eight mile, sec.	8.07
terminal speed, mph	85.38
Standing one-quarter mile, sec.	12.96
terminal speed, mph	102.38

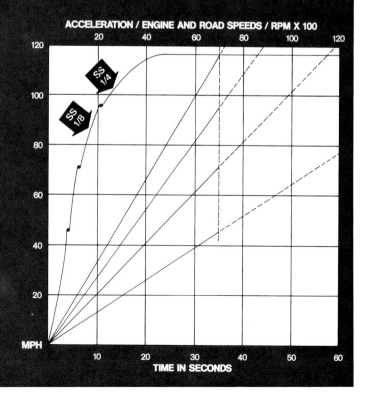

ACCELERATION / ENGINE AND ROAD SPEEDS / RPM X 100

start wind

NORTON 850

large intake ports, terminating at inlet valves with valve stem oil seals.

With the exception of the Kawasaki 650-RS, which is not being imported into the U.S. now, the Norton Commando is the only four-stroke vertical Twin being manufactured with a separate engine and transmission. In spite of the additional complication of having a two-piece primary chaincase, and additional castings for the transmission, the Norton system works very well. A rubber gasket effectively keeps oil in the primary chaincase and the transmission weeps only a tiny bit of oil from the kickstart and gearchange shafts.

A couple of interesting features are found inside the primary chaincase. First, a triple-row primary chain transmits the power from the crankshaft to the clutch with a minimum of power loss, and a huge eight-plate clutch unit features a diaphragm spring.

This spring was designed for Norton by the Laycock de Normanville firm, and has several advantages over the multi-spring arrangement found on most motorcycles. First, the spring maintains its tension equally at all points around its periphery, eliminating the chance of uneven clutch plate action. And, with the clutch actuating mechanism used by Norton, it is possible to arrive at nearly twice the spring pressure of a conventional clutch, without adding significantly to the clutch lever pressure required to disengage the unit.

Aside from the slight lowering (raising numerically) of the second gear ratio, the transmission remains unchanged from earlier Nortons. This was done to reduce the distance between the low and second gear ratios, making for smoother downshifts. Clutch action is excellent, and no slippage or dragging occurred even after a dozen runs down the drag strip.

Considering the number of old-fashioned designs found on the Commando, one of the most up-to-date and outstanding features of the motorcycle is the frame. Conventional in appearance, it is basically a single cradle design with a large,

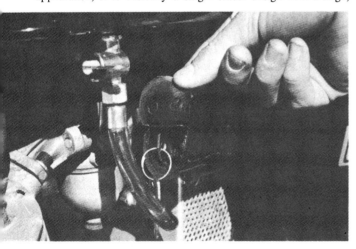

2.5 in. diameter toptube, which runs rearward from the steering head to a point under the seat. There it merges into smaller diameter tubes, two of which extend rearward, forming a loop which the seat rides on, and to which the rear fender is attached. Two others curve downward and forward, eventually terminating at the steering head, finishing the loop.

The unusual part, however, is the method by which the engine, transmission and swinging arm are attached to the "main" frame. Resilient rubber mountings are employed at the front of the engine, at the top, rear end of the transmission and at the top of the engine.

Advantages of this mounting system are twofold: the rider is effectively insulated from the greatest part of the engine's vibration, adding to his comfort immensely. And, by mounting the swinging arm directly to the engine/transmission cradle, the rear wheel is not pulled out of line with the countershaft sprocket during hard acceleration, improving handling characteristics and reducing rear chain side wear by a marked degree.

The electrical chores are once again handled by an alternator/coil/battery system, which works just fine. Although a 12 volt system, the twin ignition coils are 6 volt units with a ballast resistor. Starting and high speed operation are aided by this setup which is often used in automotive ignition systems.

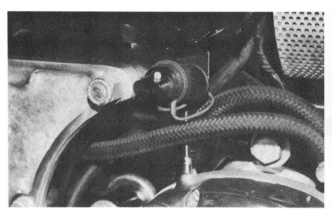

External socket allows connection of battery charger without removal of seat.

Also, there is an external "live" two-prong socket which may be used to connect a battery charger without removing the seat—or, you can use it to plug in your electrically heated riding vest or suit!

What the Interstate is, then, is an intriguing blend of carefully updated antiquated design (the engine), and innovative technology (the frame). What you get is a long distance hauler that's a superbike for sure, but that's not a bike for the masses. The masses will no longer tolerate the lack of electric starting, oil leaks, "Mickey Mouse" Lucas electrical control switches, and the like. But for those with a more tolerant disposition, for the purist with sport in his blood, the Norton Interstate has been, is, and will continue to be, a favorite. ◙

MM TESTS THE LATEST BIG TWIN FROM NORTON-VILLIERS

NORTON

MM SUPER TEST

Having hit a successful formula with their one and only road machine, Norton-Villiers have been doing some really good thinking.

Starting with the basic Commando, winner of much acclaim from the public and industry, they set about making it many things to many people. First came the updated Combat motor, then simply by switching around seats, tanks, pipes, handlebars they can produce a PR, Fastback, Interstate and even slightly more specialised jobs like the Interpol and High Riser.

That's good because they can supply a wide range of the big-capacity market this way and still only have to make what is virtually one machine.

Even so, you can't get it right on for everybody—one Interstate we looked at down at Andover was far from standard. It had been used for some pretty extensive roadwork by one of Norton's executives who has altered it about a little to suit his own tastes.

I understand that N-V intend to produce some sort of pannier arrangement soon—that's why the Interstate has those silencers, to make room for the panniers. My only comment is that it's about time—it's a bit of a cheek to produce a Big Tourer (literal translation from the Italian) and then leave the customer to go and find his own luggage carriers.

Still, I like this train of development and no doubt there will be better things to come, but there are still a few places where I've got reservations.

I know that the Isolastic suspension has won prizes, but I'm still not convinced by it. I've seen machines with more play in the swinging arm than would ever get past a scrutineer or even an MoT test on any other machine.

And even with this principle of having the rider rubber-mounted, there are still vibration problems. At least, ours had them—around 3000 it was felt mainly through the footrests and at higher revs it started to shake

the handlebars. Cruising along main roads the control levers and indicators could be seen vibrating merrily away, and a closer inspection during traffic-light stops revealed other parts doing the same thing.

Perhaps the knowledgeable will say it wasn't shimmed properly—but this was a machine which had just left the works and I'm sure that it was. Also, parts like swinging arms and engine mountings shouldn't need attention more than once a year, if that.

N-V ought to realise that you can't build a high-revving, 360-deg. 750 cc twin without vibration—I wonder why they haven't used a 180-deg. crank.

As a GT machine the Interstate is not without fault. Access and ease of maintenance should be good on such a machine. But the tool-box cover is difficult to replace, the horn is impossible without removing the rear wheel, and despite the widely spaced silencers the offside one has to come off before the wheel will come out.

I still haven't worked out how you remove the air cleaners and why they use those plastic clips to hold the wiring on to the frame—they have to be broken to be removed.

Our engine started easily enough, but the kick-starter was heavy in operation and I would like to see an electric starter. The throttle also needed two handfuls to get it open, something I never could get on with.

One thing Norton always have managed to make is nice noises; the Interstate is no exception, but they could turn the volume down a bit.

That just about covers the complaints except that I would have preferred the footrests set back two or three inches—or possibly put a bit further forward. As they were, the rider was neither leaning into the wind nor sitting back comfortably.

The five-gallon tank on the Interstate makes the machine feel big and wide and gives it a range of way over two hundred miles, even driven hard. The

INTERSTATE NORTON TEST

Unmistakably Norton, the Interstate is a massive hunk of machinery which co benefit from an electric starter, as kickstart action was rather heavy when c

Handlebar layout was neat and controls sensibly placed, if you had double-joint hands! The switches need altering so that only a flick of the thumb is need

"the Interstate is one hell of a

seat is fairly high, and this, combined with the tank (and the performance), makes sure you never forget you're riding a Big Bike.

It's a bit unwieldy if you have to push it around a parking space, but as soon as it's moving, all you're aware of is the width. It can be wiggled through traffic more easily than you'd expect, and with the big tractable motor pulling bottom gear it's often easier than managing a lightweight.

Ours had the standard 19-tooth gearbox sprocket, but one of the mods on the bike I rode at Thruxton—which you wouldn't spot from the photograph—was a 21-tooth sprocket.

Personally, I preferred this set-up—it probably loses a second over a standing quarter, but for everyday use it gives more scope in the lower gears and more of that long-legged feeling at high cruising speed. No matter what gear, the motor would pull away from 1000 rpm with no trouble—this is a machine where you *never* have to slip the clutch.

In either case, medium-speed performance is shattering for a

roadster. In fact I'd been riding the Interstate for two days before I discovered the dreaded two-handsful-of-throttle complaint—even with one handful it was moving like most bikes go flat out.

To comment on the handling is not so easy—the Interstate goes around corners quite well and copes with bumps and rough surfaces very well.

It's not the easiest of machines to chuck around, mainly because of the riding position and the sheer bulk of the thing. Yet despite this, the steering is very light. There's a tendency to twitch on long bends, especially when changing from overrun to drive.

I think basically the handling is good enough, but it does take some time to get used to. After some initial qualms I was able to lay it into slow or fast bends with complete confidence.

Ground clearance is good for a roadster—the footrests will graze the floor if you push it hard enough, but normally you never need to go that far.

It also took a little while to fully appreciate the front brake.

The hydraulic disc is rather heavy in operation and has very little movement at the lever end. This, coupled with some initial timidity, didn't produce the most inspiring results. Later on the brake really came into its own and, when the rider knows what to expect from it, turned out to be gently progressive, but very powerful.

The back brake isn't powerful, instead it's nicely balanced with the front one making it ideal for gentle braking or for steadying the machine under heavy braking when all the weight is on the front wheel.

dominant feature

Throughout the test the dominant feature was the engine. From virtually any speed you can put power on to really drive out of a corner, even in the higher gears. Top-gear acceleration is good, but once you've experienced what it does in second gear you get a bit blasé about the rest.

The ratios are nicely spaced, giving the choice of plonking along in third or fourth or dropping a cog or two for mighty

acceleration. Under normal riding conditions top gear is something of an overdrive—even with the 19-tooth gearbox sprocket the Interstate doesn't like going over 6500. With the larger sprocket, high-speed cruising is even more effortless—you can sit all day with the tacho nudging four and a half and just watch it eat up the miles.

Fuel consumption is also very good, considering the performance on tap. Driving in and out of London we were getting around 50 mpg; on a long run this could be improved to over 60 if one could resist the temptation to use the gears. Using all the power all the time removes a gallon in just under 40 miles—I imagine that the alternative higher gearing would also improve these already satisfactory figures.

As the Interstate is intended for quick cruising on long runs, that huge tank should give it a range of some 300 miles. We never actually ran the tank dry, but it would seem that reserve only gives about 20 miles riding, and for long motorway journeys I think that a little more warn-

...sic roadside toolkit comes with the Interstate. The seat was QD for ...s to the oil tank. A lot of thought has gone into this machine

...tly progressive, but very powerful, the front disc took some time to ...e into its own as action was rather heavy. It is a first-class unit

grand tourer"

ing would not be a bad thing.

The electrics, apart from the maintenance factor, are good enough, although the lighting doesn't really meet the machine's performance and it's all too easy to find yourself going a little bit too quickly. Layout of switches on the handlebars is neat—starting at the right, there is a cut-out and indicator switch, on the left the dipswitch, horn and headlamp flasher. While all the switches can be reached fairly easily, it would be nicer not to have to bend thumbs through unnatural angles, especially when they're heavily gloved and numb to boot. Still, I've seen very few machines which have all the controls comfortably to hand.

There's plenty of room for a pillion passenger, but bearing in mind that the Interstate is a long-distance touring machine, I have some suggestions for Norton-Villiers.

First, the riding position needs altering. If high, wide bars are essential, the seat should be welled and the foot-rests moved forward; or, short flat handlebars with the foot-rests moved back. The pillion seat could be a bit more luxurious too, and have a back rest. The switches need remounting so that only the flick of a thumb is needed—when you need to use the horn, flasher, indicators, etc., you usually need to brake or change gear as well.

Panniers ought to be standard —may I suggest GRP mouldings which slide into place and are located by quick fasteners? Then for loading and unloading, the pannier can be lifted out and used like a suitcase. There's room for a glass-fibre glove compartment cum map case on the tank as well. And there should be more room for tools.

I think the Interstate could pull a much higher gear—at 70 to 80 mph the 750 doesn't really need to be burning at more than 3000 or so. Perhaps an extra gear would do the trick.

Finally, more parts need to be QD, and those which already are should be QR!

I hope this is the way N-V intend to develop their machine, because even in its present guise the Interstate is one hell of a grand tourer.

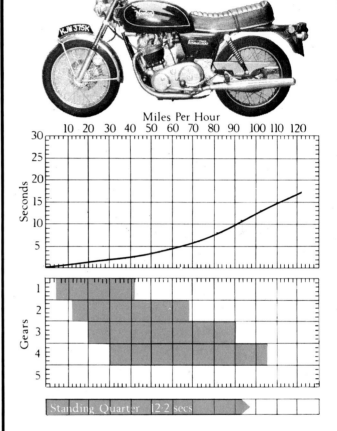

ROAD TEST

Miles Per Hour

Fuel consumption (average)   **55 mpg**
Braking from 30 mph, both brakes on dry tarmac   **28ft.**

Standing Quarter   12·2 secs

SPECIFICATION

Engine: Twin-cylinder four-stroke, ohv. Bore 73 mm, stroke 89 mm, giving 745 cc capacity, compression ratio 10:1, claimed bhp 65 at 6500 rpm.

Transmission: Four-speed gear-box driven by triple-row chain running in oil bath through a four-plate diaphragm spring clutch.

Electrical equipment: A 10 amp/hr. 12-volt battery with positive earth is supplied with current by a Lucas RM21 alter-nator via a rectifier and Zener diode. Ignition is by battery and coils with twin contact breakers and has a 12-volt capacitor in system.

Carburation: Twin Amal 32 mm Concentrics.

Wheels: Front and rear are fitted with 4.10 × 19 tyres. Brakes 10.7 in. diameter disc front and 7-in. single-leading-shoe on alloy drum rear.

Suspension: Front, telescopic forks; rear, swinging arm with adjustable dampers.

Dimensions: Fuel tank 5 gallons, 20-mile reserve capacity. Overall length 87.5 in., wheelbase 56.75 in., width 26 in., weight 395 lb.

Price: £693·31, plus £6 delivery charge.

Manufacturer: Norton-Villiers Ltd, Walworth Industrial Estate, Andover, Hants.

PHOTOGRAPHY BY ERIC RICKMAN

Norton
750 Interstate

MOTORCYCLIST TEST BY TONY MURPHY

NORTON ALWAYS HAS STOOD
FOR QUALITY, DEPENDABILITY
AND SPEED. THIS ONE
ENHANCES THE MARQUE.

When you have a garage full of test machines, among them some of the newest, most sophisticated multis with electric starters and five-speed transmissions, and one machine proves popular enough with the staff to find them sneaking away early to be sure they get to it first, that machine demands some close scrutiny. So it was with the Norton Interstate.

When the specification list is compared with the lists of some of the other 750's, it seems a little surprising that it could be so popular. It is a twin, doesn't have an electric starter, and although a five-speed transmission is optional, the model we had was a four-speed. And yet, when quitting time rolled around at *Motorcyclist*, the Interstate was always the first machine to disappear, the only evidence that it had been in the garage at all was a tell-tale puddle of oil that it left any time it was parked for more than a half-hour.

What appeal does it have? The summation of everybody's feeling about the Interstate, and for that matter, the Commando Nortons in general, is that they instill a feeling of confidence that few other motorcycles seem to accomplish. The rider feels as though he's part of the machine all the time. Nothing comes as a surprise. The rider finds himself doing exactly what he planned to do, whether it's turning around in a crowded parking lot or bending through a high-speed turn. It has 100% controllability 100% of the time.

This feeling results from the successful blending of two things; the tried and proven 750cc vertical twin engine and the unique Isolastic suspension. Down through the years, the Norton folk have always resisted change for the sake of change, and when the 750cc boom hit and everyone else ran to the drawing boards to design new, multi-cylindered engines, Norton stuck with the 750cc twin that was then available in the Atlas model. The Norton factory was in a transitional period, having been taken over by a huge holding company, Manganese Bronze, and been reorganized as Norton Villiers, to manufacture, distribute and sell both Norton and AJS motorcycles. At this stage they would have been hard pressed to start from scratch even if they had wanted to.

Instead, they stuck with a concept that had proven a reliable performer since the early Fifties. Although the concept is the same as the old 500cc Dominator; twin-cylinder, pushrod-operated OHV engine connected to a separate transmission with a primary chain, the parts that make up the 750cc powerplant are all new, beefed up where necessary to withstand the added loads of an engine with 50% more displacement. Internally, the cam followers

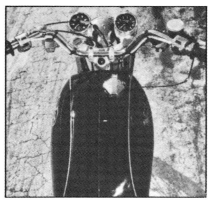

• *All new disc front brake was developed by the Lockheed brake people just for Norton. Caliper is mounted behind fork leg for better steering.* • *Huge 6-gallon tank doesn't look that large thanks to good styling. Tank has snap-open gas cap and twin petcocks. Dual instruments are easy to read and well lit for night riding.* • *Left side cover conceals tool kit and battery. Cover is fiberglass, snaps in place.*
• *Front engine mount is Isolastic rubber pads in tension; eliminates all vibration.*

and cam drive chain are interchangeable with the old 500, but nothing else. On the outside, the rocker inspection covers are the only items that will fit both the new and old, even though the appearance is nearly identical. It may be a 20-year-old concept, but it's a brand new engine.

It's what used to be called a stroker, with a bore of 73mm and a stroke of 89mm. Tradition has it that such a set of dimensions provides an engine with lots of grunt power but not much horsepower. The Norton bears out that theory, falling short of some of the claimed horsepower figures of the competition but putting all of them down at the dragstrip. In the last year or so that same engine has got the race treatment from several tuners and is always a threat and often a winner on the dirt tracks from coast to coast. At Daytona this year the same engine concept powered the fourth place machine ridden by World Champion Phil Read. It can't be all bad.

In street form the power comes in way down the scale, enabling 15 mph speeds in high gear without any hesitation or balking. Just roll the throttle on and it pulls away. Such flexibility contributes greatly to the feeling of confidence when riding the Interstate since there is never any panic stabs at the shift lever to keep the machine running. When the transmission is used, it's flawless. Every change is positive and neutral easy to find at all times.

While the engine concept has survived the 20-year span, the once famous Featherbed chassis is a thing of the past. That got the heave-ho a few years ago when an engineer named Bob Trigg came up with the Isolastic chassis used today. The Featherbed's claim to fame was absolute rigidity that virtually assured that the machine would have to hit the side of a building before any misalignment of the wheels would occur. The Isolastic system is just the opposite, causing many to be skeptical upon close examination. It combines vibration-free rubber mounting of the engine and transmission with good handling. The rider is completely isolated—thus Isolastic—from engine vibes, and yet the good handling characteristics of a solidly-mounted powerplant are still in evidence.

The engine and transmission are bolted together in the normal manner for Norton, via engine plates. However, the swinging arm is also bolted up to those engine plates, forming a very strong engine/transmission/rear wheel combination bolted together as an assembly. The rest of the motorcycle is then attached to this assembly by means of pre-tensioned rubber mounts. This means that to satisfy the demands of high-speed handling, the engine and rear wheel are always in line, and to

Continued on page 203

Norton 750 Interstate
SUGGESTED RETAIL PRICE: $1839

ENGINE
Engine type • Four-stroke twin
Displacement • 745cc
Bore and stroke • 73 x 89mm; 2.875 x 3.503 in.
Claimed crankshaft hp @ rpm • 65 @ 6500
Compression ratio • 10:1
Carburetion • Twin Amal 32mm concentrics
Air filter • Replaceable element
Ignition • Coil
Starting system • Kick
Start in gear • No

DRIVE TRAIN
Primary drive • Triple-row chain
Clutch • Multi-disc with diaphragm spring
Transmission • 4-speed
Overall ratios • 1st 12.40:1; 2nd 8.25:1;
3rd 5.90:1; 4th 4.84:1.
Shift pattern • Right, up for low

CHASSIS AND SUSPENSION
Frame • Patented Isolastic
Forks • Norton Roadholders
Shocks • Girling, 3-way adjustable
Brakes • Disc front, single leading shoe rear
Rims • Steel
Tires • 4.10x19 front and rear

EQUIPMENT
Sidestand • Yes
Steering damper • No
Kill button • Yes
Tool kit • Yes

DIMENSIONS AND CAPACITIES
Wheelbase • 56½"
Length • 87½"
Seat height • 32"
Ground clearance • 6"
Weight, wet • 460 lbs.
Tank capacity • 6 gals.
Oil capacity • 6 pints

FREEWAY FLIER

Legends are nice but performance is better and Norton has them both.

Racing success always has and probably always will create a following—one structured of varying intensities, producing the desired result: customers. The mystique built up about a winner is a natural spur to the consumer who wants to be associated with the victor. And the older that mystique, the stronger it becomes and the harder it is to yield, even in the face of adversity—the irrefutable fact of an unsatisfactory product. That's the nice thing about

the inexorable sands of time, the good things remain and get brighter and bolder while the bad times fade into distant corners on life's pages.

The success of Norton in European road racing dating back more than half a century created that kind of pervading legend. Most memorable of all was the Norton Manx, a 500 cc single. It was a boss mover in a time when life still had some simplicity. And superior handling quality was the greatest factor in keeping the Manx

competitive until its withdrawal from the racing scene in the early sixties, a victim of the multiple cylinder racer. That Norton handling was the stuff of which legends grow.

At about the same time the death knell for the racing Manx was being tolled, enthusiasts noticed a drop in quality of the over the counter product. A name that had been synonymous with good reliable performance and road holding ability acquired a bit of a tarnish. Well, a whole lot of

tarnish. But legends often stubbornly resist their own demise, and pride in a time and presence that once was can spur renewed efforts and success. The mystique, if not the on-the-street opinion of Norton, lingered on during its hiatus of sorts so that the name still conjured the image of a leaned over streak that tracked like it was riding a rail.

For the younger enthusiast, who may have been introduced to Norton after spying those ads with the fetching, sloe-eyed maiden entreatingly gazing out from the magazine page with an invitation to come and try us, history may have meant little or nothing. But whatever the instigator, a legend or a nubile lass, anyone who saddles the current product can touch upon both bases—pride in a time tested name and satisfaction with an eye appealing contemporary go-machine.

The comeback really began a few years ago when the team of Beaur, Trigg and Hooper combined their talents to design Norton's exclusive Iso-lastic anti-vibration construction. This system joins the engine, transmission, swinging arm and rear wheel together as one unit. The unit is then insulated from the frame in three strategic places with heavy resilient rubber washers. A system such as this has a couple of interesting advantages. First of all, no vibration is transmitted through the frame from the engine —result, a super smooth ride. Sec-ondly, the life of instruments and light bulbs is lengthened. Also, be-cause the rear wheel sprocket and countershaft sprocket are always in perfect alignment, even under heavy loads, chain wear is greatly reduced.

There is no doubt the Isolastic sys-tem utilized by Norton performs as well as they claim. At idle the whole machine shakes and jumps with each power pulse of the engine, but this condition is non-existent as soon as you twist the throttle. There is a small amount of vibration in the foot pegs at seventy miles per hour, but other than that, the Commando is smooth as glass. You can't imagine how grat-ifying it is to see only one image in the mirror at 70 mph or to be able to ride for hours at a time without having your hands and feet go numb

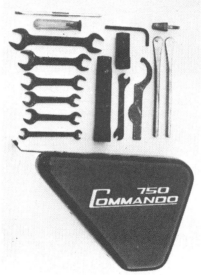

The 10.7 inch disc brake required a bit more pressure than expected, but delivered quick, fade free stops.

The 750cc OHV engine rests in a double loop frame. The cast iron cylinders help reduce engine noise.

The seat is attractive but too narrow for comfort. Excessive slope at the rear and the passenger strap also hinder comfort.

Although fully functional, placement of accessory hand switches was deemed poor. Horn, high beam and high beam flasher are shown.

Norton offers the best factory supplied tool kit we have yet encountered.

from vibration.

For a while we thought the near legendary handling qualities attributed to Norton over the years had come a cropper with this particular model. It took two trips back to Norton Villiers to finally diagnose the cause of the problem and effect its simple and complete solution. After having heard so many glowing reports on the tracking ability of the Commando we initially experienced a big let down. Before ferreting out the rascal, riding solo at seventy mph was a pleasure, but at seventy-one the front forks began to undulate with ever increasing frequency, directly proportional to the increase in speed. This condition was so bad it was impossible to get full potential out of this super bike

in the quarter-mile. After adjusting the tension of the shocks to the softest possible position we were able to accelerate to 80 mph, with the lightest touch on the bars, before this oscillation took place.

After this "hairy" experience we returned the roadster to Norton to see if they could find the cause of the problem. They checked the machine thoroughly for loose nuts and bolts, correct tire pressure and they even made sure both wheels were tracking in a straight line. To our disappointment they found nothing out of the ordinary, but we were told one of their executives and his wife had spent an enjoyable weekend riding the highways and byways and didn't encounter even a hint of a wobble.

This completely dazzled us. How could an inexperienced rider run her wide open when we didn't feel safe over eighty miles per hour? Then we figured they had found something wrong and weren't letting on what it was.

Back out to the drag strip for one burst of speed and, as before, instant wobble. Now we were really at a loss. Just for the heck of it we put a passenger on behind, and to our surprise the 750 was rock steady. Imagine, ninety-seven pounds of passenger made a night and day difference. Speeds of one hundred mph and faster could be reached with no concern about losing control.

In view of the circumstances, we could only come to one conclusion.

Ignition switch is located just in front of left side cover. Note the side stand tucked completely out of the way beneath the exhaust pipe. Upswept mufflers give more than adequate ground clearance. Kill button, turn indicator switch (there are no turn lights) and electric starter button (there is no electric starter) are placed on left handlebar along with conveniently located choke. Speedometer is minus trip odometer.

After all, Norton had told us everything was as it should be, so who were we to argue. We figured that the added passenger weight increased the trail a fraction of an inch which stabilized the handling. On the other hand, increasing trail in this manner will also lighten the front end which you would think would lead you right back into the same problem. Needless to say, we weren't satisfied with our findings or our speculative solution to the problem. We made one more trip to Norton with hopes of finding the troublemaker. As before, nothing wrong could be found until, in desperation, the rear wheel was replaced. Presto, just like magic, the Roadster was able to smoke down the road at eighty, ninety and one hundred miles per

hour with one rider and no wobble. We found the original tire so far out of balance that it began to hop off the ground at speed, causing the front end to wobble from side to side. The passenger weight tended to hold the wheel on the ground. We are certain that if a high enough speed had been obtained with two up on the old tire the same wobble would have occurred.

Back on the street, with a balanced tire, the Norton gave a ride that can't be equalled by many motorcycles. The rear shocks are inclined forward at a considerable angle which makes for an ultra smooth ride. The front forks are just stiff enough to resist any nose dive under hard braking and also offer a good firm ride over any road.

These units topped out when putting the Commando on the center stand. This never happened while riding.

The 750 cc overhead valve engine is relatively quiet compared with other British twins. The cast iron cylinder takes part of the credit on this count.

Hopefully, in the near future, the 750 will be fitted with an electric starter. It would be an easy matter of fitting one just behind the cylinders, since it appears that the case is already cut out for just that purpose.

A broad power band, along with plenty of horsepower, makes the Roadster a very enjoyable and easy unit to ride in the street under any conditions. The power is smooth and constant under acceleration.

As with many large capacity four-

The double damping forks, dubbed the Roadholders by Norton, are an exclusive feature of the Commando.

stroke machines, a five-speed gear box could be used as a sales feature, but for normal street riding the four-speed was found to be quite adequate. The clutch and gear box are other areas in which Norton excels. Clutch lever pull requires little pressure and is smooth. Shifting from one gear to another was smooth as silk. The constant mesh gear box has four well spaced gears that more than meet the requirements of any road condition.

You and your next door neighbor will be pleased at the sound of the exhaust. It not only has authority, but it is one of the quietest four strokes sold. The two chromed, slightly upswept mufflers give the machine a sporty look and do an excellent job of reducing noise.

Both side and center stands are tucked well out of the way of the ground. It was next to impossible to touch anything when cornering. The side stand is so out of the way that it is difficult to find when you need to prop the bike up. The Commando is easily hoisted upon the center stand.

Seating accommodations produced mixed emotions. The relative position of the saddle and handlebars is comfortable, with the foot pegs being a little too high. This is somewhat cramped but not unbearable. The seat itself is actually uncomfortable. It is soft enough, but it seems a little narrow to properly distribute the rider's weight. After a hundred miles we were ready for a rest. There is a seat strap provided for the passenger to hold, but it was located just beneath what for us was a comfortable riding position. This made it both awkward to get to as well as giving a bit of a lumpy feeling. One of the first things we did was to remove it from our machine. For the passenger the seat is really a sore spot. Not only is it narrow, but it is sloped forward at quite a steep angle, causing the passenger to always hold himself back so as not to crowd the rider. The seat sort of crowds two large people even before considering the forward slope. As with the rider pegs, the rear set is mounted rather high, which is another factor contributing to passenger discomfort. The seat, too, is relatively

high, making it difficult for anyone with short legs to touch the ground flatfooted with both feet. This height is actually good once you are moving because you have the feeling of being in full command of the Commando.

The gas tank is a sporty looking fiberglass unit which is painted in solid colors (blue, black, yellow, red, tangerine, purple, bronze) with the name Norton spelled out in modified Old English print. It is very simple but quite striking. Gas capacity is 2¾ gallons which is good for one hundred miles with some left over for reserve. Gas consumption was an easy to take forty miles per gallon. Running down the freeway wide open or cruising around town produced the same average.

The tool kit supplied with the Commando far exceeds the quality of those fitted to any other machine. Those riders who enjoy doing their own maintenance work will greatly appreciate the effort Norton has gone to in selecting the proper tools for this job. One thing missing, though, is a pair of pliers. That's easy enough to remedy at the local hardware store. Three cheers for Norton for putting together a tool kit the rider can really work with.

The front disc brake does its job well. We had the impression that a bit more than normal pressure was required to bring the 750 to a stop from speed. One reason for this could be the distance from the brake lever to the grip. The lever needs to be pulled only a fraction of an inch to actuate the brake. Possibly a longer pull would increase leverage and make stopping easier. The rear brake will get you by in a pinch but it isn't anything to brag about. It is our guess that nothing was wrong with this brake; it just works that way. Don't get us wrong; it does work but it could be better.

The two instruments, tach and speedometer, are located several inches apart. There is no mistaking one for the other but it is hard to read both at the same time. There is no trip meter on the speedo.

The chain, as on most large motorcycles, stretched no more than expected. Lubricant from the oil tank is dripped onto the chain to reduce wear and tear. The flow can be adjusted by pinching off the tube from the tank with the two hose clamps on the small filter in the line. Lubricating the chain in this manner does increase chain life, but also presents some problems. For instance, anyone riding as a passenger should wear either old clothes or something dark to hide all the oil spots. As the chain rotates it throws oil all over the rear of the motorcycle and passenger. Also, a big puddle of oil is left on the ground because the chain oiler keeps siphoning from the oil tank after killing the engine. Norton is working on a check valve to stop this drain problem but until then we get used to the puddle. Actually we suggest not using the chain oiler. Instead, carry some good chain lube with you and lube the chain at every gas stop. Its just a little more trouble, but it will increase chain life and hopefully keep your passenger clean.

Electrics on the Norton are of course by Lucas. In the past that wouldn't be saying anything. Today, now that the dealers are more aware of proper maintenance techniques and the improvement in quality, Lucas electrics are among the finest. The headlight illuminates the road quite well and affords good visibility at all times. The taillight is easy to see from behind and the difference between it and the brake light, even during the day, is quite distinguishable.

The balance and feel of the Roadster is very good. It handles like a dream and can be flicked from side to side with ease. This is no doubt due to the steering geometry and weight. Norton's 750 is the lightest super bike on the market weighing in at about 390 pounds.

Nortons have traditionally been fitted with Avon tires, but sales have increased to the point where Avon can't meet Norton tire needs. It is now possible to buy any of the Norton 750's with either Dunlop or Avon tires, 4.10x19 front and rear. We feel the K81 Dunlop tire is superior to anything sold for the street. We also think the Avon is a good tire but doesn't offer the traction and wear that the K81 does.

The quality of the Norton has steadily improved over the past few years. Perhaps Norton's finest feature is the almost total lack of engine vibration. Until one experiences the featherbed ride the Commando offers, it is difficult to express just what he is missing. It is definitely one of those try it, you'll like it situations.

Straight ahead freeway fliers will experience only one of the Commando's two major assets—the vibration free ride. They miss out on its super handling. With its light weight and strong double cradle frame the bike is as agile as a gazelle over the most demanding mountain road.

There is no doubt the Commando Roadster is a true super bike. It is light, fast, handles well and is vibration free. We feel certain that anyone looking for one or more of these qualities should take a close look at any one of the Commandos.

Bob Braverman/Walt Fulton Jr.

NORTON 750 ROADSTER

ENGINE

Type	two cylinder ohv four stroke
Bore and stroke	73x89mm (2.88"x3.5")
Displacement	745cc
Compression Ratio	10.1:1
Max. horsepower	65 @ 6800 rpm
Ignition	6v coil
Carburetion	two 32mm Amal
Lubrication	dry sump

DIMENSIONS

Length	87.5 in.
Seat height	31 in.
Wheelbase	56.75 in.
Ground clearance	6 in.
Dry weight	395 lbs.

WHEELS AND BRAKES

Front tire size	4.10x19 in.
Front brake type	disc, 10.7 in.
Rear tire size	4.10x19 in.
Rear brake type	internal expanding 7 in.
Tire pressures	25-29 psi

TRANSMISSION

Type	4-speed constant mesh
Clutch	dry multi plate
Internal gear ratios	lst, 2.56:1; 2nd, 1.7:1; 3rd, 1.22:1; 4th, 1:1
Final ratio	4.84:1
Countershaft sprocket	19
Rear wheel sprocket	42

PERFORMANCE

Indicated highest one-way speed	109.5 mph
Acceleration 0-60	7.0 sec.
Braking distance 30-0	29.6 ft.
Quarter-mile acceleration:	
Top speed	103.68
Elapsed time	13.09

GENERAL

Air filtration	dry paper
Battery type	12v

CAPACITIES

Fuel tank	2.75 gal.
Fuel reserve	25
Oil tank	6 pts.
Gear box	1 pt.
Fuel consumption	40 mpg

FRAME AND SUSPENSION

Front suspension	telescopic hydraulic double damping forks
Rear suspension	adjustable shocks
Frame type	double cradle

COLORS

Black, blue, purple, bronze, red, orange, yellow

PRICE AS TESTED

$1,784 FOB West Coast

DISTRIBUTOR

Norton-Villiers
6765 Paramount
N. Long Beach, CA.

Few motorcycle manufacturers can boast of a history as illustrious as Norton's. And perhaps no manufacturer still in existence can boast (nor would they wish to) of almost total financial disaster following close on the heels of unqualified success. A great number of exciting and revolutionary bits and pieces were generated by Norton on their way to the ashcan. Like "Old Miracle," a 490cc Norton side valve factory development workhorse, which garnered 112 world and British speed and endurance records before it was retired to a museum. And there were the overhead cam engines that broke motorcycle racing wide open, such as the

94

In 1951 Rex McCandless put the cap on it for Norton when he designed the "featherbed" frame, the standard of excellence in motorcycle

TEST: NORTON'S '50 COMMANDO

CS1 "single knocker" which in its very first year carried Alec Bennett to a first place in the Isle of Man and Stanley Woods to Grand Prix wins in Holland, France and Belgium. About ten years later, Norton gave motorcycling the "double knocker," the redoubtable Manx, racing's all-time evergreen that is still finding its way to the winner's circle.

chassis design that is only recently being approached by other manufacturers. (There are holdouts who contend that no one is even close to improving upon the "featherbed," but there's also an Edsel owners club.)

Accompanying the "featherbed" in its debut was Norton's popular 500cc vertical twin, the Dominator, which would be stretched to 600cc, to 650-

cc, and finally to 750cc, first as the Atlas, and then in 1967 for the Commando.

Norton's near-terminal financial malady entered a crisis in the mid-sixties following a steady, seemingly irreversible downhill slide in production, sales and profit. Many factors conspired to bring about Norton's near demise. Their facilities were old and inefficient. Tooling and

machinery, too, had seen better days. Labor costs and troubles seemed to be ever increasing. And, of course, there was the perpetual motorcycle making machine operating far to the east, in the land where the sun rises; as Japanese motorcycles grew in displacement and improved in performance they cut deeper and deeper into Great Britain's market abroad,

MAKE NORTON
MODEL 750 COMMANDO
PRICE AS TESTED $1784.00
MAXIMUM SPEED AS GEARED 108 mph
WEIGHT 385 lbs. DRY

Distributor .... NORTON VILLIERS CORP. 6765 Paramount Blvd. Long Beach, Calif. 90805

ENGINE

Engine Type	VERTICAL TWIN, OHV
Bore	73mm
Stroke	89mm
Displacement	745cc
Compression Ratio	10:1
B.H.P. at R.P.M.	65 AT 6,500
Carburetor	32mm AMAL CONCENTRIC
Ignition	BATTERY, COIL
Starting System	KICK
Lubricating System	PRESSURE (DRY SUMP)

FUEL AND OIL

Oil Capacity	6 PINTS
Oil Recommended	SAE 30
Fuel Capacity	3 GALLONS
Fuel Recommended	PREMIUM
Approximate mpg	44

FILTERING SYSTEMS

Air	PAPER
Oil	FULL FLOW
Fuel	SCREEN

FRAME

Frame Type	DOUBLE LOOP
Weight Distribution	FRONT: 48%, REAR: 52%
Wheelbase	57 INCHES
Ground Clearance	6 INCHES
Peg Height	14 INCHES
Seat Height	33 INCHES
Handlebar Width	33 INCHES

SUSPENSION-TYPE

Front	TELESCOPIC FORK
Rear Arm	SWING ARM

SUSPENSION-TRAVEL

Front	4.5 INCHES
Rear	2.5 INCHES

DRIVE TRAIN

Clutch Type		DIAPHRAGM
Primary Drive		TRIPLEX CHAIN
Countershaft Sprocket		19 TEETH
Final Sprocket		42 TEETH
Final Drive		2.22:1
Gear Ratios	Internal	Overall
1st	2.75:1	12.40:1
2nd	1.83:1	8.25:1
3rd	1.31:1	5.90:1
4th	1.08:1	4.84:1

TIRES AND WHEELS

Front	4.10x19 BLOCK
Rear	4.10x19 BLOCK

IMPRESSIONS

	Poor	Good	Excellent
Throttle Response			●
Acceleration			●
Power Band			●
Starting		●	
Engine Noise		●	
Muffling		●	
Vibration		●	
Handling			●
Choice of Tires			●
Suspension			●
Rider Comfort		●	
Transmission			●
Instrumentation		●	
Lighting		●	
Toolkit		●	
Paint and Chrome			●
Styling			●
Mileage		●	
Braking		●	

and finally at home. Norton was ill-equipped to withstand the attack; the end appeared close at hand. Indeed, Norton would have closed their books for all time but for the financial hand extended them by industrialist Dennis Poore.

Merged with Villiers, Norton became a division of the enormous Manganese Bronze Company. Plucked from the jaws of receivership, into which they had already fallen, Norton, now Norton-Villiers, was to rise 'once more, if not Phoenix-like, certainly with a new stability and the financial muscle to sit out the lean times.

The plan of action for the "new" company was characterized by streamlining—both of operations and product line. The plan manifested itself in the appearance of essentially two motorcycles where previously there had been several. Norton-Villiers' new line consisted of the AJS 250 motocrosser and the 750 Commando—with its several variations. Along with the streamlining went a policy of careful product refinement, utilizing existing major engine tooling for the Commando coupled with chassis design innovations growing out of the sound engineering base provided by the "featherbed." Now, just five model years later the plan seems to be paying off, not so much in thousands of units sold as in revival of the prestige enjoyed by Nortons of times long past.

In its present form the Norton Commando is a very special, highly desirable motorcycle. First, its displacement makes it sales competitive. Backed up with performance that truly qualifies it as a superbike, the 750's age can be faulted only in academic arguments. It's still a strong and very capable engine, no matter how long it's been around. The Commando is presently offered in two stages of tune, the normal and the Combat. The normal engine is standard in all of the five road models, including the handsome, all-white Interpol police model. The Combat engine, standard in the production road racer for which it was developed, is available, along with a front disc brake, as an option in the new Interstate and the Roadster. As its name implies the Interstate is the long distance member of the line, with a 6¼-gallon fiberglass fuel tank or a 6½-gallon steel vessel, an ample two-up seat, lower placed mufflers to accommodate panniers, directional lights and a complement of optional touring accessories including panniers, a luggage rack and a touring fairing.

The Roadster, our test bike, is more spartan, in the interest of sportiness. It, too, is offered with either fiberglass or steel fuel tank—2¾ and 3 gallons, respectively. Its seat is several inches shorter than the Interstate's and not as heavily padded. The mufflers are swept up in the best Dunstall-inspired cafe racer tradition and directionals are offered as an option.

The engine is a classical vertical twin, 360-degree crankshaft design utilizing roller mains and plain bearings for the connecting rods big

ends. Husky through-bolts are used to secure the rod caps. The gear-driven oil pump has wider gears fitted to the return side than on the feed side to maximize oil scavenging from the dry sump. The net effect is that the very low oil volume in the crankcase obviates blowby induced by the pressure created in the crankcase as the pistons descend together. The entire lubrication system is quite sanitary and oil tight, due in good part to heavy-duty reinforced external lines.

Much of the Norton's performance strength derives from the clean flow characteristics of the cylinder head. The intake tracts are close together to accommodate wide spacing of the exhaust tracts while at the same time permitting a near-cross-flow relationship of intake and exhaust ports with a minimum of port bending. The wide spacing of the exhaust ports enhances cooling in these critical areas. In fact, while not as generously finned as most of its contemporaries, the Norton runs very cool, and as the text books tell us an efficiently cooled engine will experience denser and potentially stronger fuel charges. A
(Please turn page)

definite plus resulting from the Norton design is a narrow upper engine package with less weight up high and a lower CG. As further evidence that this is a real concern we point out the forward inclination of the entire engine to lower the CG.

No doubt, most of the Commandos ordered will be with the Combat engine and disc brake. In this form the motorcycle is completely civilized; it starts willingly, pulls well at low speed and accelerates like a house afire. With its excellent power-to-weight ratio it is one of the strongest of the superbikes. And with the front disc brake fitted it is also one of the safest. Both brakes work well together and pull the motorcycle down quickly, in full control during hard braking.

Counter to present common practice, the Norton does not have a unitized engine/gearbox. Despite what we have come to believe is proper design, the Norton arrangement is virtually without fault, and a definite benefit is realized in that primary drive chain adjustment is simply accommodated by undoing a single locking nut and manipulating two smaller adjuster nuts. The alternative, short of a gear primary drive, is a pony-stealing tensioner which wears the primary chain which in turn wears down the tensioner.

The transmission has been so completely sorted out over the years that it rates as one of the strongest, easiest shifted and most predictable assortment of gears to be found. Missed shifts just do not occur and neutral is found each time it is sought. The shift pattern — one up and three down—is another matter; the logic as well as the safety of this scheme has always been tough to defend and it is even more so now with the bulk of the world's motorcycles arranged with one down and the rest all up, ostensibly in the interest of standardization. Interestingly, the pattern is reversed on the production racer version of the Commando which is set up with rear-set footrests requiring that the gear selector point aft rather than forward.

As a final bone of contention with the gearbox we wouuld like to see it fitted with one more cog. Our test bike, set up with the standard 19-tooth countershaft sprocket, felt undergeared in fourth at highway speeds. Optional 20 and 21-tooth countershaft sprockets can be specified at time of delivery but the low and medium speed characteristics are so good with the 19, particularly with two up, we'd hesitate to recommend the optional ratios. A close-ratio five-speed is available in the racer and it would be nice to see Norton-Villiers extend this to the Roadsters, although there's little doubt that the extra gear represents a significant portion of the $800-plus price differential between the trick-engine Roadster and the production racer.

The Commando's most touted feature, Isolastic construction, is something that N-V are justifiably proud of. It consists of coupling the engine, gearbox, swing arm and rear wheel together in a unit, and attaching the unit to the rest of the motorcycle with three resilient mounts. The rider, main frame, lights and instruments are thus insulated from engine vibration—most of the time; at slightly above idle, just prior to the beginning of the Isolastic phenomenon, a slight vibration is apparent (enough to make one's nose itch) but instantly disappears as the engine enters the useable speed range. Weigh this against the hours of foot, hand and backside numbing we've all grown to accept in the past and it's a small price to pay. On the whole the Isolastic thing is a pleasant experience because there is really nothing to experience —no tingling vibration periods to pass through—just constantly smooth power flow that is more like a multi than a 360-degree twin. Nice touch, N-V.

The dessert for this mechanical feast is some of the finest handling it has been our pleasure to experience. The Commando is nothing short of brilliant as an ear holer and its limits are a match for the talents —and courage—of a competent, experienced road racer. This is not to say that it can't be appreciated by riders of average experience; its excellent integration of the components and concepts that make up motorcycling are apparent from the moment the Commando is first straddled and continue through and beyond that point at which reason wisely cautions that one has experienced the limits of his ability. The Commando's handling performance is so good that few owners will ever realize its full potential—nor will they be disappointed in not being able to put it on the spot. It's a proper vehicle from the moment it begins to move and it just simply continues to get better.

The Commando was not without annoyances. The tachometer on our test bike was erratic and gave no clue of what the engine was up to. Small dollops of oil appeared on the ground when the Commando was parked for a few hours, and they became larger when it sat overnight. The rear chain coated the back of the motorcycle with oil and did nasty things to passengers' shoes. The lighting controls were awkward and offered no hint of their purpose.

But, the Commando is not simply another motorcycle to be analyzed feature for feature. It's a concept— at the very least an archetype of the full-all sporting motorcycle. The Commando harkens back to another time, a time when one could ride all day and not meet another motorcycle. The Commando is what everyone imagines his first real motorcycle to have been. But unlike kind memories which so often suppress the bad and embellish the good, the Norton Commando is real. And it is the best of all those wonderful memories tied into one package.

In today's competitive, innovation filled market the Norton Commando has a rough row to hoe. Its substantial price doesn't improve its position. For the rider who values overall performance above all else, however, for those unique enthusiasts who are concerned with what it does rather than how it does it, the Norton Commando is at least one answer— perhaps one of the best. ●

NORTON 850 COMMANDO

Norton's long-lived twin is in its second decade—and still growing!

COLOR PHOTOGRAPHY BY BILL DELANEY; BLACK & WHITE PHOTOGRAPHY BY DALE BOLLER

● Guided by the simple verities of a period most motorcyclists are not even old enough to remember, Norton goes its own way. And against all odds, against the insistent logic of a thousand warbling computers, Norton's way works. Without an overhead camshaft to its name or so much as a nod toward current fashion in multiple cylinders and transmission ratios, the Norton Commando holds its place among the seeded players in the Superbike game. That place was won, and is held, with an engine old enough to vote. It began life as a 500, was stretched to a 600, then to a 650, and it became a 750 well in advance of the brilliant bit of improvisation that gave us the 1970 Norton Commando. The engine, with its two big cylinders, pushrod-operated valves and stand-offish relationship with its clutch and transmission, is a kind of living fossil. It's a dinosaur, and just about as ponderously strong.

On the other hand, this ancient engine has been put to work in a chassis that is as modern as you can imagine. Big-displacement vertical twins shake, unless fitted with Yamaha-style contra-rotating bobweights—and there simply isn't room for all the necessary machinery inside crankcases that fit the existing crankshaft and rods tighter than a gigolo's pants. So Norton's engineers improvised, and brilliantly. They correctly reasoned that just because an engine shakes one need not meekly accept an extension of that shaking to the whole motorcycle. All that is needed is some means of isolating the engine from the motorcycle's chassis, and Norton found a way. The Norton engine and gearbox are tied together with a pair of flat plates, and these were extended back to provide a mounting for the swingarm pivot. The sub-assembly thus created was then fastened to the frame through thick rubber bushings that allow considerable flexibility in the vertical plane, this being coincident with engine vibrations. But flexibility laterally would have had a disastrous effect on handling, so broad bearing surfaces were provided to prevent side motion, and a system of shims hold side clearances to only .010-inch.

The frame into which this engine/transmission/swingarm sub-assembly fits is built around a large-diameter backbone tube. It's not nearly as appealing to the artist's eye as the "Featherbed" frame that was a Norton staple for years and is still accepted (with uncharacteristic irrationality) in Japan as the ultimate. But it does offer a very high level of efficiency in terms of weight and rigidity. Norton has been willing to deal with the fuel tank mounting problems introduced by the presence of a great, fat tube reaching back over the engine, paying a small price in that area to get the kind of structural stiffness that banishes the dread wobbles. They did make the mistake initially, of assuming that drum brakes would satisfactorily stop the Commando, but that mistake was corrected by switching to a Lockheed disc brake on the front wheel. So by 1972 Norton

The 750 was pumped up to 828cc by punching the 73mm bores out to 77mm.

had itself a Commando that would go, stop and hare around corners with the best of them, and the 750 Commando sold well enough to lend new vitality to a company that had once seemed fated for extinction.

Now, in 1973, the 750 Commando is gone, replaced by the new 850 Commando, and the biggest difference in physical terms is a four millimeter enlargement in bore diameter (from 73mm to 77mm). That raises the Norton engine's displacement from 745cc to 828cc, but doesn't do much for peak horsepower. A return to the "S" camshaft of the recent past, with milder timing

than that employed in last year's Commando 750, bolsters mid-range power at the expense of what would otherwise be a bigger surge up near the redline. In consequence, an engine noteworthy for muscular thudding and chuffing at comparatively low crank speeds has had this basic character intensified.

Other engine changes have been made, but none aimed at more power. The crankcase has been strengthened to cope with the increased pressure from above, and there's a new flywheel made of an "upgraded" material and a few ounces heavier than the one for the 750. Early 750 engines had their cranks supported by a roller bearing at the output end and a ball bearing on the timing side. That arrangement was abandoned in favor of two roller bearings in 1972, but the lack of any center mainbearing and resulting flex in the crankshaft have prompted a switch to German-made "Superblend" roller bearings in the 850 engine. Flexing of the crankshaft tends to concentrate bearing loads on the ends of the rollers, and in a very narrow contact line along the races. The Superblend rollers have a rounded taper ground at their ends to spread the contact area when the crank begins to whip, and that will be good for long-term durability. Of course the crankshaft doesn't get whippy unless plenty of revs and throttle are being applied, but then from what we've seen that is precisely the riding style of most American Commando owners. Along with the changes already noted, Norton's venerable twin has been given thicker valve guides (which we are assured do not bell-mouth and dribble oil into the intake ports like the earlier guides) and the phosphor bronze camshaft bearings that have worked better than any of the alternative materials Norton has tried.

Push-button starting is not likely to appear on the Norton Commando 850 any time soon. Item-8 on Norton's technical specification sheet tells us that "the kick starter crank has been toughened, to prevent distortion, and lengthened to improve leverage." That should tell you a lot about the level of pressure needed to crank the Norton 850 engine. Small riders are going to wish that the kick starter *pedal* had been lengthened too,

NORTON 850 COMMANDO

Price, suggested retail . . . . .West Coast, POE $1,879
Tire, front . . . . .4.10 in. x 19 in. Dunlop TT100
      rear . . . . .4.10 in. x 19 in. Dunlop TT100
Brake, front . . . . .10.71 in. x 1.65 in. x 2
      rear . . . . .7.0 in. x 1.25 in.
Brake swept area . . . . .122.3 sq. in.
Specific brake loading . . . . 5.09 lb/sq. in., at test weight
Engine type . . . . OHV four-stroke vertical twin
Bore and stroke . . . . .3.03 in. x 3.50 in., 77mm x 89mm
Piston displacement . . . . 50.5 cu. in., 828cc
Compression ratio 8.5:1
Carburetion . . . . .2; 32mm; Amal 932
Air filtration . . . . .Paper element
Ignition . . . . Battery and coil, breaker points
Bhp @ rpm (claimed) . . . . 60 @ 6,200 rpm
Mph/1000 rpm, top gear 17.43
Fuel capacity . . . . 3 gal.
Oil capacity . . . . 6 pts.
Lighting . . . . 12v, 104 watts
Battery . . . . 12v, 8 ah
Gear ratios, overall . . . .(1) 11.20 (2) 7.45 (3) 5.30
                                              (4) 4.38
Wheelbase . . . . .58.6 in.
Seat height . . . . 32 in., with rider
Ground clearance . . . . .6.0 in., with rider
Curb weight . . . . .462 lbs., with full tank of gas
Test weight . . . . .622 lbs., with rider
Instruments . . . . . Speedometer, Tachometer, Odometer
Sound level, Calif. Std. . . . . .85.5 dB(A)
Standing start ¼-mile . . . . . . 13.06 seconds 100.78 mph
Top speed . . . . 122 mph (at 7,000 rpm redline)

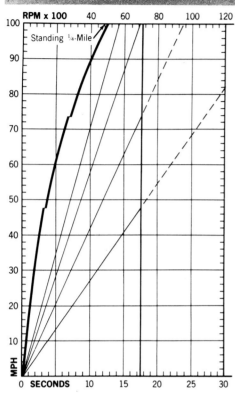

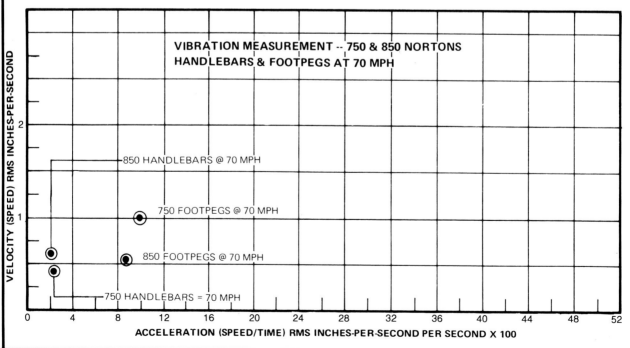

so they can jump on it with both feet. Both feet is what it takes when the engine is cold, and its pistons glued in place with chilled motor oil. It is God's own blessing that the engine really isn't reluctant to start, once you have persuaded the crankshaft to rotate. Twirl it fast enough to draw fuel into the cylinders and it fires. You have to be careful not to flood it with over-enthusiastic use of the carburetor ticklers, but even then it will clear itself with a couple of sooty coughs and settle down to business. Starting it warm is no trick at all: one kick and it's running.

Sadly, the Norton's willingness to start is matched by a willingness to stall unless the idle is set rather high. Its Amal concentric-float carburetors (devil take them) refuse to be adjusted for a low, even tickover. You can fiddle the idle mixture screws and throttle stops until everything seems perfect and the engine is thudding away with a wonderfully even beat—but as soon as you blip the throttle one time your perfect idle is transformed into a case of the blind staggers. Af-

ter a while you learn to settle for a ragged, busy 1,200 rpm idle which drives you crazy when the bike is stopped for a traffic light, but at least keeps the engine from stalling.

You are entitled to wonder why a fast idle is such a bad thing. Here's the reason: the 850 engine's vibrations are more than the rubber mountings can handle at some engine speeds. Indeed, at certain speeds the Isolastic mounting makes things worse, and the worst condition is encountered between 1,500 and 3,000 rpm, with some really interesting pulses coming up through the chassis as low as 1,000 rpm. Still, it is tolerable at 1,000 rpm, but it will drive you right off the bike at 2,000 rpm—at which point the oscillations are so bad that the taillight vibrates vertically with an amplitude of nearly two inches and one's vision tends to blur slightly. There isn't quite that much shaking with the engine under load, but you get it in fulsome glory when waiting for a traffic light to change and nicking the engine to keep it from stalling.

There isn't much positive to be said for the 850 Commando as an around-town motorcycle, except that it lunges and stops pretty well. The vibration at low speeds forces you to do a lot of riding in the lower gears, which keeps the engine spinning above 3,000 rpm and stops the shaking, but seems overly dramatic in light of the exhaust pipes' tendency to resonate themselves into a window-rattling fit above that same 3,000 rpm. In this connection we should point out that the 85.5 dB(A) noise level registered by the Norton under the CHP test procedure is deceptive. In this test you run past the instruments in second gear, accelerating from 30 mph, and the plain truth is that the tall-geared Norton gets just beyond the range of the sound meter's microphone before working itself up to full bellow. So when you hold it in second gear in fast traffic, keeping the revs up to keep the vibration down, you raise a lot more commotion than anyone wants to hear.

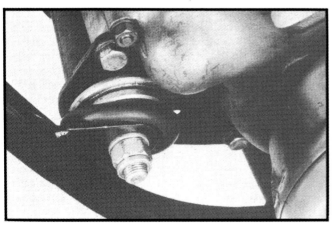

Pictured here is a front engine mount in the Isolastic system. The mounts allow the engine to shake in a vertical plane—but not in a lateral one.

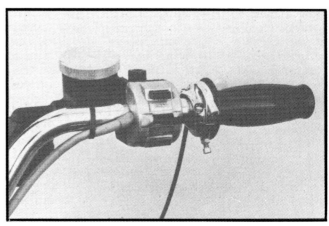

Hopefully, some day British bikes will rid themselves of these confusing, uncomfortable, and hard-to-use handlebar switches. The day can't come too soon.

NORTON 850

On another level, the vibration at low engine speeds to some extent cancels one of the 850's best features. The engine pulls like an elephant all the way from about 2,000 rpm, but you find yourself always reaching for another, lower gear any time the revs fall below 3,000 rpm. The result is that the theoretical advantage provided by the extra displacement and a milder camshaft remains theoretical; you have to do just as much shifting, or more, than was required with the 750 Commando and is required when riding a high-revving Japanese multi. The 850 doesn't shake any more than the old 750, a little less in fact, but it does its worst shaking at lower revs and the change in overall gearing means that the engine is always turning more slowly. The net result is that you do get more vibration at anything short of freeway speeds.

Where the 850 Commando engine shows itself to best advantage, and is really impressive by any standard, is away from the urban crush, out on the open road. There the engine is always above that critical 3,000 rpm and the bike feels glassy smooth. At 70 mph it's burbling away happy as Christmas at 4,000 rpm, and feels as though it would lope along that way forever. It is as pleasant an Interstate flyer as you are likely to find this side of an air-conditioned Cadillac, and a lot less dull.

Even so, it is not zapping along the straight-line Interstates that the Norton does best. Where it shines, and edges out most other Superbikes, is hooting along zig-zag mountain roads. The 750 did that sort of thing with real flair, but it yields primacy to the new 850, which incorporates subtle changes in steering geometry. The 850 Commando is a big motorcycle, with a 58-inches-plus wheelbase and a weight of 462 pounds, but you'd think maybe it's a lightweight judging by the way it can be flicked around on the road. When you first start riding it that way, there is a temptation to begin mentally composing letters to Norton-Villiers' Managing Director asking why the 850 Commando was given so little side clearance, why the centerstand drags in left turns, and why the exhaust pipe develops a big flat spot from making turns to the right. One thinks, too, that the engine really isn't doing all it might with 828cc, that the bike isn't rushing along the road like other Superbikes. But then you notice that your familiar 20-mile loop of mountain roads has been travelled in minutes less than is usual, and when you stop for a breather you notice that the tread blocks on those fine Dunlop TT100 pavement grippers show a feathered wear pattern right out to their edges. The evidence is clear and conclusive. The Norton has been going genuinely fast, making maximum use of a pair of very good tires and getting from point to point with rare dispatch. And effortlessly, too. The engine hasn't been pressed any-

where near its redline. The handlebars seem to turn themselves as the bike sweeps into slow corners and the Commando does most of its own aiming through fast turns, making any rider feel just a touch better than he actually is.

Would that the Commando was as comfortable as it is fast and agile. That backbone tube mentioned earlier reaches back from the steering head just a little too straight and level, and the underside of the seat is grooved for clearance in a way that leaves the padding too thin up near the front. When you're trying to ride briskly you'll be sitting right where the padding is especially thin. Fast riding demands that your weight be placed over the footpegs, and these are too far forward, which brings you right up against the back of the Norton's fuel tank and straddling what feels like a bare backbone tube. As one of our staffers put it, "It's like having a bunch of rowdy friends ride you out of town on a rail: it's fun, but that doesn't keep your tail from getting sore."

What the Commando badly needs is to have more padding over the front part of the seat, and to have its footpegs moved back a couple of inches. When the pegs are moved back the shift lever will have to be shortened, but that will help cure another problem. That old Norton gearbox definitely has it over more modern transmissions in terms of smooth, low-effort action, but there simply is too much travel. Human ankles don't swivel far enough to handle the distance the lever has to be moved, so you sometimes miss gears and hit neutrals just because your ankle hinge reached its limit-stop before the gears fully engaged. Apart from that, the gear change mechanism is a marvel—and so is the clutch, likewise with one qualifier. This new Norton's clutch is substantially the same excellent diaphragm-spring unit used in the Commando since its inception, with a couple of extra plates (now a total of five). The clutch's all-metal plates make it nearly bullet-proof and the over-center action of the diaphragm spring give it a lightness others with the same torque capacity are lacking. However, its engagement point is speed-sensitive: use lots of revs and full engagement does not occur until the lever is almost fully released; try easing away at low revs and you'll get full engagement as soon as the lever starts moving away from the grip.

Sometimes the Commando's suspension feels as though you're getting hard contact with the bump stops as soon as the wheels move. It has enough travel, but seemingly has an excess of springs and a shortage of damping. Expansion strips on the freeways jolt the Norton harder than any other Superbike, and the suspension harshness is the only handling deficiency. Fast, bumpy turns make the wheels dance and chatter enough to impose a lower limit on speed than do the tires or general stability.

Drag-strip testing the Commando 850 was fun, and a frustration. Fun, because

the bike scampers through the quarter-mile very quickly. Frustration (of a sort) because no rider skill is required. The 850 engine's power band is so broad that you can make your upshifts anywhere from 6,000 rpm to 7,000 rpm (the redline) without changing the numbers more than a tenth either way. The Commando is also the most consistent drag-strip performer we've ever had, turning run after run at almost exactly the same speed and elapsed time. Its brute torque removes any real need for refined technique in getting underway—you just whiz the engine up to about 6,000 rpm and drop the hammer. The Norton takes off like a shot, runs straight and true, and turns the same times every time.

Norton's 850 Commando has great visual appeal for anyone who likes the lean, rangey look. Its 19-inch wheels make it look spidery, and they've done wonders getting 3.5 gallons into a container that has to straddle a big frame tube and still looks small. The only jarring note in the bike's appearance is the engine itself, which has a cylinder and head that look too puny for 850cc worth of piston displacement. The reason is the very minimal finning, which is too scanty for a balanced appearance and perhaps even too scanty for adequate cooling. We also think the handlebars are too wide to look right, and they don't feel right to us, but the chaps at Norton-Villiers say their dealers keep asking for precisely the sort of bars they've put on the 850 Commando. In any case, handlebars are a matter of individual preference and easily changed. Owners may also want to do something about the dangling throttle cable, which hangs down in a loop right where it can snag on a bush or something if you get sloppy and cut the inside of a righthander too close. Snag that cable and the throttles will be jerked wide open. That certainly will move the bike away from the inside of the turn, and it is likely to be more of a readjustment in line than you really wanted.

We also don't care much for the handlebar-mounted switches and buttons, which are—all claims for ergonometric design notwithstanding—a study in confusion. The high/low beam switch makes sense, but the up and down action of the identical turn-indicator switch does not. And then there are the two buttons above and below each switch, four in all, and all identical. It is a confused layout, and it confuses.

Finally, there is the traditionally-British weeping of oil. The Norton engine left puddled proof of its presence back when they used a timed crankcase breather; it does so still with the new open breather pipe—which carries crankcase fumes to the aircleaner. The current switch to plastic sump-plug washers, replacing those infamous and failure-prone fiber parts we all know and loathe, may dry up the seepage around the sump plug—but our bike was fiber-washered and it drooled and slobbered all over its belly. There was also a

Continued on page 157

NORTON'S BIGSTER

Test:
John McDermott

Photography:
FOTOFAST /
Vic Barnes

THE last purely motorcycle show to be held at Earls Court was back in 1967. Norton Villiers got the lion's share of the press reports with a large, sleek grey job — silver grey frame, silver grey cycle parts, a modified Atlas engine on rubber mountings, a large, bulbous green eye on each side of the fueltank and unholiest departure of all, a bright orange dualseat. They called it the Commando.

The first full production prototype, a more sober offering than the show model was taken down to a service station on the M2 one bright October morning that year and I was amongst the half dozen riders to test it on the tarmac alongside the orchards of Kent. As NV's publicity man I had access to many such perks and did all I could to get roped in for a day away from the office testing and trying motorcycles. Later, when faults were found with the frame, steering geometry and gearbox, I did my stints at MIRA and Thruxton on destruction testing. I even managed to seize a gearbox as instructed by changing up and down for three days solid without using the clutch and doing all manner of silly things that even a half witted three legged nurk with lead boots on would find hard to equal. In consequence, having been in on the Commando project from the start, and having done around 40,000 miles on various Isolastic models, I reckon I know Norton's 750 as well as most.

The 850 version though, I did not know. I'd taken a ride on Paul Dunstall's 850 last summer and with the exception of a few minor faults, that had proved a very creditable machine. But would the factory's attempt at mass-producing a bigger Commando be better than Paul's hand-built,

small batch production? The stories I'd heard about Norton's 850 led me to believe that there was a big gap of unfulfilment in my life and that I was in for a treat. After many months of conversational badgering, I eventually got the Andover company to let me have one for test.

One thing was certain as I rode out of the Andover factory's drive: it was a heavy motorcycle — at least it felt heavy, heavier than anything else I can ever remember riding. Most of the weight seemed to be around the front end, very high up and making 'U' turns and creepy-crawling through traffic light queues on the 850 relegated me to a footing, incapable novice. It seemed that without the support of a stiff leg on each side to hold it up, the machine wanted to keel over. And even a 34in inside leg is put to the test on a machine that seems a mile high. The riders' manual states seat height (rider seated) as 31in but the seat is so wide, unless you have a funny tunnel-shaped crutch, those 31 inches are the equivalent of around 35. Anyone built smaller than 5ft 10in had better fit training wheels as the Commando won't accept a sidecar.

As a youngster and proud 'L' plate carrier, I was not aware of the RAC/ACU training scheme but being the son of a London copper, a copy of Motorcycle Roadcraft was available for me to read, and read and digest every word within that excellent manual I did over the years. One of the first snippets of roadcraft wisdom it imparted was "don't drag your feet when starting or stopping, as soon as the motorcycle is in forward motion, get your feet up on the footpegs, and don't put them down until the bike has stopped." All nice and tidy and, it suggested, a good pointer as to how good a motorcyclist you really are. The 850 Commando though, deprived me of this tidiness and within a few hours of taking delivery, I was well on the way to becoming disenchanted with it. With time I managed to control the nodding, ill-balanced beast a little better, but when a machine embarrasses you and takes away even a small percentage of your dignity when first you get together, there ain't much chance of love blossoming.

Quick she is. Like a sunburnt bat out of Hades. Quick that is, not particularly fast (maybe you use the terms differently to me, but in my book quick equals acceleration, fast equals top speed) and certainly not 100cc faster than the 750s I remember.

Steer, however, she did not. She would just refuse to behave herself at the back end under any circumstance. The rear suspension seemed to be at fault, for after a 50 mile gallop over good 'A' roads the left hand Girling was decidedly warm whilst the right hander was no more than luke warm. Over normal, well maintained road surfaces the back end was a mite wallowy, the symptoms worsening through moderate bends, but over badly patched surfaces with seams and sunken manhole covers the suspension was stiff and unyielding. That led to the back end chopping and moving out, even when travelling two up. Over bumps it was at best uncomfortable, at worst spine cracking and I finished most long runs in need of a Radox bath.

I had decided to give the Norton a run around the TT course in early August and test it under conditions that I — and you — are familiar with. Derestricted roads, a superb conglomeration of bends, straights, uphill sections, downhill rushes, heavy braking points — the TT course has the lot, so my bookings were made before I picked the bike up. If I'd had a choice after collecting the machine I would not have gone, but to reschedule the trip was impossible. So the following morning I strapped a few things on the bike in preparation for the run up to Liverpool. Sure enough, there in the morning light, underneath the machine was a pool of oil. Geez, how I hate and despise a bike that can't hold its liquor. The engine was filthy from the tacho drive union all the way back to the rear wheel with oil oozing from the tacho drive take-off point, the oil junctions at the back of the timing case, the top of the gearbox — well, just everywhere. To cut a long story short I went to the Island, I stayed a while, got madder and madder with this bloody awful heap of a motorcycle, came back and fumed in the office for a day and a half, wondering whether to write about it or shove it back at NV and ask for another. Surely this particular bike was not truly representative of the marque. No, it couldn't be, my three years riding NV's press bikes in the past were full of happy, no-trouble memories with only one puncture to mar the

picture. All I did was pour petrol and oil into the machines and point them into the sunrise, and maintenance was no more than adjusting the odd cable and pumping air into the tyres. I asked for another machine but was told there wasn't one available.

This one was such an old nail, a noisy, oil leaking, clutch slipping, gearbox-full-of-neutrals, bad handling mess that I did not have one good word to say about it. No, that's not quite true, the handlebars, designed by NV's Barcelona agent Juan Rhodes (who won the Barcelona 24 hour race for them in 1968) were delightful. Low, almost straight and just wide enough for comfort, they were only imperfect by virtue of the fact that the footpegs could not be adjusted back a shade to complement them.

A lot of readers might criticise my wish to hand the machine back to NV, take another and keep quiet about the first, but I would defend my action by saying quite simply that there are, in all manner of produce, ''friday'' units, freaks of human frailty that are bolted together badly because the factory was too hot, too cold, or made just before the weekend, or built by a man whose wife had cold-shouldered him the night before. These units are not representative of the marque and make up maybe one percent of the total manufactured, so by damning every unit made because the one percenter happened to come my way would be unjust. One has to be fair to the manufacturer *and* the potential customer at the same time.

Having drawn a blank with the official source of press supply, I looked around for another 850. Alas, it was Wednesday and the South London Norton Owners Club meet on Tuesdays, so unless I was prepared to wait another week, I would have to scrounge one from elsewhere. Whammo! It came to me in a flash, Peter Williams has one for his own use — well, officially that is, but it seems to be used as the JPN race shop runabout when Peter's not looking. I 'phoned him and he very kindly obliged, loaning me NOR 850L to complete my test. But he issued a warning: it had done 2,300 miles and had not been properly looked after — it's the old story my headmaster used to tell when I was late for school ''Johnny'' he would say ''the

nearer to church, the further from God'' and that's how it might be with Peter's bike. In the midst of all that engineering talent, it lay neglected, but 2,300 miles is not really enough to destroy a new machine, so I gladly went down to Thruxton and picked it up.

The first 850 I had was an Interstate job, NOR 850L is a plain Roadster with the small tank and short dualseat. She looked a picture with her cherry red and silver stripe paint job but I could see the oil stains from the tacho drive smeared along the crankcase and the rear wheel was also covered in black filth. One thing's for sure, if you own a Norton you can forget about rust — at least on all the bits abaft the exhaust ports.

This one at least did not feel top heavy, she was easier to steer at low speed than the former, but she did wave her head a bit under acceleration and there was a whisper of noise from the transmission. The handlebars were better suited to half mile racing at Ascot Park and presented the full width of my torso to the raging wind, a wind strong enough above 90 mph to cave my skinny chest in. She was a bit

unsmooth in a way — I didn't know in which way at the time — but a real flyer, pouring out bags of torquey power all the way up from 2,000 rpm to the red line mark at 7,000. Six and a half was more than enough for normal road blasting and I felt more comfortable keeping the top 500 rpm on the shelf should I need them for overhauling a long string of traffic. Barely an hour had passed from my leaving Thruxton when I rolled it off for Kingston — and I had taken the more pleasant old road, the A303/A30 in preference to the M3 — and taking my place in the outside lane crossing the Thames bridge, she began to cough, splutter and wheeze. I checked the ignition switch for looseness, the plug caps, the coil connections, the carb connections and one or two other bits but she persisted in getting worse. Within a few miles I was being shuddered along unevenly, unable to use more than 3,000 rpm without creating a backfiring loud enough to waken the dead.

I walked into the office in a worse fury than before. Christ, two out of two. At least Norton were proving consistent. Maybe all those stores I'd heard about

how good the 850 was were all put round by spares stockists, the Communists, the Mafia — I don't know, but someone with a sense of humour that doesn't match mine. With the Interstate I had called in to Taylor Matterson and asked Sid to adjust the clutch and after checking it he had declared ''It needs a bloody sight more than adjusting,'' so I was loth to creep round there again with more problems. I had to run in to the West End later in the day so I called in to Gus Kuhn's and asked an extremely busy Vincent Davey to help me out. They were well overworked but not wishing to stand by and see me slate the Andover factory without doing something about it — there's loyalty for you, full marks Vincent — John and Peter were taken off customer work to check the bike over. What was to be a quick job at no cost to anybody turned out to be a two-hour plus overhaul and I hope Vincent Davey sends a big bill to Andover. Loyalty comes from the heart and not from the wallet, and this was beyond a joke. Take a look at the faults found on a machine that left the production line just 2,300 miles previously:

Carburettors loose/one N57G and one N60 racing plugs fitted/Timing on one cylinder 40 degrees, the other 32 degrees (where it should be 28 degree to each)/the offside points gap 10thou instead of 15/Kickstart lever loose on the shaft/Tacho drive union spewing oil/Primary chain excessively loose/Two lots of bared wiring burnt out by exhaust pipes/Balance pipe clamp bolts chewing into frame downtube.

The last two items are the most infuriating. The wiring — from the contact breaker to the coil was so badly sited that the breeze generated by forward motion blew the wires back onto the exhaust system's balance pipe and burnt (thus shorting) it out. The clamps holding the balance pipe to each exhaust pipe had been removed (in order to weld up a split pipe) and had been put back wrong way round and the vibration of the engine on the Isolastic mountings had allowed the bolt to chip away at the offside downtube and actually chew a hole out. If the machine was mine. I would take it off the road until the hole was welded — or dump the frame and fit a new one. I would not be happy with a mere pinhole in any frame of mine.

So there I was, gassing to the ever-helpful Kuhn crowd — a pleasant enough pastime in itself but I was in the way and I had planned a busy schedule as this was the last day I had to test the machine before flying to Germany to try BMW's new 900 cc model. Believe me, as I stood there in the workshop champing at the bit, the trip to Munich was an oasis of delight dangling like a carrot somewhere in the near future.

It was a beautiful day, a scorching sun burnt into the pavement and the indentations in the hot tarmac outside the Kuhn shop witnessed a steady flow of customers. It occurred to me that I wouldn't mind having shares in a Norton spares/repairs business and being able to afford a little beach hut out in St Tropez or the Bahamas. A voice behind me (and one I won't point a finger at by naming names) said ''There y'are, I told you I've never seen a rusty Norton rider'' and as I turned to find out to what the voice was referring, saw a finger pointing at my back. I was dressed in jeans and a snazzy JPN race team jacket, mainly white with the red and blue 'lazy S' John Player motif down the front, very kindly given to me by Ted Macaulay of

BIGSTER

Stanbury-Foley the JPN publicity agency. All the way up, down and across the back was the black filth of an oil slick, cast upward from the rear wheel. The jacket was absolutely ruined in just ninety miles of riding. Ironic that a smart, mobile advertisement for John Player Norton was ruined on its first ride on a Norton. Thanks anyway chaps, I liked it while it lasted.

By this time I was fresh out of fury. Get mad too often in a short space of time and the next blow doesn't seem to matter. What the hell. Kick John McDermott in the teeth more than four times in one day and it don't hurt any more. Anyhow, the bike had been taken around the block for a final check-out and it was now back having the carburettors fettled and I would be on my way shortly, getting more muck thrown up my neck. And Munich was two hours nearer by this time.

The carburettors — or at least one of them — was duff. John, Kuhn's mechanic told me they had come across quite a few over the past months and there was nothing much that could be done except change them. But the main problems had been cured and apart from an unevenness at low rpm, the bike was running as best it could. I tripped into town to finish my business before taking a run into the country and it most certainly was annoying. All jerky and uncomfortable, and it was more than I dare to let the thing tick over at traffic lights — that was asking for a stall.

I eventually did get my last run out on it before stowing it in the garage and packing my weekend bag. And by that time the unevenness had got worse, traffic on my way back into London had got denser and restricted me to less than 3000rpm whereas the shudder only disappeared above this point.

The bad handling of the first bike was not echoed in the second, even though Peter had swiped the Girlings off NOR 850L at Brands Hatch when he crashed his racer, replacing them with the bent Konis from the crashed machine. True, the racing Konis gave a very stiff ride and being bent did not help, but bearing this in mind, the bike handled well. It could be laid down until the stand scraped, lifted up and laid down the other way with total ease, but she did wave her head a little under these conditions. The motor was torquey and fluid from the

word go and she started easily, one prod on the kickstart being enough under any circumstances.

The one thing I was not in the mood for though, especially with a picture of that punctured downtube fresh in my mind, was finding out her top speed.

It didn't — as I said earlier — seem any different from the 750s of yore and I would rather not guess and decieve you. She was happy to cruise at ninety plus for hour after hour (just two that I tried) and as the Interstate got me from Liverpool to London in three hours ten minutes travelling time, I feel sure the Roaster would have equalled this. The brakes were good but far from excellent. One could squeal both tyres even at fairly high speeds but the amount of energy required at the handlebar end of the front disc was excessive. Off-motorway riding at high speed resulted in a right hand with a puffy pre-blister look due to the amount of work it had done. The feeling of retardation was progressive but not commensurate with the leverage applied. The rear stopper was good enough for the job but did not, I feel, have anything in reserve. A 430lb projectile with one or two passengers and about 40lb of fuel aboard needs some stopping from the three-figure speeds it is capable of. A rear disc would comfort me in this respect.

Summing up the Commando 850, I think it has had its day. I don't think Norton can go on its way to the still-expanding markets of this world with this egg in its basket. Customers will buy one and only one before getting fed to the teeth with too-regular maintenance sessions, a bike that needs a lot of Gunk to make it presentable, oily boots and a messy garage floor.

It's a pity that they are so badly built: the performance is exhillerating, and although they don't have the "Roadholder" tag of the Featherbed models, they steer fairly predictably. But so do many other modern bikes, and "Japanese" is a word held in ever-growing respect. I feel personally that Norton Villiers have let me down. My memories of so many fast, fun-filled gallops on the early Commandos has been dealt a body blow that I shall recover from, but with less glamorous recall. As I sit here bleaching my jacket and scrubbing the oil from my boots I feel tired and a little bit sick. I wish I could have said how good their motorcycles were. Ⓜ

COMMANDO 850 SPECIFICATION

Engine: Vertical twin, bore 77mm, stroke 89mm, capacity 828cc. Comp ratio 8.5:1, peak power at 5,800, maximum rpm 7,000.

Transmission: Diaphragm clutch:

Ratios: 1st 11.21
2nd 7.45
3rd 5.30
4th 4.38

Primary chain 3/8in Triplex, secondary chain 5/8in x 3/8in.

Carburettors: Amal 932 32mm.

Electrical: 12v coil capacitor, 8 amp/hr battery, zenor diode between alternator and battery.

Capacities: Oil tank: 5 pints
Gearbox: .75 pint.
Fuel tank: 2.5 gals (Roadster)
5.8 gals (Interstate).

Wheels/tyres:
Rims: WM2 x 19in
Tyres: 4.10 x 19in.
Pressures: 24lb/sq in front.
26lb/sq in rear.

Dimensions:
Length: 87½in
Wheelbase: 56¾in.
Ground clearance: 6in.
Weight: 430lb (dry)

Price: Roadster: £726
Interstate: £726

BIG BORE

Five years 'Machine of the Year'... Can the 850 Interstate retain the title? MCM rides, tests and reports on the new Norton...

BLAST OFF!

There's no substitute for cubic inches! The 750 Commando has been the Machine of the Year for five years running and the 850 is the first real development of the basic Commando since it was introduced!

The 850 is very much the same as the standard Commando with its cycle parts, but it's the motor which is most interesting. The new iron barrel has a bore of 77 mm while the standard 750 is only 73 mm. It is simply this increase in size which gives the extra power.

One of the most important points about the new motor is the effort Nortons have made to make it more reliable and easier to ride.

The compression ratio is lower than the 750: 8.5 against 8.9:1 and the carburettor size is the same at 32 mm. This helps produce not only more power than the 750 but, very important, more usable power.

Other firms have produced big-bore kits for the Commando, but they have never made any attempt to beef up the bottom end. The 850 is strengthened considerably where it matters. The four outside cylinder-head bolts pass through the barrel and screw into the crankcase. This should reduce the possibility of the barrel trying to lift off the cases and also cuts the loading on the cylinder-barrel base.

The main bearings are what Nortons describe as "high-capacity, super-blended, large-diameter, roller main bearings", which apart from sounding like an advert for margarine means that the bearings are normal roller bearings with a slight taper on the ends. This will give the advantages of the roller bearing for load capacity and the advantage of taper rollers for isolating the crankshaft from too much endfloat.

These modifications to the motor should result in a longer life. But it is not only in this department that Nortons have been busy. The crankcase breathing system has been revised. The breathing is now done from the back of the timing cover.

It was found with the old system, that when the engine was being held at high revs for any length of time, that a lot of oil came up the breather and this resulted in a build-up in pressure in the cases, which caused oil leaks.

The new breathing system will be more efficient, and with legislation becoming more strict about emission control, the new 850 Norton should have no trouble complying. The silencers, too, have come in for some development. They are really quiet and certainly won't give the Noise Abatement Society anything to complain about.

What's it like on the road? Really good. The motor is smooth and flexible and there is so much usable power, I never

MM ROAD TEST

had any trouble when overtaking.

The really impressive feature of the motor is the way it doesn't seem to matter what gear you're in when you want acceleration. More than once I managed to get into second gear instead of first at traffic lights because the gearbox works the opposite way round to that which I am used to, but even in second gear there was no need to slip the clutch to get really good acceleration.

To find out the standing-start quarter-mile times, we took the 850 to the Santa Pod Drag Strip.

We entered the Norton at the season opener meeting on April 1 and the results were very impressive. On the day there was a headwind of between 30 and 40 miles an hour, which was slowing the times of all the bikes and causing some of them real handling problems. Fully road equipped, that means including the baffles in the silencers, a full tank of petrol and full toolkit.

The Norton was running in the 13.9-second bracket all day long, and, there is no doubt, that without the headwind the

Norton would have no trouble in getting down to about 12.8 or 12.9 seconds.

In a straight race against a 750 Commando, the 850 was a lot quicker over the first eighth mile and was still pulling away slightly on the last part of the strip. I apologise to my pit crew of Colin Sanders and Denis Gawler and the *Motor Cycle Mechanics* fan club for pulling a red light in the first round, but I think the Norton did prove that in standard trim it has a lot of acceleration, especially as it was racing against machines, most of which have been set up especially for Drag Racing.

Although the drag racing session was interesting, I don't expect the majority of owners are really interested in a split second difference in standing quarter-mile times, but I did use the Norton as much as possible under very varied road conditions—London rush-hour traffic to deserted twisting country lanes—and the motor was always perfect. However, there were one or two minor complaints about the handling.

On the rare occasion I had to shut the throttle halfway round

a corner, the frame felt like it was hinged in the middle. And when I checked, I found that the swinging arm had enough play in it to fail the MoT test.

When Charles Deane rode the bike, he thought the front end was too light and, if the power was put on hard going round a corner, the front wheel became light enough for the bike to want to go straight on. Charles and I are about the same size and weight and yet I had no problem with a light front end, which either means that we ride a bike differently or, more likely, that "the Ed" goes a lot faster than me!

I used the bike quite a bit for night riding, and fortunately our model was fitted with a quartz halogen headlight. This light was so good that I would not consider buying a Commando without one.

Although I really enjoyed riding the Norton, both the editor and I have two identical complaints. The first is that the seat is far too high, and although it only measures 32 in. off the ground, it's so wide it feels more like 36 in.

It would be no problem for

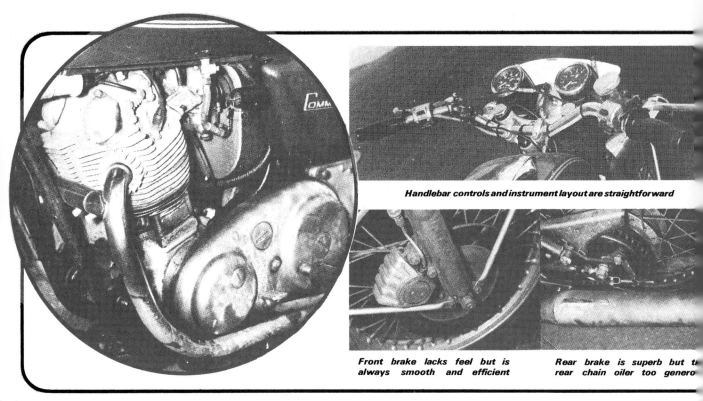

Handlebar controls and instrument layout are straightforward

Front brake lacks feel but is always smooth and efficient

Rear brake is superb but the rear chain oiler too generou[s]

MCM on the drag scene. Mike Cazalet takes the big-bore Norton to Santa Pod . . .

Nortons to lower the seat on this bike as there is enough room for it to be dropped at least 2 in. All that needs to be done is to make a new seat base.

The other complaint is also caused by the seat height. The only way I could get a good swing on the kickstarter was with the bike on the centre stand. When I tried to start it off the stand, it turned into a Sammy Miller balancing act, with the likelihood of me and the bike toppling into the gutter!

Once underway, the height doesn't matter, in fact the riding position is really good. The footrests are high and the tank is wide enough to grip comfortably between the knees. Also, the seat is well shaped to stop even weak-armed riders like me from falling off the back.

With its fantastic, performance, the Norton would be dangerous if it didn't have the brakes to match. The front was deceptive, because it had a very wooden feel. However, it never locked the wheel and I never felt that there was any chance of the bike not stopping in time.

The lack of feel could probably be overcome by giving the brake slightly more leverage, at the same time providing a method of adjusting the gap between the lever blade and the handlebar.

The back brake is superb. The design is the same as that used on Nortons since the days

of the Featherbed Dominators. Odd to say, but in those days it never used to work particularly well and, although there are no *obvious* improvements, the brake is very smooth and does not suffer from fade no matter how hard it is used.

Neither the clutch nor gearbox could be faulted. No matter how much the clutch was slipped it always took up the drive cleanly. Gear selection was always positive and never once did I miss a gear, even when I did clutchless changes. This is one bike that does not need the complication and expense of a five-speed box.

Nortons are the only firm still making a gearbox with a one up three down pattern and this can cause confusion. Perhaps it is time they changed the pattern to be the same as other manufacturers.

This new Commando would be my choice for the "Machine of the Year" if it wasn't for so many points of criticism over quality control. Maybe our model had been badly treated by whoever had tested it before, but we had considerable trouble during the first week we had the bike.

One of the bolts which holds the inner chaincase to the crankcase had come undone because its tabwasher had not been properly done up.

The bolt had smashed its way through the inner chaincase.

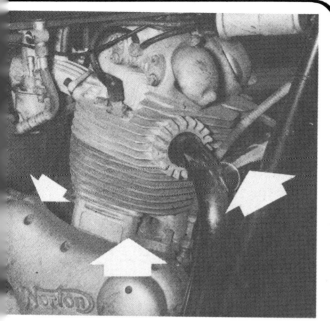

...e-away points on the new 850. Balance tube between the ...es, studs through barrel, breather in timing cover

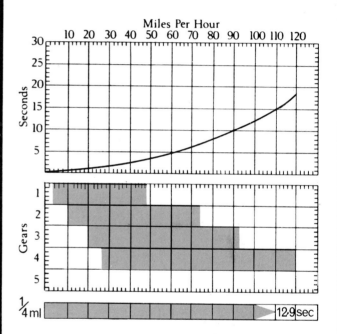

When we took the outer cover off, there was an even bigger horror inside. Somehow the triplex primary chain had only been fitted to two runs of the engine and clutch sprocket. I would have thought it impossible for the chain to have jumped a complete row of teeth, which means the chain must have been put on wrongly.

We are never sure if the bikes supplied to us for road test are the best of the range or if the manufacturer cleans up a development model just enough for "mad" journalists to wreck. But if the Commando was supposed to be a good example of this model, then Nortons have some rethinking to do on their quality control.

Within 1500 miles our Norton was starting to look very second hand. We had rust on the cylinder-head bolts, rust on the barrel and on the centre of the front disc.

The exhaust pipes had turned a very attractive shade of blue and the motor was running slightly rich. In places, the frame appeared to have no paint on it. The cross tube under the motor and the front engine mounting had started to rust.

The rear chain oiler had lubricated everything from the pillion footrest back, except the rear chain. There was no possibility of the nearside front fork leg rusting, there was too

much oil leaking for that to ever happen and the white lining and top layer of paint on the back of the fuel tank had been worn away by the riders' knees. All this on a very expensive motorcycle which should be an advert for the quality of British engineering. It's not good enough!

I like the Norton, but if they are hoping to sell this new model to anyone apart from founder-members of the Norton Owners' Club, they are going to have to crack down on the standard of workmanship. The design is very good, it combines the best of the traditional; separate gearbox, a reliable fuss-free motor that is easy to work on, with enough new features to make it an attractive bike. But who wants to buy a new bike and have to spend time working on it instead of riding it?

Would I buy one? Yes, if someone will buy my Drag bike off me at the right price. The idea of having a bike which is quick enough to be competitive on the strip and the occasional clubman's road race and still be able to use it for touring and about-town transport, makes the Norton my sort of motorcycle.

Words: Mike Cazalet
pix: Dave Kennard

SPECIFICATION

Engine: Twin-cylinder pushrod-operated four-stroke. Bore 77 mm, stroke 89 mm, giving a capacity of 830 cc. Compression ratio 8.5:1. Power output 60 bhp at 5800 rpm. Maximum safe revs 5900 rpm for continuous cruising.

Transmission: Four-speed constant-mesh gearbox with ratios 11.20, 7.45, 5.30, 4.38. Primary-drive ratio 2.19:1. Multi-plate diaphragm clutch with triplex chain drive.

Carburation: Twin Amal Concentric 32-mm-bore carburettors.

Wheels: Front: 4.10 × 19 with 10.7 in. hydraulic disc brake. Rear: 4.10 × 19 with single-leading-shoe 7 in. drum brake.

Suspension: Front telescopic forks. Swinging-arm rear suspension with adjustable rear dampers.

Dimensions: Fuel tank 5 gallons with $\frac{3}{4}$-gallon reserve. Oil tank 5 pints. Weight 430 lb. Seat height 32 in. Length 88 in.

Price: £726 inc. VAT.

Manufacturer: Norton Villiers Ltd, Andover, Hants.

THE NEW BIG NORTON

Commando 850 has many changes from the 750

THE NEW 850 Norton incorporates a considerable number of detail improvements over the current 750 Norton range, in addition to basic structural and dimension differences. These modifications, as detailed by NVE, are outlined below as a general background introduction to the new model :

1. The 850 is distinguished by a restyled cylinder barrel, through-bolted to the crankcase. The petrol tank and side panels carry a double line.
2. A "candy apple" finish (metallic red) to tanks and side panels will be a new option.
3. The Interstate model is fitted with Veglia instruments. The speedo meter incorporates a trip.
4. A new seat of different interior density and "aerated pattern" exterior offers more comfort. Chrome grabrails are fitted to all 850 Nortons.
5. The latest Lucas switches are fitted, incorporating longer flasher and dipping controls. The push-buttons extend more prominently. A red kill button is fitted. Redesigned lever geometry lessens the amount of clutch pull required. Mirror fitting blanks are now provided in the switches.
6. A larger tail lamp is fitted to comply with regulations in certain markets. The indicator brackets are strengthened.
7. The kickstarter crank is of an improved bend-resistant material.
8. The gearbox shell has additional thickness in the area of the main bearing housing.
9. The all-metal clutch has an additional plate—making five in total.
10. All 850 Nortons are fitted with a 21t final-drive sprocket.
11. The 850 cylinder mates to the crankcase on a wide-flange design, utilizing a plastic gasket. The outer stud holes are helicoiled.
12. The exhaust pipe flanges use a thicker abutment ring and are through sleeved. The finned exhaust lock rings are more robust. A balance pipe is fitted to all 850s in the interests of noise reduction.

13. The 850 crankcase incorporates a removable gauze strainer. A magnetic sump plug is fitted. The pick-up area is modified to improve scavenging.
14. The flywheel material is upgraded. The 850 flywheel is reshaped to compensate for the heavier pistons.
15. Fag Superblend main bearings are fitted, giving a greatly increased dynamic load capacity.
16. The valves are stellite tipped at the rocker ends. The exhaust seats are widened—valve guides are retained by circlips.
17. The camshaft bushes revert to phosphor bronze, lipped at timing side, plain at drive side.
18. The contact-breaker/auto advance assembly has several detail improvements.
19. Carburettor ticklers are now of "waterproof" Spanish type. The float bowls are fitted with drain plugs. Cutaway spray tubes are fitted.
20. Hard chrome is now employed as the standard finish to fork tubes.
21. Mudguards are of stainless steel.
22. Front-wheel spoking has been revised. Non-crushable bearing dust covers are fitted to the front wheel.
23. Rear braking efficiency is improved by a stiffer brake drum.
24. The Isolastic system has several changes in order to reduce maintenance intervals. Spacer buffers are now circlipped in position. Washers are constructed of bronze-impregnated PTFE. Softer gaiters, to improve cold weather sealing, are fitted and silicone grease is now used for all Isolastic assemblies.
25. A strengthened return spring is fitted to the centre stand.
26. Pivoted-fork rigidity is increased by means of box sectioning. The cylinder head steady is modified to box section type.

Engine

Air-cooled four-stroke overhead-valve vertical twin-cylinder engine. Dry-sump lubrica-

tion with full-flow disposable element oil filter. Bolt-through cast iron finned cylinder. Aluminium one-piece cylinder head and rocker box. Hemispherical combustion chambers with large ports, valves angled for maximum power. Forged steel rocker arms. Austenitic nickel chrome steel exhaust valves. Inlet valve stem oil seals. Built-up forged steel crankshaft with centre flywheel. High capacity Superblend roller main bearings. Forged aluminium alloy connecting rods with inserted thin shell big-end bearings. Aluminium pistons. Gear and short chain timing drive to forged, hardened and Tufftrided camshaft. High efficiency direct drive to tachometer. Profiled aluminium push rods. Cam followers with stellite face pads for long life. Polished aluminium timing cover.

Capacity :	828 c.c. (50 cu in)
Bore :	77mm
Stroke :	89mm
Compression ratio :	8.5 : 1
Max. r.p.m. continuous cruising :	5,800
B.h.p. at sea level at 6,200 r.p.m. (SAE) :	60

Clutch

Multi-disc metal to metal with hardened centre and large diaphragm spring, the special design of which ensures light hand operation.

Transmission

Wide-tooth four-speed gearbox with medium-close ratios in heavy-duty casing. Precision gear pinions of high alloy nickel chrome steel for dog strength. Triple row heavy-duty primary chain drive within streamlined aluminium housing. Oil feed pipe to rear chain. Cush drive with reinforced polyurethane pads in rear wheel.

Primary drive ratio :	57t clutch sprocket
	26t engine sprocket
	2.19 : 1
Final drive ratios :	
Rear sprocket teeth :	42
Gearbox sprocket teeth :	21
	Ratios :
Top gear :	4.38 : 1
Third gear :	5.30 : 1
Second gear :	7.45 : 1
Bottom gear :	11.20 : 1

Alternative final-drive sprocket sizes available on order.

Dimensions

Wheelbase :	57in (145cm)
Length :	88in (223cm)
Width :	26in (66cm)
Ground clearance :	6in (15cm)
Dry weight :	415-430 lb (189-196 kg) depending on specification

Performance

Under best conditions :*

Top speed :	Approaching 125 m.p.h.
Acceleration :	
0-60 m.p.h.	4.5 seconds

* Figures provided by Norton Villiers Europe.

NORTON COMMANDO REBUILD

Supertwin assembly at Norton's experimental workshop

Five times machine of the year and one of the favourites to win the award again this year — the Norton Commando. Since Norton-Villiers produced the Commando from the ashes of the old AMC empire, the big Norton engine has proved itself capable of producing high power and long life. The engine unit has been used to power the TT winning John Player Nortons and two of the engines supply the go for T. C. Christianson's world record breaking drag bike.

To find out what was involved in working on one of these engines we went to the Norton-Villiers experimental department at Wolverhampton . . .

NORTON COMMANDO REBUILD

● The most important point to check when rebuilding these engines is that every part must be perfectly clean before it is refitted to the engine. If the crankshaft is taken out of the cases then it must be split, after marking the parts to make sure they go back the same way, and the inside of the shaft must be cleaned out. Another job that must be done when the engine is stripped down is to put an air line through all the oil ways in the cases.

All gaskets on the engine must be assembled dry, or with a thin smear of grease, apart from the head gasket. This is fitted with a thin smear of red Hermetite on the cylinder head side. Dry joints like the crankcase mating surfaces are sealed with plastic gasket.

Before any work is done on the engine there are a few special tools that are needed.

The most important of these are the clutch compressor and the extractor for the engine sprocket. Also essential when working on these engines is the proper workshop manual, available from any Norton distributor.

Ignition timing on these bikes is critical and must be set with a strobe. If you do not have one, then take the bike to a dealer who will do the job for just a few pence.

The engine we used for this article is the new 850, but the assembly procedure is the same for the 750 apart from a few small points.

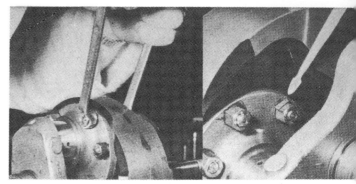

Crankshaft must be split and cleaned out during a rebuild. New bolts and nuts must be used when crank is assembled.

Make sure these lockwash are replaced and that they pushed firmly over the ho ing nuts. Oil the cranksh

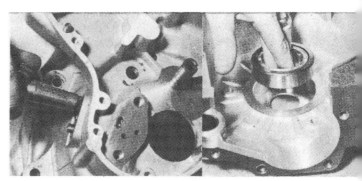

Blow all the oil passages in the cases out with an air line. Any dirt here can damage the pump and block the oil feed.

New main bearings are fitt to hot cases. Use bear Loctite to make sure th the bearings cannot mov

CAM TIMING

Mark on crankshaft pinion should be at the 12 o'clock position. This is supposed to line up with a mark on the rear . . .

. . . pinion on the half time pinion. The two marks on the chain wheels should be set with five chain outer links . . .

. . . between them as in the picture. With everything lined up slide the half time pinion and the cam sprocket on to . . .

. . . their shafts. Set the cam drive chain so that there is very slight play in the chain in it's tightest position.

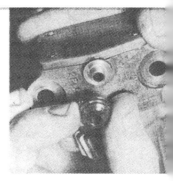

This eal governs the c pressure. Take no chances Replace the seal when th pump is off the crankcases

850 bolts should be torqued down. Pull the 750 base nuts down evenly. The cylinder head gasket is assembled . . .

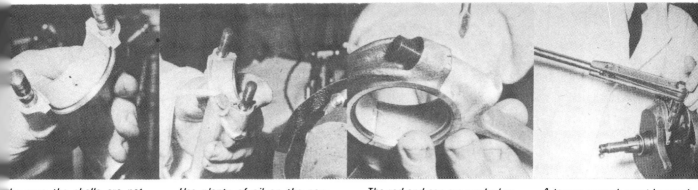

...ke sure the shells are not ...ud of the rod. Check that ...e in the shell lines up ...h the hole in the conrod.

Use plenty of oil on the new shells when the rod is bolted back together. New conrod nuts and bolts must be used.

The rod and cap are marked so that they can not be refitted the wrong way round. Do not exchange the caps between rods

A torque wrench must be used to get the big-end bolts done up correctly. Check on the correct setting from book.

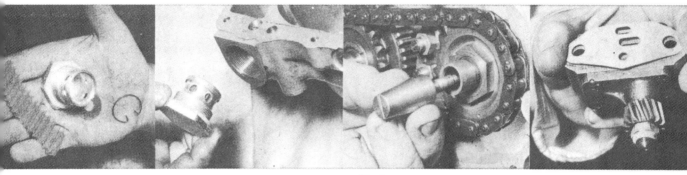

...ip the crankcase filter ...t and clean it with petrol ...d an air line. Check that ...o is perfect before fitting.

Filter is refitted with a new washer and Loctite. Shaft is then fitted to the cases using oil on the bearings.

Fix the cam timing. Remember to use the oil seal guide when fitting the timing cover to prevent damage to seal.

Oil pump gasket only lines up one way. Check that the oil holes are clear before fitting the pump into the crankcases.

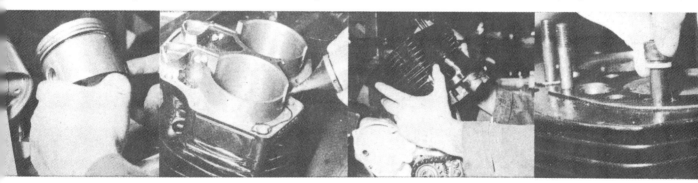

...at pistons before fitting ...the conrods. New circlips ...st be used every time the ...tons are taken off rods.

Barrel to crankcase joint is sealed with plastic gasket. Bore is soaked in oil before the barrel is fitted . . .

. . . over the pistons. Use ring compressors to prevent damage to the rings and the pistons are supported on blocks.

The 850 barrel is held to crankcases with these through bolts. 750 barrel is held down with base studs and nuts.

. . . with a thin smear of red ...rmetite on the barrel side. ...n't overdo the cement or ...d removal will be difficult.

Centre push rods, the inlets, are the longest ones. Make sure that the rods are fully seated before fitting head.

Do centre bolt of the cylinder head up first. Slip the push rods on to the rockers and then tighten the head bolts in . . .

. . . sequence. Make sure that the tappet settings are right. Tight tappets are going to burn the valves out very quickly.

Road Test

Norton Commando 850 Interstate

"It's not supposed to be a performance bike" claim Norton Villiers. Our test bike was, most decidedly, NOT.

TESTERS: MICHAEL RICHARDSON, JULIAN SCULLIN.
PIX: BILL MEYER, MICHAEL RICHARDSON.

WHEN WE FIRST HEARD last year about the new Commando 850 we thought that Norton-Villiers, possessed of a lust for power, were about to unleash an even more powerful version of their already super-quick 750.

And news that a supposedly standard 850 had run the quarter in 12.356 at an international sprint meeting in Holland confirmed our belief.

We were mistaken. The 850 is not an out-and-out performance machine; nor is it intended to be. It has been designed to rectify many of the reliability problems associated with the Combat 750 (see CA, Issue 1), yet still have comparable power.

We think that Norton have succeeded, but only partially. The new 850 is neither as fast nor as quick as the Combat 750; in fact, our test bike would have been hard pushed to beat a standard 750 in a performance test. But it accelerates, handles, and cruises so easily, so lopingly, that it seems as if it would run forever. It is a pretty fair assumption to make that the 850 has closed the reliability gap.

You can instantly distinguish the new 850 by its bolt-through barrels; the 750's head studs did not go right through to the crankcases; the 850's do. This should prevent the all-too-common "popping" of head studs prevalent on earlier models.

There's little room under the solid single back-bone to increase the stroke of the parallel twin engine; besides which, with an 89 mm stroke, the Commando already has one of the highest piston speeds in the business and wears out rings in about 22,000 kilometres.

So the bore has been enlarged from 73 to 77 mm, which, in itself, increases the engine capacity from 745 to 828 cm³. Claimed maximum b.h.p. is 60, developed at 5900 r.p.m., as opposed to the 750's 58 b.h.p. at 6500 r.p.m.

The other major external difference between the 850 and the earlier model Interstate is the balance pipe between the two headers — a Dunstall development aimed at reducing exhaust noise and increasing mid-range torque.

There are, of course, other changes to the motor. Perhaps the most important of these is the redesigned crankcase breather; the breather pipe now exits from the rear of the timing cover (where the maggie used to go in pre-Commando days and where the

Our test bike tracked straight and true round corners.

Road Test

long-awaited starter motor will eventually slot). The old breathing system caused crankcase oil pressure to build up over the safe limit, causing oil leaks. The new one worked well for us; the crankcases didn't leak a drop of oil, even after 50 hard laps at Sydney's Oran Park circuit.

The crankcase also incorporates a removable gauze strainer and magnetic sump plug to pick up iron filings. The flywheel has been modified to compensate for the heavier pistons, and Fag Superblend main bearings (rollers with a slight taper on the ends to eliminate end-float) fitted. The valves now are Stellite tipped for longer life and the valve guides — previously a heat press fit — are retained by circlips. Compression ratio is down from 8.9 to 8.5:1.

There are several other changes but these are only of minor importance. What becomes evident in this list (and there are even more changes to the bike as a whole — 26 of them in all) is that NV are really trying to build a Superbike that will keep on Superbiking — just like the Japanese and Italian machines.

Stylewise the new 850 differs little from the established models. Two 850s will be offered; a roadster and an Interstate. Our test model was the Interstate, finished in candy apple red with double, not single contour lines on the petrol tank.

Breezing through Norton's latest pamphlets we notice that the Fastback — which we regard as the best-looking Norton ever — has been dropped from the range, and won't be available in either 750 or 850 versions. On the positive side, there is a short-stroke 750 in limited production (primarily for racing) which will rev to 8000 and churn out up to 80 b.h.p.

Still, the Interstate 850 is a very pretty bike. The instrument mounts are now longer and finished in black, not silver; there's a grab rail for the pillion passenger and the stop-light has — at last — been enlarged to a reasonable size.

Starting the new 850 gives no indication of the lowered compression; you still have to give a big, healthy heave. It's always best to tickle the carbs before lunging; the new 32 mm Amals are fitted with "water-proof" tickler buttons that are, if nothing else, easier to use than the earlier type. We noticed that the float bowls are fitted with drain plugs too, a big advance.

As long as the correct procedure was followed the big engine would usually spring into life at the first kick, although when warm it becomes a little harder to fire. Then the familiar bobbling and joggling of the Commando motor at idle ensued — a

distinctive trait of the Isolastic suspension set-up.

Very briefly, this is simply a method of rubber mounting the engine and swinging-arm together, thus isolating the engine vibrations from the rider and maintaining good handling characteristics. Everything—engine, gearbox, swinging arm, rear wheel, is suspended from two rubber frame mounts, a torque bracket on the head, and the rear Girling shocks.

A change in the Isolastic system from last year's model is the use of bronze-impregnated PTFE shim washers instead of steel ones. Circlips now hold the spacer buffers in position, and softer, better sealing gaiters are fitted.

All this is very fine, but if the tolerances as specified in the workshop manual are not strictly observed, the bike won't handle and it will vibrate like an Atlas.

Unfortunately, the mounts weren't shimmed up properly on our test bike. The front mount was too tight; the rear one too loose and there was a slight kink in the rear wheel. All of this added up to bad vibration (by to day's standards) at speeds over 64 km/h (40 m.p.h.) and a very insecure feeling at low speeds. In fact, when dawdling through peak-hour traffic the Norton felt like it was hinged in the middle — although it tracked straight and true round corners. The suspension though — a combination of Roadholder forks and Girling shocks — could not be faulted.

Still, all this wasn't sufficient for us not to enjoy the test, particularly the section round Oran Park. The only thing we couldn't get used to was the front brake, which had plenty of feel but just didn't seem to want to stop the bike. Our later braking tests showed that the 850 stops as well as most Superbikes, but that didn't help our lap times, which were extremely disappointing. The Interstate 750 we had along for a comparison check was considerably faster — although that was due in part to its lower gearing (19 tooth countershaft sprocket to the 850's 21).

The 850 also has one degree more rake — 28 instead of 27. This increases the trail slightly and makes the machine more stable at high speeds. We did, actually, find the bike very stable at speed, but coming out of Energol into the main straight it twitched quite noticeably. It wasn't enough to make you alarmed, but you knew it was happening.

On the circuit, we didn't notice the vibration unduly, but when we picked up the bike for the second part of our road test it became far more marked.

However, this is not a distinctive characteristic of the Commando, so

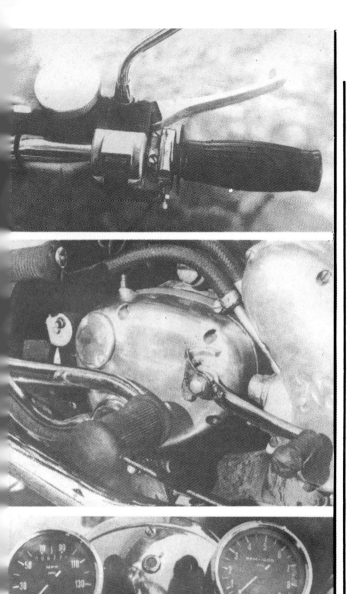

Opposite, top: Narrow profile belies the Commando's capacity.

Opposite, centre: Head studs bolt through to crankcases.

Opposite, bottom: Disc had feel. Note redesigned instrument surrounds.

Top: Lucas' new switches aren't much better than before.

Above: Gearbox and footrest are still the best in the business.

Left: Speedo is hopelessly optimistic. Veglia instruments will soon be standard.

Bottom: 850 bogged badly at the drag strip: 14.00 seconds was the best we could run.

we won't harp on the subject. Suffice it to say that there was some vibration throughout the rev range.

Comfort in other areas was not exceptional, either; the handlebars were too high; the huge 27 litre (6 gal.) tank too wide and the new "aerated pattern" seat too hard. We understand that NV are shortly to bring out an Interstate with scalloped tank which will improve things considerably.

On the positive side, the torque of the 850 was such that taking off from the traffic lights in second or from idle was a snack, and once in the country you just put the bike in top (fourth) and let 'er rip.

The transmission has been upgraded as well as the engine; once again for reliability (it couldn't have been for ease of operation; Norton's AMC gearbox is the best on the market). The gearbox shell is thicker near the main bearing, for more support; the kick-starter is stronger (and, we hope, the pawl at the end of it!) and the clutch has an extra plate.

This clutch is of a diaphragm type, and has always been one of the best. Where the plates used to have friction inserts, however, the five 850 plates are now all-metal. And there's a tab washer to keep the mainshaft bolt inside the clutch itself from coming loose (a 20-minute repair job previously, and impossible without special tools).

Our clutch was reasonably light, though nothing like a Honda Four's. Adjustment of the ball lever on the kick-starter side of the gearbox could have made it even lighter.

Speaking of the clutch lever brings us to the controls and instruments. The instruments were good. The controls were terrible.

Our test bike was fitted with Smiths tacho and speedo, although further 850s will have Veglia instruments. The trouble in Britain is that, both with switches and with instruments, for motor-cycles, there's a monopoly situation. You can go to Smiths and Lucas or you can go jump. In desperation, NV have gone to Italy for their dials; it might make them cheaper but it will do nothing for accuracy. The speedo on our test bike was as accurate as a police unit. If it said you were doing 40 m.p.h. (64 km/h), then that's what you were doing.

On the negative side, the instruments weren't very easy to read during the day and at night things became worse. The tiny bulbs behind the instrument faces illuminate only one side of the dials; you operate in the dark if you want to run the motor faster or travel at more than 80 km/h.

The Lucas "space age" switches are supposed to have been improved.

Actually, all that has happened is that the blinker and light switches have been lengthened. It hasn't made them any better. On the right-hand bar are a kill button (only kills the motor while your thumb is on it), a nothing button, and the indicators (a mistake, this, it makes throttle operation coming into crossroads very difficult). On the left-hand bar are the headlight switch, horn and headlight flasher buttons. Only the latter two are satisfactory. If we bought a Norton we'd be tempted to replace the lot.

Between the instruments nestle an alternator warning light and the high beam indicator which, for some abstruse reason, is green. There's also a switch for the headlight.

When you come to park the bike you'll find another good thing, and another bad thing, about the Norton. The good thing is the main-stand, which has been revamped with a stiffer return spring and is easy to lift the bike onto. The bad thing is the side-stand, which is easy for anyone over 6' 3" to operate, but nearly impossible for anyone shorter. We finally got the hang of it — you push it down nearly as far as you can while sitting on the bike and then kick it. Most times it will travel forward and stay there.

Oil leaks have always been a problem with the Commandos, but the 850 was pretty well oil-tight. The only problem was the rear chain oiler, which was very much over-active and blanketed the area behind the rider's feet with lubricant. Quite a bit also ran down the underside of the primary chaincase and dripped onto the ground.

The oiler is supposedly prevented from this sort of thing by a length of plastic pipe stuffed with absorbent material. If NV can't make the padding thicker they'd be better off removing the oiler completely, and letting the owner look after the chain himself.

The exhaust pipes are the now-familiar Interstate type but kinked in more; although we ground the left-hand foot-peg down considerably at Oran Park the pipe did not touch. Not so, however, the main-stand; it took a hiding.

The bike emitted an even more subdued sound than the Interstate, which in turn was more subdued than the Roadster. The pipes look a little odd, but they seem to work. The header flanges are fastened more securely, now, and are stronger (stories of pipes coming loose on the earlier models are legion).

The mudguards are stainless steel, rather than chromed steel. This may be a step forward, but the shoddy, matt silver stays are definitely retro-

grade. They spoil what is otherwise the nicest front end in the business.

Materials have also changed for the tank and side-covers. New laws in England prohibited the manufacture of fibreglass fuel tanks so Norton changed to steel, and they obviously decided to throw in the side-covers for good measure. The bigger bore and other changes, though, mean that the 850 Interstate weighs in at 196 kg. (430lb.), some 16 kg. more than the 750 Combat model we tested last year! Fortunately, this is still well below most other 750s, and the 850 did not seem to be an unduly heavy bike.

One side-cover can, with some difficulty, be removed by undoing a Dzus fastener. Inside are the sturdy, if somewhat crude-looking tools. The other houses the oil tank. You have to lift off the seat to fill or check the tank — relatively easy, just undo the knurled knob on either side and pull backwards; the first Nortons had slots going straight up and down the seat brackets and the seat could work loose. This seat won't, but it rocked under hard acceleration. Carrying a pillion passenger pushed the seat firmly down into the frame rear guards, obviating the rocking.

Well, that's the Norton in general terms. It shaped up pretty well, although machine preparation was not all it could have been. And neither, as it turned out, was the state of tune.

Our bike was pretty lean on kilometres when we took it to Castlereagh International Dragway for some quarter-mile runs. The clock showed just 1000 km. (615 miles), but the thrashing round Oran Park under NV's supervision had loosened it up quite well and the machine was showing no signs of ill-running.

We were looking for 12s. We couldn't find 13s. Our first run was the best — 14.00/91.46. We tried two riders, and varying tyre pressures, and a number of different off-the-line techniques, without much success. The terminal speed improved to 95.23 m.p.h., but the e.t.s. slowed to 14.20. It was disappointing, to say the least.

The main trouble was that the 850 bogged terribly coming off the line. Slipping or feeding the clutch was not the solution. The quickest quarters came from revving the engine up to around 6500, leaning right forward, and dropping the clutch. But about ten metres out of the hole everything stopped happening and the revs dropped to about 3000 before picking up again.

There were a number of things operating against the bike. Firstly, the paucity of kilometres on the clock. Secondly, the Dunlop K81 tyres (which were great for handling but

aren't sticky enough for quick e.t.s) And thirdly, the 21-tooth countershaft sprocket, two teeth up on the optimum 19-toother.

Still, terminal speeds were not such that we could have dropped into the 12s, even with those things remedied. And our (later) top speed runs showed that the bike's poor drag strip showing was no random error.

At Oran Park the bike had refused to run past about 6200 r.p.m. in third — a little over 150 km/h (93 m.p.h.). And with well over a kilometre run-up, it would not go past 161 km/h (100 m.p.h.) in either third or top. That was it. 6600 r.p.m. in third, 6000 in top.

In a way, that makes sense — but only in a way. Peak power and torque are both developed below 6000 r.p.m., meaning that there's less to push you along at higher revs. Still, overseas tests have reported speeds of 193 km/h (120 m.p.h.) without too much effort. And 161 k.p.h. is pretty poor for a Superbike. To say nothing of a Superplus bike.

Low-down acceleration was still up with the best, though, despite the bogging. We recorded a best 0-100 km/h time of 5.2 seconds, well up in its class.

Our brake tests were slightly below average, once again indicating that our earlier feelings about the bike at Oran Park were fairly correct. Average stopping distance from 50 km/h was 8 m (26' 4"); from 100 km/h, 38 m (124' 10"). The trouble was, you needed too much lever pressure to get the front wheel to slow (it never locked). At least you can be sure that those figures are accurate; the disc stopped just as well each time and even the s.l.s. drum rear brake only faded slightly over a number of crash halts. We understand that NV have beefed up this rear brake a little.

Well, that was it. What sort of a package does the Commando 850 add up to?

The engine improvements should do a great deal to make the bike more reliable. With a fuel consumption of 17 k.p.l. (48.1 m.p.g.), the machine has a range of at least 450 kilometres (280 miles), putting it in the real long distance touring category.

For the round-town playboy, there's also the roadster version with the 11 litre (2½ gal.) tank — not the best for touring but it won't suffer from altered handling as the tank empties.

We believe that the 850, properly set up, will run both faster and quicker than our test bike, that it will handle better and have less vibration.

The disturbing thing is that there are a lot of bikes around today that will also do all those things. And many of them will do them for less than $1735. ●

engine

Type	parallel twin o.h.v. four-stroke
Bore and stroke	77 x 89 mm.
Displacement	828 cm³
Compression ratio	8.5:1
Claimed max. b.h.p.	60 @ 5900 r.p.m.
Claimed max. torque:	N.A.
Carburation	two 32 mm. Amal concentrics

dimensions

Length	2230 mm. (88 in.)
Wheelbase	1450 mm. (57 in.)
Width	660 mm. (26 in.)
Weight (dry)	196 kg. (430 lb.)
Fuel tank	27 litres (6 gal.)
Oil (dry sump)	5 litres (3 pts.)
Tyres (front)	4.10 x 19 Dunlop K81
(rear)	4.10 x 19 Dunlop K81

Norton Commando 850 Interstate

In an effort to make their Commando reliable, Norton seem to have slowed down what was a very fast bike to a mediocre level. Handling and braking are good. But we'll reserve our judgement until we get a chance to ride the machine again.

transmission

Primary drive	Triplex chain
Clutch	wet, five metal plates, diaphragm-type
Gear ratios (overall)	1st: 11.20:1
	2nd: 7.45:1
	3rd: 5.30:1
	4th: 4.38:1
Primary reduction ratio	2.19:1
Secondary reduction ratio	2:1
Brakes (front)	272 mm. (10.7 in.) disc
(rear)	180 mm. (7 in.) s.l.s. drum

performance

Ss ¼-mile	14.00/91.46 m.p.h.
0-100 k.p.h.	5.2 s.
Top speed	161 km/h (100 m.p.h.)
Braking: 50 km/h-0.	8 m. (26' 4")
100 km/h-0	38 m. (124' 10")
Fuel consumption	17 k.p.l. (47.7 m.p.g).

distribution

Test bike suppliers	Norton Villiers Motorcycles Pty. Ltd., 25 Moxon Rd., Punchbowl, N.S.W. 2196.
Price	$1735 without reg. and insurance
Options fitted	none
Warranty	6 months/5000 miles

NORTON COMMAND

BY PETE SCATCHARD

NORTON'S lone runner in the roadster motorcycle stakes has been with the buying public for some seven years now.

The Commando 750 having now been replaced by the 850, readers may question the value of a long-term assessment of the former. However, the two machines do share the bulk of components, so we felt that many of the remarks appertaining to the little 'un could be read across to big brother, and such a report could thus prove of value to those contemplating the purchase of a new machine as well as those scouring through the second-hand market.

Heart of the machine is a pushrod OHV vertical twin engine, unfashionably over square, driving an equally unfashionable four-speed box via a triplex primary chain and dry multi-plate diaphragm spring clutch. The engine/transmission package is mounted in a spine type frame via the patented Isolastic rubbers, permitting movement in the vertical plane, thus absorbing engine vibration, wide thrust faces allied with close (10 thou) clearances in the mounts preventing movement in the horizontal plane that could otherwise make for interesting handling. A stripped down version of the long established Roadholder fork clutches a Norton-Lockheed disc braked front wheel, while the rear end is suspended by a pair of Girling shocks. Onto this basic machine is bolted a variety of tanks, seats, exhaust systems, side covers, handlebars and headlamps to form the current range of Roadster, Interstate, Hi-Rider and JP Replica versions, although Fastback, LR, S Type and SS variants have also been produced.

Despite the antiquated design, based on Bert Hopwood's 1947 Model 7, there's no shortage of effort from the big motor, whatever its detail form. The standard

750 mill runs on an 8.9 to 1 cr, a thicker solid copper or aluminium head gasket offering reductions down to below 8 to 1. The Combat motor uses the same pistons and a remachined head to achieve a cr of 10.2 to 1, breathing through two 32mm Amal Concentrics in place of the standard 30mm affairs. Perhaps the most unusual feature of the Norton Heavyweight twin motor is the integral head and rocker box, the rockers being located in the main head casting through the tappet inspection covers on press fit spindles sealed by small cover plates. Exhaust pipes are located in the head by large finned gland nuts, screwing directly into the casting. These form probably the biggest single source of irritation in the engine design, since despite the adoption of solid iron gaskets and a tab washer to lock gland nut to head, the exhaust pipes can be found jangling merrily away every 1,000 miles or so, whereupon a special spanner of monstrous proportions is required, plus a modicum of care to avoid overtightening and stripping of the threads. Solid skirt pistons featuring two compression rings, the top one chromed, and a Triflex oil control ring run in a bore machined directly from the cast-iron block.

Bore wear is minimal, the large paper element air filter effectively preventing the normal air-borne abrasive particles from doing their usual worst. Stellite tipped valves run in cast-iron guides, the inlets fitted with oil seal caps to overcome oil burning problems experienced at one time, large diameter aluminium push rods transmitting the cam lift via cam followers running in bores machined in the front of the block. The camshaft, buried in the front of the crankcases, runs in phosphor-bronze bushes, driven by a short chain. This requires checking for tension every

O 25,000 miles on

10,000 miles or so, and replacing about every 30,000 — no large expense or great effort is required, but it's another niggle regarding the engine design, and by the time twin sprockets, a chain and the necessary slipper adjuster had been fitted it would surely have been cheaper from a production angle to utilise gear pinions to transmit rotation from crankshaft to camshaft.

If chains are to be used, an external and preferably automatic tensioner should be incorporated, as per Honda OHC drive systems, as the present set up requires the contact breaker unit to be removed, and thus the engine retimed every time the tension's checked! The valve actuating mechanism is virtually bulletproof, although there are the occasional tales of stellite tips coming adrift from the followers, accompanied by interesting noises!

Major source of Commando engine problems has been the crank assembly, a forged steel bolted up crankshaft running in roller bearings. Being but a two-bearing affair, crankwhip occurs at high revs, causing the edges of the rollers to take more than their fair share of the load, breaking up the hardened tracks. The problem's been eliminated by the adoption of Fagg "Superblend" bearings, the rollers featuring a slight taper, thus eliminating the line contact. Con-rods are forged aluminium with steel big-end caps, the big ends being white metal backed plain bearings. Gudgeon pins run direct in the small-end eye, this and the big-end assembly being accepted as almost 100 per cent reliable.

End result of all this is a motor producing a claimed 60 bhp (SAE) at 6,500 rpm, redlined at 7,000, with peak torque at approx 5,000. These figures, allied to a dry weight of 415 lbs should mean some very adequate performance, and sure enough it

goes! Quick rather than stunningly fast, there's a regular indicated 110 mph available, with the bonus of approaching 120 with everything set as per book, and some mucho rapido acceleration up to 90 or so, at which point things start to quieten down. Norton claim a 0-60 time of just under five seconds, but as with most such figures it's a trifle academic — you need a nice Shell Grip surface, a quarter mile of straight, clear road and a healthy lack of mechanical sympathy to achieve such figures. Suffice to say that there's little, if anything, that'll stay with you out of the box, initial acceleration being rather quicker than a Honda 750's, but tailing off a little earlier than the Four.

The outstanding engine characteristic is the tremendous torque that the tall motor produces. It'll pull from a mere 1,000 rpm, while at two grand the throttle can be opened back to the stop without inducing a trace of fluffing, pulling smoothly until at about 3,500 the engine note changes and the mill really starts to soar away. Such willingness to pull from low revs proves a real boon in heavy traffic, and is ideal for winding through mountain roads, when the machine can be left in third gear all day, providing a 15-90 mph speed range.

It is therefore unfortunate that, while isolating the rider from the ever-present vibration at higher revs, the Isolastic mount's limited flexibility allows the large amplitude, low frequency vibration at low revs to be transmitted to the cycle parts. To be fair, this is hardly felt as vibration, more as a low down rumbling judder, and that's not apparent on small throttle openings below 2,000 rpm. The judder's at its worst when accelerating from low revs up to 3,500, when the mirrors are really a-tingle, then all of a sudden, the rhythm of the engine

matches the resonance of the Isolastic units and, just like flicking a switch, the "bad vibes" are but a memory, remaining so from there on up.

Above 3½ grand, the mounts really do their work, and the rider's totally isolated from the still vibrating engine, although still, of course, subject to shocks and judders from the suspension, this being more noticeable than usual due to the absence of other rider stimulii! The price to be paid is in the maintenance of the Isolastics, as the gap twixt spacer and mounting requires frequent checking and adjustment by shimming if the normal standard of handling is to be expected. Not a difficult job, the manufacturer recommends checking at 10,000 mile intervals, but this is little short of ludicrous — a 2,000 mile interval is about the maximum one can manage before excessive sideplay becomes apparent and a few more, very cheap shims are required. This kind of constant need for maintenance is one of the things one seems to have to accept on British bikes, though it would seem technically quite feasible to design either a no wear or self adjusting system.

Long regarded as the mass production experts on handling, and with good reason with such stalwarts as the Garden Gate and Featherbed frames under their belt, Norton dropped the long established full duplex frame in order to introduce the rubber mounted Commando, a complete re-design being essential to enable the swinging arm to be joined rigidly to the engine/gearbox unit, thus preserving the fixed relationship between the transmission components, yet permitting this "powerhouse" package to be flexibly mounted in the frame via the Isolastic bushing. Not unnaturally, the first question asked was not the usual "Wot'll it do?" — after all, the

engine was basically Atlas, but "Wot's it 'andle like?"

Comparisons were invariably made with the Featherbed, mostly uncomplimentary, but after a while many previously Featherbed owning riders started to revise their opinions. To judge, it's perhaps wiser and fairer to do so by performance, rather than by comparison. In its day, the Featherbed ruled supreme, together, in my opinion, with the Velo, marked by a very heavy front end, giving rock like stability on bumpy bends; today, the Commando must come right at the top of the heavyweight's handling tree, although its characteristics in this department are totally different.

A light front end produces a slight waggling of the bars at low speed, noticeable when riding one handed, and a delicate feel at high speed — a new approach is required, a sensitive one, reliant more on backside and foot than arm steering, but once one's learnt the technique and one's initial anxiety at this rather nervous feel to the steering reassured, it's predictable and very, very good. Ground clearance is positively massive, although large bumps when heavily laden and laid down round steep left handers produces interesting noises from the centre stand's roll-on extension.

Bumpy bends tend to cause the machine to wander a little, while heavily loaded it's possible to be nearly flung off hitting deep ruts when well cranked over and screwing it hard, though this only happens when one's perhaps asking a little much from a machine loaded to the hilt, set up for long distance touring and being caned hard, when the rear end goes coil-bound.

Suspension is in the normal British tradition, taut and hard, perhaps not to quite the extent

NORTON
COMMANDO 25,000 miles c

practised by the Italians, but a far cry from most Japanese machines' characteristics. Minor road irregularities are transmitted straight through to the rider, while larger craters frequently require longer travel than is provided. Heavier riders may find the ride rather better, as matters improve immensely two up (10 stone rider, 8½ stone pillion) and the bike loses much of its "tip-toe" feeling. Taken all round, the suspension proves adequate for nearly all riding conditions, only the worst Continental potholes, crossed two up and heavily laden producing bottoming, but not actively comfortable.

Comfort could also be improved in the seating department, there being inadequate padding to cope with 300-mile plus runs without the old numb . . . , though Interstate and Roadster versions feature somewhat thicker foam. Overall riding position's reasonably good with the European bars fitted, a slight forward lean, footrests about right for my five foot eight inches, though taller riders usually complain they're too far forward, the penalty for non-adjustable pegs, and the foot controls are easily fitted to the individual's requirements.

Any machine's handling characteristics being to some extent a compromise between low speed comfort, soft and wallowy, and high speed stability, the Commando obviously opts for the top end of the spectrum. It's disappointing, therefore, to find that just when the discomfort of the low speed hardness should pay off in terms of rock steady high-speed handling, there's that nervous, twitchy feeling. However, the trick's to relax and *not* to fight it — all's OK once one accept the fact that there's nowt dangerous about it, but it does require getting used to, and doubtless explains the varied accounts of Commando handling.

Most of the braking action's provided by the front disc, hydraulically actuated by a handlebar mounted master cylinder. Fluid is pumped to the twin pistons in the heavily ribbed cast aluminium caliper unit bolted to the right-hand fork leg, applying the two circular disc pads to the cast-iron disc. Lever pressure's on the heavy side; it's thus easy to come to a finely controlled

gradual halt, with no risk of sudden wheel locking on nasty surfaces, although emergency retardation requires considerable effort.

However, under such conditions there's never any difficulty in obtaining maximum retardation, and it's always possible to lock the front wheel up under really hefty braking. One becomes rapidly used to the pressure required, the relationship between lever pressure and braking force being totally predictable, and this rider's never run out of brakes in nearly 25,000 miles of hectic riding, other than through brake failure, of which more anon. Pad wear, however, it extremely rapid in poor weather conditions, three sets of pads having been chewed through at approx 3,500 mile intervals, this increasing to a 10,000-15,000 mile life in rain free conditions. At £1.20 a set, it's no great expense, but a retro-fit stainless steel wiper blade system is being introduced, and pad life should undoubtedly be greatly improved. The cast-iron disc, dull chromium plated, rusts at the slightest opportunity, and this surface rust is scattered all over the front end of the bike when the pads are subsequently applied.

Despite the excellent coefficient of friction afforded by cast iron, it's high time that an answer was found to this problem, and indeed stainless steel discs are rumoured to be on their way. Oval cross-sectioned front fork legs, massive spokes and a substantial spindle prevent fork twist under heavy braking, and this together with the grippy 4.10 x 19 TT100 boot enable full use to be made of the braking power. Maintenance is extremely simple, a clamp bolt and one nut securing the front wheel, whose removal enables pad changing to be accomplished in a couple of minutes. Pad wear can be checked without removing either wheel or caliper assembly, a task which must be accomplished regularly in wet weather as it has proved possible to eject pads under braking before the warning singing of metal to metal, disc on pad backing material, occurs — result no brake!

At the back, a 7 inch single leading shoe stopper is incorporated in the final drive sprocket. Operated by cable, it's an unex-

citing contributor to the overall braking. There's little or no risk of a clumsy hoof locking the rear end up under heavy braking, and its real use is limited to preventing the back from hopping around too much, and to coming to a gentle halt in traffic. The combined brake/chain wheel, allied to a system of paddles, enables the rear wheel, complete with transmission shock absorbing pads to be removed by merely withdrawing the rear wheel spindle ie one nut — at least, that's the theory, but the exhaust system gets in the way, so the silencer rubber bolts have to be disconnected, a further two nuts.

However, it's still a genuinely QD system, eliminating the need for realignment etc on replacement. Like the easy front wheel removal (necessary for frequent disc pad renewal) it's just as well the task's a doddle, as the plastic shock absorber inserts require inspection at 10,000 mile intervals, and believe me, at 10,000 mile intervals, they require replacement! Again, not expensive at £1.20 the set, or difficult to achieve, but a niggling annoyance, a poor substitute for a properly thought out, decently constructed shock absorber.

Rather on the heavy side, the clutch nevertheless can stand hefty abuse, and although long periods of clutch slipping like on rough tracks results in excessive lever clearance appearing, with subsequent drag, when cool normal clearances are restored. Plate wear in 25,000 miles is practically nil despite several attempts at burning the thing out, while the new all-metal clutch promises even longer life. Clutch dismantling can only be achieved with the aid of a diaphragm spring compressor, but as compensation there's no need to adjust springs to achieve parallel plate disengagement, thus effecting considerable maintenance time savings.

Adjustment is simplicity itself, a cap in the primary chaincase allowing access to the operating pushrod adjusting screw and locknut. Cable adjustment is at the handlebar end, and can be easily accomplished whilst on the move. The Achilles heel of the clutch department is the cable itself, exposure to foul weather rapidly converting a clutch already on the heavy side to a real bicep

developer, eventually resulting in nipple popping, the cable's that is! With no provision incorporated for oiling the cable, it's an unwelcome fag to strip out the cable, connect up lubricator, etc, etc, ad nauseam. Whilst appreciating that the incorporation of an oil nipple would doubtless add immeasurably to the factory's costs, it would result in far fewer complaints being directed at the clutch, although the current 850s include modifications to the withdrawal mechanism, lightening the actuating pressure.

Primary chain tensioning is achieved by checking through one of the aforementioned caps, then moving the gearbox back or forth by means of a draw bolt — sounds simple when you say it fast and indeed is, but for the location of the engine feed and return oil pipes, which effectively prevent a spanner being placed on the adjusting nuts! It's fortunate that the triplex chain rarely requires adjustment, perhaps every 5,000 miles, the final drive chain seemingly absorbing all the punishment. At 25,000 miles approximately half the gearbox adjustment has been utilised, and a primary chain life of 40-50,000 miles is thus entirely practicable. Rear chain is rather a different kettle o' haddock, 7,000 miles having proved about the limit, not bad by current standards, especially considering the relatively small dimensions of the Renold's unit, due doubtless to the frequently over-enthusiastic chain oiler fitted, which also protects the rear of the machine from any suspicion of rust, and effectively waterproofs pillion riders' boots.

This problem is intensified by the totally inadequate chain guard fitted, its straight top edge preventing any of the oil flung off by centrifugal force where the chain wraps itself round the final drive sprocket from being retained, though the Mk 1A 850s are slightly improved here — when, oh when, will we get away from these foul exposed rear chains? MZ, on machines costing around the £200 mark have shown everyone that a full enclosure chaincase can be simple, effective, and damn it all, actually *attractive*, unlike some of the rather heavy looking examples of the late 50s and early 60s.

The gearbox dates from the

above period, but despite its white hairs performs as well as any. A little sensitive to clutch adjustment, chain tensions etc, cog swapping's a delight when all's in harmony, the clutch a superfluity once under way. Standard ratios are semi-close, revving the motor to 6,500 or 7,000 rpm in each gear before changing dropping the revs to 4,500-5,000, smack into the maximum torque band.

Overall gearing may be altered by swapping gearbox output sprockets, this necessitating the removal of the primary drive, a simple enough task providing a sprocket puller and the previously mentioned diaphragm spring compressor are available, but hardly encouraging frequent monkeying around — still, at least gearing can be altered, which is more than can be said for many machines. On the 21-tooth sprocket that's normally fitted on UK models, gearing's very slightly on the high side, max revs only being available in top with everything absolutely spot-on, but making for relaxed cruising, 90 mph representing 5,300 rpm. For the maximum practical acceleration for road use, a 19-tooth sprocket is fitted, but this limits top speed to around 108 mph, lowers the comfortable cruising speed and adds to tyre, fuel and chain bills.

All in all, the transmission is robust and pleasant to use, simple to maintain and theoretically easy to adjust, but it's spoilt by a lack of cable oiler, oil pipe obstruction of the primary chain adjustment mechanism, and rather irksome rear wheel adjusting screws. It's a pity that the rear brake outer cable stop is mounted on the swinging arm, rather than on the brake plate, as cable readjustment is therefore required each time the chain's adjusted, about every 500 miles. Allied to the torquey engine characteristics, the four speeds are totally adequate, first low enough to all but eliminate clutch slipping in heavy traffic; while maximum revs can just be reached in top with everything set 100 per cent as per book, a speed of almost 120 mph, yet no gaps are apparent in the flow of acceleration through the cogs.

Long the subject of innumerable bitter jokes, the electrics of the Commando are 100 per cent Joe Lucas, with the exception of the battery, now a Yashua. Standard equipment is a resin encapsulated alternator, silicone rectifier and solid-state zener diode providing the charge side of the picture, a seven-inch headlamp with integral pilot bulb, stop/tail lamp, currently of immense proportions to comply with our Transatlantic friends legislation, trafficators and instrument illumination all attempting to discharge the battery, aided by the twin point, twin 6-volt coil, ballast resistor ignition set-up. Controlling this little lot is a four-position switch, off and parking lights only allowing key withdrawal, ignition only and lights and ignition retaining the key.

Switching to lights and ignition brings a headlamp shell mounted switch into the game. The usual left-hand Lucas handlebar switch flips from dip to main beam, with headlamp flasher button above and horn push below. A matching console on the right bar controls the indicators, one button killing the ignition, the other sitting idle at present, waiting for the long promised electric starter to be fitted!

The lights are all more than adequate, the optional Lucas QH 60/55 watt headlamp being a real beaut, punching out a great tunnel of pure white on main beam, with a fairly well defined dip pattern illuminating the kerb without provoking protests from

NORTON
COMMANDO 25,000 miles on

other road users. An idiot light mounted in the headlamp shell warns of main beam, while matching ignition and trafficator lamps are also fitted. These are well chosen, being bright enough to see in all but the most brilliant sunshine, without being distracting at night. Brake light switches are fitted to both front and rear operating mechanisms, the rear a sprung-loaded plunger, the front a hydraulically operated one.

The generating system is simple but effective, having no moving parts but for the alternator rotor, and no bearing surfaces to wear. One complaint that can be directed here is the relatively low output of some 110 watts which prevents the running of a two-beam or second headlamp unless a large capacity battery, capable of sustaining a slight discharge for reasonable periods of time is substituted for the standard 7½ amp hour job. Another gripe is the quality of the twin leaded cable emerging from the encapsulating material of the stator. Subjected to considerable heat and continually splattering with hot oil, the cable rapidly becomes extremely brittle and great care must be taken should alternator removal be necessary to prevent cracking. This has been the case since Lucas introduced the bike alternator, back in the 50s, but in these days of advanced plastics technology there can surely no longer be any excuse for this sort of thing.

So far, the Lucas electrics have acquitted themselves well, being functionally excellent and reliable, but they're let down in the sparks department. The contact breaker unit has caused many a holed piston and burnt valve in the past, through timing slip due to mechanical wear, but Lucas have beefed up the unit and claim to have licked the problem. Having fitted Boyer's tranny ignition, it's not been possible to verify the claim, but general opinion is that there's justification for it, though matters could still be further improved. Timing, thanks to a built-in scale viewed through a cap in the primary chaincase, is simplicity itself, permitting stroboscope readings to be made in seconds.

Final moan must be regarding the awful, tatty after-thought of a wiring harness that's fitted, Lucas apparently supplying but one

loom, to also fit the Triumph Trident triples, so various wires are surplus to requirements on a twin pot motor left hanging loose, their ends "protected" by silly strips of insulating tape.

Returning to the bike as a whole, detail finish is poor, but for certain exceptions. The major engine castings are rough and ready sand castings, cheap and easy to alter it's true, but presenting a surface cratered like that of the moon on the cylinder head and barrels. Some, however, are nicely polished out, like tha chaincase outer and the fork legs, but even they have their rough spots where the buff couldn't reach, and certainly don't present the razor-sharp finish and consistency of die castings. Unlike most Japanese machines, the polished ally has no plastic coating to protect it from attack by the elements, OK if you're a Solvol freak, not so good if, like me, you believe that a bike should come up gleaming after but a sudsy wash and hose down.

However, there's therefore not the problem of removing peeling plastic once the coating breaks down, as inevitably it does. Paint and chrome, too, are delicate

finishes on the Norton, exceptions being at the lower end and at the back where the copious chain oiler and blown back engine drips see to protection. Spoke and spoke nipples suffer terribly, being but cadmium plated as are most of the nuts and bolts, soon reduced to hideous rust. Only real praise that can go to the finish is offered to the glass-fibre ware, the tank, tail faring and side panels, this being of great thickness, has a lovely deep, smooth, colour impregnated surface and is nicely tidied up round the edges.

So how's it all behaved over some 25,000 miles? Well . . . we started with oil all over the right boot but 10 miles from picking it up — porous cylinder head casting, though how it wasn't picked up during the famous final road test given every bike leaving the factory I'll never know. Replacement was accomplished the next day, top marks to the factory's service department. Replaced under warranty were a number of components whose finish just disintegrated, notably the chromed fork stanchions, the flaking chrome then wearing out the fork oil seals. At 8,000 miles an exhaust valve burnt out, probably

my fault, setting too tight a tappet clearance.

At about about 11,000, the transmission shock absorbers packed up, then rear wheel spokes started to snap at regular intervals, and despite a rebuild, continue to do so today when travelling fast, two up and loaded. The kickstarter pawl then wore out at 14,000, at 18,000 the oil control rings called it a day and were replaced, and at 20,000 one of the main bearings threw in the towel. Add to that oil leaks here, there and everywhere, prop and centre stands breaking and sundry other minor niggles, and one could hardly accuse the Commando of being dull! Most of these faults were accelerated by the long, fast, heavily laden travelling being done, but under similar circumstances I very much doubt if say a Honda 750/4 would have suffered as badly.

Servicing wasn't neglected, although that too is required rather more often than I'd like, especially chain and Isolastic adjustments. Fuel consumption under such conditions varied between 40 and 50 mpg, pretty reasonable by current standards, and could be improved up to the 60s with careful riding. Even trying, I doubt if it's possible to get much below 40 to the gallon, one of the four stroke's advantages. Oil consumption, assuming rings and seals OK, worked out at around 1,000 mp pint, most of that going through the rear chain oiler.

In summing up the Commando one can best perhaps describe it as cheap and cheerful. Cheap in price (for these inflated days), cheap in finish, but also in consumables like tyres and chains, not as disastrously priced as some, nor so often required, and at least readily available. Cheerful too, when it's going — I still know of very, very few bikes that are as nice to ride as a properly set-up Commando, R90S, Honda 4 etc included, while the performance is as much as most can use. As a functional piece of machinery it's got some excellent points, but it's let down by silly faults, poor attention to detail, and poor quality finish. At current prices, it's probably a fair buy; after all, you can't afford to make a silk purse out of a sow's ear!

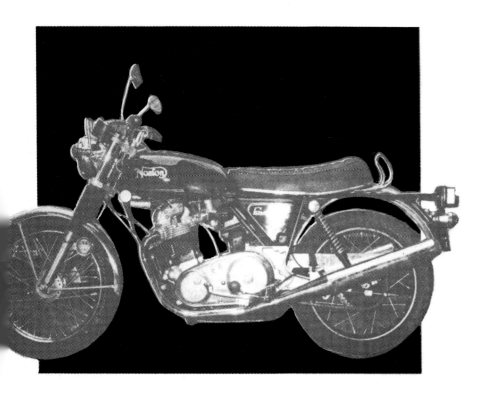

If anybody ever needed a cure for a power complex, Norton have just made it. After only a few miles the latest Commando variant lets you know that you've got more on tap than anyone else in the county. The message comes over so strong that even a megalomaniac would be content just pottering about, secure in the knowledge that it's there when he needs it.

Traffic light type performance is the kind that makes owners of Dino Ferraris start looking at the small print in their guarantees.

If you think this sounds a bit sensational and also, quite rightly, that there are other machines with as much going for them, there's an answer. When you start really trying, as opposed to the traffic light stuff, there's lots more to come. Have a look at Sport Scene on page 27 and you'll see how Dave Rawlins on a slightly modded 2A ran an 11.53 quarter. And by raising the gear-

CATCH THE 850

Norton introduce the uprated mk 2A Commando

ing and lowering the rider he pulled over 142 mph not long ago.

The results of the 850's development are now in the shops, the most obvious refinements being the new styling. The new tanks, handlebars and upswept pipes make the 850 look a lot better than earlier models, and I hear that you can now get the wheel spindle out without stripping the exhaust.

The tank on our model was the small 2½ gallon one, but the larger Interstate tank is available. On the new models the big tank has had a section removed from the centre, it still looks the same but isn't so uncomfortably wide at the rear. The tank on our demonstrator gave an adequate range, but had an irritatingly small reserve which allowed less than 10 miles before drying up.

. Starting the Norton up required something of a knack, especially from under a layer of frost, but things were definitely hindered by the low-geared kick-start. Doing things properly and having the machine off the centre-stand concentrated all the kicking effort into squashing the rear springs. An electric start would at least have saved the neighbours from some pretty original exclamations.

The 850 needed careful warming for a minute or so and a little juggling of the choke once under way. Half a mile down the road it would start responding properly and the choke could be backed right off.

The riding position is an improvement on earlier models, mainly due to the flatter bars which give much more comfort at speed, and the narrower tank. The footrests could have been an inch or two further back, and it would have been nice to have some adjustment on them. The seat has also been changed, the new one being harder — there is still more than enough room for a passenger and it gives a comfortable ride in the main. Over very rough surfaces the seat,

coupled with the firm rear suspension does let the rider get jolted about.

The front suspension seemed a little soft, in comparison, and tended to top too easily. It could either have been underdamped on rebound, or possibly just too soft to match the rear springing.

For pottering about, or weaving through traffic, the bulk of the 850 was no problem. The front had a tendency to wander slightly at low speeds, especially when a passenger was carried, but it could be manoeuvred easily enough. It pulls a high gear, and while the motor would pull away from an indicated 1,500 rpm, it didn't like being plonked, which meant that in traffic it spent all of its time in the low gears. (1,500 in top is about 26 mph anyway.)

The gearing is now higher overall, a feature which suits the long-legged character of the 850, and the four ratios are just about right for fast road riding.

The motor hit a vibration peak at around 2,300, where it gets really chunky and everything shakes. But as it pulls up through 3,000 it smooths out and the shakes disappear never to be seen again all the way up to the red line. This high speed smoothness seems to be a function of the big Norton motor, I've ridden three versions, all of which showed the same characteristics.

The almost uncanny smoothness coupled with the equally efficient intake and exhaust silencing perfectly matches the swift, silent character of the 2A. It also lends a gentle deceptiveness to the machine's performance; once the motor is under way in the tall top gear, you are really moving.

6,000 rpm in top is a quiet 106 mph and there's only the wind to let you know about it.

The throttle still has to be turned too far to get it right open, but using anything over half-throttle will whisk you up to the 100 mph level with no hesitation. As we said with earlier Com-

mandos, acceleration is *the* strong point even when overgeared.

It is geared to pull 124 mph at 7,000 in top. For practical purposes this allows 100 mph cruising, and on the track we reached a true 110 mph.

Some time back Norton altered the head angle, and improved the handling by cutting down the tendency for the front to get light and wobble. The 2A still shows this tendency slightly and the handling takes a little getting used to. Once the rider has got some confidence in the machine it can be thrown about quite happily. I discovered on the track that the harder you push it the better the handling gets. It only fights back when the rider gets a bit indecisive and starts to ease off halfway through a turn.

Roadholding is very good, you can put the 850 on a line and it will keep its nose pointing just where you aimed it no matter what. For normal use there's ample ground clearance, on the track we found the prop stand would ground on left handers, while the spring lug on the stand would dig in on bumpy left-handers.

Both brakes are good, well-matched and up to the performance of the machine. Initially, the back brake seemed over-keen, later it improved but it's debatable whether this was the rider getting used to it or the brake bedding in. The front one was strong enough to make the tyre moan and could lock the wheel up at virtually any speed, although we didn't press this point too far.

One point I didn't like was that the non-adjustable front brake lever was heavy in operation, like all of the other controls. While they all work smoothly and sweetly, in particular the clutch, they have this heavy operation — even the gearshift was a bit notchy. On one occasion I had to ride back and forth across central London a couple of times and after an hour or two of that kind of

traffic the controls got fairly tiring. In traffic or on the open road the fuel consumption was fair, averaging around the 50 mpg mark if you weren't being very economy conscious. The small tank gave no problems in and around town, but I wouldn't trust it on a motorway run without keeping a very careful check on the fuel level.

The detail finish on the 850 could be better; the switches are not positioned very well, the mirrors give too blurred an image at all speeds and the ignition switch, with its soft plastic shroud (presumably to keep out water) is almost impossible with cold fingers, while fumbling about with the key it is also too easy to switch on to parking lights.

The lights themselves are excellent. Norton fit a QH headlamp which really lights up the way and has a nicely spread dipped beam with a sharp cut-off. In fact all of the electrics are well up to the job, if a burst from the flasher doesn't clear your way, a blast on the horn will.

Back on the subject of details I gather that Norton are *still* planning panniers or some form of luggage carrying equipment for their machines . . .

During our test the oil consumption was almost negligible, the motor losing some through the tank breather and showing slight leak under the chaincase.

The 2A, as a refined version of the earlier 850, is a quicker, quieter and generally better thought-out machine. There's still room for detail improvements, but the basic machine fits very nicely into the slot reserved for long distance runners with as much power as you need, or can legally use.

JOHN ROBINSON

DEVELOPMENT

The Mk. 2A Norton 850 is the result of nine months' hard work by the Wolverhampton Experimental shop. Information

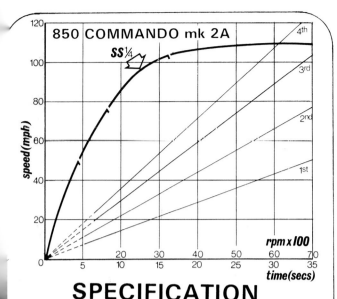

850 COMMANDO mk 2A
SS¼

SPECIFICATION

braking distance from 30 mph	29 feet
fuel consumption	50-55 mpg overall
engine type	360 degree OHV twin
displacement	828 cm³
bore x stroke	77 x 89 mm
compression ratio	8.5:1
claimed output	58 bhp at 6000 rpm
lubrication	dry sump, feed/scavenge from gear pump
carburettor	two 32 mm Amal Concentric
ignition system	twin cb and coil with CD
lighting system	12V ac/dc from alternator via
charging system	rectifier and Zener diode to 10 a-h battery
clutch	single plate, diaphragm spring
gear ratios, overall	10.71, 6.84, 5.10 and 4.18
primary drive	triplex chain, 2.19 reduction
secondary drive	single row chain, 1.91 reduction
gearbox sprockets	16, 17, 19, 20, 21, 22 (std), 23 and 24
wheel sprockets	42
engine sprockets	26
clutch sprockets	57
mph/1000 rpm in top	17.7
fuel tank capacity	2.5 gal inc. 2 pts reserve (4.5 gal optional
oil tank capacity	5 pints
tyres, front	4.10 x 19 Dunlop TT 100
rear	4.10 x 19 Dunlop TT 100
brakes, front	10.7 in disc, hydraulically operated
rear	7 in. single ls drum, cable operated
wheelbase	57 inch
ground clearance	6 inch
seat height	31.5 inch
dry weight	410 lb.
test weight	430 lb.
front/rear ratio	not available
suspension, front	two-way damped telescopic forks
rear	s/a with three position dampers
castor	62 degree
trail	4.36 inch
speedo error	4 mph fast at true 70 mph
tacho error	zero
tool kit quality	very good
parts prices (NOT including VAT)	
front mudguard	£7.18
handlebars	£1.87
speedo cable	£1.64
exhaust pipe (each)	£11.83
set of points	£0.93
set of pistons (complete)	£10.54
list price	£770 inc. VAT
original equipment	two wing mirrors, grab rail, headlamp flasher, kill switch, indicators, QH headlight
manufacturer	Norton Villiers Triumph Ltd., Marston Road, Wolverhampton.

Catch the 850

obtained from road testing and Dave Rawlins' Street Class Drag Bike has been collected and analysed and built into the new bike.

First object of the new version was to cut down noise levels to comply with all known future American, European and British laws. This had been done partly with the new peripheral discharge silencers but mostly with the new, high volume, low air speed air box. As a point of interest the intake ears on the bottom of the air box are detachable, and if taken off push the power up and the noise level with it.

Lowering the noise level had the side effect of reducing the power output, but lessons learned from the drag strip showed that a change of inlet port shape put the power back up. The Norton now carries the same 32mm Amal Concentric carbs but on basically 30mm ports. As a bonus this has eliminated the power loss which the Mk. I suffered between 3,000 rpm and 4,000 rpm.

As well as developing the engine Norton have taken the opportunity to refine the bike. Points that we commented on in the road test of the Mk. 1, like oil coming off the chain onto the rear tyre and the number plate have been prevented by putting a small extension to the end of the chainguard.

Another result of this development has been the sports kit. During the test programme the experimental department have found that it is possible to get over a 10 per cent power increase by fitting the SS camshaft and raising the compression ratio to 10:1, and it is in this condition that Dave Rawlins was able to get his standing start quarter mile time down to 11.53 seconds at the MIRA test track.

It looks like the Norton 850 has reached the point where only detailed development can be done to it. The problem is now, what have Norton's got left up their sleeve? They are after all the only British Motorcycle manufacturer left.

MIKE CAZALET

129

With the primary chain cover off, the first thing is to unplug the generator wires from their snap connector behind the inner chaincase. The wires are . . .

. . . pulled through the ru gromet in the inner case then the alternator stator removed. Note the spacers the three studs under s

■ *If you are ignorant or old fashioned, the first thing you do when you take off a Commando primary chaincase is start looking for the spring link in the chain.*

The second thing you do is discover it hasn't got one!

Why this should be, I'm not quite sure. The manufacturer's party line on the matter is that spring links are weak links, and therefore they very kindly don't fit 'em — but I must confess, I've never been able to see why a triple row spring link, with no less than four fish-plates holding the shafts together, should be any weaker than the single row ditto which they are quite happy to fit to the rear chain.

Anyway, the result of having an endless primary chain is, of course, that you have to take off clutch, engine sprocket, chain an' all as one unit if you want to replace anything. We wondered just how much of a job this was on the Commando — so we went along to Gus Kuhn Motor Cycles, in Clapham Road, London SW9, to find out. There, Dave Potter stripped out and rebuilt a Commando drive side in just over an hour, even hampered as he was by yours truly leaping around taking pictures. This would seem to indicate that the job isn't very arduous after all but on the other hand, Dave had both the knowledge and the special tools going for him, which the average owner certainly won't have in such profusion.

After taking the primary chain case off, the first thing is to disconnect the generator wires from their snap-ins behind the inner case and pull them out through the rubber grummink in same. You can then remove the alternator windings, undo the crankshaft nut, remove the rotor, tap the rotor key out of the shaft and take away the spacer and shims which go between the rotor and engine sprocket.

Turning attention now to the clutch, the next step is to remove the adjuster from the centre and then sit back on your haunches wondering how the hell you're

going to compress the diaphragm spring so that you can get the big securing circlip out.

Dave had the correct spring compressor, which screwed into the adjuster hole, and I suppose the owner could make up something like it: in fact, the owner would jolly well *have* to, because while you might get the circlip *out* without it, you sure as hell won't get it back.

With the spring and the clutch plates out of the way, the next step is to undo the clutch securing nut, which leaves the clutch ready to slide off. The engine sprocket fits the shaft on a taper, so you need another extractor for that before you can remove the

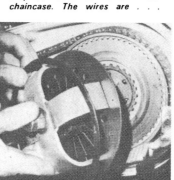

The spring and spring-hub come off as a unit, and expose the innards of the clutch. Dave Potter hooked out a few plates before they fell out, and . . .

. . . then knocked back the washer on the clutch and undid it. On re-build don't forget to use a new arm the tab-washer to secure the

TRIPLEX TROUBLES

whole gubbins. When you *do* get everything away, note that the clutch has a thrust washer and a few shims behind it. These are to align the sprockets properly, so don't forget to put 'em back. Don't over-tighten the clutch centre nut, either: you might crack the circlip on which the thrust washer rests.

The one good thing about all this, of course, is that you don't have to do it very often. Triple row primary chains are very reliable and Dave told us that he very rarely finds either chain or sprockets seriously worn.

Cracked rollers are more common than the usual chain problems of hooked sprocket teeth and stretching.

Re-building is the reverse of dismantling. With rotor and stator bolted up, make sure you have .008in. clearance all round rotor. If you haven't . . .

. . . try changing position stator or have rotor skimme Primary chain tension is 3/8 at the tightest point of chain. Adjust by moving cogb

the crankshaft nut is undone the generator rotor removed. to tap the rotor locating out of its keyway on the ...kshaft without damaging it

Underneath the rotor is a spacer and two or three shim washers. Don't lose these, or forget where they came from — there are similar-looking jobs elsewhere

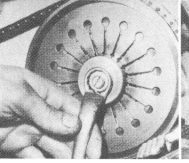

Now the clutch adjuster locknut is slackened off, and the central adjuster screw removed altogether. The diaphragm clutch is secured by a big circlip, and . . .

. . . in order to remove this you must compress the spring. The only way to do this is with a special tool: a nuisance, but you could always make one up

engine sprocket fits on the ...nkshaft on a taper, and an-...er extractor is needed to ...ak the fit. Tighten down ... extractor, then tap bolt

The primary chain, clutch and engine sprocket now come off as a unit. Don't loose the engine sprocket key, which stays on the shaft, or the shims . . .

. . . behind the engine sprocket and the clutch. These are there to align the sprockets, and the wise man checks this alignment before putting it all up again

Behind the clutch shims is the thrust-washer that the clutch bolts up against. This bears on a small circlip, so don't tighten the clutch nut too much

Dave Potter shows how to change a Commando chain in the Gus Kuhn workshops . . .

Triplex chains don't wear much, but check by trying to lift chain off sprocket like this. Any movement is bad. Check sprocket teeth for "hooking", as well

Cracked rollers are more common than old-fashioned stretching on a Triplex chain. Look for separating link plates, caused by sprocket mis-alignment, as well

...efore replacing the clutch ...djusters, make sure operating ...rm hasn't slipped down in its ...lot. Then slacken handlebar ...ver adjuster right off . . .

. . . and screw in clutch centre adjuster until there's about 3/32 in. play at the operating rod. Finally, take up cable slack with the cable adjuster

Use a new primary chaincase sealing rubber — the old one will inevitably have stretched, and you won't be able to get it in. Use a little non . . .

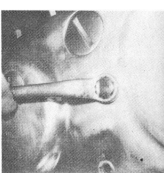

. . . setting goo on the cover, and be careful not to over-tighten the cap nut securing the case. If you do, you'll distort same and increase the usual leakage

WHATEVER the reason, MCI and Norton don't seem to meet quite eye to eye with respect to Commandos.

Remember four years ago when Alan Aspel and I attempted our first Land's End John O'Groats run on a pair of specially prepared 750s? Disaster after disaster. Wrong sized and patched innertubes, unbalanced wheels, loosening exhaust flanges, cracked exhaust pipes, oil leaks and high oil consumption and so much else that we finally had to abandon everything despite hours and hours of work and riding on our part. "A Fine Ride To Failure" we called it. Remember it, Alan? How we rode? By the gods that was a ride. Running before time, being passed by it during the many roadside repairs then thundering after it, matching it and then relaxing a little as we found our tight schedule once more.

We tried, but we failed, and the report was not good for Norton. Machines were promised by Norton Villiers for the following year and then withdrawn as the date approached. More recently, you probably read John McDermott's own unhappy experience with Britain's pride and joy.

All in all, it begins to rankle both factory and magazine, and both "sides" wonder whether or not there might be some ulterior motive behind it all. Do we antagonise Norton because we cannot have machines for test, or does the factory refuse us machines because the fear our experience of their machines? Either way, it's rough on everyone and altogether totally inconsequential.

I know full well that it affected me, and I found myself refusing to believe *anything* good about them at all and have turned to the Continent for the satisfaction that once I had from British bikes.

But Norton has its champions in Britain, one of them being Sport Motorcycles in Manchester. Steve Wynne and John Gear the directors of the company, who I know as friends of fast things motorcycling, thought that maybe MCI had hold of the wrong end of the stick with Norton and that they were not the rotten bikes we thought they were. I asked for a long ride on their own demo' machine and the figures to prove it. They gave me an 850 and opened their Commando warranty files.

The warranty matter can wait a little. The fact is that I had a great day's riding . . . First time on a Commando. Which seems to back up John McDermott's claim that Commandos *can* be good.

Steve has run his own Commando for years. Production raced it, toured right around Europe on it, and would have bought another only he has just taken on a Ducati agency and felt that he should do the right thing by them and so he uses a V twin just now.

"Where are you going," they said.

"Scotland," I said.

"Straight up Deansgate," they said, "and right on that way."

I went "straight up Deansgate", and had I known the area better would have kept clear of main roads immediately, but I hate map reading on a bike, especially in a crowded part of the world, so I took the M61 to Preston. Then the M6 to the A65 junction below Kendal, and from there on rode East into the Pennines.

The way things are now, it's risking too much to blast on totally disregardless, so I left the needle on 80 and sat back to enjoy the sun and scenery, because around that part of the world it is pretty good.

The big Norton laughed on, its deceptive smoothness making light of its road speed, and I sat there in a new set of snug fitting leathers cheating the wind and trying hard not to exceed 80 — all too easy on the 850.

Few other vehicles were on the motorway, a car every mile or so and practically no lorries. At one point I fell in behind a 127 Fiat — identical to mine, all 900 revvy cc of it, travelling perhaps one mph slower than me, but reluctant to allow me past. I played the old trick of allowing its driver to keep ahead by increasing my speed so slowly that he imagined himself to be in control of the situation. Imperceptably our speed crept up to 90, me still behind, and him proudly leading.

The best of it was that I knew his car's performance to the last degree and knew full well that for the last 12 miles he had been cruising flat out, which in a car developing its maximum power at 6250 revs — 90mph, and a cheaply made tin box at that, it could not last for long. At 90mph in a 127 Fiat you feel like Biggles breaking the sound barrier in a biplane. Nothing happens to the engine, they take to revs like a Honda, but the experience is shattering, and despite a few brave tries the poor chap was beaten by his own car.

Not until my turn-off point came up shortly afterwards did I realise that the Norton was still on 90, plus a little something. Great riding, but one of the machine's big weak points, or rather, one of the prime factors causing its weakness. Fact is that my Commando was riding like a bird and I was ripping off time and tarmac like silk ribbons from a naughty girl's party frock.

The idea of rubber mounting a vertical twin is a fine idea, without any doubt the best arrangement yet made marrying all the advantages of a vertical twin with all those of a multi without the disadvantage of width, expense and what

have you.

Trouble is that the old Norton power unit is creaking with age, and however well it might go in short bursts — and that it does incredibly well — and however smooth it might feel — and that it also does incredibly well, no engine of its age is going to hang together for long, in ownership terms, if it's pushed along at damn near its maximum regularly. 5800rpm is maximum power output, and that is 100mph in Commando terms, one of the reasons the bike is such a lolloping eager beaver up top. Forget all about its 7000rpm maximum recommendations. Try that with a long stroke pushrod engine for long and it's going to crack up very prematurely.

I met a chap on a 500 Suzuki — probably on his way from Eddie Crooks' at Barrow-In-Furness, and after a bit of shuffling about with both of us winking and nodding in a deceitfully friendly ''biker'' style, just as though we fully understood that going quickly was all a bit infra-dig y'know, let off.

I love 500 twin Suzukis, very much. They are probably the finest motorcycles, in practical and real quality terms, to have ever left Japan, but to my immense surprise the Commando, without hesitation, rapped away and forever from the moaning stroker without a second's thought, and not simply along the straights. Chop chop chop we went, bend after bend, and I swear, cross me heart and hope to die (but make it quick and painless) that I was line chopping as quickly on that bike as I would want to on any, be it from Munich or Milan.

Obviously, I was well away from the M6 by then, going East along the A686 across the Pennine spine of England, towards Hawes. One of my favourite roads is the 686. An A road, but free of traffic, and stupendously tortuous, although not in the Welsh mountain road sense, but expansive and curling. Chummy on the Suzy disappeared and I enjoyed my big huggy bear bike trip all alone on a road without borders more than the edge of high moorland.

Something that has only struck me since the ride was the way I was ignored by the few people I saw who were not actually looking my way. Fact is that the 850 was, and is, very quiet. more than that I think. Somehow, I understand, although not how, Norton and its technical advisers have not simply killed each combustion explosion noise, but broken it up so that it doesn't all get out at once. You listen to a Commando sometime with the latest silencers and you'll hear what I mean. Each pulse is spread over a longer period than is usual, sort of drifting from the silencer rims making the noise a deep, hushed boom.

What with this, and the galloping torque available, the 850 is probably one of the fastest roadster motorcycles around. Sure, a Mk1V Kwacker would trample it under given its head, so would a 3c Laverda, but on both of these there is exhaust noise to consider. Give either a big brave handful in anything but someone else's empty streets, and you've got to be a pretty big and brave fellow to return for another go. What's more, gear changing on the 850 is more than a bore, being just about unnecessary providing the bike is actually moving.

From Hawes I turned north and rushed up hills without number — far more than I came down it seemed — and rode to Keld and then to Brough and on to the A66 to Penrith and from there north again on another smashing bit of switchback, the A686 to Alston. Then via an incredibly devious route to Haltwistle on the A69 where I had a quick look at Hadrian's Wall and flashed back to Manchester, most of the way by M6 because it was getting late. And I didn't want to be late because the promise of dinner at one of Manchester's best restaurants loomed large and persistent before my hungry eyes.

The 686 was good, the equal to a good many famous Continental mountain roads, albiet shorter, but seven miles of steeply climbing, hairpin cornered road are not all that easy to

find in Britain, especially within a couple of hours reach of a major *English*, I repeat, *English* city.

I suppose I saw 12 cars on that road, including one chap who came running over from his ditching to help, a look of horror on his face. I had stopped to wipe my goggles clean of a big, fat, squashed flying bettle smeared bloodily over my right goggle lens. He had seen the thing burst and had thought something unimaginable had happened to my eye . . .

Going up was a cinch. Nothing to report other than solid shove all the way, but coming down was another story.

I'm a great believer in downhill runs. Nothing sorts out roadholding like a few dropping bends. Maybe I was becoming used to the Norton by now, and was taking a few liberties, but I think not, having ridden a few previously. The first thing that became obvious was that 850 Commandos do need the power turned on during cornering, and they don't like lots of sudden throttle and braking work. Given that, they move unpleasantly, all sly and devious, making you/me wonder whether or not anything really happened.

Equally obvious was that much of the inherent corrective powers of the bike are due to its superb steering geometry and suspension. I mean to say, you put a rubber bungee between the wheels of a Kawasaki, for instance, and then live to tell the tale and you *will* have a tale to tell. I did not like the roll of the 850, but it all seemed to be under the control of the machine itself once I accepted it. But I still don't like it, and I have ridden commandos far worse than this one on its short one day thrash. Enough time to evaluate a bike? Maybe not. But enough to convince me that good 850s do exist.

To prove a point, part way down I tried freewheeling and sans power went whizzing around a few bends at around 60 with the tyres scrubbing and humming away (I never knew that bike tyres did that before. No wonder they wear out!) but gave

SOME FACTS ABOUT COMMANDOS

it up very quickly as on one right hand upswoop I bounced right across the road.

On the M6 too, long three figure speed-bends brought out the worst. Not too much, but unsettling enough for me to want an alternative arrangement. But then, the engine would not be as smooth and I would not have been as comfortable because of it, at least, not at £800 I wouldn't.

Even so, the ride back was a good one. Cooling evening sun, orange and fat, and a sky clear of all but the white 'cuts of jetliners. .

The good life. The first ride of the year. Flirting with a smiling girl in the back of caravanette. Jamming a finger at a couple of aimiable yobs in an old Mk II Zodiac. One eye always in a mirror. A neck aching against the buffeting of my own gale. Thinking world moving thoughts and forgetting them. Accelerating from 100 at race pretenders. The sting and pop of flying insects.

Ah! I'm back fellers; on a black Norton and the road goes on for ever.

*OPINION is all very well, and providing it is well stated and conclusive, no less important than the logistics involved. Figures, as has so often and boringly been said, can be made to prove anything. So they can, as shown by the various methods of "factual record" stated by the airlines, railways, road hauliers, tram drivers and Motorway Pedestrian Users' Association. All of them "proving" conclusively that theirs and **only** theirs is the safe travel system.*

Me? Well, I'm like any other rider, and despite brave attempts to remain icily detached from the various stories, rumours and personal relationships drifting around the bike trade, am as receptive to them as anyone. The difference is that being caught up within the drift of the industry I hear more than most and see the truth of them, or otherwise. In doing so I have cultivated a healthy cynicism about the whole business, which is why I dug a little deeper than my own feelings about Commandos.

I rode one, admittedly for a short distance, and liked it, to my surprise. (Give me another one, Norton, for a week, and let me knock up 1500 miles only don't expect a report. Do what a few others do. Lend me a bike, let me enjoy it, think about it so the experience matures and begin to "think" Norton like I do BMW and Laverda. Educate me, but don't leave me to do my own Buy British campaign again). These are the figures and facts supporting my change of mind. They are true in all respects and due entirely to the enthusiasm and persistence of Sports Motorcycles, who Norton should thank enormously after this.

● ● ●

Sport Motorcycles are the second largest Norton dealer in the country, lying second to The South London people who do a lot of racing and who sell BMWs as well. These figures have been taken from the last 100 machines sold by Sports Motorcycles. That figure was chosen because of its convenience. You will see why in a moment.

You will, I hope, forgive the lack of dates concerned with the bikes but Sports Motorcycles have no wish to expose themselves completely to trade competitors who would love to discover the retail sales of others.

Bike 1: Ignition switch failed mechanically. This has since been modified and strengthened by Lucas.

Bike 2: The mainshaft gear wore because of freak machining and finishing.

Bike 3: Exhaust pipe and rear spring unit chrome peeled.

Bike 4: One loose valve guide due to overmachining.

Bike 5: Poor chrome on silencer, mudguard and brake pedal. (Mudguards are now stainless steel).

Bike 6: Corrugated cylinder bore developed after a few thousand miles. Exactly why has never been discovered.

Bike 7: Silencer cracked on weld joint.

Bike 8: Porous barrel casting.

Bike 9: Centre stand leg snapped off.

Bike 10: Warped front disc developed after 800 miles.

Bike 11: One bonded brake lining broke loose from shoe.

And that is the complete list of warranty claims dealt with in 100 bikes. Just 11 per cent.

What did I learn from this? Firstly, that whatever I might like to think about inherent faults, the record, at least, this record, shows that there is no pattern at all to the warranty work carried out, and none of it points to any design flaw. All appear to be very ordinary manufacturing faults.

*Neither can this list be dismissed as being unrepresentative and that all the troubles showed themselves **after** the warranty period, because Sports Motorcycles work a very unusual system indeed. They completely overide whatever guarantee manufacturers might offer by extending their own to cover all parts and labour for a customer until they feel he's had a good run for his money. After that, customers buy parts at trade price. When the bike is old or has covered a big mileage then the operation is open to negotiation for obvious reasons.*

"We lose £100 a week running that workshop, but I reckon that it all evens itself out in the end because we have no spares shop to staff and run, and no job cards to make out. No costing of repairs, and no arguments with anyone about money. We only deal with people who buy new bikes from us, obviously, but they like it, so they always come back next time for another machine."
Steve Wynne.

135

NORTON INTERSTATE

The 850 not just a good motorcycle – but an outstanding one

THE MEMORY of our unhappy ride to Cologne two years ago, when we seemed to spend much of the trip at odds with our Norton Interpol, is still very clear. The whole episode left relationships just a little strained between us and Norton and it took perhaps eighteen months for the dust to settle.

A chance meeting with Mike Jackson who has, among his many other tasks at Andover, responsibility for the Press bikes, gave us the chance to clear the air. He accepted that we could do nothing but write about the bike as we found it; and we accepted that the bike *was* supplied at short notice and was no more than a hack that had seen better days. This was back in June. "Look," said Mike, "why don't you take a Commando to the Cologne show this year and give us the chance to redeem ourselves." He thought for a minute. "We'll even supply the tow rope." He was grinning as he said it. We accepted on the spot. We would be only too happy for the Norton to come through with flying colours and we also wanted to go to the Cologne show. It would make a change to have a bike arranged three months before, and not three days, as we usually manage things.

True to Norton's word, the Norton was ready for collection when we telephoned Andover a week before the date. It was to be the Mk 11A 850 Interstate. Not new, far from it in fact, for it was the one used by Peter Kelly of *Motor Cycle* for a Land's End to John O'Groats trip in the summer. Peter Williams had also taken it to the continent and it showed just over 5,000 miles on the odometer. That was no bad thing for if the bike did have any little idiosyncracies, one of the two Peters would have found them by now.

There has been a breath of fresh air blowing through Norton-Triumph these last few months. A few staff changes had changed attitudes also, and, at last, we had the feeling that someone realised that all too often the general public's opinion of a machine was influenced by what they read in the technical press. It makes sense to ensure, then, that the bikes given to the press are

good examples rather than bad. There is nothing dishonest in that, indeed they would be fools if they did not. Certainly, when we ride a machine we try to bear in mind that it has been supplied by the manufacturer, and we expect it to be good.

The Norton had been prepared for a long ride. A spare clutch cable was taped in position, spare plugs and disc pads were in the tank bag and a spare fuse was taped to the frame. Only the fuse was needed, and that was not the Norton's fault. It was comforting, though, to know that someone was interested enough in the bike to take the trouble. Perhaps readers might think that we are making an unnecessary thing about what ought to be a perfectly normal situation. Believe us, it is not as usual as all that and we were gratified to find that the sole remaining British manufacturer could at last hold its own with "the rest". Also supplied was the excellent French luggage carrying equipment that was first shown at the Racing and Sporting Motorcycle Show earlier this year. A tank bag and two tank-side bags clipped to a skin stretched over the tank. A smaller, ugly, bag was permanently fixed on top, like a wart, the only blot on otherwise handsome equipment. Made in some sort of vinyl, it looked in fact better than it was, for the finish was poor on our set. The design was brilliant, though. It held enough luggage for my wife and myself for the weekend (with the assistance of an old Craven top box that just happened to fit the carrier also supplied. This was used for maps and suchlike). My share was the wart on top. As a matter of interest, they are available in this country to special order, for the Interstate and /5 or /6 series BMWs, from Gus Kuhn at £35 or so a set.

The story of the Norton Commando must go right back to the 1940s, earlier if you want to compare it with the Edward Turner Triumphs. Introduced as a 500 it grew to 600, then 650 and, with the arrival of the Commando concept about six years ago, to a 750 before finally arriving at its present 850 c.c. capacity. Generally it is admitted, even at Nortons, that the design is getting towards the end of its useful life. Long in the tooth is an oft

heard term. By that token, BMWs are also in the same boat, for their design has been around since 1923! The problem with Norton is not so much that the basic design is old but that within the limits set by available tools and jigs, there is nowhere left to go to strengthen the motor to accept considerably increased power. That is not to imply that the present motor is going to fly apart at the first sign of hard work, more that we doubt if Norton will be upping it to a thousand!

Power. For the past five years it has been the god worshipped by nearly all manufacturers. Perhaps at last we can see an end to this trend for top speeds are down on many machines, as the emphasis shifts to a search for "cleaner" engines making less noise. Norton are at pains not to make any claim for maximum power for their machines, which is perhaps better than some of the fairy stories we hear, aided by having different "standards" for measuring the power. What they do say is that maximum torque is 56 ft lb at 5,000 r.p.m. with a "red line" on the tachometer at 7,000 r.p.m. giving a useful spread of power. Certainly one of the virtues of the Norton is its unhurried approach to travelling quickly.

They have been saying for years that the vertical twin has had its day, but still it retains its popularity. As well as Norton, Honda, Yamaha, Laverda and Bennelli make large capacity (500 c.c. or over) twins and one or two others make smaller ones. Vibration is the bugbear and various

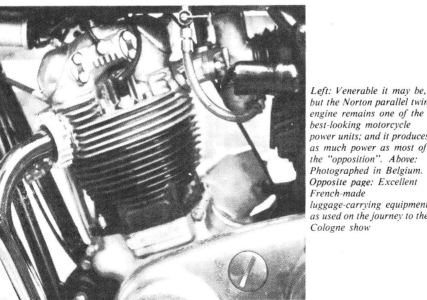

Left: Venerable it may be, but the Norton parallel twin engine remains one of the best-looking motorcycle power units; and it produces as much power as most of the "opposition". Above: Photographed in Belgium. Opposite page: Excellent French-made luggage-carrying equipment as used on the journey to the Cologne show

walls are lubricated by mist from the big-end feed and valve gear, pushrods and followers and timing case by the residue from the rocker feed returning down the pushrod tunnels. A breather runs from the rear of the car crank case back to the oil tank and another breather vents the tank to air. The gearbox has its own separate $\frac{1}{4}$ pint reservoir.

The contact breaker assembly is housed, under a removable cover, at the front of the timing case with the contact braker unit being a taper fit on the end of the camshaft.

On the left-hand side of the engine we have a good old-fashioned primary chain case, the gearbox of course coming as a separate package. We think perhaps it is the only one remaining in this unit construction age. Removal of the cover, catching the oil as best you can as there is no drain plug, reveals the alternator rotor mounted on the left-hand end of the crankshaft and drive to the gearbox via a massive triplex clutch. It is possible to remove the engine sprocket/clutch/and primary drive chain as a unit, should replacement be necessary. Again the accent is on functional simplicity. The clutch is of the diaphragm type, and very pleasant it is too.

Now to the gearbox. Like the engine a classic in simplicity. It must remain as the last bastion of the four-speed school and, frankly, it is ample. Nortons have always been famous for their gearboxes, and this one is a superb example. Its only drawback was its much publicised inability to cope with the power under racing conditions. Among the advantages of having a separate gearbox is that of having its own oil reservoir, ensuring good, clean, comparatively cool oil all the time. This can mean less gear-change "stickiness" after a prolonged spell of high-speed work. And of course it can be hoisted out very

easily for repair jobs. Again the theme of simplicity.

The gears are in "extra-tough" nickel-chrome steel. The kickstarter drives through an internal ratchet on the layshaft first gear, which in turn drives the mainshaft and clutch. That is one of debits. If you stall it in traffic neutral has to be found before restarting.

The carburettors are Amal 932s, 32mm and, again with Triumph, have the distinction of being equipped with ticklers. They were needed, too. At least that's one less hole in the gloves to worry about if you are among the majority of riders without these (essential) items! One of the oft-heard complaints about the Commando is a tendency for the nuts holding the exhaust pipe to the head to come undone. Now they are securely retained by a locking washer and ours didn't budge. The pipes were blue when we took delivery of the machine, a common enough occurrence these days on most bikes.

methods are used to try to cancel it out. Norton, of course, use the much publicised Isolastic system wherey the engine and gearbox and exhaust systems are isolated from the cycle parts and rider by rubber mountings. That it works in most conditions there can be no doubt but, because the rubber has to be "tuned" to absorb the vibration at normal running speed, it is less effective at lower speeds, when it allows the engine to shake. That limit can be set by the designer without too much difficulty but if he moves it from one place he has to lose it from another. Norton have settled on a lower limit of 3,000 r.p.m. Below that the engine shakes considerably. It still does not transmit vibration as such to the rider, this is still absorbed, but he is very conscious of the movement of the engine and it is possible to feel it occasionally clunk against something solid down below. It seemed to be the inside of the left-hand alloy footrest casting. From 3,000 to the top of the scale there is not the slightest trace of vibration evident to the rider and within this range the Commando must rate as one of the smoothest motorcycles in the world.

The Norton engine has been much maligned over the past few years because it has not changed in basic design since the days of the Model 7. One thing is often overlooked when criticising it. Because the design is unchanging it has the real virtue of simplicity. It is a twin-cylinder parallel twin with pushrod-operated

valves. In fact it is so simple that owners can actually decarbonise it in an afternoon! The cylinders have an alloy cylinder head and an iron barrel. Compression ratio is 8.5 to 1. Each piston has three rings, and no ring is used at the skirt of the piston. The pushrods run in tunnels cast in the barrel and operate the pistons by a conventional rocker arm. Valve closing is controlled by coil springs. Cylinder head removal can be accomplished with the engine in the frame.

At the bottom end the crankshaft, a hefty bolted up assembly, uses car-type big end shells, also bolted up, to house the connecting rods. Removal and replacement is a relatively simple operation. The camshaft, a single one being used to operate all four valves, is at the front of the engine with the drive by chain. The sprocket for this drive is on the right-hand end of the crankshaft and free play is taken up by a slipper tensioner. Behind the camshaft drive sprocket is the oil pump drive pinion, the oil pump being of gear type with a pressure release valve should the pressure rise above 45/55 lb/sq inch.

One of the less common features of the Norton is that, with Triumph, it uses a dry sump, the oil coming from a separate five pint tank under the dualseat. A replaceable filter is built into the return flow, accessible from behind the gearbox. Oil flows from the tank to the pump and from there by separate feeds to the big end, and main bearings and to the rocker spindles. Cylinder

The frame is of duplex-cradle type, twin down tubes looping under the engine and sweeping back up to meet the large-diameter top tube at the rear of the fuel tank. A secondary tube runs from the bottom of the steering head to just over half-way along the top tube. Two more tubes run from either side of the gearbox at the top mounting point to meet the top tube at much the same point as the secondary tube. No gusseting is used at all. The dualseat is supported by a sub-frame. The rear swinging-arm assembly pivots to the rear of the gearbox and the footrests, front and rear, are attached to a beautiful cast-alloy plate on either side.

Controversial from the day it was introduced, the Isolastic engine-mounting system has certainly had its fair share of press comment, favourable and otherwise. Norton feel that often it is blamed for other problems, i.e., incorrectly fitted or unsuitable tyres and they feel that, provided that it is set up by the book, it handles and performs as well as the best. The engine is "suspended" at three points, by a plate from the top of the cylinder head by two rubber mountings to the frame; by two bonded and two more rubber mountings at the bottom front of the engine, either side; and by three bonded and two rubber buffers above the gearbox, to complete a triangular mounting pattern. The whole essence of the system is that the shimming, i.e., play between the engine and frame, must be right. The ideal gap is given as 10 "thou". Too much play and the engine shakes in the frame, affecting handling – too little and vibration makes itself felt. The exhaust system remains in isolation with the engine by way of rubber mountings at its only point of contact with the frame, at the rear.

Front forks have the fashionable skinny look and the rear suspension units are adjustable Girlings, both conventional enough systems. Since we last tried a Commando the disc brake has arrived on Nortons, a well-made and effective unit by Lockheed offering a braking area of 18.69 sq. in. The drum rear brake gives an effective area of 13.60 sq. in. The wheels use Dunlop TT100s, 4.10 x 19 in. front and rear, with the rear wheel offering that most unusual asset, a genuine q.d. removal. Until 1971 the wheel was held to the brake drum by three studs which passed through the hub. Since then these have been replaced by polyurethane shock absorber segments which let into the hub. To remove the wheel all that needs to be done is remove the spindle, drop the speedometer drive housing and lift the wheel out. It is such an asset to have a q.d. rear wheel; it could well be enough to swing the balance towards the Norton if the prospective buyer were unable to make up his mind.

The petrol tank, finished in black and having "Norton" boldly emblazoned on the sides, held just under five gallons, an excellently large amount. As for the dualseat, that too earned high praise for it was still comfortable after 10 hours' riding. One last asset were mudguards made in stainless steel. Very nice.

Our look at the Norton has been more comprehensive than usual and, to our delight, the closer we looked the more there seemed to be to commend the bike. Half the battle when writing about a bike is won if the manufacturer helps the tester to understand it; Norton sent us not one but two comprehensive workshop manuals to peruse at our leisure. Most other manufacturers consider they are being generous if they give us a sales pamphlet! Such helpfulness gave us the chance to appreciate some of the features of the Commando, not least its classic simplicity. The

number of special tools needed to complete every major task on the bike is minimal and an enthusiastic owner would have no difficulty in acquiring the lot.

THE RIDE

Our normal practice is to report on a bike as we find it over a period of time but, in this case, we will just talk of one ride we had on the Commando, the aforementioned trip to Cologne.

Our trip to Cologne was to be as part of a club run, a dozen bikes meeting at Dover to journey to Germany. It could have been an interesting situation for the other 11 were all BMWs! As a BMW owner myself, I should have shrugged my shoulders and apologised for my thoughtless choice of transport (at least if I was conforming to the popular image of BMW owners). Almost to my surprise, I became defensive about the Norton. I had already covered a couple of hundred miles on the bike and was both astounded and overjoyed to find that I loved it. It suited me to perfection and I was determined that by the time we returned to England the Interstate would still be able to hold its head high.

To tell truth, it got off to a most unfortunate start for we had gone barely five miles when part of the headlamp glass fell out! A flying stone, presumably, had caused a freak break and there we were at eight o'clock at night with a hole in our light – and our timetable. Where were we going to get such a unit at that time of night? As luck would have it, we were directed to a late night accessories shop in Kennington, Stockwell Motors, where the man in charge, a motorcyclist, after much searching came up with a quartz halogen unit that was more or less the same as we needed. We breathed a sigh of relief that we were on one of the few bikes for which it was possible to get replacements late at night. Within an hour we were on our way to Dover and caught the midnight boat in good time.

By the time the ferry steamed into Ostend, at 4 a.m., a ghastly hour, we had discovered only one aspect of the Interstate that we didn't like. It needed one hell of a swing to start it. Eight hundred and twenty-eight fairly highly compressed c.c. shared out between two cylinders, and no valve lifter, is just too much and I am bound to say that starting the bike was never much fun. Especially at 4 a.m.!

The real surprise came from the Interstate th moment we heard it start. It was so quiet! Jus about on a par with a BMW 900. They hav really done things to the silencing arrangement on this bike. Mechanically it had barely a rattle the air was effectively drowned by a new ai cleaner system, and the silencers, with a blac cap on the end (to pronounce death to noise? were superb. Of course, there had to be a snag Norton did not do this entirely out of concern fo the ear drums of passers-by. Pending Unite States legislation gave them a hearty shove in th right direction and they came up with the goods The price to be paid is a falling off i performance, with top speed reduced from claimed 122 m.p.h. to a hard-to-find 110 m.p.h For my money it matters not one whit, for who really cares about an extra 15 m.p.h. at tha dizzy end of the scale? Let us hope that the paying customer takes the same view. The othe effect is psychological. The Norton Interstate n longer makes a very "fast" noise. It never seem to be hurrying and bystanders, or pillion passengers, could be forgiven for thinking that i is a bit sluggish. Certainly its initial acceleratio is a little down, now it is more content to make haste quietly. More power to its elbow; or rather not, for I'm very content with it the way it is.

Winding through Ostend streets before dawn meant that we could do so without being assailed by Belgian toots and in no time the bikes were pointing towards Brussels. I was last away and a prolonged spell of 90 m.p.h. cruising showed that the Interstate was very happy at that speed, and that it was damned chilly! Brussels came and went without our getting lost, thanks to the leader, whom we had now caught, knowing where he was going. Our destination was Stadtkyl, a village in the Eifel Mountains, a club meeting place and stopping-off spot for many riders at the Elephant Rally. After a stop for coffee and fuel, where a tankful showed that we were averaging 59 m.p.g., a figure that was to be repeated constantly, we completed the 200-odd miles to Stadtkyl just after most were leaving the breakfast table.

A couple of hours to try and remove the sand from our eyes and then a massive German lunch followed by a tour of some of the local beauty spots, the Commando behaving itself magnificently. Naturally, being in Germany, wherever we stopped it was the "foreign" bike

Is the Norton now unique in having an old-style separate gearbox (four-speed too, which is getting rare) with primary drive by chain? It's a setup that works very well, with several practical advantages

...hat caused most interest and I was genuinely ...appy that it still looked pristine. No oil was ...eaking and it sounded great. Starting wasn't ...etting any easier, though. It *started* well, to be ...air. My only problem was to spin the engine. I ...sually settled for putting the bike on the centre ...tand and standing alongside. At least that way I ...educed the chances of thumping my knee on the ...oil tank.

It was 50 miles from our village to Cologne, a ...retty, sunny ride that was made more ...pleasurable by the company, increased later when ...the rider of a 250 NSU joined us. Arrival at ...Cologne coincided with countless thousands of ...other motorcyclists and there was a long, ...slow-moving queue into the exhibition hall where ...IFMA was being held. Not once did the Norton ...object and it was happy most of the time to plod ...along, clutch out, in bottom gear at about 2 ...m.p.h. I wouldn't have believed it. It was at ...variance with its tickover which, when ...stationary, had a tendency to increase to 2,000 ...r.p.m. where it normally would settle at a steady ...thousand.

It was dark when we returned to the mountains. And chilly too. The Norton's 60/55w lights were not as good as I recalled due, I later discovered, to a badly located bulb but the switches and control layout were excellent and I had become used to them. I wouldn't go so far as to say that I like the long-eared Lucas dipswitch/indicator switch but it worked and gave me no trouble, so perhaps I am allowing my initial dislike of them to linger unfairly.

More substantial German food and a glass or two of the magnificent local wine left us well armed to retrace our footsteps to Ostend the next day and we bade our German companions goodbye and once again enjoyed the trip through southern Belgium, passing the remains of the Siegfried Line just before we left Germany. Once again passports were not required, nor insurance, and we were delayed for only seconds. The more I rode the Norton the more I was enjoying it. It was still returning 59 m.p.g.; top speed, not outstanding at 110, was ample, more than ample in fact for *everywhere* seems to have speed limits these days, and the comfort was outstanding. Even the luggage equipment was playing a part by keeping the wind off my knees.

Sunday riding in Belgium was to be avoided, we were warned, but I am bound to say I much preferred it to the English equivalent. Not once were the Norton's excellent brakes called upon to work unduly hard. The squeak that they had from delivery was beginning to disappear and only in the wet did they worry me (as do *all* disc brakes). As we never had a drop of rain that was not a problem. The big engine was more than happy at the 80/85 m.p.h. that we tended to cruise at. This speed settled the tachometer needle to 5,000 r.p.m. and the sensation to the rider was that of sitting on a smooth, but icy, magic carpet. At that speed the miles were fast disappearing and we stopped just before Ostend for a meal, confident that there was no boat for hours. There was, of course, but enquiries beforehand had assured us otherwise.

The crossing was accomplished without incident, if one can ignore a Force 8 gale and, finally disembarking at Dover and going through the usual customs queues, we had a high-speed run to Surrey and arrived, after a very long day, with not an ache or twinge between us. I was still enjoying myself and could, happily, have gone on as long as I could keep my eyes open. The trip meter said that we had done 720 miles in the last three days, hardly as far as Newcastle, but different, somehow. In that time I had not adjusted the chain (I hadn't needed to), the merest trace of oil leaked from the clutch cable entry to the gearbox and a drip came from the primary chaincase. Not a drop of oil was needed during the trip and no adjustments were made, excluding the headlight of course, and a blown fuse when we got our wires crossed in the dark replacing it.

As a long-distance touring motorcycle the Norton Interstate had shown itself to be ideal. The only detail criticism that could be made was regarding the ignition/light key mounted inaccessibly under the tank. Starting was, of course, always an irritation but in its defence I am afraid I will have to tell the story of how I took the Norton along to the local training scheme one Sunday morning and a slim young lady who is instructor there asked if she could have a ride. "Of course," I replied, "if you can start it." She did. First kick. Exit one tester with egg on his face. I forgot that she owned a 650

Triumph. That is the last time I take her to the TT in my sidecar.

Another aspect of the starting situation is that the long-promised starter motor is now nearing reality. One of the weeklies has carried a picture of it and an electric-starter equipped bike was reported as attending the FIM Rally in June. If it is man enough for the job, and Lord knows it ought to be, the time taken to develop it, it removes just about the last obstacle to the Norton breaking through as a top seller. In every other respect it is good. Its handling is steady at high speed, it goes around corners without twitches or complaint and it is light enough (430 lb) and has a short enough wheelbase (56¼in) to be able to be flicked through bends with more ease than its apparent bulk suggests. In fact, by today's standards, it is a lightweight, and most riders enthused over its typically British good looks. A handsome bike rather than a pretty one. The suggestion that it is a long-distance tourer is a considered one. The engine does not become really smooth until the bike is doing 50 m.p.h. (3,000 r.p.m.); riding around town was not unpleasant, just not much fun. Certainly a bike for the open road, and one to be ridden quickly.

One only needs to return to British tyres for a week or two to discover that there really is a difference between them and Japanese ones. We had no rain on the German trip but plenty after, and the bike was rock steady in the wet. Dunlop TT100s suit the Commando well.

Perhaps readers will consider that we have dwelled too long on the Norton's virtues and we, too, were a little surprised to find that we had so much to say about it. We did ask ourselves the question: How much of our enthusiasm for the Norton was genuine and how much was dictated by our desire to see it succeed? It would be an easy trap to fall into. Norton-Triumph are the last bastion of British motorcycling. Without them we have nothing. "So what, you may say. Look at it from the selfish point of view. Without Norton the home industry loses a valuable, indispensable almost, buffer against the worst excesses of the politicians. The incentive to go easy on the motorcycle because we still make them and sell them abroad is removed. That matters to all of us. From an unselfish point of view, none of us wants to see the last rites administered to a once great national industry. Perhaps you, like us, love motorcycles and love the contribution that we have made to the worldwide development of it. Take Norton away and that contribution stops.

Certainly we were not unaware of the political considerations of Norton's success or failure but, with this in mind, we still came to the honest conclusion that the Norton Commando Interstate that we tried was not just a good motorcycle, it was an outstanding one. Now we are aware of the problem. Not *all* Nortons leave the production line as good as ours. Quality control is something that the Norton-Triumph management have to get to grips with before they can claim to be among the best in the world. When they do and all Nortons are up to the standard of the one that we have just returned to Andover they will have a winner. And we will be there cheering for it.   B.P.

• There is a natural selection in motorcycling. Consider the kickstart lever of the 850 Norton. Some nine inches in length, the lever demands real muscle or weight to swing it through its arc. Those who can't drop the lever down smartly, or those who don't want to learn, or those who don't want to be bothered—they all will pass to less formidable motorcycles. It's a peculiar process of natural selection. Under-achievers may want a Norton, but find themselves unequal to the starting task. You may choose it, but bikes like the Norton must also choose you.

Understand that the Norton 850 is an elitist's motorcycle. For he who has learned *the drill*, the Norton will rumble into life with a single well-coordinated swipe. The Norton man shrugs off effete electric starters and invites his quarrel-some friends to demonstrate their expertise at the lever. Most likely they'll turn pasty under a nice moist sheen of perspiration without bringing the engine to life. There's a secret. Being a good Norton man is like being a magician; the magic is in a few well-rehearsed drills. Learn the routine and proceed to center stage.

The John Player Special is the most elite Norton of all, and it takes a little extra knowledge, like the ignition key trick. The starting procedure begins at first with a frustrating attempt to insert the ignition key into its slot. The standard Norton switch nearly fouls the trailing edge of the fiberglass cowling. You can't see the slot which is protected by a rubber cover, and

initially you can't quite remember which way the key's toothing should point. But after you've fumbled your way through a few times, you learn the trick. You know where the slot is, and how to hold the ignition key in your left hand between your thumb, index and middle fingers. The key slips right in. You can do it—because you must do it—blind. Of course it's a dumb place to have the switch. But when did you see a magician with all his cards up front?

Tickle the 32mm Amals carefully. One must top up the float chambers without gushing them over. Fold the right footpeg up. The kickstarter moves the Norton's two 77mm pistons slowly through their 89mm strokes. Bring the engine up past compression on one cylinder. Use the clutch to free the kickstart lever and position the cranking arm at 10:30. With the bike on its centerstand (or on its wheels, if you're the confident type) smoothly rise up, roll your weight over on your right leg, lock your knee, roll your eyes to heaven and drop the lever down.

Unless the engine is hot, the lever won't exactly plummet. On a chill day, when the oil is thick and the engine cold, the kickstarter descends more with an ooze than a swoosh. On such occasions, use the

choke and count on three or four cranks. When the Norton's warm, one stab will suffice. It's all in the sorcerer's handbook.

The John Player Norton has a certain illusionary character. It's the namesake of the Norton factory bikes which race under the banner of the John Player Tobacco Company. What's in a namesake? Not a production-racer replica of anything, the Player bike is a standard Commando dressed up in race-track clothes. The outfit has come from the same tailors who created the John Player Norton F750 racers, so the style and cut follow an intentional pattern. The upper part of the JPS fairing mocks the F750 racer, though the street Player has two huge eye sockets for headlamps. The street fairing is a three-quarters midi, a style which no doubt will become fashionable just as soon as the back-street entrepreneurs begin to build molds off the Norton's Avon fiberglass. To complete the racer-image, the JPS sports a high-back mono-posto seat, clip-ons, rear sets, black exhaust system, and a tank canopy.

Tank canopy? Yes, the real steel gas tank hides under the spreading fiberglass cover. At its lower reaches the canopy-cowling flares out and meets the fairing, connecting up with four Dzus fasteners

NORTON 850
JOHN PLAYER SPECIAL

The Norton 850 Commando arrives at an intersection . . . somewhere between Brands Hatch and Tobacco Road.

COLOR PHOTOGRAPHY: LARRY WILLETT   B/W PHOTOGRAPHY: BILL DELANEY

on each side. Fiberglass tanks are now illegal for road-going motorcycles in England. Nevertheless, Norton didn't want the JPS bike to lose its racer-image, hence the thin fiberglass canopy over a steel gas tank. Does it offend your sense of race-crafting? Where, you might ask, is a strictly functional lightweight aluminum gas tank? Where indeed. Most likely such an idea got trapped at a deadly juncture—between two sheets in a cost accountant's ledger. So the JPS's racer-looks are literally gel-coat deep.

Hmmmm, you ask, if the bike has no more poke than the standard 850, and if it's just another pretty fiberglass face hung on a dear old girl, is the John Player deal all a steam-blowing shuck? Quite to the contrary. The street Player is refreshingly and beguilingly honest.

No one at Norton is shouting "production racer." Nobody is claiming that you'll get a piece of Peter Williams, or a section of Parliament Square, or even an odd chunk of the Isle of Man. The JPS has no extra power, no special speed, no monocoque frame, no trick gearbox. It's zip-zero-zip for a straight-up reason. The basic 850 Norton Commando is the end product of a British system of development and refinement. That means the basic Commando is both the factory's best, and only, Norton. If the John Player cafe-racer had trick ignition, a special gearbox, high-compression pistons, and high-rpm camshaft *(specialitis ad nauseum ergo undo)*, Norton would be selling something considerably less than its best motorcycle. Better that Norton's cafe customers have flashy John Player glasswork and a good Commando than flashy John Player glasswork and a basket of incipient shrapnel under the cowling.

Lift off the tank cowling and you'll find a modified Commando Roadster gas tank with foam rubber squares gracing its surface at strategic points. The treatment prevents the shroud from rattling about on the steel tank. This vessel, which even a polite Anglophile would label "cobby," holds 3.2 gallons. That's a bit more than the standard Commando Roadster (3.0 gallons) and far less generous than the Interstate Commando (6 gallons).

The JPS shows some rearranging immediately behind the engine. There's a new air filter box, a large molded plastic container with air intake scoops on the bottom and a wet foam filter inside. The new airbox really hushes down the intake noise of the big vertical twin. The larger airbox has forced other components behind the engine into another formation. The battery on the cafe-racer has been rotated 90 degrees so that it mounts transversely (that is, the long sides of the battery go across the bike).

The new intake plumbing is part of the so-called Mark 2A sound-control system. The 2A specification also includes giant mufflers. Although the ends of the silencers appear to be sealed, the exhaust actu-

NORTON 850 JOHN PLAYER SPECIAL

Price, suggested retail	West Coast, POE $2995
Tire, front	4.10 x 19 in. Dunlop TT100
rear	4.10 x 19 in. Dunlop TT100
Brake, front	10.71 x 1.65 in. x 2 (272 x 42mm x 2)
rear	7.0 x 1.25 in. (180 x 32mm)
Brake swept area	122.3 sq.in (795 sq.cm.)
Specific brake loading	5.3216/sq.in., at test weight
Engine type	OHV four-stroke vertical twin
Bore and stroke	3.03 x 3.50 in. (77 x 89mm)
Piston displacement	50.5 cu.in. (828cc)
Compression ratio	8.5:1
Carburetion	2; 32mm Amal 932
Air filtration	Wet foam
Ignition	Battery and coil
Bhp @ rpm (actual)	48.27 @ 5500
Torque @ rpm (actual)	46.73 @ 5000
Rake/trail	28°/4.36 in. (111mm)
Mph/1000 rpm, top gear	16.4
Fuel capacity	3.2 gal. (12 liter)
Oil capacity	6 pt. (2.8 liter)
Transmission oil capacity	9 pt. (4.2 liter)
Electrical power	192 watts @ 7000 rpm
Battery	12V, 8AH
Gear ratios, overall	(1) 11.78 (2) 7.52 (3) 5.61 (4) 4.60
Primary transmission	Triplex chain 26/56 2.15:1
Secondary transmission	⅝ x ⅜ Renold chain 22/42 1.90:1
Wheelbase	57.75 in. (146.7cm)
Seat height	29.25 in. (74.2cm)
Ground clearance	4.25 in. (10.8cm)
Curb weight	476 lbs., with full tank of gas (216.3kg)
Test weight	651 lbs., with rider (296kg)
Instruments	Speedometer, Tachometer, Odometer
Sound level (California Standard)	80db(A)
Standing start ¼-mile	14.123 sec. @ 94.33 mph
Top speed	115 mph (est.)
Average fuel consumption	44 mpg
Speedometer error	39 mph actual 31.17 60 mph actual 62.76
Braking force (actual)	.979

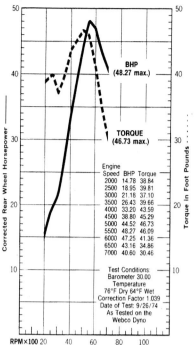

Engine Speed	BHP	Torque
2000	14.78	38.84
2500	18.95	39.81
3000	21.18	37.10
3500	26.43	39.66
4000	33.20	43.59
4500	38.80	45.29
5000	44.52	46.73
5500	48.27	46.09
6000	47.25	41.36
6500	43.16	34.86
7000	40.60	30.46

BHP (48.27 max.)
TORQUE (46.73 max.)

Test Conditions:
Barometer 30.00
Temperature
76°F Dry 64°F Wet
Correction Factor 1.039
Date of Test: 9/26/74
As Tested on the
Webco Dyno

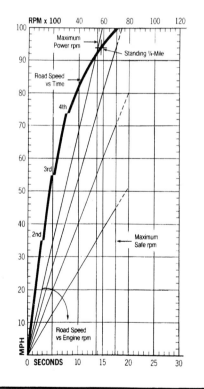

ally escapes around the circumferences of the end plugs. The 2A hardware has already been marketed in Europe where Germany and Sweden have the toughest noise-control laws. The whispering John Player bike sneaked past *Cycle's* decibel meter with an 80-db (A) reading. Credit for the new-found silence is shared by the effective intake and exhaust systems and by the fairing and cowling which contain upper-end engine noise.

The seat has normal padding by cafe-

racer standards. Judged on a touring scale, the seat would get high marks for misery. Two snaps at the top of the tail section permit access to the compartment behind the padding. This must be Norton's version of the Yamaha Cycle Camper—there's an enormous amount of room.

Up front the Avon midi-fairing dominates the motorcycle with its two six-inch headlamps. In order to provide sufficient energy for the dual lamps, Norton has fitted the JPS with a high-output alterna-

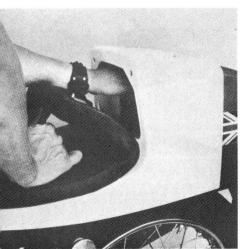

The seat cowling seconds as storage compartment. Access is simple and protection afforded superb.

Location of the ignition switch demands that Norton owners learn yet another trick.

tor. In certain cases, the double headlights work better than the best single lamps. For example, the double lights are excellent for straight-line Interstate driving. But for night-time riding on winding roads, they're not significantly better than the Kawasaki's Z-1 headlight.

Above and behind the headlights, the fairing has a handsome instrument deck which carries the tachometer, speedometer (which strangely lacks a tripmeter) and the indicator lights for ignition, signals and high beam. The fairing interior and deck are finished in a matte black.

Customers better love the way the John Player bike looks, because the fairing (though attached by a U-bolt, bracket, and stays) is an integral part of the bike's concept. One can't just subtract the fairing and find ready solutions for instrument and headlight remounting. And without the fairing, the tank cowling would have no anchors. Dispensable the midi isn't—but vulnerable it is.

Street Player owners will undoubtedly exercise some riding caution just to protect the beautiful lightweight Avon fiberglass. We would advise care. During a photo session, we propped the JPS away from a wall of background paper with a 12-inch ruler. The ruler slipped out of place and the bike fell against the wall. The thin fiberglass surrounding the clip-ons fortunately distorted on impact and did not break. In fact, the blow didn't put any cracks in the gel-coat of the glass. However, the right-side mirror, which bolts directly into the fairing, punched a hole through the glass around the mirror's mounting boss. You can't have a fiberglass fairing which is light and resiliant (within limits) and still highly resistant to pinpoint blows. The Player Norton fairing will absorb minor blunted assaults which would crack thick fiberglass. But in any real sky/ground/Dear Lord/sky/ground episode, no fiberglass is tough or resilient enough to survive intact. A street Player will likely endure a minor fracas in its garage. But if you ditch it with enthusiasm somewhere, draw your money-gun and start shooting.

Minor surface scratches in the color-impregnated gel-coats can be rubbed out with a careful balance of elbow grease and polishing compound. You'll not be running off to your local hardware store for touch-up paint. The red and blue stripes aren't paint either; the colors are pre-cut sections of pressure-sensitive tape. Ditto for the seat decor. There's good reason for using tape. Most paint dries very brittle, and it would flake and crack off the fiberglass surfaces of the bike.

Any cracks in the gel-coat surface show up more in light colors than dark ones. Some cracking developed in the tank cowling which is so thin and lightweight (five pounds) that it's very bendable. Nevertheless, the Avon glasswork is almost flawless; it's in a different league from most other factory-supplied fiberglass which we've seen. By comparison, Italian glass looks like it was laid up in a brown paper bag.

For short periods the Norton engine reminds its rider that he's aboard a big displacement vertical twin. The Isolastic system allows the 850 engine to shake the entire motorcycle below 2500 rpm. The shaking ranges from very little to severe. At 1800 rpm, for example, the engine vibration reaches exactly the correct amplitude and frequency to rattle the JPS with amazing ferocity, and white fiberglass becomes a ghostly blur.

The street Player did not quake so fiercely as the 850 Commando which *Cycle* tested in July 1973. That bike had a set of round-town troubles. When it was set up to idle nicely, the 1973 bike would stagger and stall off-idle. To eliminate stalling, the Amal carbs were calibrated for an unhappy 1200-rpm idle. To avoid the shaking range on the 1973 bike (idle to 3000 rpm), staffers used second gear in fast city-type traffic, where muffler noise proved embarrassingly loud.

The Player Norton is a real turn-about. It becomes smooth at 2500 rpm. Thus the JPS has a broader, more useable powerband. The Player is geared a little shorter than earlier 850s (20-tooth gearbox sprocket instead of 21- or 22-cogs), making both second and third gears workable for 30-45 mph city traffic. And the JPS had the best Amal carburetors that *Cycle* has tried in a long time. Norton now uses its own special carb needles. The engine chugs softly at its idle speed of 900 rpm. Sometimes there's a tiny hint of a glitch and a fleeting trace of hesitation right off idle, but compared to other Amals the set on the JPS was a near revelation. Kickstarting at the stoplight, like rowdy Norton mufflers, appears to be history. In city traffic, the JPS behaved as unobtrusively as Casper the Ghost.

On the open road, the Norton's silence remains impressive. The bike almost radiates a BMW R90S character. In part the silence creates that impression, but it's also in the easy gait of the engine, the torquey punch which a throttle roll-on produces, and the remarkable smoothness above 2500 rpm. The Isolastic buffer system allows the engine—and transmission and swinging arm—to vibrate in a sub-section isolated from the rider and the main running gear. At some intervals up the rpm

band, such as 3000 rpm, the rider can feel some faint trembling through the footpegs and seat, but nothing severe enough to call bothersome. Furthermore, as the brand new (and tight) 850 engine bedded in, the exact rpm-points of the tremors shifted around a bit.

Hooking down a winding road is probably the most pleasant thing you can do with the JPS. Assuming you're willing to lean on the 55-mph limit, and assuming you haven't picked a knotty road with tight, vicious corners, then you can click the Player into fourth and proceed with a sense of calm grace. The bike feels light and agile and precise, something like a big road-going single. The Norton's agility and the TT100 tires give the rider a confident feeling. The bike suggests that a rider could change his mind in a corner should his line intersect with a suddenly-discovered rock on the road.

The Player lacks the cornering clearance for moderate (side- and centerstand left-side) to proper (right-side pipes) heroics. Especially swinging left, you wouldn't want to bore into a corner too hot—and have to crank the bike over harder to stay on the road. In that situation you might have to trust both the macadam and dirt capabilities of TT100 Dunlops. JPS owners should do themselves a favor: remove the whole sidestand assembly and file off a corner of the centerstand. That still leaves the pipes, but most riders might well be approaching the tape-and-bandage state of public highway riding when they start grinding flat spots in the pipes and mufflers.

Cafe racers are never really comfortable; there are simply levels of pain or its absence. Riding positions are particularly critical. Dimensions that fall an inch short, for example, may spoil a touring machine's riding comfort while an inch's error can make a cafe racer all but unbearable. Furthermore, what fits a rider who is five-ten and 160 pounds may put a six-foot 185-pound rider in sheer agony. Even two people who are the same height and weight may disagree about the "bearability" of the same motorcycle. Differences in arm, leg and torso measurements can result in far different judg-

ments about comfort. Anyone who buys a cafe racer should expect to do some individual tailoring.

Cycle's larger staffers felt both stretched and cramped on the JPS. The bars were too far from the saddle, and the stretch produced sore arm and neck muscles after an hour in the saddle. Most American riders would probably welcome clip-ons which could be located about three inches higher and two inches rearward from their present position. As the JPS bars pulled riders forward, the footpegs seemed too far back. Larger riders started to hang their boots on the pegs by the heels. This, in turn, dropped the toes down too far for brisk riding. In a series of corners the boots had to be pulled back on the pegs and up out of the way.

Big feet combined with the gearshift lever to create an awkward situation for some riders in right-hand corners. With the JPS clicked over hard to the right, the gearshift lever is so close to the pavement that a big foot can't get under the lever to change up a gear. What's worse, you could get a size-13 toe caught between the road and the lever, and that shocking experience is guaranteed to widen your line through any righthander.

The Norton's hand controls remain as before: wing switches for the high-low beam and the directional signals, and a half-turn throttle which should be a quarter-turn one. As always, the clutch pull is light, thanks to the diaphragm-spring clutch. And the Lockheed disc brake has a firm, progressive feel at the lever which translates into a lot of stopping power with the Dunlop TT100 front tire. Two staffers complained that the front brake lever started working too soon—the lever hadn't arced back sufficiently for some riders to get a grip strong enough for a tire-howling stop from high speed. Big-handed staffers scarcely noticed the problem. Yet in this age of disc brakes, there's little reason for brake levers to be positioned as far away from the handgrip as the clutch lever, unless manufacturers find symmetry a compelling argument.

Down in the foot department, the four-speed Norton transmission, once

Continued on page 203

● Amal lovers, grit your teeth. This is yet another feature which suggests how British Amal carburetors might best proceed from some cylinderhead to the refuse-shelf. On the other hand, those enthusiasts who love their Norton Commandos —but mistrust Amal mixers—may wish to read on.

There's an Amal legend in motorcycling. According to tradition, the instruments work pretty well when new and then begin, with varying degrees of rapidity, to develop annoying habits. One distressing feature, present from new, is leakage. Unless the petcock is turned off when parked, a gassy dew collects on the carburetors and relentlessly drips off. Even worse, open petcocks allow the Amals to hemorrhage internally: gas runs down the manifolds, washes the cylinder walls, and primes the engine for a hard start.

Real bothers come with use. Though good dealers can synchronize Amal carburetors precisely, the slides fall out of unison as the cable lengths change slightly. Moreover, the adjustment screw controlling slide height and the air-mixture screw for the idle circuit fit loosely in the carburetor body. Indexing the screws helps to maintain the positions but even the best lock does not guarantee unending accuracy. The slides and carburetor bodies wear against one another, and after a certain time and mileage—such as 5000 miles or more—the slides get loose in their bores. This sloppiness eliminates almost any chance of getting the carburetion straight and consistent. Don't

NORTON COMMANDO
THE MIKUNI CONVERSION

PHOTOGRAPHY: BELA LUKACS

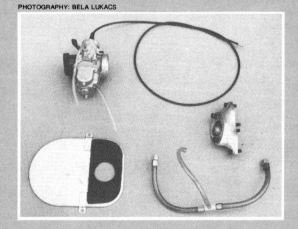

laugh if some British bike owner tells you that he can hear the slides ticking inside the carburetors when the engine is idling. He's not kidding.

Amals, then, are almost living things; they change with age. Typically, owners of Amal-carbureted products will first notice a deterioration in the idling mode. Very simply, the motorcycle either refuses to idle, or idles irregularly and erratically. Though the throttle may be snapped shut, the engine speed will only drop to 1500 or 1800 rpm; then it tapers off slowly to 800 or 900 rpm, whereupon the engine burps and dies. The owner normally cannot take his hand off the twist-grip at stoplights. And as he accelerates away, he'll notice a small hesitation or flat spot

in the carburetion just above idle speed. These constant changes encourage many owners to delve into the Amal adjustment business. Of course the results depend upon the resourcefulness and ability of individual owners. And luck. In general, Amal owners learn to live with imperfect idling. Rather than sinking more time into the bottomless pit of adjustment, they build and polish some extraordinary rationales. To wit: "It doesn't idle perfectly, but that's no more serious than a Japanese bike which has a lot of sloppiness in its driveline. Naturally, because any idiot can identify an idling problem (the engine stops), that seemingly makes it more serious in the scheme of things. Since people buy motorcycles according

quarter-mile performance suffers a bit.

As a rule of thumb, twin carburetors better fill the Norton cylinders at high engine speeds (near the peak) because the inertia ram effect, which helps to stuff the charge into the cylinders, can be more easily exploited inside individual intake tracts. However, were some bright and enterprising individual willing to spend enough time and effort flow-testing single-carburetor manifolds for vertical twins, he could devise manifolds which would flow mixture as well as—if not better than—dual carburetor systems with individual intakes.

The 34mm Mikuni carburetor must work twice as hard as either the 32mm Amals it replaces. That should present no problem. A 360-degree vertical twin draws fuel/air mix into the cylinders at separate intervals anyway, so twin carburetors spend much of their time loafing.

Hard work, however, doesn't account for the increased size of the Mikuni. The elbow in the Y-manifold slows down the air velocity from the carburetor to the cylinderhead. Moving air always takes the shortest possible path it can find. This mad rush along the shortest path creates turbulance elsewhere inside the manifold, and beyond a certain level, the turbulance begins to foul the main current of air.

If you begin moving the fuel-bearing air at considerable velocity through the elbow, not only will the air become confused and lose its way, the air actually will drop the fuel it's carrying. The world's best manifold, as designed by our bright and enterprising flow-bench artist, wouldn't have this problem. He could maintain a high gas velocity through the manifold, and the air would stay well-behaved enough so that it wouldn't spit its fuel load out.

A straight commercial adapter/manifold isn't flow-bench designed. That means slower air velocity through the manifold. Within limits, if the velocity is reduced, you still can get more fuel into the system by increasing the carburetor area. The 34mm Mikuni carburetor provides that area increase.

Stripping off the Amals is easy. Remove the tank and seat, disconnect the cables from the handlebar controls, and unbolt the air filter. The allenhead screws on the outside of the two manifolds are a cinch to take out. More difficult are the inside allenheads, since there's very little maneuvering room between the carburetors. As the Norton manual advises, "a shortened socket key is needed for ease of removal." Tough it out.

Having dispatched the Amals to the appropriate shelf, the Do-it Engineering manifold can be bolted straight on. Don't forget to sandwich the gaskets between the manifold and the cylinderhead. Clumsy workers should replace the inside socket screws (with lock washers) with great care. In the single-carb manifold the inside socket screws actually go in the interior of the manifold. Thumb-fingered folks could lose a socket screw or lock washer right down an inlet port. If you anticipate trouble, stuff small rags in the

Main electrical line passes over the Mikuni; any fouling can be avoided by using very little of cap's cable adjuster.

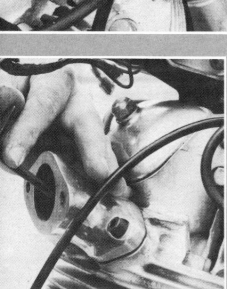

Proceed with care when fitting the inside/interior socket bolts. One slip could drop a washer or screw down an inlet port.

to individual preferences, majority vote shouldn't determine what is or isn't a serious handicap. The majority can only tell you what an obvious problem is."

For Norton owners who would rather switch than argue, Do-it Engineering (1135 Barkley, Unit H, Orange, California) offers a cure. The remedy consists of an intake manifold, matched on one end to the Norton intake ports and on the other to a single Mikuni carburetor. It's a bolt-on operation to the cylinderhead, and the 34mm Mikuni plugs into the Do-it manifold *via* its own rubber mount. The set-up costs $89.00. The single Mikuni provides a slight gain in miles-per-gallon, improves the 850 engine's throttle response, strengthens fourth-gear acceleration (50 to 80 mph), makes starting easier, produces a reliable idle, and does not leak. There are two drawbacks. First, you must build your own air cleaner adaptation, and

NORTON COMMANDO THE MIKUNI CONVERSION

ports. Then should you drop a screw or washer, you won't need to remove the cylinderhead.

A universal cable, silver solder and small torch will allow you to build a cable to the precise length. Because the Norton twistgrip uses a single-cable roller drum, you can use the stock item. Get the cable length as close as possible. You don't want to use very much of the screw-adjuster at the top of the Mikuni carburetor. If the adjuster is screwed out a fair distance, then the throttle cable and adjuster will foul the electrical trunk line which passes above the carburetor. The throttle cable should be no longer than necessary and carefully routed. The Mikuni spring

Existing fuel lines can be used; the only extra parts needed will be a T-junction ($1.00) and an extra length of gas line ($.25).

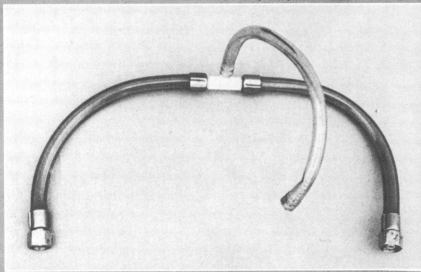

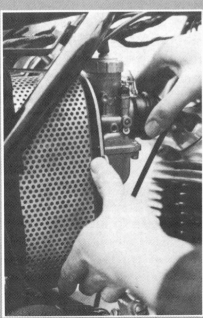

Final assembly requires air cleaner panel to be mounted to the Mikuni; lack of room requires carb to be detached from the manifold.

Modified air cleaner panel features closed-cell neoprene sheet glued into place with a liberal dose of silicone sealant.

isn't nearly so strong as the twin Amal springs. If you route the cable carelessly, or leave it super-long, or don't lubricate it, then the Mikuni carburetor slide will close reluctantly. It won't stick, but it won't close unless you roll back the throttle.

Pull the fuel lines off the Amal carburetors. Both lines should be fed into a T-junction. The single lead coming out of the T-connector feeds directly to the Mikuni float bowl.

There's a simple way you can keep the present air cleaner—and you should, because pleated paper elements provide superior filtration for street motorcycles. Just remember that the Norton engine shakes a lot on its Isolastic cushions, but the air cleaner has a solid mount. The carburetor must be connected to the air filter box with a soft mounting. We built a straightforward system with a hacksaw, a file, silicone seal, and a small piece of closed-cell neoprene sheet.

A quick lash-up will show you where the Norton filter cover and the rear of the Mikuni will meet. Saw an opening *larger* than the mouth of the Mikuni. Remember that the Mikuni will be shaking, and the air-filter cover will remain stationary. You'll find that you have opened up the area between individual holes through which the Amals drew air. Smooth the ragged edges of the cut with a file.

Closed-cell neoprene sheet makes a good cover and connector. It's flexible and glueable, and the closed-cells won't pass air. The round hole in the neoprene sheet must not be too large. You want a snug fit around the Mikuni mouth. Cut the neoprene so that it covers all the open area on the air-box cover. Attach with silicone seal. On the interior of the air box cover, apply silicone seal liberally around the cut edges—just for insurance against any air leaks.

Assemble the set up. It's a tight fit. You must unbolt the Mikuni at its rubber adapter, put the paper filter element in place, slide the air box cover on the Mikuni, slip the carburetor and cover in place, and bolt up the carburetor.

Our Mikuni required only one adjustment. Having set the idle, we left it alone. The engine started easily, settled into a dependable 1000-rpm idle and became wonderfully responsive. The strong spring pressure of the Amal carburetors had been replaced with the velvet softness of the Mikuni.

Dragstrip testing revealed no real shocks. As a temporary expedient, we had mounted a green filter sock on the Mikuni. After a couple of runs (13.7 and 13.8 at 92–93 mph) we pulled off the green sock. The time dropped to 13.65 and the speed improved slightly. The best run with the Amals delivered 13.4 at 96 mph. Times did not change when we removed the air filter, so we concluded that the huge Norton air cleaner does not impede performance one bit. That convinced us to retain the standard cleaner with the Mikuni set-up.

Another day of experimentation yielded more information. There's no discernable difference between the Mikuni and the

Amals on a fourth-gear pull from an indicated 50 mph to an indicated 70 mph. The Mikuni is more responsive, but responsiveness is not the same thing as horsepower. The Amals even took time out to hesitate momentarily when the throttle was snapped open. But once under way, the Amals pulled the Norton very smartly to 70 mph.

A four-gear pull from an indicated 50 to an indicated 80 mph did establish a margin. The single Mikuni carburetor would accelerate to 80 mph more quickly. The difference in distance amounted to three or four bike lengths. The gain was hardly overwhelming. In short, the Mikuni works equally as well, or slightly better, between 50 mph and 80 mph (3200 rpm and 5000 rpm). Clearly the Amals hold an advantage between 5000 and 7000 rpm as shown by dragstrip testing.

Performance-junkies will look at the quarter-mile performance and laugh at the Mikuni adaption. Norton owners who use their 750s and 850s on the road and who never tweak their engines beyond 5000 rpm will opt for the Mikuni. There's no doubt which carburetion system *Cycle* staffers prefer: the Mikuni. In every way, save two-tenths or so in the quarter-mile, the Mikuni is far better.

Cycle pitted the Mikuni carburetor conversion against a fine set of Amals which had been put in perfect fettle. *Cycle*'s test mule was an 850 Norton Interstate with 2000 miles on the clock. As noted earlier in the John Player Special road test (December, 1974), Amal carburetion on current Nortons, as provided to *Cycle* Magazine, is outstanding. Though present metering is much improved on new Commandos, there's no reason to believe the current batch of Amals won't develop woes after 5000 miles. Indeed, a couple of Norton owners who had far more than 5000 miles on their bikes tried our test mule. They were amazed. They had never ridden a Norton with such accurate Amal carburetion, though they allowed that early-on, their bikes had been almost as good. Time and mileage, however, had debilitated their carburetion.

Cycle's best advice amounts to this: If you have a new Norton, and the carburetion is satisfactory, there's no point in buying a Do-it Engineering manifold and kit. When your carburetion does get fuzzy and reaches an incurable stage, then the single-carburetor Mikuni makes sense. If you already own an older 750 or 850 Norton which you plan to keep riding, the Do-it Engineering adaptation is a worthwhile improvement.

Though we built our own, the $89 shot now includes a throttle cable. You'll also find in the kit the Mikuni carburetor, rubber manifold, mounting bolts, and the Do-it Engineering aluminum manifold.

To those Norton owners who are sensitive about putting a Japanese carburetor on a British machine, just relax. With the standard air cleaner, your Anglophile friends will only notice the modification with a close second look. And why would they look again? Easy. Your Norton will idle, and theirs still won't. ◉

NORTON
Text continued from page 40

Norton motorcycles have long been noted for good handling and the Commando S is no exception. The bike is fitted with Avon tires that resemble road racing covers. The rear tire is semi-triangulated and the front boot is ribbed. Both tires, a 3.00 on the front and a 3.50 on the rear, are mounted on 19 inch chromed rims. A twin leading shoe brake is fitted at the front, this 8 inch diameter unit is supplied with an air scoop and pressure relief holes. The brake at the rear of the machine is a standard Norton component. The brakes on out test machine proved to be up to the demands made by the potential of the bike.

(The owner's handbook supplied with the Commando S states that the machine is . . . "equally at home on the highway or on rough trials." Elsewhere, the handbook warns against fitting any other types of tires. Have you ever tried to ride in the dirt with what are essentially road racing tires? It's quite an experience!)

Handling and suspension on the Commando S are virtually impossible to fault. The front forks appear to be the famed Roadholders with the gaiters and metal covers removed. Girling shocks, with the lower covers removed, control the movement of the swing arm. The Norton is one of the select group of machines that is equally at home on the freeway or on a twisting mountain road. You can power the machine through a sharp turn with a degree of steadyness rarely found on a touring machine. Everything feels rock steady and the suspension transmits precise information as to the state of adhesion.

Much of our time with the Commando S was spent on the twisting roads that lace the mountains surrounding Los Angeles. One good indication of the handling of the machine was that our riders would return after an hour or two in the mountains and comment that they weren't tired. That's a sign of really good handling; the bike does most of the work giving the rider the opportunity to enjoy the ride.

Basically, motorcycling is just that: enjoying the ride. The Norton Commando S is the kind of machine you can enjoy at both ends of a six hour ride, it's truly one of the super bikes!

NORTON COMMANDO mk3

We bought it at random, right off the showroom floor. We rod[e] it non-stop for three days, covering 3,000 miles – like riding cle[ar] across the USA! We completed our 10,000 km test mileage [–] that's equivalent to a year's normal use – inside three months. An[d] after 5,000 miles we put it through the most exhaustive perform[ance] tests ever. How did it rate? A Beauty or a Beast? Our four [–] page test report gives you all the answers.

solo

ACCELERATION ON GRADIENT

FROM REST

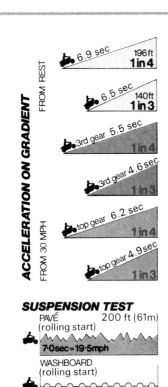

6.9 sec	196 ft	1 in 4
6.5 sec	140 ft	1 in 3
3rd gear 5.5 sec		1 in 4
3rd gear 4.6 sec		1 in 3
top gear 6.2 sec		1 in 4
top gear 4.9 sec		1 in 3

FROM 30 MPH

SUSPENSION TEST

PAVÉ (rolling start) 200 ft (61m)

7·0 sec = 19·5 mph

WASHBOARD (rolling start)

9·0 sec = 15·2 mph

ACCELERATION OVER STANDING ¼ MILE (400m)

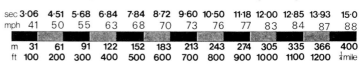

sec	3·06	4·51	5·68	6·84	7·84	8·72	9·60	10·50	11·18	12·00	12·85	13·93	15·0
mph	41	50	55	63	68	70	73	76	77	83	84	87	88
m	31	61	91	122	152	183	213	243	274	305	335	366	400
ft	100	200	300	400	500	600	700	800	900	1000	1100	1200	¼ mile

ACCELERATION FROM REST

0-30 mph	2·7 sec
0-40	3·0
0-50	4·51
0-60	6·0
0-70	8·72

SPEED RANGES IN THE GEARS

1st gear	4 mph	48 mph
2nd	10	73
3rd	13	92
4th	19	107

BRAKING FROM 30 MPH

Front	47 ft
Rear	58
Both	35

SPEEDO CORRECTION

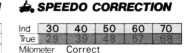

Ind	30	40	50	60	70
True	29	39	48	57	68
Milometer	Correct				

FUEL CONSUMPTION

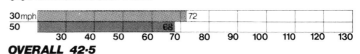

| 30 mph | 72 |
| 50 | 68 |

| | 30 | 40 | 50 | 60 | 70 | 80 | 90 | 100 | 110 | 120 | 130 |

OVERALL 42·5

with passenger

ACCELERATION ON GRADIENT

FROM REST

6.2 sec	1 in 4
7.0 sec	1 in 3
3rd gear 6.3 sec	1 in 4
3rd gear 6.2 sec	1 in 3
top gear 8.4 sec	1 in 4
top gear Failed	1 in 3

FROM 30 MPH

ACCELERATION OVER STANDING ¼ MILE (400m)

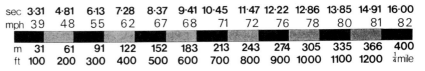

sec	3·31	4·81	6·13	7·28	8·37	9·41	10·45	11·47	12·22	12·86	13·85	14·91	16·00
mph	39	48	55	62	67	68	71	72	76	78	80	81	82
m	31	61	91	122	152	183	213	243	274	305	335	366	400
ft	100	200	300	400	500	600	700	800	900	1000	1100	1200	¼ mile

ACCELERATION FROM REST

0-30 mph	2·8 sec
0-40	3·6
0-50	5·8
0-60	7·1
0-70	10·3

SPEED RANGES IN THE GEARS

1st gear	4 mph	48 mph
2nd	10	73
3rd	13	92
4th	19	102

SUSPENSION TEST

PAVÉ (rolling start) 200 ft (61m)

6·0 sec = 22·7 mph

WASHBOARD (rolling start)

7·0 sec = 19·5 mph

BRAKING FROM 30 MPH

Front	53 ft
Rear	68
Both	38

Norton

850
Commando
ELECTRIC START

NORTON
COMMANDO MK3
'Marathon 1'

IT was 8 o'clock in the morning on Thursday, August 7, when Steve Hackett straddled the Norton outside his home at Sutton to set off on the first stage of our Motorway Marathon.

We had chosen, for this non-stop three-day run, the circuit formed by the M4, M5, M6, M62 and M1 motorways. That meant that, on each lap, our riders would go either from London to Bristol, Birmingham, Manchester, Leeds, and back; or, to ensure a different set of conditions, in the reverse direction. The result was a stamina-sapping course of just over 500 miles per lap — stamina-sapping not just for the rider, but also for the bike. We were scheduled to cover it twice each day — one day run: one night run — and the engine would never grow cold for three whole days or nights. The longest stops would be on the change-over at the end of each lap, when the incoming rider was briefed and any necessary maintenance carried out — our testers were on their own; no back-up cars or service vans on this effort!

In practice, a stop only once exceeded an hour. With 45-minute halts for meals — and pull-ups for refuelling — this meant that daytime laps were of around 9½ hours duration. That gave a road average of 54 mph for 510 miles. Understandably, the night-time laps were a little slower.

Steve was the first to find that the Roadster's tank capacity of 3 US gallons — only 2½ Imperial gallons — was hardly ideal for sustained speedwork. North of Bristol he went on to reserve, and spent an anxious 25 miles waiting for the next Service Area to turn up. Mind you, he *did*

have a spare gallon in the can we had thoughtfully strapped to the back, and he needed it right at the end of his lap, when he only *just* contrived to reach the Watford Gap area on the range provided by the spare fuel and the reserve combined. . . .

At Scratchwood, with the bike running well and 515 miles covered, Steve handed over to Phil Mather for the night shift. Apart from a high-speed weave, which was to trouble us throughout the rest of the Marathon, Phil had no bother — though he, too, had some unkind words to say about fuel reserves that last only 20 miles, when Service Areas can be 30 miles or more apart.

However, it was during this lap that oil leakage was first noted. Right at the start, the rev counter drive had been seeping: during the night, more and more lubricant began to cover the outside of the engine. A pint of oil was added after 138 miles, and a further pint 353 miles later.

The leaking connection was tightened at the end of the lap, and the drive chain was adjusted before Charles Deane set out on the second daylight stint. He reported a near-faultless ride, except for oil leaks — where the rev counter's efforts were now being reinforced by a hit-and-miss tank cap seal which was spraying lubricant along the whole off-side rear — and for chain trouble. Severe vibration at speeds above 60 mph was attributed to a dry and stretched chain, and a new one was fitted at the end of the lap, with 3,446.9 miles on the clock. Another pint of oil was added, too.

By 7.30pm on Friday, the Norton had covered 1,537.9 miles in 35½ hours, and Steve Hackett was in charge of the night's 'milk run'.

Riding down the M4, he encountered heavy holiday traffic. Then, nearing Bristol, came the first streaks of lightning. Before long, he was ploughing through thunderstorms, heavy rain, and the spray from cars and caravans. Reduced to a 50mph cruise, despite the Norton's excellent lights, Steve kept pace with the rain all the way to Manchester. And he found out, the hard way, that night-time riding on the motorways can be a cold business, as well as a wet one!

By the time Phil set off on the last daylight circuit — on Saturday morning — the Norton was a somewhat grimy sight. At 3,955 miles, it had covered just over 2,000 miles in two days — and it looked it. The offside was saturated with oil and road dirt, and though Phil cleaned the fouling from the rear disc brake it was oiled up again within 17 miles. The filler seal had done its worst by then — it took three pints of oil to get a reading back on the dipstick! — but only one further pint was needed during the rest of that 500-mile lap. By then, though, the tick-over was becoming erratic.

Some people are devils for punishment: for the final circuit Charles had a passenger — his daughter. Must run in the family. . . .

Riding by way of Leeds and Liverpool, and loping along at an easy 70 mph, Charles reported "no complaints" from the pillion during the entire trip. The extra load made little difference to either speed or fuel consumption, but Charles was the second of our test team to be caught out by that restricted tank capacity, running dry after covering just over 100 miles from fill-up.

Well before 8 am on Sunday morning, Charles brought the travel-stained Norton to a halt outside his house in South London, and the most ambitious road-test for years was over.

Our Norton, with no special preparation, had covered 3,147.1 gruelling miles in just under 72 hours' total time. At running averages of upwards of 50 mph it had returned daytime fuel consumptions of 42.8 mpg. On the quieter night laps, its thirst had dropped to around 50 mpg. There had been no major mechanical trouble: the electrics had gained nothing but praise: and the only dull note was that curse of the British motorcycle, oil leakage.

We were almost inclined to forgive the Commando that one aberration. . . .

DELIVERY FAULTS

After collection from Lewes, the Norton was ridden five miles to our Editor's garage, and checked. The following delivery faults were found:—

1). The top Dzus fastener on the battery cover was insecure. When the fastener was opened, the lower part fell off.
2). The battery cover had paint "curtains" along its leading edge.
3). The seat lock was reluctant to open due to excessive play in the catch.
4). The nearside footrest hanger

had an area of discoloured chrome.
5). The gear pedal had 5/16-in. vertical play.
6). The nearside pillion footrest pivot was so tight that the rest could not be lowered.
7). Rust was forming at a spot weld on the rear chaincase bracket.
8). Drilling swarf had not been cleared from the holes in the air filter box.
9). The offside fuel tap was loose in the tank.
10). The offside fuel pipe was finger-tight at the tap union.
11). There was a right-angle bend in the throttle cable where it passed round the steering head. The radius of this bend was approx. a quarter of an inch.
12). There was a sharp bend in the choke cable, next to the lever.
13). The offside carburettor drain plug was weeping.
14). The speedometer dial was completely obscured by a running-in label set over an almost illegible label referring to the use of the trip knob.
15). The speedometer dial was set off-centre to the left by 5°.

16). The rev-counter dial was set off-centre to the left by 15°.
17). The cylinder head upper fin was cracked from its centre point to the first head bolt fixing hole. Later, examination by the dealer showed that the head casting was also porous.

SUBSEQUENT FAULTS

1). Within 50 miles, oil leaks developed from:—
   a). The front lower timing chest joint.
   b). The lower joint of the primary chaincase.
   c). The crankcase strainer body joint.
   d). The plug beneath the gearbox.
2). Within 75 miles, engagement of neutral from a standstill became almost impossible.
3). Up to 1,000 miles, operation of the starter usually failed to turn the engine unless the kickstarter was used at the same time.
4). Front brake squeal set in after 75 miles.
5). At 106 miles, the speedometer light unseated itself and the speedo trip reset spindle fell out.

6). At 160 miles, the neutral indicator light failed.
7). At 209 miles, the exhaust pipes and the balance pipe were turning straw-coloured in the area of the ports.
8). At 302 miles the primary chaincase gasket started to creep out of the joint about halfway along the top run.
9). At 400 miles the gasket was fractured, allowing oil to leak from the case: oil was leaking from the front of the timing chest: and brake fluid was seeping from the handlebar reservoir.
10). At 800 miles, the kinked throttle cable jammed. with the engine opened up — luckily at a standstill. Cutting it open revealed that half the cable strands were fractured, acting as pawls on the inner casing.
11). At 980 miles, the machine was beginning to smoke heavily for about five seconds after starting.
12). At 1500 miles, oil was leaking past a badly-fitting filler cap on to the rear forks, rear wheel, and tyre.

150

JFG 664N

*. We first saw our road test Norton on a Sunday morning. It was standing in the showroom of Redhill Motors Ltd. in East Street, Lewes, Sussex. To be honest, it was not our first choice: that had been a beautiful Interstate, in traditional Norton silver, black and red, at the North St., Brighton, branch of the same firm. Unfortunately, one of the snags in testing "the bike the reader might have bought" is that on occasion the unfeeling reader may nip in ahead of you and buy it before you can lay hands on it.

And that's why you are not now reading a test of an Interstate. It was sold before the ponderous IPC bureaucracy could bring itself to sign away £1200 or so. Result? We had to settle for a second-choice machine — which at least proves that when we say we buy 'em off the showroom floor that's precisely what we do . . .!

Our Mk.3 Roadster was delivered on May 22, 1975. It had engine Number 330171 and frame Number F130740. The odometer reading was 00006 miles.

After 740 miles, it was returned to Redhill Motors Ltd. for the free first service and correction of faults under warranty.

After collection, it was ridden a matter of 20 miles before the driver of a Mercedes 350 took an instant dislike to all motorcycles — and our Norton in particular — and charged out of a side road straight into the left-hand side of the Norton. The Merc's wheel put several dents and scrapes into the Commando's nearside silencer, and pushed it off line on to a collision course with approaching cars.

Luckily, the rider was able to keep control and to ride, at 30 mph, up a two-foot bank on to a grass "island" between the three roads converging at that point. Understandably, he was unable to maintain control afterwards, and the Norton dug in its right-hand footrest. The damage was:—
1). Right footrest hanger bent.
2). Brake pedal bent.
3). Rear hydraulic cylinder brake rod bent.
4). Right-hand front indicator smashed.
5). Right-hand fork shroud bent.
6). Fork stanchions misaligned.
7). Left-hand silencer dented and scraped.

The machine was, nonetheless, still ridable and it was returned to Redhill Motors. It remained off the road until mid-July — five weeks later. According to the dealers, this was due to non-supply of parts by the factory: and though Redhill Motors were able to make the machine roadworthy by straightening some of the original units they were still awaiting a footrest hanger and silencer in early September.

This delay robbed us of nearly six weeks' testing: nonetheless, the Norton was ready to embark on our Motorway Marathon by August 7, the only replacement part necessary in the interim being a faulty throttle cable. During the Marathon, we also made a precautionary chain change.

Apart from normal maintenance items — the fitting of new oil filter elements, for instance — JFG 664N completed our 10,000km (6,250 miles) test with no further failures.

13). At 2,500 miles the rev-counter drive began to leak oil.
14). At 3,955 miles, the top oil tank mounting bracket fractured.

TOOLS

★ The tool kit was checked on delivery. We found that it contained no spanner capable of loosening the rear wheel spindle nut — just how *is* one supposed to adjust the chain? None of the spanners would fit the front fork filler plugs, nor the crankcase gauze strainer body.

The kit was packed into a thin plastic tray and it was awkward to get the roll back tightly enough to enable the seat to be closed down.

The seat lock was laughable. The lock's hook was located on a squared section of the catch and held by a single central bolt. It took roughly 20 seconds to insert a suitable open-ended spanner behind the lock, undo the bolt, flick off the hook, and open the (in theory!) still-locked seat.

TYRES

★ As standard, the Norton is equipped with Dunlop Roadmaster K 81 (TT 100) tyres. The tread depth was measured on delivery, and again at 5,417 miles, and the following wear pattern established:—

Front tyre.
Measurement at valve: tread depth in mm.

	Left		Centre		Right	
Outer	Inner			Inner	Outer
5	6	7½		6	4½
Measurement after 5,417 miles					
4½	5½	7		5½	4½
Measurement opposite valve					
4½	6	7½		6	4½
Measurement after 5,417 miles					
4½	5½	6½		5½	4½

Rear tyre.
Measurement at valve: tread depth in mm.

	Left		Centre		Right	
Outer	Inner			Inner	Outer
5	6½	8		6	5
Measurement after 5,417 miles					
5	2	2		4	5
Measurement opposite valve					
5	6	7½		6	5½
Measurement after 5,417 miles					
5	4½	2		5	5½

From this, we would postulate a life of some 25,000 miles for a front cover and 6,300 miles for the rear.

Although the Commando had barely notched 1,900 miles on the clock before our marathon began, we decided to run through the recommended 3,000 mile service schedule as well as checking out the usual day-to-day items such as tyre pressures and battery level. Though we have a well equipped workshop, we figured it worthwhile seeing just how far we could get with the Norton's own tool kit, but the bated-breath routine had to wait because on the first job — adjusting the rear chain — we couldn't find a spanner to fit the wheel spindle nuts!

For chain lubrication, Norton supply an aerosol of Ambersil spray, so we gave the links a good dousing — the handbook recommends lubing at 500 mile intervals — and added the can to the list of essentials to take with us. Unfortunately, it contained only enough for six man-sized applications.

Next we changed the engine oil and replaced the cartridge-type filter. Draining the tank is easy enough, provided you have a piece of cardboard handy to channel away the oil, but again there was no spanner in the tool kit suitable for removing the tank and crankcase strainers.

The oil filter itself is disposable and tucked away behind the gearbox. Unless you have a bike lift (like us), or a convenient hole to stand in, removing the filter is a grovelling operation and we found it necessary to punch a screwdriver through the filter to enable it to be unscrewed from its fixing.

Ignition timing can be checked either by strobe or with the engine stationary. Either method requires two people, the timing indicator plate being mounted in the primary chain case on the opposite side of the motor to the contact breaker points. The stationary method also requires a 'special washer', which is not supplied with the machine, to lock the auto advance unit. There is, however, a feeler gauge for gapping the points.

Removal of the fuel tank — secured with four Nyloc nuts — facilitates access to the rockers. Adjustment here is a straightforward operation which owes much to the cut-away design of the rocker box itself.

The primary chain is oil-bath lubricated, the correct level being determined by a plug set in the outer primary cover. Likewise, a level plug in the rear of the gearbox cover determines the oil content. Topping up is done through the filler cap, which also allows for inspection of clutch push rod adjustment.

To determine the correct amount of play in the Isolastic engine mountings it is first necessary to support the machine under the main frame tubes, leaving the centre stand folded. The clearances can then be checked, the front on the righthand side and the rear on the left. The Isolastic adjusters are well protected from moisture and road dirt by rubber gaiters, and a small tommy bar is included in the tool kit for altering the clearances. However, the handbook *does* recommend that, if disturbed, the main mounting bolts are retightened with a torque spanner to 30 lb/ft.

★ HALF of the Commando's mileage was accounted for by the Marathon: the rest was divided almost equally between open-road and town riding, with something like 250 miles of track testing thrown in.

PERFORMANCE

Without so much as bending a law, the Commando would put up road averages of 40-plus and combine them with a fuel consumption better than that obtainable from quite a few smaller-engined bikes. A 96-mile trip from Lewes to Andover, for instance, took 140 minutes to complete on 1.8 gallons of fuel. Average speed, 41.4 mph. Consumption, 53.7 mpg. Quite creditable for a twisty journey, mainly on single-carriageway roads.

On running such as this, the Commando was as nearly single-geared as made no difference. The engine was operating nowhere near the speed at which maximum torque would be produced — nearly 85 mph — but there was ample power in top gear above 45 mph, and third looked after the rest. Tweaking the grip, in either gear, produced immediate and very satisfying acceleration with no fuss. Though top-gear vibration had been troublesome below 3,000 rpm initially, it lessened considerably during the first 1,000 miles use, and 50 mph top-gear cruising on restricted roads gradually became positively restful!

In towns, unfortunately, it was a different story. The Commando was not — and is not — a pleasant machine to use in congested areas. Really, it is under heavy traffic conditions that the Commando begins to show the age of its basic concept. Even at 20 mph in bottom gear, the engine is below the critical 3,000 rpm at which vibration becomes an annoyance. Top gear is almost impossible to engage, and even third a bit fraught, at traffic speeds. It is the old story of vertical-twin inflexibility writ large.

Unfortunately, in the Commando's case there are more snags too. The clutch is ferociously heavy and — worse — engagement of neutral with the machine at rest is guaranteed to produce an immovable pedal and a palpitating Commando stuck in first gear. The *only* remedy, if tentative prods at the pedal to get into neutral on the roll fail, is to cut the engine, select neutral, and then restart. Even that is sometimes more easily said than done, since the electric starter has only just enough power to swing each 414 cc cylinder over compression, and dabs on the button are not invariably successful. You then have to kick the thing *and* press the button at the same time, since kick-starting alone requires the leg muscles of a centre-forward allied with the weight of a young elephant . . .

A commuting Commando is also thirsty. We recorded 39.8 mpg on suburbs-to-centre work, compared with over 45 mpg on runs from Lewes to Central London.

HANDLING AND RIDE

Oddly, the handling improved noticably as the mileage mounted. At first, the Commando handled as well as, but no better than, any one of half a dozen comparable superbikes. It was safe, predictable, and reasonably accurate. It was *not* outstanding. But after 6,000 miles it was noticably tauter and responsive, maturing like a vintage wine.

The riding position is good, though the lack of adjustable footrests is a nuisance, and the bike does not tend to tire the rider so long as the speed is kept above the low-frequency vibration band. Also, its firm suspension gave a good ride, though track tests disclosed limitations. It coped with pavé, but on washboard surfaces pushing the speed up induced steering vibration that could have become a tank-stopper. Not the bike for the outback!

We found, on the track, that with a carrier fitted the Commando would weave noticeably. Around 85 mph appeared the threshold speed for this, and above 90 mph it felt as if it might well go out of control. The oscillation disappeared if the rider crouched over the tank with knees and elbows well tucked in. Curious!

Continued on next page

NORTON
COMMANDO MK 3
IN BRIEF

ENGINE ★★★★

Apart from the oil leaks, it was the Norton's big torquey, gutsy motor that won over everybody who rode it. And for the way that mill performed we'll forgive it most of the oil-spattering we endured. . . .

Bore 77mm × stroke 89mm = 828 cc. Single-lipped roller main bearings; plain big-end shells. Cast iron block. RR 53B light alloy cylinder head, alloy connecting rods. Overhead valves operated by Dural push rods. Inlet valve 1.49in., exhaust 1.302in. Twin 32mm Amal 932 carburettors with oil-impregnated foam air cleaner. Max. torque 56 lb/ft. at 5,000rpm. Max. power 62 bhp @ 5,800rpm on 8.5:1 compression ratio.

TRANSMISSION ★★

Basically an over-development of the old-time AMC gearbox, the four-speed Norton box is notchy in operation and not improved by the new remote linkage necessary to give left-foot operation. Heavy clutch — at least it won't slip! — and fast-wearing chain now that the oiler's been discontinued complete an uninspiring story.

Internal ratios: 1st, 2.56:1; 2nd, 1.70:1; 3rd, 1.21:1; 4th, 1:1. Overall ratios: 1st, 12.40:1; 2nd, 8.25:1; 3rd, 5.90:1; 4th, 4.60:1. Standard sprockets: engine, 26T; clutch, 57T; gearbox, 19T; rear 42T (USA/Canada, gearbox 20T) other export markets, gearbox 22T). Primary drive: 92 pitches, 0.375in. × 0.250in. triple row chain. Secondary drive: 100 pitches, 0.400in. × 0.380in. single row chain. Clutch: diaphragm spring type with five friction plates.

FRAME AND FORKS ★★★★

Tough and stiff — they're built by Norton, after all — the Commando frame and forks form a unified and unique chassis. The Isolastic system is one of those devices that just shouldn't work; but it does — and though the result is not an outstanding steerer it is certainly among the top half-dozen.

Isolastic frame, with 13-in. Girling suspension units. Spring fitted length: 8.4in. Spring rate: 126 lb/in. Single-row ball steering head bearings. Telescopic front forks with 1.3589/1.3574in. main tubes. Spring free length (75½ coils): 18.687in. Spring rate: 36.5 lb/in. Total fork movement: 6 in.

WHEELS AND BRAKES ★★★

Norton-Lockheed discs at front and rear had a curiously "dead" feel to them, but they were smooth in opera-

tion and had little tendency to lock even on heavy application. They were not unduly affected by rain, and the rear one even survived its periodic baths of oil.

Hydraulically-operated 10.70in. discs front and rear. Pad friction area diameter: 1.65in. Wheel rims: WM2-19. Tyres: Dunlop K81 TT100 4.10×19in. front and rear. Pressures: 26 psi both.

ELECTRICS ★★★★

Apart from early failure of the neutral indicator light — never cured — the electrical system was first rate, and the headlamp outstanding, lighting up the road for at least a quarter of a mile ahead, yet cutting to a clean 150-yard dip with little diffusion of light. The switchgear, too, is neat and logical, though the upward movement of the headlamp flasher switch came in for criticism.

Battery: 12v 13 AH Yuasa, positive earth. Alternator: RM23 180 watt with rectifier and twin Zener diodes. Twin 17M6 coils with ballast resistor. Prestolite MGD 4111 starter motor. Lucas Type 463 quartz-halogen headlamp. Plugs: Champion N7Y. Gap: 0.023/0.028in.

EQUIPMENT AND FINISH ★★★

The pipes blued, but for the rest the Norton was singularly free of defects at the end of the test. The chrome appeared to be unmarked, and there were no rust patches on the paintwork apart from an area rubbed by the spare keys on the top fork yoke. We would have preferred a larger fuel tank, but the slim Roadster unit at least gives a more comfortable leg position than with the somewhat bulky Interstate.

We also liked the subdued exhaust note from the well-finished 3.5in. diameter silencers.

DIMENSIONS ★★★★

Almost full marks to NVT for keeping a machine of the Commando's size down to manageable physical limits. But for the over-small tank, they'd have had five stars.

Incidentally, the Commando must be the easiest machine ever to place on its centre stand — one press of the foot and up she comes . . .

Length: 87.5in. Wheelbase: 56.75in. Seat height (unladen): 33in. nominal. Width: 26in. Height to bars: 40.75in. Ground clearance: 6in. Turning circle: 17ft. 10in. Fuel tank capacity: 2.7 gal. Oil tank capacity: 5 pints. Gearbox capacity: 0.75 pints. Primary chaincase capacity: 200cc. Front fork capacity: 150cc each leg. Recommended lubricants: Engine: 20W50. Gearbox: SAE 90EP gear oil. Chaincase: 20W 50. Forks: 10W 40. Hubs: Multi-purpose lithium-based grease. Swinging fork bushes: 140 EP gear oil. Rear chain: Graphited or Moly grease.

GOOD BUY?

At face value, we would not class the Commando as a good buy. For less outlay, you *could* buy a far more sophisticated, smoother and advanced machine. The Commando is old-fashioned; still prone to oil leaks; intractable at low speeds.

However, face values are not everything. Despite the faults we found in 10,000km. testing, every member of our test team liked and respected the Commando. We would not recommend it for use mainly in built-up areas — or even where a substantial town mileage has to be covered before open roads are reached. However, where it can be used in its designed role — as an effortless high-speed touring bike of enormous stamina — we think it would justify its admittedly high price of £1,161 inc. VAT.

It is the motorcycle equivalent of a Morgan sports car — sometimes harsh, but always exciting. If you are the kind of rider who aims to end his days driving a big Ford, then the Commando is not the machine for you. If you prefer sportier but starker vehicles, then this could be close to your ideal.

By the way, we reckon that the Commando is one of a select band that will be the classics of twenty years' hence. What's more, given reasonable attention it will probably last that long too. . . .

Overall, then, our star rating for the Commando is: ★ ★ ★ ★

A NEW BREED OF NORTON FOR GENTLEMEN?

THE CLEANCUT COMMANDO!

Chocks away! But electric start regardless, the Mk III still needs an understanding touch to get it alight.

Meet the Mk III double-disc, electric start Commando — and forget the oil on your white socks, the purple bruise on your right instep and the maddening vibration at cruising speeds. DAVE MINTON has found the new breed Norton is a lean, clean machine!

FOR YEARS British bike enthusiasts have patiently tolerated oil leaks and inferior electrics for the sheer pleasure of riding some of the finest-handling road machines in the world.

Now, finally, the enthusiasts' tolerance has paid off, because at last the rest of the bike is up to scratch — the new Nortons really are superb!

Although I have never been a fan of the big woofling twins, until now I think my doubts have been reasonably well-founded. In the past a hard-driven Commando soon became a shaky Commando. Blown gaskets, burned oil, leaked oil, turning bearing races — you could bet your boots that something would give out sooner or later. Fortunately, the new Commandos are different — and perhaps a little tale I heard accounts for Norton's timely changes.

It concerns Dennis Poore and Hugh Palin, top executives in the Norton-Villiers-Triumph group. Poore is Chairman of NVT — a man of incredible determination and willpower who has seen his company through a traumatic period that would have defeated lesser men. That's why I like this story and believe there's more than a grain of truth in it.

FIRST RIDE!

Poore and Palin were motoring down through Italy to Imola a couple of years ago in Poore's big Mercedes. A fast car that Merc, with a big fuel-injected V8 under the bonnet, and its occupants were making the best of its high speed cruising. Now, if there is one thing Poore understands it's fast motoring, he being an ex-racing driver of considerable ability.

Just occasionally, a small group of hardened and experienced big bike pilots managed to get past him. Even more frequently Poore overtook gaggles of fast riders. Their speed was around 160 km/h. Poore said to Palin, "Why are none of them riding Nortons?" Palin admitted that Nortons were not popular with Continental riders because they would not cruise reliably at continual high speed.

On Poore's return to England two things happened. Norton engines were considerably beefed-up all round to get over the mechanical unreliability, and Bob Manns was made chief tester.

Bob is one of those rare men — the professional enthusiast. His riding dates back to the days when Britain won the ISDT and he was in the team on a Matchless 650. Being chief tester for Norton still means what it used to in the days when men like Edward Turner and Val Page were in charge of testing for their factories. They rode their products and took note of what

their test riders told them. To be a tester then you had to be a skilled, analytic engineer with a bent for racing — and combine all this with incredible patience.

Such a man is Bob Manns. What he says goes — on personal command from Dennis Poore. Nothing passes the test department unless they agree. Bob rides every day in all weather, piling up kilometres like most people take breaths.

His effect on the Commando has been very noticable. In two years it has emerged from its rubber suspended "Atlas" engined days into a punchy roadster of quality.

All told, 138 new components have gone into the '75 Commando, most of them associated with the electric start and gearbox. Basic appearance remains traditionally appealing. Note changeover of front disc to left hand side with the caliper in front of the fork leg. Apparently racing experiences have suggested this is a better setup.

The new model's motor is even more impressive on low-down torque — and has lost a lot of vibes as well! This is as much a result of the fixed gearbox and hydraulically tensioned primary drive as it is the new Isolastic setup (visible on rockerbox). Wider flange faces on engine cases are said to have eliminated oil seepage problems.

THE CLEANCUT COMMANDO!

With the advent of the 850 two years ago, heavier and much stronger engine components eliminated unreliability, but oil leaks remained. Even they have disappeared and it now appears the new Commando is capable of cruising at 130 km/h plus as well as any other bike.

Major oil leaks around that old trouble spot, the chaincase, have been totally eliminated. In place of the centre nut housing is a more conventional series of periphery crosshead bolts. These combine with wider gasket joint faces to keep this area of the bike clean. On the other side of the engine the timing cover has also had its joint faces widened for the same reason. A third alteration contributing to the outer cleanliness of the engine would be the improvement of the lubrication system.

The oil pressure relief valve inside the timing case cover has also been modified. At low engine speeds, when oil is thick, high revs can build up extreme pressures in oilways and a by-pass valve has been built in to prevent this. It also discourages frothing during high temperature operation.

The latest crankcases are a new casting with more webbing around the new, bigger main bearings and also greater wall thickness. This is the second time this has been done to the 850 crankcases. The crankshaft has also been strengthened with heavier webbing.

The performance increase is due to an improved air cleaner and larger carburettors. Another old bogey, loosening — or worse, cracking — of the exhaust pipe flanges has been prevented by a special design that allows the pipe to find its unstressed position after the other attachments have been clamped up, and so remain free of fractures.

In the words of John Hudson, the factory's most experienced maintenance and service engineer, "We've got it beaten now. There are no oil leaks anywhere, except maybe on the rev counter take-off gearbox and that is next on our improvement list. It will be changed for the production models."

Obviously oil leaks have had to be eliminated with the decision to use a hydraulic rear disc, but no one except the marketing men seem to know why the disc is there. Evidently the public wanted it — so they got it, but I'm damned if I can see the reason why. The old drum unit was effective enough; nothing special, but what rear brake is for that matter? I leave my final judgment until I have ridden a lot of Commandos over a lot more ground in widely-varying weather conditions.

One of the more interesting changes has come about through the factory's concern with private owners and racing teams. It was discovered that some machines offer improved handling with the front disc brake transferred from the right to the left side. Why this should be is a matter of conjecture but it's real enough for all new bikes to come equipped as standard with left side disc brakes.

Even the engine breather has been painstakingly designed to stop every last misty particle of oil escaping. From the crankcase it is directed into the oil tank, where initial separation of the mixed oil/air mist takes place. Finer particles that do not sink into the main reservoir are then trapped, with the air, in a simple filter system. The trapped oil then trickles into the main tank. Clean air passes into the airbox which contains the ordinary air filter. Whatever remaining oil mist is still in suspension gets burnt.

It would have been easy enough for Norton to have simply stuffed the crankcase breather tube into the induction tract and allowed the engine to burn it all.

Rear brake is a disc with the hydraulic reservoir tucked in behind footrest and right hand brake mounting plate. Probably the most significant change is the "two piece unit" setup with engine and gearbox mounted firmly together.

Slightly changed but still traditional. New switchgear is good. Front brake reservoir still gets in the way if you like a brake lever position much different from the one offered — but that's not a problem common to Norton!

THE CLEANCUT COMMANDO!

The improved system ensures that only the minimum of dirty air is inhaled into the combustion chamber. This guarantees greater efficiency.

Unlike its zippy cousin, the Trident, the Commando uses an American Prestolite starter motor. If you kick over a well-maintained, warm 850 Commando you will understand why the less powerful Lucas starter motor wasn't suitable. It also explains why the Commando requires a 150W alternator to the Trident's 120W.

The Isolastic mounts which encapsule the power and transmission train into a single isolated unit are well known enough to require no further explanation. The difference for the '75 model is that they are supported by a duplex coil spring mounting at the front of the rockerbox, just under the steering head. Aware that the three rubber bushes were to blame for vibration at low revs, Norton devised this complementary system to eliminate the low frequency, low engine speed resonance. Its damping effect is immediately noticable. Not only is the low speed vibration reduced but it dies away at low revs so that

by the time the engine is turning freely at 2000 rpm it runs smoothly.

Some of this improvement can be attributed to the hydraulic slipper tensioner within the primary chaincase and, as all backlash is eliminated, the transmission of power is considerably smoother. The hydraulic pressure for the tensioner comes from the engine oil pump.

In fitting a duplex chain, Norton has killed a few dirty birds with one stone. The system offers increased chain life and also simplifies the fitting of an efficient tensioner — but a duplex chain can only be used with a fixed engine and gearbox unit.

Sliding gearboxes are a bind. They can move of their own volition if not correctly tied down and they make chain adjustment difficult. Norton has now bolted the gearbox firmly to the engine making it a type of unit construction. Because the Americans demanded a left side gearpedal the old sliding gearbox would have been impossible anyway, as the pedal shaft now projects right through the primary chaincase just forward of the clutch. Like the Triumph system, it works through a long shaft which engages with the old selector mechanism at the other side of the transmission housing.

"Prod the starter button once only," I was told. "If the engine doesn't catch, release it immediately, wait a second, then try again."

A valuable tip, because the big twin with its two big pots and huge flywheel has a strong inertia resistance. To spin the engine would need a much bigger battery and starter motor. Mike Jackson, Norton's sales director, claimed the only starter motor powerful enough to spin the engine came from a V8 Cummins diesel and left no room for the engine itself!

Mike's got a weird sense of humor anyway. The "prod" starting system allows the engine to rebound back from compression after an abortive attempt to fire it up. The trick seems to be to switch on the fuel, tickle the carbs and with the air lever shut just "pop" the engine over. No more.

With a hot engine, exactly the same applies but without the cold start procedure. I tried the kick starter crank as well, but only to prove it really worked. It's strange, seeing a starter unit resembling the old magneto in exactly its old place once more.

Although the medium and top end power delivery of the Commando was good, it was the bottom end which most impressed me. Commandos always shook at

under 3000 rpm but smoothed out when spinning freely. They no longer shake at low rpm because of Norton's careful reappraisal of the unique "Isolastic" engine mounting and also the effectiveness of the new hydraulic primary chain adjuster-cum-auxiliary shock absorber.

Unlike its Trident stablemate the Commando is definitely not a sportster. High speed cruiser if you like, luxury tourer, but without that indefinable sharp edge so vital on a true sports machine. Like so many modern big machines it escapes any clearly defined classification.

The power output of the Commando is best used at low to medium revs, like the Harley Davidson Sportster. Despite its stretch from 750 being in the bores alone, it is nonetheless a long-stroke engine with all its inherent punch and fun at low speeds. The optimum power delivery speed might well be 5900 rpm but I never went above 5000 rpm on the road. This felt like the least strained and most comfortable maximum. I have no doubt that 6000 rpm produces more power, but the high piston speed and super-low speed "umph" suggests that owners might be advised to steer clear of prolonged high revving.

The bike is geared for a theoretical top speed of 193 km/h. Crouching over the tank in a winter riding suit, however, the best I was able to get from the machine was 177 km/h at 5400 rpm.

Some danger lies with insensitive riders not appreciating that smoothness does not necessarily indicate a lack of stress. For this reason most guys are going to have to keep an eye on the tacho because there is simply no other way to gauge top cruising speed.

Acceleration in top gear was incredible — quite incredible. I have always favored V-twins for their gearless method of fast riding, but, quite honestly, the Commando is equal to just about anything around. From 2000 rpm in top alone, which is 62.7 km/h (39 mph), the thing pulls like a truck and even from below it, but from there on about the only way to describe acceleration is to call it massive. Not wicked like a Mach III, but a smooth liquidity of motion.

During a couple of initial acceleration runs I found it impossible to use the clutch because I simply could not let go of the handlebar. Then I learned that the clutch was unnecessary. This gearbox beats most five-speeders in nifty shifting, clutch or not. Yet because of the power style of the big twin, wheelspin in the lower ratios was extremely difficult to provoke.

The front end did become light during "limit" riding around fast curves when gearchanging was attempted. Thanks to the wide power delivery period such a style was experimental only. No ordinary buff, however keen, is going to need the additional revs from a chop down to provide more power. It's all there in top!

Handling, as always on Nortons, was impeccable. Roadholding too was entirely a matter of rider experience and not limited by any machine traits at all. Stability, too, was much better than I have experienced with a good many other Nortons and I think it might stay that way.

Until now old Nortons, plus a few new ones, have that nasty built-in shimmy induced by slack Isolastic bushes, the trouble with press test bikes is that they all have correctly-shimmed rubber bushes and the rubber is new and therefore firm. Unfortunately, their engines are often not fully run-in either, which generally results in the test report suggesting a much more stable yet slower machine than a well-used Commando actually is.

Like most European motorcycles, a Commando is not properly run-in until it has covered at least

Continued

6500 km — by which time its Isolastic mounts are sloppy. I was never more amazed than when I borrowed a factory "hack" for a few weeks not so long ago. It had 8000 km up and that thing tramped on! It was so fast I thought the speedo was wrong, whereas all I was riding, for the very first time, was a well-worn 850.

Wisely, Norton has slung out the shim system of adjusting the Isolastic bushes. Now a coarse-threaded cone, adjustable by means of a simple peg issued in every toolkit, takes up the slack. Time taken for each bush is said to be less than a minute. The effect could be to ensure that the new Commando's stability will not deteriorate with age, due to the easy new adjusting method.

For all that I did notice the tiniest twitch during fast cornering and power changes induced by whatever method, including gear-changing. It was much less serious than anything Japanese, for instance, but more noticeable than a Trident or Ducati reaction.

If anything, the Commando was faster than the Trident around ordinary roads at speeds up to 128 km/h (80 mph) purely on the strength of its lighter weight and superior engine power low down.

Fuel consumption was pretty good. Normally I got slightly better than 17.7 km/l. Faster stuff (private roads you understand, chaps, private roads) reduced this to 10.6 km/l.

Thanks to Lucas' excellent new switchgear incorporating all the essential switches used during riding on the left side, leaving the right hand free to grapple with the brake and twistgrip, at last Britain seems to have reached success. Without exaggeration, it's the best switch setup I have used in many years of riding.

The quartz-halogen headlamp is truly brilliant, the riding position more comfortable than ever before thanks to footrests put almost 25 mm rearward from previous positions, the silence of the bike is bettered only by BMW, and its smoothness is uncanny.

All in all it's a great package that at last is going somewhere. I had my reservations about Commandos until recently, but the MK IIIs are something else.

It's not just "excitingly traditional" now, but very practical as well!

Continued from page 102

creeping wetness around the oil hoses, which simply slip over stubby tubes and are clamped in place. Maybe next year Norton will have proper, crimped-ferrule fittings on the Commando.

But those are the kind of minor aggravations you'll encounter all over the Norton Commando 850, along with pegs placed just a bit too far forward and a seat without quite enough padding. To the right kind of man, these pale to insignificance beside the Norton's virtues. It is, above all else, a sporting rider's motorcycle, and offers more sporting fun for that kind of rider than any other Superbike. Norton takes a different, and sometimes unfathomable road to total performance, but it gets there all the same. Riding the Commando 850 is a return to the sounds and sensations, to the verities, of a thoroughly entertaining (and sometimes exasperating) past—but at today's performance levels in terms of braking and sheer, thrusting speed. ◉

NORTON 850 INTERSTATE

■ Norton. Nearly a dinosaur by present-day motorcycle definition, an anachronism to many who do not believe a 25-year-old design can exist among throngs of space age technology and modern day influences. Yet it has existed healthily through the superbike era and come out the other end fairly intact, perhaps proof that things learned over two decades about motorcycle design are not to be forgotten amidst other progress.

But tradition and purist logic do not survive an age in which volume and production line blandness couple to produce an everyman's motorcycle. Throw in overbearing labor problems, and motorcycles like the Norton teeter on the precarious brink of becoming nothing more than fond memories.

And this is precisely what is happening at present. For some time you've no doubt read and heard about the many troubles of Norton-Villiers-Triumph (Norton-Triumph in the U.S.); and those troubles are brewing again.

The Meridan factory where Triumph Twins have been produced is presently in operation making parts only for the Twins, which were in very short supply because of the workers' co-op lock-in of more than a year and a half. The Wolverhampton factory has been placed in receivership and has been closed; and Norton production will move to the Small Heath factory in Birmingham where Triumph Triples are now produced, *if* everything goes according to NVT plans.

Current problems developed when the British government refused to loan the NVT people any more capital, leaving them behind the eight ball and owing quite a bit of money. This meant a giant cutback in expenses, particularly for Norton-Triumph in the U.S., putting many out of work and Norton-Triumph back on the endangered species list. If NVT can get a private loan from a British bank and consolidate all Triumph Triple and Norton Twin production in the Small Heath operation, and if the buying public continues to demand British machinery at the rate it always has, and if the feds don't regulate the once exciting performers into meek ghosts of what they once were, then the British motorcycle industry will survive. That's a pile of *ifs,* and there're more. But in the meantime, prices of the large displacement machines have been lowered to bargain basement levels. . . meaning there're a lot of people out there who are going to have to make some big decisions.

Should you buy British now and risk having a motorcycle that might be hard to get parts for in the not-too-distant future? Or will parts be that difficult to come by? The opposite may happen. You might wind up with a motorcycle that will increase in value each year. . .a collector's item. Afraid that no dealers will be left to service or repair the once famous brand? Shouldn't be a problem, as today there are specialists all over the country with parts and repair service for Matchless, Royal Enfield, Indian, ad infinitum. In other words, if the company should fail, and if you love British machinery to any degree at all, it'll be worth the extra bother to possess a motorcycle that is rare and different, particularly at the price you will have paid. And if the company goes on into the

future of motorcycling successfully, you've still got your British bike, and you got it for a song compared to the rest of today's values.

We looked at the modern-day Triumph Triple two issues back (Sept. '75), now let's take a healthy gander at the latest from Norton, all other considerations aside.

Hard to believe, but this motorcycle has a heart a couple of generations old. As a baby the big Twin started life as a 500, growing to 600, 650 and then to its most famous stage as a 750. Performance-oriented motorcyclists remember the 750 fondly, as do we; the 1972 model was our all-time favorite. But one can reasonably wonder how a performing, but nevertheless antiquated pushrod Twin could carry on into the '70s against the multitudes of Japanese computer printouts that produced overhead camshafts, five-speed gearboxes and multi-cylindered, multi-carburetored engineering exercises that for the most part worked better than fine for the average rider.

What saved the quaking, shaking and vibrating vertical Twin from demise was a brilliant improvisation. . .Isolastic suspension they called it and still do. . .which isolated the engine/transmission/swinging arm sub-assembly from the rest of the motorcycle. . .and the rider. A super rigid chassis and proper geometry made Norton handling an example for others to follow, and its all-around exceptional performance kept it well up there on the highly desirable list for many people.

Come 1973 and the bore was increased 4mm, which, of course, made the 750 an 828, or, to better fit people's desire for even numbers, an 850. The new engine was generally beefed up throughout, though power-wise no real increase came about where it counted. . .on the Chrondek timers at the drag strip. A host of improvements popped up in 1974 (April '74 CW), but the 850 Interstate remained a long-distance *sporting* machine not to be confused with a true tourer.

Perhaps in an effort to better the Interstate's touring image, Norton-Triumph in the U.S. was about to market a complete tour package for the latest 1975 model, the subject of this test. But the bottom fell out in Duarte, and abandonment of the idea followed. So the equipment you see on our test model (seat, crash bars and windshield/fairing), may or may not be available when you read this. Saddlebags were supposed to be a part of our package, but they too went by the wayside in the NVT shuffle.

The big news with the latest model is, of course, electric starting, left-side shifting and a new rear disc brake. And if one is at all familiar with Nortons, there is nothing weirder than throwing a leg over the latest version and discovering the brake on the right and the shift on the left! This, of course, is now a federal regulation. No doubt if the government continues at its present rate, standardization will follow on everything we say or do in the future, including our methods of making babies!

Breaking from traditional black with gold striping, our test machine was finished in silver and black; not quite as rich looking perhaps, but pleasing just the same. The fairing and safety bar struck us as strange, but only because they were fitted to the Norton. We just don't see that many touring-equipped Commandos. More so than the options, were other new items that hit the eye.

Highly welcomed, maybe even prayed for by many, are new handlebar switches and ignition key location. Abandoning the old Lucas razor blade devices, Norton has gone to a perfectly positioned horn button, beam changer and direction indicator on the left, all within easy and comfortable reach of the

NORTON 850 INTERSTATE

SPECIFICATIONS	
List price	$1995
Suspension, front	telescopic fork
Suspension, rear	swinging arm
Tire, front	4.10-19
Tire, rear	4.10-19
Brake, front, eff. dia. x width, in.	9.87 x 1.5
Brake, rear; eff. dia. x width, in.	9.87 x 1.5
Total brake swept area, sq. in.	161.6
Brake loading, lb./sq. in. (160-lb. rider)	4.3
Engine, type	ohv four-stroke Twin
Bore x stroke, in., mm	3.03 x 3.50; 77 x 89
Piston displacement, cu. in., cc	55; 828
Compression ratio	8.5:1
Carburetion	(2) 32mm Amal
Ignition	alternator/coil
Oil system	dry sump
Oil capacity, pt.	6.0
Fuel capacity, U.S. gal.	6.3
Recommended fuel	premium
Starting system	electric; kick, folding crank
Lighting system	12V alternator
Air filtration	oil-wetted foam
Clutch	multi-disc, wet
Primary drive	triplex chain
Final drive	5/8 x 3/8 single-row chain
Gear ratios, overall:1	
4th	4.60
3rd	5.57
2nd	7.83
1st	11.79
Wheelbase, in.	57.0
Seat height, in.	31.0
Seat width, in.	10.0
Handlebar width, in.	32.0
Footpeg height, in.	12.5
Ground clearance, in.	6.0
Front fork rake angle, degrees	28
Trail, in.	4.0
Curb weight (w/half-tank fuel), lb.	522
Weight bias, front/rear, percent	47/53
Test weight (fuel and rider), lb.	700
Mileage at completion of test	2985

TEST CONDITIONS	
Air temperature, degrees F	96
Humidity, percent	29
Barometric pressure, in. hg.	29.90
Altitude above mean sea level, ft.	383
Wind velocity, mph	0
Strip alignment, relative wind:	NO WIND

PERFORMANCE	
Top speed (actual @ 5672 rpm), mph	94
Computed top speed in gears (@ 7000 rpm), mph	
4th	116
3rd	96
2nd	68
1st	47
Mph/1000 rpm, top gear	16.5
Engine revolutions/mile, top gear	3636
Piston speed (@ 7000 rpm), ft./min.	4083
Fuel consumption, mpg	46
Speedometer error:	
50 mph indicated, actually	48
60 mph indicated, actually	60
70 mph indicated, actually	69
Braking distance:	
from 30 mph, ft.	31.0
from 60 mph, ft.	130.5
Acceleration, zero to:	
30 mph, sec.	3.0
40 mph, sec.	3.5
50 mph, sec.	4.2
60 mph, sec.	6.0
70 mph, sec.	8.2
80 mph, sec.	11.8
90 mph, sec.	18.3
Standing one-eighth mile, sec.	8.9
terminal speed, mph	72
Standing one-quarter mile, sec.	14.929
terminal speed, mph	85.95

ACCELERATION / ENGINE AND ROAD SPEEDS / RPM X 100

TIME IN SECONDS

start

thumb. On the right is a thumb-operated button for the new electric starter motor, an engine stop switch and a rocker switch that isn't hooked up on U.S. models.

If you were like us and had bad dreams about Norton's old ignition key location—it was cleverly concealed under the left side of the seat—fret no more! Moved to a central position between the speedometer and tachometer in a small console, the key operates the taillight for parking in full left position, is off and locked in the central position. Ignition only turns on with one click to the right; two clicks to the right gives you ignition and lights both. Warning lights include ignition on, high beam, turn indication and neutral; the neutral light does not necessarily mean the transmission is in neutral, however. . . at least not on our machine. A separate key operates a steering lock that proved difficult to use for us, despite repeated dousings with WD-40 and the like.

Fuel petcocks are now easier to understand and operate; one side operates the reserve system and the other side is simply an on/off arrangement. The tank is one of the largest you'll come across on a stock motorcycle, holding roughly 6.3 gallons. Our fuel consumption average of 46 mpg was under a variety of conditions, equaling our last Norton 850 figure despite more restrictive silencing all the way around.

This, Norton calls the Mark 2A intake-exhaust system; it's far more quiet to meet today's very strict noise level requirements. The airbox is molded plastic and all new, containing oil-wetted foam filters and a method of collecting oil mist residue from the engine breather tubes and redirecting it into the cylinders where it is burned off rather than deposited in the air. The pipes are now *pronounced* upswept, with those funny little end caps that make it appear as though someone plugged the tips when the rider wasn't looking. Very

Photography: Bob Atkinson, D. Randy Riggs

quiet, with a most unNortonlike sound. So much for tradition.

And tradition goes all to hell with the addition of that electric starter, to be sure, but especially when one considers where the starter motor is manufactured. . .in the U.S. Sure enough, Prestolite makes it, but it was a bit more than a bolt-it-on operation. A new die casting was made to accommodate the motor, which sits behind the cylinders and connects to the primary chain. The chain case is new, as well.

Nortons have always required a fairly hefty kick and a certain starting sequence for best results. Stall the machine at a traffic signal and you once had your hands full with the horn honkers. Now that's all changed. Simply push the button and things start turning. Once in awhile the starter motor labors a bit, but remembering the force of the kick required on earlier Nortons to get the crankshaft rolling, it's not hard to understand why the motor struggles.

PARTS PRICING	
Warranty	6 mo./6000 mi.
Major Tuneup	$37.50, plus parts
Air Filter Element	5.18
Rear Tire (standard)	39.57
Drive Chain	26.25
Headlight Bulb	2.32
Taillight Bulb	.76
Turn Indicator Bulbs	.78
Battery	21.50
Clutch Cable	5.30
Throttle Cables	5.45
Ignition Parts	
Points	2.40
Condenser	2.99
High Tension Coil	19.72

Of course, the Amals still require the messy tickling before the engine is started; a choke lever need only be used in very cold weather.

They've also beefed up the crankshaft and the crankcases have thicker walls; inlet ports have been enlarged from 30 to 32mm, helping out mid- and top-end performance. The timing cover is new and a hydraulic chain tensioner is fitted to keep primary chain tension right at all times. New seals are used throughout to help prevent oil leaks, threaded adjusters are now used in the Isolastic system for easier maintenance.

To further improve the already good handling characteristics, the swinging arm is enlarged and stiffer and the rear axle is a larger-diameter piece with new rear-wheel adjusters. The relocation of shift and brake pedals necessitated a slight change in footpeg locations. . .about three-quarters of an inch rearward, but still not enough to keep them from fouling the rider's leg when stopped at a light or standing still.

The footpegs will also touch ground fairly readily in hard cornering, and their non-folding attributes can cause a moment of thrills. If they folded they also wouldn't be nearly as annoying to the rider's legs when he's stopped and holding the machine upright.

The new rear disc brake mounts on the right with the front unit being switched to the left for supposedly better braking balance, but the caliper has gone from the back of the fork leg to the front, meaning an increase in steering mass and a loss in the fine touch department. Brakes on our machine were disappointing, particularly the rear unit, which only worked to a sufficient degree when it got very hot. When cold. . .forget it, the front would have to be the savior. Master cylinders are positioned in conventional locations, the front on the handlebars and the rear just behind the gearbox.

The 1975 models also sport a new cush-drive rear hub assembly with a pre-loaded vane damper. The rear wheel can be removed without touching the chain or rear sprocket, ISDT-style, but it's more difficult in practice than it is on paper. The front, however, comes off and goes on with little>

NORTON 850

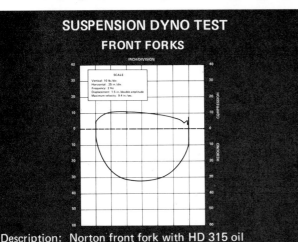
bother, helped by an adequate centerstand that holds the bike securely in position when either wheel is taken off. The sidestand, however, is long and awkward to use.

In the workmanship and quality departments Norton has slipped a notch since we last gave one a going-over in 1974. Thank goodness the seat on our test model will not see production, for it was of far too soft a density, allowing even lightweight riders to bottom out on the seat base, and movement was restricted by the "hump" separating rider and passenger. The engine remained fairly oil-tight, with the exception of the tach drive mechanism emanating from the engine case.

None of our testers liked the padded "falsie" handgrips or the odd rear view mirror shape, and the touring package seemed out of place on such a sporty machine. Too, four-speed gearboxes are rare on large-bore streeters these days, but the 850's rhino-like torque more than makes up for the lack of an extra transmission ratio. Clutch pull was medium-hard, but full engagement was obtained very close to the bottom of the lever squeeze. At times neutral was easy to find, rolling or stopped. Then, inexplicably, it became as elusive as Howard Hughes, though shifting action usually remained positive. But long throws are the rule rather than the exception.

For touring work, suspension compliance was unsatisfactory up front; the forks are harsh and stiff and could give a hoot about giving rider or riders an easy time of it. And the rear shocks acted only slightly better, for the most part ignoring the small bumps and yielding a tad to the big stuff. But away from the straight touring aspects and into the sporting realm, where the Norton belongs, the suspension is much more fun, and contributes much to *twisty-turny* handling. We'd like more ground clearance on both sides, but particularly on the left. Other than that, the Norton's easy, light and positive steering was a welcomed blessing. . .though expected. Hell, it's *British*.

Around-town, low-speed handling is clumsy and imprecise; mechanical noise from the engine also becomes apparent. Low-rpm vibration or, rather, earthquaking, rattles and shakes everything but the neighbors' windows; traffic around you is apt to wonder if the machine is going to wiggle itself into a pile of warm scrap iron before the light turns green. But it doesn't, and an occasional blip of the throttle will assure people that it's a motorcycle and not a Vic Tanny reducing machine. It will also keep the engine *running,* because Amal carbs and slow idling don't always make a predictable combination, meaning the engine likes to stall a lot. Tinker with the carbs all you want, and just when you think they're adjusted perfectly, a mere blip of the throttle will throw things out of kilter once again. Yeah, Harry, Mikunis do a lot of fixin', and they'll cure the Norton of a few ills.

Performance is a far cry from that of the famed Commandos of 1972, but we showed our readers how to make present-day Nortons run like the wind in our May 1974 issue. Those same techniques still apply today. In the course of refinement, Norton has lost some of its personality, but will no doubt appeal to a new group of riders.

So the modern-day Norton has a few minor aggravations to contend with, most of which are easily solved. Riders who formerly balked at kickstarting the big, healthy Twin need not worry with the latest from England, which makes it far more desirable for the masses. Serious touring is a bit out of its realm, which is really purely sport and purely pleasure. It's a motorcycle that entertains. . .and we all know that it takes a *real* motorcycle to entertain. Norton still makes a *real* motorcycle. . .ain't that just dandy!

Power choice

The New Commando 850 Mk3
New for '75

- ■ **Electric start**
- ■ **Rear disc brake** Hydraulic operation
  - ■ **Improved Isolastic**
    Sprung head – steady for even better isolation
  - ■ **New seat**
    Hinged, lockable, improved contour and comfort
    - ■ **New control switches**
    - ■ **Left foot gear change**
      Incompliance with
      USA legislation

Norton Triumph

Norton Triumph Europe Limited
Andover, Hampshire SP10 5BD
Tel : Andover (0264) 61411

the INSIDE story, 1
NORTON COMMANDO MK3

How the engine of our stock test bike stripped — and how we stripped it

STRIP one Commando and you've stripped them all — and this includes the latest 850 electric start model. .

Obviously, there are slight differences, but none that any proficient amateur mechanic would find difficult when it comes to stripping and rebuilding.

Our Norton had completed 10,000 kilometres — over 6,200 miles — during the course of 'New Motorcycling's' road test procedure.

Apart from an oil leak from the rev counter drive connection on the crankcase, and slight weeping from a porous cylinder head casting, there appeared to be nothing wrong with the motor, except that the tappets were beginning to rattle a little. We presumed that this was due to the normal slackening or wearing-in of components; later, during the course of the strip, we were to discover otherwise. Surprisingly, in spite of correctly maintaining the machine, with regular oil and filter changes, one of the lobes on the camshaft showed serious signs of scuffing and wear. Approximately 10 thou had been ground off the cam by the follower, and with the face-hardening obviously giving way it was certain that inside another 5,000 miles there would have been a major repair bill — including the cost of the new camshaft!

A number of special tools are required to dismantle the Norton motor. They include a clutch diaphragm spring compressor, plus extractors for the engine sprocket and the half-time or engine pinion. Also, to reach down into the cylinder head, a long 3/16in box spanner is essential. However, providing you have a reasonable socket set, plus open-ended and ring spanners and a set of Allen keys, you should be able to carry out the following work without too much difficulty.

We were able to hire the special tools for the job from Gus Kuhn with a deposit of £6, and you can probably do the same at your Norton main agent. Oh, by the way, don't forget to get a complete engine gasket set before you start work, plus the necessary gasket goo. Now, on with the job. . . .

Stage One

FIRST stage in stripping, before removing the motor from the frame, is to take off the petrol tank and then **(1)** remove the carb slides and carbs from the cylinder head. The oil feed to the cylinder head **(2)** is then disconnected. Note there are soft alloy washers either side of the unions.

The cylinder head steady **(3)** is next to be removed, after first freeing from the Metalastic bush on the frame tube.

With the head steady out of the way, the ignition coil pack **(4)** is unbolted from its mounting and placed on top of the frame, out of harm's way.

A C-spanner is available to un-screw the exhaust pipe rings **(5)**, but a drift can be used on the ring as shown. Also disconnect the exhaust system and footrests at the rear of the motor.

With all fuel, exhaust and electrical connections broken from the motor, the stripdown proper can begin. Take off the gearchange lever, drain all oil from the primary chaincase, and remove the chaincase retaining screws. On rebuilding, fit a new gasket and refill with SAE 20/50 oil (7 fl.oz=199cc) to the level plug. Lift off the cover **(6)** as shown.

With the engine in gear, and the back brake locked on, the rotor nut can be undone with a sharp tap on the spanner. Undo three nuts on the stator plate, lift off the complete unit **(7)**, and prise out the Woodruff key. Note that there is a spacer **(8)** behind the rotor.

Four nuts hold the electric starter drive pinion housing in place. Remove the nuts and

NORTON COMMANDO MK3

housing (9): the intermediate gear (10) will now pull straight out. Note the location piece on the end of the shaft. The main drive pinion (11) also lifts straight off, complete with its bearing.

At this stage, it is also possible to remove the starter motor (12) by disconnecting the electrical connection and unscrewing two screws.

The retaining plate for the hydraulic chain tensioner is next to be removed (13) and by undoing two nuts the chain tensioner (14) itself can be pulled off its studs. Note that it is possible to reverse the shoes on reassembly, so take care to keep them in their correct positions.

The sprag clutch which turns the motor is located in the centre of the engine sprocket. It pulls out (15), with a spacer behind it. Note that the grooves face outwards.

By removing the clutch pushrod adjustment, the diaphragm spring compressor tool can be screwed in to release clutch tension (16) so you can remove the retaining circlip. With the clutch outer plate removed (17), the clutch pushrod is pulled out.

Next knock back the clutch nut tab washer and, with the machine still in gear and the rear brake applied, give a sharp tap on the spanner to undo the nut. Note nut, tab washer and spacer location (18).

The second of the special tools required is the engine sprocket extractor. This is screwed by two bolts to the sprocket and then the centre bolt tightened (19) to free the sprocket on the crankshaft.

Lift off the primary drive (20) complete, as shown. Note that there are shims behind the clutch to set the primary chain alignment. Ensure they are replaced on assembly. The primary starter gear (21) is next to be lifted out, and then the crankshaft key (22) has to be prised off. Finally, to complete the dismantling of the primary drive, pull out the gearchange shaft, undo the inner case retaining nuts, and lift off the case (23). Renew all gaskets on re-assembly.

Before starting work on the timing side of the motor, disconnect the breather pipe (24). Next remove the contact breaker cover plate, undo the two nuts retaining the assembly, and remove as shown (25).

By undoing the cam retaining bolt two or three turns, a sharp tap with a light hammer will free the cam and auto-advance unit on its taper (26). Note that it's not keyed and will require careful adjustment on re-assembly to obtain the correct ignition timing. Also, check that the auto-advance unit is not showing signs of wear and that the springs are not stretched.

With the breaker unit out of the way, the timing cover screws can be removed and the cover lifted off (27). Have an oil tray handy to catch spillage.

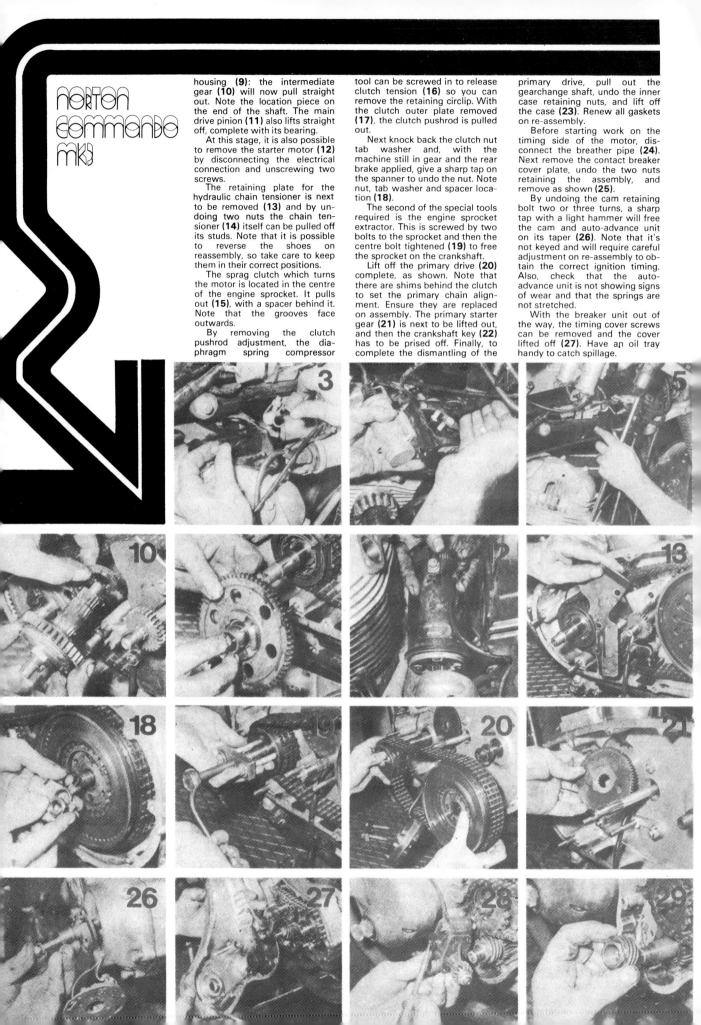

The oil pump (28) is next to be removed, by undoing two bolts. Check that the rubber washer indicated is in good condition, as this seal ensures good oil pressure to the big-ends. There is a reverse thread on the oil pump drive (29), so don't try undoing it the normal way.

The camshaft drive chain (30) is on a pinion/sprocket drive. Note that the camshaft is keyed, and the timing mark on the chain pinion must match up with that on the halftime/crankshaft pinion. Also, the two 'pop' marks on the intermediate and camshaft sprockets should be <u>ten</u> chain rollers apart.

The half-time pinion is keyed and is a tight fit on the crank, so a special extractor (31) is required. Don't try to lever it off or you will damage the casing.

Behind the pinion is a spacer (32) and oil retainer. These easily pull off. Finally, disconnect the oil pump feed at the rear of the case (33).

RE-ASSEMBLY DATA

Crankshaft
Big-end journal 1.7509/4 in. = 44.473/44.460 mm
End float 0.010/0.024 in. = 0.254/0.61 mm

Connecting rods
Side clearance 0.013/0.016 in. = 0.33/0.406 mm
Big-end clearance Less than 0.001 in. = 0.0254 mm

Pistons
Standard diameter (bottom of skirt) 3.028/3.0271 in. = 76.91/76.888 mm
Top ring (fitted gap) 0.010/0.012 in. = 0.254/0.305 mm
Middle ring 0.008/0.012 in. = 0.203/0.305 mm

Valve timing
Inlet opens BTDC 50°
Inlet closes ABDC 74°
Exhaust opens BBDC 82°
Exhaust closes ATDC 42°

Ignition timing
Fully advanced 28 degrees BTDC

Contact breaker
Points gap .014/.016 in. = 0.356/0.406 mm

Torque settings

Cylinder head nuts/bolts (⅜ in.)	30 lb. ft = 4.15 kg. m
Cylinder head bolts (5/16 in.)	20 lb. ft = 2.75 kg. m
Cylinder base nuts (⅜ in.)	25 lb. ft = 3.45 kg. m
Cylinder base nuts (5/16 in.)	20 lb. ft = 2.75 kg. m
Cylinder throughbolt	30 lb. ft = 4.15 kg. m
Connecting rod nuts	25 lb. ft = 3.45 kg. m
Rocker spindle cover plate bolt	8 lb. ft = 1.11 kg. m
Crankshaft flywheel nuts	30 lb. ft = 4.15 kg. m
Oil pump stud nuts	15 lb. ft = 2.07 kg. m
Rocker feed banjo bolts	15 lb. ft = 2.07 kg. m
Engine mount bolts	25 lb. ft = 3.45 kg. m
Rotor nut (crankshaft)	70 lb. ft = 9.68 kg. m
Alternator mounting stud nuts	15 lb. ft = 2.07 kg. m
Clutch/mainshaft nut	70 lb. ft = 9.68 kg. m
Mainshaft nut	40/50 lb. ft. = 5.50 kg. m
Countershaft sprocket nut	80 lb. ft = 11.06 kg. m
Gearbox inner cover nuts	12 lb. ft = 1.66 kg. m
Top gearbox fixing bolts	55 lb. ft = 7.60 kg. m
Oil pressure release valve	25 lb. ft = 3.46 kg. m

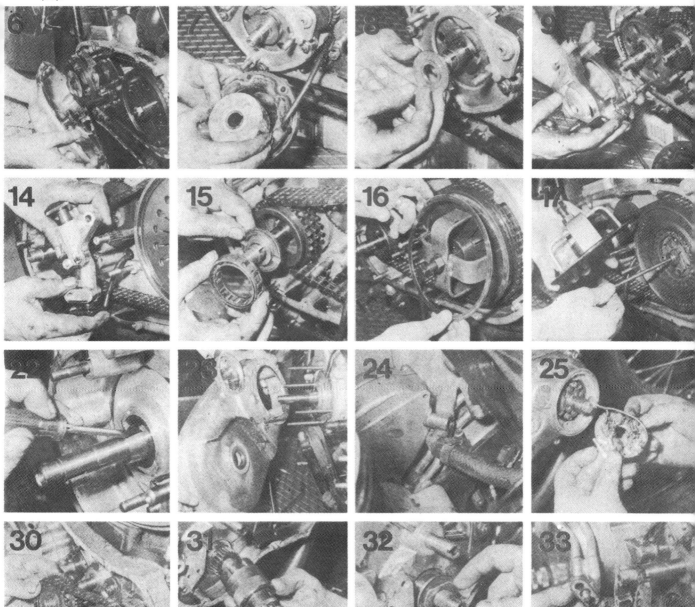

WORK may now begin on taking off the 'top end'. There are ten retaining nuts and bolts to undo, the most difficult of which is the 3/16in. nut **(34)** shown being undone with a long box spanner.

With the head free, set the pistons at TDC to ensure that the cam followers are in their lowest position and then, lifting the pushrods as high as possible in their tunnels, tilt the head backwards and lift it off **(35)**. The head gasket may be used again if it is in good condition.

Four Allen screws **(36)** hold the barrel to the crankcase, and five cylinder base nuts must also be removed.

The barrel should now lift off **(37)**. Check for scoring in the bores or any sign of a lip at the top of the stroke.

To remove the pistons, first take out the circlips **(38)**; then heat the top of the piston **(39)** — we used a gas blowtorch — and simply push out the gudgeon pins **(40)**. Easy isn't it?

All that remains of the engine in the frame is the crankcase. So, undo all retaining bolts, loosen the front Isolastic mounting, and lift out the crankcase **(41)**. On the bench, you can undo the remaining nuts, bolts and screws which hold the crankcase halves together. Then, with gentle tapping using a small hide or nylon mallet, the crankcases will part **(42)**. Don't use a screwdriver to prise them apart, as it will damage the mating faces.

The camshaft **(43)** easily pulls out, but note that there is a spacer (concave side to the case) on the end of the shaft. Ensure it is placed the correct way round on re-assembly.

The crankshaft will now lift out of the other crankcase half **(44)**, leaving the main bearing in place. The inner part of the race stays on the crank and requires a special extractor for removal. Again, don't try chiselling it off!

The big-end nuts are self-locking **(45)** and should always

be renewed on re-assembly. The big-end shells must be checked for scoring, and if necessary replaced. If you don't have a micrometer or vernier, take the crank to a Norton main agent. There you will find out if you need a regrind and oversize shells. Any signs of scoring will usually mean this — so take your rods too.

If your main bearings have been rumbling, the only way to get them out is heat the cases **(47)** until they are just too hot to touch, and then drift them out with a large socket spanner. Remember that it must be a perfect fit around the bearing, which will then gently tap out **(48)** along with the oil seal. Make sure the seal is fitted the correct way round on reassembly (wire spring inwards). To fit new bearings, heat the cases again to expand the seatings. It will also help if you put the bearings in the freezer compartment of a fridge for a couple of hours, so causing them to contract.

Stage Two

norton commando mk3

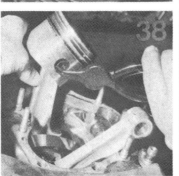

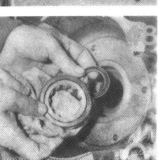

Time passes slowly for monuments . . .
The Norton on the rugged coastline of
Port Campbell.

Riding out the Norton legend...

AN ERA ON THE ECLIPSE

This is about a road — and about a bike.

It's also about the day when you realise sophistication doesn't always improve things; about the day when you realise there will be no more reprieves for the fabulous Rhino powerhouse Nortons you have ridden for 16 years; that the solid image of the Norton has been toned into a soft blur of emasculated sportster and general everyman's tourer. And as such it can no longer offer that total handling/sporting feel it once generated . . .

THE NORTON Commando no longer sits among the very fleet of two wheels and it is no longer the nimblest of them all. Technology and computerised designs have, with the arrival of the Suzuki GS750, created mass-produced multi-cylinder dohc bikes which provide equal, and possibly better, handling and far more go at the top end.

But if, after 26 years, the Norton has dropped behind in the handling and power stakes it still in its final form as the Mk III, provides a solid, heart-warming and comforting companion for those who buzz on tradition and style. For if any bike on the roads retains class with tradition and style it is the guilt-edged, black and gold 850 Interstate which caters not only to the whims of the Great Standardised Rulings, but also to a new level of Norton owners who want Tradition with some civilities.

And that is what you get. Who can imagine a Norton with an electric start? One that works, believe it! Or one with the gearlever on the left side with a one-down and three-up pattern! All of which really does not affect forms of Pure Riding — which is what the Great Ocean Road on the south-western coast of Victoria is all about!

It is one of the few roads on the mainland that reminds riders of Tasmania. It is one of the few fun riding roads which has lots to see and, if you pick the right time of year, is a road with only light to negligent traffic. It is a road that at times appears one continual turn, either entering one, exiting one or sorting things out in the middle of one. Try it, with 78 left and righthand bends between Lorne and Wye River. Yes, 78 bends in 16 kilometres! As a friend once said, "It's the sort of road where you throw that baby down on the peg and nail it on."

The GOR (Great Ocean Road) has been around a long time; not as long as Norton itself, certainly longer than the venerable twin in the final concept of the big Commando. The GOR was built to commemorate the services of the soldiers and sailors of World War 1 and

One of the lookouts built during the '20s when the GOR was completed. Between Lorne and Wye River, and 78 turns therein!

although the GOR Trust was founded in 1918 by one Howard Hitchcock the road was not completed until the late '20s. Actually some road purists have rudely said it isn't finished yet as there is still one short dirt section of about 21 kilometres through the rugged national park/forest of the Cape Otway region, south-west of Apollo Bay.

In all, the real riding section covers 243 km. The GOR starts about Bellbrae, 16 km past Geelong. From there it is On. The official start is marked by a tree drive and wood plaque over the road at Aireys Inlet, which is a few kilometres past the surfing and trail riding township of Anglesea, and by then you are locked in the mind-bending rhythm of the Real Thing.

We were lucky. We had a real reason for going during the week, and somewhere to go to, although neither should be a pre-requisite for riding the GOR. Five days ahead with three bikes. Two new Japanese multis and the big black Norton 850 Mk. III. The boring part is covering the law-enforced dual "freeway" (not if you are caught) from Melbourne to Geelong, then through that city and off Highway One towards Bellbrae and the Start-Of-Something-Good. It's a 74 km *cool-it* ride to the start.

The Norton is loping along. All the bikes are. Then from Bellbrae a sprint to wake up, letting the Avons hunt a little on the sweepers, flicking sand up into the rider following. Not a fast run to Lorne, as the others have not ridden the GOR on big bikes before. It's the sort of road that expects some care, and gets it.

Lorne is only 40 km along the road from Bellbrae. Very neat. Very trendy.

Port Campbell, a niche in the rocks and made for surfing. Rugged when windy, no foolin'.

AN ERA ON THE ECLIPSE

It closes up in winter like most of the fishing villages, sulking in the shadows of the Otway ranges as the young keen winter surfies pass through waiting for school holidays. There is some stirrings during the weekends of late spring, then warming to the rush of summer. The hard-core fishermen keep things going all year round as well as the dedicated surfers.

The second major port along the coast is Apollo Bay, 43 km of fabulous riding away from Lorne. Less expensive and less trendy for the Melbourne and Colac wealthy, it is just as good a spot to stop. But the heart of the GOR, the power of the coastal surges and the best buzz, is found around little Port Campbell, a hole in the cliffs some 50 km further on from Apollo Bay.

In early November the weather was still cold, the places still almost closed up, the road fairly clear. The villagers are among the friendliest in Vic, better than the heavy highways, and far more trusting than city people can believe.

Example. Three heavily-garbed lads arrive in the township of Lorne. Dump the gear at the in-laws' house, but as the food and camera gear is coming down by F100 the next day, plus the super-cook camera girl, why not eat out? The night is cool and a steady drizzle makes things slippery across the bridge into the main street. Three restaurants! Wow. Three hotels. The best is the Pacific for swingers. Not much swinging on a bleak Friday eve. Check the price lists at two and decide

to miss it, so down past the main shops to the Arab.

It's been there for years. Bloke named Steve is bitchin' about selling out to two chicks and a guy, semi-student types. We order, coffee first while waiting. However after the three student types leave the Steve is anxious. Appears there are things happening in the town council with the "Youngies" trying to grab the power from the "Old Established" (seems like it happens everywhere).

But the move is to get everyone in to vote who is eligible. So Steve says do

you mind if I go to the meeting? Why not! Leave the place. She'll be right! Christ! He just zaps a radio out on the counter for music, dims the lights and tells us to leave the door closed when we finish. We ask about locking it and Steve replies, "I never lock it, just close it!!! No one comes in!"

It shattered us, three half-heavy looking types at that. With three Big Bikes parked at the front. One forgets that not all people are sharp sticks all their life. Country sea air must do something to people. Like make them honest?

We are embarrassed at being left. We eat and make comments. It's good. It was a good meal as well.

Saturday is mostly photography and riding. Sunday much the same. Monday and Tuesday riding longer, more relaxed checking out the GOR. It has been a long time, but even if it was a trip every second week it would never be boring. It is a little run all by itself, another dimension.

The Norton 850 Mk III is quite different from the Mk IIA ridden for a year. Quite different from the other Mk IIs. And a world away from my two early '70s British Racing Green 750s. The reasons are obvious. Weight. Power restrictions, due to legislation. The speed has gone. The latest 850 is totally unromantic. And Nortons were always,

Graded section of GOR through the Otway forest includes lots to look at, giant trees, cool ferns, as well as tourist drivers using all the road. New highway will soon make all the GOR paved for the scratchers.

especially from the Commando series made for the romantics. And for those who appreciate high speed handling. The long-stroke twin, which has a history extending back 26 years came to initiate the superbike era then found it had lost its buyers and tried to compete with the multis. And paid the ultimate price.

The name lives on. And will live on with products to buy and parts for 20 years. But not in quantities. They will be for Purists. There are 10-year-olds who will spend their whole lives riding Japanese machines and never know what Norton really means. Will never know that digital gear read-outs, neutral lights, beeper indicator, stainless steel disc brakes that don't work in the wet and sundry look-nice sales gimmickry are not necessary, to create a mobile riding machine that can do things well. Very well. Among the very best. Some people will spend their lives looking AND TRUSTING the green neutral indicator light!

Norton went soft with the Mk III. The isolastic frame remains the same, with stronger swinging arm region. It still works well, separating engine vibes from the rider and pillion. The extra strength in the swing arm region is about the only change needed; the isolastic design was the brilliant improvisation which gave the Norton another 10 years of life — but apparently not quite long enough for the British industry to get it together. The beefed up swinging arm includes a larger diameter axle with new rear wheel adjusters and a modified mechanism for adjusting the isolastic shimming. The new rear hub incorporates the disc brake, set on the right side and thus the front has been moved to the left hand side to even up the braking forces. The change of the disc to the left side of the front means the caliper is now mounted forward of the fork leg instead of behind it. This move is minor but despite the Lockheed performing very nicely the steering is just a fraction out compared with previous models. The old Lucas switches have gone. The ones which caused one on-the-spot fine in the rain in heavy traffic when I would not take my hand off the throttle and brake to use the indicators ... $25 and two points. The new switches on the Norton Mk III are Americanised and easy to use. The indicators, high/low beam and horn are on the left. Starter, killswitch are on the right. A central cluster between the large Smith speedo and tacho sports ignition key, four idiot lights, the neutral turn signal, high beam and ignition.

The large Interstate fuel tank holds 28.5 litres. It remains one of the top features of the Traditional Norton. The fuel taps are improved. The left one is reserve/off. The other side is on/off. The minor changes include the moulded plastic airbox with oiled foam element.

Norton has kept the strange upswept Mk II exhaust and mufflers with the black caps set into them. Dull and quiet and restrictive. The big change for most is the electric starter. The unit works while the bike has a healthy battery and good tuning. Cold mornings are for the owner to warm himself up with a few kicks and then use the starter. Tickling the carbs is still necessary. The primary chain gets a tensioner now that things are fixed permanently (no more moving the gearbox rearwards to adjust things). The gearlever runs right through and exits the left side. The brake does the opposite, providing riders with standardised rightside brake and leftside gear changes. One down and three up movement.

Suspension is the same, Girlings rear and roadster-forks that cope with most things at the price of a firm ride. I like them. Lots of small changes have made the Norton as oiltight as it will ever be, and improved the bike in many respects. But these changes have added a weight burden which takes the frame past the sportster feel.

The 750 Commando was the lightest big gun. The Mk II 850 was about the lightest although weight was up. The early 750 weighed in around 195 kg (431 lb). The 850 Mk II was only up a bit to 202 kg (446 lb). But the 850 Mk III scales in at 236 kg (522 lb) and this extra 34 kg takes the frame into the realm of average instead of outstanding.

Continued

AN ERA ON THE ECLIPSE

Continued

Mark you, it is good enough for fast touring but no hard scratching any more. The bike is no longer happy at the edges of traction. Ground clearance and the weight combined with less power have stunted the performance, have castrated the black shining Trad British bike.

Lighting is still excellent, among the better night stalkers to be with. Handling is predictable but slower than ever. The sharp GS750 Suzuki was the first Japanese bike (apart from an RD350 ridden in the Black Spur road years ago), well, the first Japanese multi sportster machine, which could run away from the Norton on the GOR.

It was surprising. Annoying.

And a points loss for the Old Loop, the ride we once used for sorting things out years ago. The roads have not changed much, little improvements and some deterioration in spots.

You start at Lorne. Down the GOR road past the small village of Wye River, to Apollo Bay. Then north to Forrest in the heart of the Otway ranges, on to Colac for a break.

Colac on the Princes Highway is the cosy satisfied matron of the western wealth. Leave there quietly heading east toward Geelong on Highway One eight km, then right onto a secondary road which runs fast and hard through Deans Marsh then up into the forest and ranges, tight, hard dangerous racing boys! Down to Lorne. Total is 170 km. Try it at night!! Be sure you know and trust who you are riding with.

We did the loop again. And also detoured to Red Hill north from Colac to check out the eclipse. Storm clouds made pics hard but afterwards the clouds cleared and we raced home in the crisp late evening filled with life. A huge fire that night at Lorne, a few rounds and what else ...

One of the guys took off Sunday, sweeping north to Bendigo. We did some photos around Lorne and watched the people filling the roads and villages. Missed out on two incredible hitch-hiking fems by not having helmets with us! A Major Down for the weekend. People kept mistaking the Suzuki 750 and the Kawasaki 650 as the same bikes. No-one ever mistakes the round lumpy lines of the great Rhino Norton. Pure grunt and classic tradition in the silver and black engine and the black and gold pinstriped paint job.

At the Lorne Pier we struck two hard chargers on their fours, keen riders from Geelong on their way round 'n about. A chat there about the bikes. Then later in the afternoon I had the Norton just cruisin', looking for some sun and a last shot of the bike. Some denim-clad hoons had passed us going the opposite way early in the day. They were parked in town. Checked them out.

A ratty BM 90S, orange. But that BM leaked oil from every orifice it was possible to leak! A hot 550 four, couple of 650 Yams, a 750 Honda. Ragged bunch. Half from Finlay in NSW. Down to work at Ford in Geelong. Down to ride with the others who were hard core Geelong. Smokies and small monos in main street. Good trick! The BM had been down the road a few times, rocker covers were well worn, he rode hard. They all liked the Norton.

And still later cruising back from down the coast a bunch of three riders getting into their wet weather gear. Said hello. Checked out the 900SS Duke, rider in full-house leathers, a brand-new spankers GT860 Duke and an old, battered 650 Yamaha. Melbourne bunch who were enjoying the brisk Sunday air on the GOR. Heading for coffee before heading home. Lucky those who had two more days.

Monday and the coast was dead once again, the sudden surge of early activity during the weekend had sapped its strength. Up and away in the early sun. Prue cool on the back of the 850 Interstate. She likes the twin, more than any other bike. Not because it is Trad. She doesn't like pillioning on the

GS750, the Kawasaki 650 nor the 1000. Nor the Laverda 1000 or the Honda 750. The Norton lopes along and doesn't give her bumps, grinds and pains. It's the feel that counts and the Norton has it. That's important. Loaded with camera gear. Cruising during the early part (counting the bends between Lorne and Wye River).

Then scraping the pegs, side and centrestand and mufflers all the way down to Apollo Bay. A high wind making the seas foam and surge. A good day with no traffic. Into the Cape Otway forest, the first section which is tricky all the way with hair pins, very narrow and slick. The new road will destroy the old . . .

Finally out to Glenaire and onto bitumen again, a very fast section in a river valley, green and with cattle around the road edges. Edging 85 on corners (that's mph). The tank, the instruments, and the whole appearance of the bike is the same but the feel is different. The Norton doesn't react as accurately, is not as fast and seems a bit ungainly. The thoroughbred feel is missing.

Up to Lavers Hills, a T-intersection with another route to Colac on the north. We turn south and plummet off the ridge towards the rugged cliffs of the grand coast of the GOR at its best. Rolling plains to the edge of the cliffs, the road turning and twisting to conform. Fast here, flat out downhill to get the Mk III past 105 mph. The old Nortons would go 10 to 15 mph better!

Up one hill the Norton coasts to a stop. A check for gas, roll back down. Nothing. The kill button is off. Hard to see how the thumb nudged it. Maybe the bumps. Fire up and away. One long down hill, left right left, again and again. One tight S with sand all over it! That keeps you awake.

Hard chargers jawin' at Lorne Pier. Two riders on seasoned fours check the new Japanese offerings . . . and talked a while about the Norton. On the Great Ocean Road all bikes are equal . . .

Finally strung out along the edge of the coast and into the region of Port Campbell, Victoria's best. The bike falters, petrol this time.

We eat and head back to the park area. The names interest me; Trumpeter Steps, Marble Arch Steps, London Bridge, Sentinal Rock, Bakers Overn Rock and the Blowhole . . .

All impressive. But the one to see is Loch Ard Gorge. Here is the Real Thing. The Port Campbell National Park is set between Peterborough and Princetown, 30 km of coast declared a national park in 1964. It is spectacular. The Blowhole is adjacent to Loch Ard Gorge. It is about 400 metres from the sea, an egg-shaped hole 30 metres deep, 50 metres wide. The sea surges and crashes into it. Mean.

The huge rock stacks form weird shapes out to sea. One called London Bridge is still connected. You can ride (if game) or walk out on this pinnacle, a metre wide and 30 above the sea. The wind tries to give the sea a chance. This coast is good for smugglers and shipwrecks. But there is no reason to smuggle here (anywhere would do along our coast) but shipwrecks have little choice. There were five big ones off the area between 1855 and 1908. The huge swell and the nasty rips and rocks make things grim for those trying to swim.

Many were buried on the windswept plains. Just near the gorge is the Loch Ard cemetery. The area is isolated, empty. Wind-swept heath interspersed with clumps of she-oak and mesmate and grasses.

The GOR continues through Port Campbell to Peterborough. A neat fishing and diving spot. I like it. A long, wooden bridge marks the village. Watch the western exit, a steady left-hander which seems to collect 300 mm of sand permanently. Lots have come undone there at night. The road continues all the way to the Princes Highway, a further 43 km to Allansford. But it has changed, no longer a cliff-hugging fast run. Just a run through pastoral and wind-swept plains. And on Highway One it is a short blast to Warrnambool and out of the magic.

The Peterborough bridge marks the end for me. The feel is from there, all the way back to Anglesea. The trip on the Norton 850 Mk III was at medium-to-fast pace with some sections done at tourist time. The big 850 has lost little of its Rhino-like torque but lacks the sheer power at high speeds it once had. Petrol consumption was around 13.8 km/l (39 mph) which means one can safely run into the night on the Interstate, knowing you can cover 375 km or therebouts.

The big Norton only had to take us back to Lorne, the headlight carving patterns on the rocks ahead or sending a beam into nothing over the water. The weekend had passed, the other bikes had gone, the eclipse had gone and Norton too had gone.

We had another day to kill; a few games of backgammon, a walk in the cold after-midnight air, wind lifting sand off the beach. The ride had been good, the weekend relaxing but busy, now it was just a time for being. For being cold and for being alone.

Walk back up the cliff, along the road and up to the house. The Norton, a sculptured silhouette angled over on the sidestand stood under the verandah/ patio. Alone . . .   *

No.1: Norton Commando

THIS feature is the first of a new series on buying second-hand bikes. In each we will be looking at one particular machine: at its history, its performance, its good points, and its bad points. Most especially we will be looking at its bad points — for the series is not intended as a mere out-of-date road test, but as a ruthless and down-to-earth guide for the person contemplating the purchase of a second-hand bike. What this person needs to know is not only how good the device is, but more importantly the weak points he must look for when buying, and what sort of snags he may expect afterwards when he comes to live with the machine.

Our intention is to aim each article at the type of person to whom the particular machine is relevant. Thus, in dealing with the Commando, we are considering the sort of rider who has some experience, and is possibly buying his first big bike. Because of this we will assume that we do not have to discuss at length the obvious standard second-hand buyer's checks such as chain condition, dampers, head races, etc. When it happens that the bike under scrutiny is more often purchased by a first-time buyer we will shift the emphasis accordingly and assume less experience on the part of the reader.

History

THE Romans used to have signs posted up in their market places saying "Caveat Emptor"; which means Buyer Beware. Historians tell us this was to warn people against buying duff togas or over-priced slave girls — but we have another theory: somewhere down in the used-chariot bazaar, some was selling second-hand Norton Commandos. Because whatever one can find to say in favour of the Commando — which is much, in terms of buying price, performance, and handling — there is no denying that the marque has had its troubles.

The Commando first poked its head round the door in '68, using the 750 Atlas engine with one or two modifications in the lubrication department. Critics at that time admitted that the Isolastic frame damped out some of the famous Norton vibration, but claimed that the chassis didn't handle so well as the old Featherbed Dominators: they also said that it wasn't so quick as the last of the Featherbed line, the 650 SS. There was considerable validity in both of these comments.

Anyway, having started it, Norton then proliferated the line. The Fastback and Commando S were introduced in '69, the Roadster in '70, and the Interstate in '72. All these models were 750s, and the Mark number of each model changed each year. Which makes things rather complicated and doesn't, when it comes right down to it, necessarily mean a great deal: so we will ignore the Mark numbers, and concentrate on the more significant factors of year and engine serial numbers.

In '73 the 850 models — or to be strictly accurate, the 828cc models — were introduced, in Roadster and Interstate forms. The 750 range ran parallel to the bigger bangers for a few months, and was then phased out before the end of the year. The 850s continue to this day (well, more or less continue, anyway) the major significant change being the introduction of an electric starter with the advent of the Mk.111 850 in Jan '75.

So much, then, for the potted history. Now let us look at the Commando in detail.

Engine

Up until the end of '71 — or, more to the point, up until engine number 151,000 — Commando engines used to suffer from a

Don't worry about seepage from the rev-counter drive. They all do it.

bottom end which was stressed to pretty nea the limit. Main bearings used to rumble int oblivion after depressingly low mileages (sometimes as low as 10,000 miles), and if on had occasion to have the crank re-ground on had to be jolly careful that the crankpins wer properly radiussed or the crankshaft woul break.

In '72, while the factory was still seeking th complete answer to the main bearing failures it was decided that what every Comando

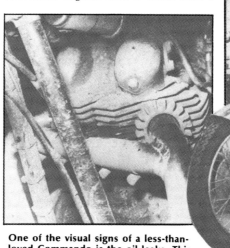

One of the visual signs of a less-than-loved Commando is the oil leaks. This one at the front and three fins above the head/barrel joint, means weeping rocker spindle covers.

BARGAIN OF

owner really needed was the tuned-up Combat version of the engine in his bike. This motor — beginning at number 200,000 and further identifiable by a letter C stamped on top of the rocker box — had a higher compression and a wilder cam, and was fitted to every Commando in the range. The crankcase was strengthened, and at the same time, in a superhuman burst of intelligence, the oil filter in the sump was dispensed with. The engine went like a bat out of hell — and main bearing life came down to 4,000-5,000 miles. This was rather tedious even by Norton standards, so Something Had To Be Done.

What was done, at the end of that year, was a composite answer. The engine was de-tuned back to its original cam and its former compression ratio of 9:1, and at the same time the main bearings were changed to a pair of Superblend roller races. (Bearings in which the rollers are slightly barrel-shaped at their ends, in order to reduce the usual disasters attendant upon a crankshaft which whips too much.) These mods, which were standard issue from approximately engine number 220,000 onwards, more or less solved the main bearing problem — and, furthermore, the Superblend bearings could be and still can be fitted to the earlier machines without any difficulty or machining. The best bearing to use is the RHP 6MRJA30.

All of which, of course, leaves the potential buyer of a pre-'73 Commando on the horns of an interesting dilemma. Looking at a possible purchase he must ask himself (a) are the main bearings silent and sound?, (b) have they ever been changed to the Superblend type?, and (c) is the engine a Combat still boasting its original high compression and hot cam, both of which were a considerable contributory factor to the main bearing mortality rate? We have to confess that we can't think of any infallible method of answering these questions merely by gawping at the outside of the motor: unless the seller can produce a service history proving that the motor has Superblend mains and the sensible cam, there is simply no way of being sure. You might shrug your shoulders and take the view that any pre-220,000 Commando with more than about 15,000 miles on the clock must have had its bearings changed; and if it's a private sale of a '72 model you might even get ever so cunning and ask the seller what he sets the tappets to (since the standard cam requires .006in inlet and .008 in exhaust, while the Combat settings are .008 and .010) — but whatever you do you still can't be sure. It all comes down to finding a seller with an honest face and/or a thick wodge of service records.

Leaving the main bearing saga now, the next thing to look at on all Commando engines is the oil-leak situation. Oil stains around the top end have three common causes: a leaky head gasket, one or more leaking rocker spindle covers, and/or a porous cylinder head casting. A leaking head gasket is fairly obvious, and the answer to it is to fit a late-pattern gasket with metal flame rings. Weeping rocker spindle covers are a little more subtle since the oil runs along the cooling fins and emerges as a stain on the front of the head about three fins up from the head-to-barrel joint. But probably the most difficult thing of all to diagnose is the porous-casting die since all you really see is the stain, with nothing to indicate exactly where it's coming from. Experienced Norton mechanics trace the source of the problem by washing the motor down, then dusting it liberally with French chalk and running it until the stain (s) starts to appear. This pin - points the starting point of a leak — but if it does prove to be a porous casting, then what? A new head is expensive and may even suffer from the same disease, and likewise a second-hand head; most people end up muttering into their beer and learning to live with external lubrication.

Another thing to look for on a Commando is a smoky exhaust, for which there may be several causes. First, the 750's will cheerfully drain a considerable quantity of oil from the tank down into the crankcase when the bike is left standing for any period of time. This produces a smoke-screen when the beast is first started up, coupled with a generally high rate of oil consumption. The latter symptom may be further aggravated by the conscientious rider checking the oil level with the engine cold, finding it needs a litre or more to bring it up to the mark — and then, ten miles up the road, discovering that the extra litre or so which was lying in the crankcase has now been scavenged back to the tank, thus overfilling same and causing the motor to breathe out the excess all over the back end of the bike. The 850's are better in this respect, having a non-return valve between oil tank and engine.

The next possible cause of exhaust smoking is worn valve guides (to which all Commandos are somewhat prone, along with relatively

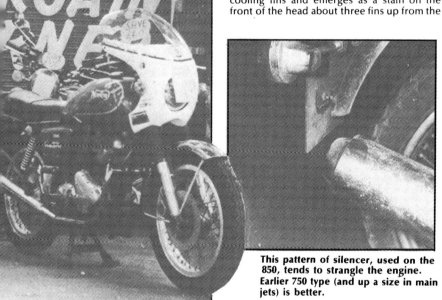

This pattern of silencer, used on the 850, tends to strangle the engine. Earlier 750 type (and up a size in main jets) is better.

All silencers tend to shed their chrome and split up like this round the mounting lugs.

BANGER?

MCM'S USED BIKE BUYERS GUIDE

short-life valve seats.) The reason for all the smoke is that with the engine inclined, oil gathers in little 'wells' around the inlet valve springs, and escapes down the guide in excessive quantities if there is enough clearance to do so. Or at least, that's what Nortons thought was happening when they changed the pattern of the guides and fitted oilseals to them at the end of '71: in actual fact, some oil was going down the inside of the guides whilst more was also trickling down the outside of them, because they weren't a terribly famous fit in the head. So the complete answer to guide-leakage is twofold: fit the post '71 pattern guides with oilseals in all cases (they are a straight replacement of the previous type), and also be sure to use a moderate helping of Loctite when you shove them into the head.

Coming back now to the oil-leak scene, you must accept the fact of a damp patch around the rev-counter drive: they all do that. But if there's a weep coming from the vicinity of the crankcase-to-chaincase joint, that's probably from the alternator cable grommet or the gearbox mainshaft oilseal. (Don't, incidentally, overfill the chaincase: the level screws are not a reliable guide, since they are set too high). The correct quantity is ¼ pint except on electric start models which take one-third of a pint.

The next thing is the auto-advance. This is again difficult to check when you're buying a bike, but at least it isn't financially crippling if you do get a duff 'un. The fact of the matter is that up until '73, the auto-advance simply wasn't man enough for the job. It used to wear out its cam-spindle, the return springs would cut through their posts, the points gap would become almost infinitely variable, the thing would jam on full advance — you name it, it did it. The one used from '73 onwards was OK, however, and can be fitted straight onto the earlier engines. The way to check which unit you've got with a minimum of dismantling is to remove the points-plate and look at the advance spring anchorages: if any of them consist of a tiny tag secured by a spot-weld, then you have the duff issue.

To sum up on the engine, then, it must be said that most pre-'73 units (or pre-number 220,000) should be regarded with considerable suspicion for a variety of reasons. The very late 750's ('73) and all the 850's are a better piece of equipment all round: Norton's even condescended to put the sump filter back in the 850 range! If we had to buy a pre-'73 Commando we would definitely want one which was proven to have the non-Combat cam and the later mains, valve guides, and auto-advance unit. If it wasn't so equipped, we'd expect to get it dead cheap.

Transmission

The Commando clutch isn't too bad, although the potential buyer would be well advised to take a few big handfuls of throttle during his road test to check for slip. Prior to engine number 220,000 the clutch had fibre friction plates, and after that they were replaced by sintered bronze. The early plates would slip if they got oil-soaked and/or worn. Glazing can sometimes be removed with a file. All clutches will slip if the chaincase is overfilled, although this can often be rectified by dismantling the unit and cleaning with petrol. In addition, the pre-220,000 clutches were somewhat sudden in operation, and sometimes used to shear the two steel pins holding the first drive plate to the clutch drum. These pins were changed for three rivets on the all-metal clutches.

The other thing about the clutch is to listen for low rumbly-grinding noises when it's disengaged: that means the centre bearing is on its last legs.

On the 750's, the primary chain is adjusted in the conventional manner, by rocking the gearbox backwards or forwards on its adjuster. The later 850's, however, have a hydraulic slipper-tensioner, which does not yet appear to have quite achieved perfection. The trouble with it is that if the bike is left standing for a long period the tensioner can drain itself of oil, which allows the chain to become very slack indeed. This produces a deep grinding rumble when the bike is started up: the sort of rumble which leads the uninitiated into thinking its main bearing trouble. The way to tell whether the racket is mains or chain is to blip the engine quickly a few times, and then bring the revs slowly up from tickover for comparison. If the racket re-doubles when the throttle is cracked open quickly but isn't so bad when the speed's increased gently, then the source is almost certainly the chain thrashing around: whereas if it sounds more or less the same however you increase the revs, it's more likely to be mains.

If the chain is slack, then the only answer is to get the spanners out, take the chaincase off, and prime the tensioner with oil. It's no use riding the bike around in the hope that the device will prime itself: it probably will, in the end, but in the meantime you'll

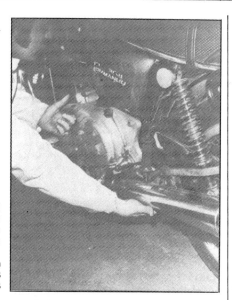

Touch the primary chain and haul rear chain up and down: if primary slackens and tightens, clutch sleeve bearing is saying goodbye.

have made a right old dog's breakfast of the transmission.

The other thing about the transmission is to listen very carefully for whining gears and rumbling bearings in the cogbox. The old Norton gearbox has really been stretched to its limits on the Commando (particularly on the 850), and the layshaft bearing and the clutch sleeve bearing are both somewhat prone to giving up the ghost. The clutch sleeve bearing can, in fact, be checked by resting a finger on the primary chain and hauling the rear chain up and down: if the tightening and slackening of the rear chain causes an obvious change in the primary chain tension, then the sleeve bearing has had it.

If the gearbox whines at all, either in some or all of the gears, you may be looking at one of a batch of Commandos which slipped through a couple of years or so ago with inadequately hardened gear clusters.

Frame and cycle parts

The first thing to check framewise on any Commando is the sideplay in the rear swinging arm. The swinging arm bearings are very much an Achilles heel on all Commandos, and we have seen examples where the slop at the rear wheel is getting on for half an inch! If the bike you're thinking of buying has more than the slightest trace of swinging arm play, then budget for a new spindle and bushes: sloppiness here plays hell with the handling.

On the 750 models the swinging arm bushes would last quite a long time providing they are pumped full of heavy gear oil (not grease) at regular intervals. The swinging arm pivot shaft holes in the engine plates would sometimes become enlarged, but Nortons flogged an oversize shaft to deal with that. On the 850 range, however, the design of the swinging arm bearing was changed around somewhat — and in this modifying process Norton's saw fit to dispense with the grease nipple and at the same time remove any practical possibility of an owner fitting one for himself. This masterly tactic has reduced the average life of Commando rear swinging arm bearings to 3,000-8,000 miles.

When testing for rear swinging arm play, incidentally, take care not to confuse bearing-wear with slack Isolastic engine mountings. The end-clearance of these should be

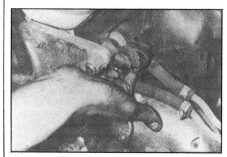

Don't confuse swinging arm play with slack Isolastic bushes: feel here for Isolastic movement. Cure is fiddly, but inexpensive.

MODEL GUIDE

YEAR	MODELS	COMMENTS	APPROX. PRICES*
1968	Commando	First model with Atlas engine. (Distributor behind cylinders).	£320
1969	Commando Fastback Commando S	Distributor dispensed with: less than reliable auto-advance inside timing chest.	£360
1970	Fastback Mk.II Commando S Commando Roadster		£380
1971	Fastback Mk.III Roadster Mk.II		£430
1972	Fastback Mk.IV Roadster Mk.IV Commando Interstate	Bad year. All models had ill-fated Combat engine.	£490
1973	Fastback Mk.IV	Dropped early in year.	£530
1973	Roadster Mk.V Interstate Mk.V	Possibly the best 750's of all. With the problems sorted but retaining the Combat's larger inlets and carbs. 750 engine size dropped in autumn.	
1973	Roadster 850 Mk.IA Insterstate 850 Mk.IA	Introduced in the spring; bored out 750 engine.	£600
1974	Roadster Mk.IIA Interstate Mk.IIA		£680
1975	Roadster Mk.IIA Interstate Mk.IIA	Dropped early in year.	£740
1975	Roadster Mk.III Interstate Mk.III	Introduced Jan: electric starters.	£840
1976	Roadster Mk.III Interstate Mk.III		£900

* Prices quoted are for machines in good condition having an average mileage of about 9,000 miles per year.

Check for side-play on the swinging arm: the bearings are often well shot.

Indicator switch is a weak point. Also, 850 with electric start doesn't have generator man enough for the job.

checked every 2,500 miles, and adjusted if necessary by reshimming: if they are allowed to become too slack, the whole engine/rear suspension complex will wiggle from side to side. Basically, play in the swinging arm bushes creates a 'loose' feeling when you move the rear wheel from side to side, while sloppy engine mountings result in a sort of 'spongy' movement.

Another thing to look for is obvious signs of pitting or wear on the front fork stanchions when the legs are fully extended: a small weepage of oil from the leg seals is normal enough, but there certainly shouldn't be any tramlines or back - and - forth play at the bottoms of the legs. There frequently will be such play, of course, since un-gaitered front forks are asking for trouble anyway.

Next on the list of possible problems is vibration damage and finish. The oil tank rear mountings tend to break, the seat pan is inclined to crack right across near the centre, and the silencers tend to fracture around the captive nuts where the mounting bolts screw in. The whole exhaust system is prone to rusting, and the clamps that secure the pipes into the head have a habit of coming undone and sometimes chewing up the threads in the head casting. If you're in any doubt about that, unscrew the clamps and have a look: new heads are expensive items!

If you're buying an 850, incidentally, it's well worth putting on the old 750-pattern silencers when the present ones cash in their chips. The latter silencer design was a good quiet chuff-box, but tends to strangle the top-end performance. The cognoscenti fit the old 750 silencers and go up a size or two on the main jets to match, according to the colour the plugs come out after a high-speed blast.

Wheels and brakes

The wheels are okay except that the chrome peels off rather easily — and the brakes are okay except that the disc brakes tend to do exactly the same thing! The discs are chromed as standard, presumably in an effort to avoid rusting, and the result is a brake which is somewhat insensitive until such time as the chrome starts to peel off. When this takes place, as it almost invariably does after not too long a period, the surface of the disc takes on the characteristic of a grinding wheel, somewhat to the detriment of brake pad life. The answer is to comport the disc along to an engineering shop before it gets too chewed, and have them skim off the chrome. Problem solved. They'll go rusty when you're not using the bike, of course — but once the chrome starts to peel they'll go rusty anyway, so what the hell.

It's not so much that there's actually anything wrong with the chrome: it's just that it doesn't stay attached to the rims . . . .

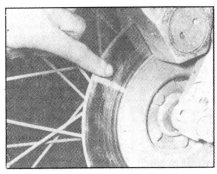

Standard chromed discs suffer from peeling of chrome, turning surface into a grinding wheel. Best answer is to have chrome skimmed off.

Servicing

We'd give the Commando about three out of ten. The basic service intervals are 1,000 miles, 2,500 miles, 5,000 miles, and 10,000 miles — which means you'll be having the spanners out pretty regularly. Some of the jobs are a bit fiddly, and things like dismantling the clutch and changing the Isolastic rubbers require special tools.

Giant Test
SHOULD THE COMMANDO DIE?

Photography Duncan Cubitt

REMEMBER 1967? It wasn't just the year of the summer of love, the season when Jimi Hendrix and Sergeant Pepper splashed into the rainbow colours of burgeoning psychedelia with crazy abandon. Even more important for the British bike scene, it marked the launch of the Norton Commando. Ten years on, the Commando may not seem much when matched against the kind of exotica spawned by the seventies' bike boom, but to the innocents of the late sixties it appeared almost like a flash of divine salvation for the British bike industry, whose decline was already in full swing.

True, the Commando was just another vertical twin, using an engine that had been in production in one form or another for almost 20 years. But it was a side-by-side banger with a difference — it didn't vibrate. Or, to be more accurate, its new Isolastic engine mounting system prevented most of the vibes from reaching the rider, because there was just no way that that 745cc long stroke mill with its 360-degree crank throws could be persuaded not to shake.

A couple of years after the appearance of the Commando came Japan's first serious big bike challenge — the Honda CB750. Not only was the Honda the first Oriental muscle machine, it also had four cylinders ranged across the frame, a layout that every other Japanese maker has since hustled to copy (Yamaha being the last with their forthcoming XS1000).

This month, the Commando becomes obsolete when the last of the 1,400 machines that were being built by NVT this summer were scheduled to roll out of Wolverhampton. Yet the CB750 continues, even though a series of newer multi-cylinder designs have constantly threatened to upstage it in recent years.

So for this Giant Test, we pulled together these two long-running favourites — the CB750 in its "original" four-pipe form, the Commando in its latest 828cc Interstate guise — to match British big twin funk against Japanese sophistication. And in measuring the Commando against Japan's most successful big bike, we asked: does it really deserve to die?

Testers: Graham Sanderson, Mike Nicks

HONDA CB750 K7

YOU'VE GOT to hand it to wily old Honda. Almost a decade ago they launched the first Japanese muscle machine, and the original concept was so good that it was able to carry the prestige of the flying H through lean periods when their obsession with car development left much of their motorcycle range looking about as appealing as the left-overs from last night's party. After the trend-setting CB750 in 1969 Honda were able to shuffle the pack and deal variations in 550, 500, 400 and 350cc sizes. While the twins in Honda's line-up looked less than exciting, the fours were — and are — good bikes. Meanwhile, caught in neutral at the lights by Honda's magnificent hole shot, the opposition stampeded to get their versions of the four-across-the-frame theme into production.

But the astonishing fact is, in an era when the Japanese lust for turnover has at times led them to trash designs still cooling from the white heat of launch publicity, the CB750 continues to cut a respectable dash. To meet the competition's new breed of fours that incorporate European-ised handling — Suzuki's GS750 and 550 and Kawasaki's Z650 — Honda offer the F2 variation. This has the new Comstar wheels, four-into-one exhaust plumbing, triple discs, an engine finished in mean black and more power and a higher rev limit coming from reworked cylinder heads and valve gear. It's a fully up-to-date sports 750.

But back in Nostalgia Flats there's still the K7. This is the bike we sought for this test because, visually at least, it's still remarkably close to the first CB750s to appear. And it's clearly intended as more of a touring, all-purpose bike than the F2, and is therefore more appropriate to match against the Commando, itself no performance fireball by contemporary standards.

What immediately differentiates the K7 from every other Japanese multi in the four-stroke division (except its 550cc K3 stablemate) is that it has a separate exhaust pipe and silencer for each cylinder. Now back in balmy '69 and the early seventies aspiring young bikers could sometimes be found crazy-eyed and trembling by the kerbside after seeing a motorcycle with four exhaust pipes passing before them *on the public road!* Sure enough, after a while fashion decreed that four-pipers were yesteryear's thing, and the new multis with lighter, less costly, easier to clean four-into-one and four-into-two systems appeared.

But when we picked up the K7 from the Ken Ives emporium in Leicester (Midlands buyers should note this shop that at the time of writing was running no less than *seven* demonstrators) we found that styling improvements over the years had added to the four-piper's appeal. It now sports plenty of chrome and polished alloy, an unashamedly garish maroon paint job on tank and side panels, and imitation brass logos on its tank and flanks. The tank itself has massive exterior dimensions with a bulbous heart-shaped outline just like a Harley Electra Glide's. So what we have in the 1977 version of the four-pipe Honda is motorcycling's Chevrolet Biscayne. It's a camped-up extension of the original CB750's styling, but the attention that it grabs from rubber-necking bikers and non-bikers alike proves that four-pipe looks have a kind of timeless appeal.

The first few miles on the K7 tell you that its riding position and general feel are as disarm-

ingly "dated" as its appearance, and by that I mean no criticism. Honda haven't attempted to shield the rider from the K7's bulk — all 540lbs of it. Instead they've supplied a lush, deeply padded seat and a set of wide but almost flat handlebars. So the rider settles *into* the bike, confronted by the broad bars with their massive black (and easily operated) switch blocks, the central console of rev counter, speedo, warning lights and ignition switch, and the twin mirrors. Behind there's the slightly raised pillion portion of the seat, and below on each side the twin pipes running back below the footrests. Yup, the K7 makes no bones about the fact that it's a big

bike, which in one way is no bad thing because many riders investing in heavy metal like to feel they've ended up with plenty of motorcycle for their money.

The sohc 736cc CB750 mill is one of the all-time classic motorcycle power units. Reliable, smooth, fast and versatile (Daytona winner to seven-second quarter-miler to favourite with the custom crowd) it comes in 67bhp form for the K7, against a claimed 73bhp for the F2. If memory serves me right, the original '69 CB750 also had 67 horses, so one might ask, what's happened to progress? It's been channeled into the F2, that's what, while the K7 remains as yer basic multi-purpose four-cylinder motorbike. On the road it feels noticeably less crisp than some of the newer fours now coming from Japan, but in a way that's typical Honda deceptiveness. Like most Hondas the K7 has more suds, than you'd suspect stacked away at its top end, as was indicated when it ripped through the speed trap at 110mph with the rider sitting up. From there on a minor clutch gremlin called a halt to the day's proceedings before we could time its all-out speed. We'd estimate 115mph with the rider prone. *(Dear Bike, contrary to your K7 test, my bike does an indicated 187mph running on three cylinders and pigeon crap, etc, etc, etc . . .)*

The K7 makes a usable tool for urban work or fast hauling on good quality main roads. The leverage offered by the bars and the tractability of a four-cylinder motor make it less of a hassle than you might expect to thread the gleaming beast past the bus queues. Out on well surfaced A-class roads the Honda moves along confidently, the motor able to cruise in the 80 to 90 bracket and the set-back footrests counterbalancing the wide bars to give a fatigue-free riding position. As it's a bulky bike, the rider tends to physically pitch it into turns with a twitch of the hips, but belying appearances, there's a surprising amount of clearance underneath those pipes before the little metal warning bubbles under the pegs hit the ground.

Out in the backroads, however, the K7 displays handling failings reminiscent of the wild old 500 Kawasakis. It really starts to mop its brow if hustled along rough and minor twisty roads as the chassis loses contact with the action and the harsh damping gives a ride like a hovercraft bashing through a stormy sea. Pretty soon the bike is heaving and wallowing, and you've got to back off. In a perverse kind of way it's fun trying to push the bugger along country roads in a hurry, but just be prepared to swallow your pride if you're passed by a GS Suzuki or a Z650 Kawasaki.

Fondling the Honda's light clutch lever reminded me just how much musclepower the Commando's clutch action demands, and therefore it's a pity that the snatchy Japanese transmission doesn't have the positive movements of the British gearbox. The K7, as well as being a little slower than most 750cc multis, also vibrates more. The tingles don't interfere with rider comfort, but they do blur the mirrors at 70 or more, which is a minor but irritating fault in these times when everyone knows someone who's been totted off the road.

The K7 has a single disc at the front and a drum at the rear, and scores highly in the braking department. The disc is beautifully progressive, and while it requires plenty of pressure I prefer that to the kamikaze instant-lock equipment fitted to all too many bikes. And another plus goes to the meaty ¾in. rear chain fitted to the latest big Hondas. Admittedly it's an endless type which will involve fitting hassles at replacement time, but its permanent lubrication facility sealed into the pin/bearing bushing by rubber O rings should ensure a long life and more miles between adjustments than on most big bikes.

The CB750 hasn't really aged, it's simply matured. And with the F2, it's clearly changed into a far more refined motorcycle than the first of the line. But such was the inherent "rightness" of the original CB750 that Honda are able to offer the K7 — a machine with no more power or performance than its predecessor of eight years ago — knowing that it still comes through as a competitive touring motorcycle.

Mike Nicks

Forward tilted motor and polished side casings give the Commando mill an up-to-date look, helping to disguise its 30-year heritage.

Unlike F2 sports model, K7 has just a single front disc. But it does a good job, offering mucho feedback.

828cc motor pumps out peak torque at 5,000 rpm, while max horsepower is churned out just 900 revs higher. Electric starter sometimes doesn't want to.

Four pipes sweeping under the motor still look classy in an era when four-into-one layouts rule. Motor still churns out a claimed 67 bhp.

Norton's discs actually work in the wet. Silencers meet stifling US noise regs, but muffle performance too.

These days ignition switch and choke control are mounted just ahead of the handlebars, far more accessible than earlier positions.

NORTON Commando Mk111

THE WIND rushed through the open door of a Cessna 180 as it circled high above a tiny grass airfield just west of the A1. Inside, three of the five occupants knelt, almost petrified, in the cramped and breezy atmosphere of the cockpit as they prepared to perform one of the most exhilarating and illogical stunts man can experience. To leap out of a perfectly airworthy monoplane and descend by parachute.

By the time the pilot, strapped firmly to the light aircraft's only seat, had manoeuvred the machine over the drop zone, I'd resigned myself to the sobering fact that within the next few seconds the instructor would issue a few brief orders in a manner calculated to instil an air of falling - off - a - log nonchalance into his three pupils.

"Cut", came the order and with the brainwashing effect of the day's training and the sense of discipline it had created I stepped onto a tiny metal step in the full blast of the propeller draught with the earth 2,000 feet below.

"Go", came the final instruction and seconds after pushing myself from the tiny foothold I was greeted with the reassurance of a vast canopy mushrooming some 20 feet above. The earth stretched out below like a gigantic model village and the vehicles on the grey vein of the A1 looked like an advert for Scalectrix. Satisfaction, relief, pride, you name it I experienced it. Even after a slightly bumpy legs-together and chin - on - chest regulation landing I had to reflect that the exercise was nothing like the ordeal I'd imagined seconds before the plane took off to dispose of its cargo, and was a whole lot more satisfying than I'd expected when toying with the idea from the safety of an

armchair some weeks before.

By an odd paradox, riding one of the latest and last Mk 3 Norton Commando Interstates reminded me of that aerial exploit undertaken as a cub reporter a few years back. Okay, okay, I'm not suggesting that riding a Commando, or any other British bike, is burdened with such melodrama, but six months as a C15 owner had left me healthily cynical about the real worth of British machinery. And to someone whose interest in bikes materialised in the sixties when the British industry was already in steep decline and Japanese motorcycles had become an accepted part of British life, the thought of an 828cc parallel twin seemed so incongruous compared to the multi-cylindered, de-toxed seventies.

Yet older colleagues said that I ought to enjoy the unique brand of motorcycling the Commando provides, and it wasn't long before The Truth filtered through their originally unconvincing promises. I found the relative crudity of the Norton quite refreshing compared to the highly sanitised Japanese fours. But the fact that I was enjoying this form of biking was even more surprising when you consider the odds stacked against the machine.

Like the latest Triumph products from Meriden, the basis for today's Commando took to the roads decades ago. In 1949, about the time Mr Honda was making his first inroads into the bike industry, Bert Hopwood's 500cc Dominator twin was announced. Since then it's been bumped up through 600cc, to the 650cc Dominator, the 750 Atlas, and the 750 Commando, yet even with its current displacement of 828cc the machine is still fitted with the four-speed gearbox AMC first fitted to their machines in 1956. But despite early setbacks, the Commando has enjoyed much success, particularly in its early years when there was less Japanese opposition to steal its thunder. This is particularly amazing considering that while at Triumph Bert Hopwood and Doug Hele went for a triple layout for the 750 Trident because they considered 650cc was the maximum capacity to which a vertical twin should be pushed.

Yet here we are with a product 178cc over the Hopwood/Hele "limit" and the Commando is still selling. And strongly. And I suspect the demand for the last 1,400 Commandos to roll out of Marston Road is due as much to nostalgia and misplaced patriotism as it is to the desire to own as good a British machine as there's likely to be in the immediate future. Ironically, it's the rejection of British machines in the sixties that assured the final glimmer of success for Norton. At a time when British-bike freaks are paying vastly unrealistic prices for machinery they once so vehemently criticised, who can blame NVT for asking £1,317 for the Commando? After all it's virtually the last mass produced symbol of the once great British industry.

At 70mph you can almost count the beats with the motor rumbling and tappets clicking at a lazy 3,800rpm, and it's this long legged, unburstable feeling that really makes the Commando a pleasing machine to ride. Mike Jackson, now NVT's marketing director, summed up the Norton's most appealing characteristic when Commandos in various guises had been cleaning up in production racing and dirt track events Stateside in 1972. His slogan on a hoarding at the Ascot Park, California, half mile read: "Lotta torque about Norton." Too right. The Commando really epitomises top gear motorcycling.

Let the clutch home and the motor will punch you past 2,000rpm with the pulling power of a steam engine. The engine shudders from 2,200 to 2,400rpm, but get all your cog-swapping over by three grand and you can forget about the left-side mounted gear lever until you're forced into an urban crawl below 25mph. By 3,000rpm the motor has settled into a relentless stride with the Isolastic engine suspension set-up filtering through just a twinge of low frequency vibration which makes a change from the high frequency massage dished out by so many Japanese machines.

With maximum torque being lashed out at a lowly 5,000rpm you'll be wasting petrol in exchange for very little extra performance should you start forcing the engine to its 7,000rpm red line. Owners will find that 5,000rpm is adequate for their daily needs, and all the Commando's slugging power seemed so easy to handle compared to the frenzied high revving characteristics of more complex contemporary machines.

Now that the British bike industry has become insignificant it's small comfort to reflect that lack of ingenuity didn't contribute to its failing. The Commando may only have been a two year stop-gap model conceived by Dr Stefan Bauer, Bernard Hooper and Bob Trigg, but it featured a major technological advancement in its Isolastic innovation which used rubber in the engine mountings, car industry style, to protect the rider from the inherent vibration of a parallel twin. But there were serious problems with early Commandos which needed constant re-shimming of the Isolastic rubbers to keep the engine firmly fixed in the frame. And since the swinging arm bearings are part of the rear engine plate assembly which was, and still is, Isolastically mounted, wild handling Commandos were common and needed constant attention and correction. Much of this problem was solved when Norton substituted a Vernier adjustment using a lockable thread for the shimming method, although when the Commando grew to 828cc in 1973 the facility for lubing the swinging arm bearings was abandoned, which meant about 8,000 miles was the limit before renewal was needed.

Anyway, with the Isolastic problem largely solved the Commando began to behave like it was originally planned. Although not as precise as the legendary Featherbed frames which it replaced, the handling on the latest chassis is still sure-footed. The bike just sits on the road like a limpet to a rock and nothing ever knocks the machine off line. Even the slight side-to-side flex that's almost inevitable over bad surfaces when an Isolastic frame is used doesn't get out of hand. Maybe the Roadholder forks are still unable to deal comfortably with small pronounced bumps in the road, but there's no such harsh and juddery feeling when the bike is gliding over more undulating surfaces.

Like many derivatives of bikes which first hit the highway in the late sixties the Commando Interstate is a slower, more refined and thankfully more reliable shadow of its once fast and less predictable self. Pre-'73 Commandos chewed through main bearings since the over-stressed crank flexed so much and literally burrowed its way into the plain bearing surfaces. Before they'd solved that major problem, Norton offered the ill-conceived Combat engine, with higher compression and wilder cam, during 1972. This 65bhp motor went like hell but so did the mains. But the bearing hassle was solved when slightly tapered Superblend rollers were fitted at the same time that compression was reduced to the original and saner 9:1.

No longer is the Commando a high performance roadster. Not with those T160 style silencers strangling top end performance it's not. Even if you replaced them with earlier silencers the genuine 51.5 bhp the motor produces wouldn't put the Norton in the superformance category. It'll lope along all day at 70 to 80mph, and even though the engine is capable of even higher cruising speeds no serious long distance rider could stand the discomfort of the riding position. It's not something you can blame on that monolithic, 5.25-gallon slab of a petrol tank but on the combination of a pair of handlebars which are too wide before turning back towards the rider, and a seat which dips in the middle. The result is that with increasing speed you slide into the dip of the seat forcing you to grip the bars with greater force. Which all makes for some pretty uncomfortable cruising if you're aiming for a constant 95-100 mph. For anything over the ton you'll have to slide your feet back onto the pillion footrests and lie on the tank, and even then you'll be lucky to get anywhere near the red line in top. Our top speed of 111.16 mph was recorded at 6,300 rpm with 700 revs to go before the red.

Considering the vastly different concepts involved, both the Norton and the Honda CB750 are remarkably similar in terms of performance. Both machines have descended from more rapid ancestors, but now that the curves on their performance graphs have been smoothed off they're more touring orientated. On the Commando there's realistic Halogen headlighting and a disc at each end with Lockheed hydraulics that actually work in the wet even if the front brake does need bags of squeeze. And they're just a couple of details which spell serious motorcycling in capital letters.

Even though the Commando is still being produced eight years after it was originally due to be phased out it's still sad that the machine reaches the end of its production line this month before it reaches its development summit. Sadder still is the fact that there's no sponsor for the Bernard Hooper/John Favill Norton '76 featured in the April '77 issue. This is a great pity since the 1¾ in single SU carb they used greatly improved petrol consumption, which proved heavy on our test bike. Screwed hard the Interstate slurped fuel through the twin Amal concentrics at the rate of 33 miles to the gallon, some 20 mpg *less* than the Norton '76's worst figure. The Italian Paioli forks fitted to the Hooper/Favill machine were an improvement over the Roadholders and styling changes, particularly the FPS cast wheels, made the machine look more fashionable, or rather less archaic, alongside smooth Japanese fours.

If time hadn't run out on Norton engineers

ROOTS: Engine from which Commando was developed was originally launched way back in '49 as a 500. Top drawing shows the 1951 model with trendy (well, for those days) plunger-sprung rear end. Bottom pic shows the first Commando as it appeared in 1967. Many would say this is still the sleekest and best looking of the variations churned out since.

before the receiver slid into the picture, they'd probably have got round to improving the American Prestolite starter motor, added by popular demand in 1975. It occasionally choked when pushing up the 9:1 pistons on cold mornings. Maybe the clutch, often a source of minor trouble rather than a major defect, could also have been revised. The pressure needed to activate the clutch on our bike was so great that it almost strained the tendons in my left hand.

As the Commando's ten-year, 60,000-unit run ends this month, owners of the 10,000 machines still in the UK can at least look forward to a fairly good spares supply. NVT have cleared out Marston Road and Small Heath and shifted £2 million worth of Commando, Trident and miscellaneous Triumph and BSA spares to Andover, which has become NVT's worldwide service centre. Whether new spares will be manufactured when the present stocks run low depends entirely upon demand. Another bonus for Commando buyers is the 6 month 4,000 miles parts and labour guarantee, which despite the receivership difficulties NVT are still able to maintain.

Graham Sanderson

SUMMARY

VIEWED DIRECTLY alongside contemporary machines the Commando may seem dated and even backward in design. The way it leaps around at tickover, the slight engine oil leak and the 2ft long spider's leg of a prop-stand may appear to belong to motorcycling of a bygone age. But the fact that there's still a small and partisan market for the bike is reason enough for the Commando's survival. Never have I ridden a machine which has inspired so many pedestrians into flowery roadside reminiscences of *their* biking days. It must be something to do with that indefinable quality: character.

It's too late to hope for a total resurrection, but in backing the far more outdated twins from Meriden and shunning NVT the Government have not only made the industry a one-horse race, but we can't help thinking they've bet on the wrong steed. We reckon that in better circumstances the Commando could have carried on for a while yet.

As it is, the bike seems likely to feed off the current wave of nostalgia for old British tin, and to become a collector's item in a very short time. Just watch those second-hand prices rise.

The Honda K7, despite its four cylinders and totally different concept to the British machine, is surprisingly similar in its touring outlook to the Commando. Both are good all round big bikes with moderate performance and handling to match the needs of a rider intent on covering long distances at a constant 80mph plus. And with only £18 between the K7 and Commando price tags the choice depends upon just what type of motorcycling you're after — the raunchy long-legged, low-revving pulling power of the Commando, or the silky smooth bulk of the K7.

Although both machines compare favourably with each other it's when you look at similarly priced motorcycles in the market that you begin to question the cost of the Commando and K7. For another £82 above the cost of the Norton the character-seeking biker could own one of the much acclaimed shaft-driven Yamaha XS750 triples, surely one of the most refreshing Japanese designs in recent years. For someone who enjoys four-cylinder biking there's the performance orientated Kawasaki Z650 for £174 *less* than the K7, the better handling Suzuki GS750 at £1,300, and Honda's own F2 at £1,379.

CHECKOUT

	HONDA CB750K7	NORTON COMMANDO INTERSTATE MK.3
Engine	4-cyl SOHC 4-stroke	2-cyl OHV 4-stroke
Bore x stroke	61 x 63mm	77 x 89mm
Capacity	736cc	828cc
Compression ratio	9.2:1	8.5:1
Carburation	4 x 28mm Keihin	2 x 32mm Amal
BHP @ RPM	67 @ 8,500	58 @ 5,900
Max torque @ RPM	44ft/lb @ 7,000	48.5ft/lb @ 5,000
Primary drive	Duplex chain	Triplex chain
Clutch	Multiplate, wet	Multiplate, wet
Gearbox	5-speed	4-speed
Electrical system	Alternator battery/coil ignition	120w alternator battery/coil ignition
Lighting	60/55w headlight	45/40w headlight

DIMENSIONS

Wheelbase	58.5in	57in
Seat height	32in	32in
Overall width	34.5in	—
Ground clearance	6.5in	4in
Kerb weight	540lbs	492lbs
Fuel capacity	4.3gals	5.25gals

EQUIPMENT

Trafficators	Yes	Yes
Electric starter	Yes	Yes
Trip mileometer	Yes	Yes
Steering lock	Yes	Yes
Helmet lock	Yes	No
Headlight flasher	Yes	Yes
Others	Twin mirrors, locking fuel flap	Locking seat

CYCLE PARTS

Tyres		
(front)	3.50 x 19 Jap Dunlop	4.10 x 19 Dunlop TT100
(rear)	4.50 x 17 Jap Dunlop	4.10 x 19 Dunlop TT100
Brakes		
(front)	11.5in disc	10.7in disc
(rear)	7.8in drum	10.7in disc

PERFORMANCE

Top speed		
(prone)	115mph (est)	111.16mph
(sitting up)	110.29mph	101.23mph
Standing ¼ mile	13.9secs (est)	14.25secs (est)
Speedometer error		
at indicated 30mph	26.6mph	29.6mph
at indicated 60mph	57.7mph	58.5mph
Fuel consumption		
(overall)	42mpg	39mpg
(ridden hard)	38mpg	33mpg
Braking distance		
from 30mph	27ft	31.5ft
from 60mph	123ft	137ft

PRICE	£1,335 inc VAT	£1,317 inc VAT
Guarantee	12 months unlimited mileage	6 months/4,000 miles parts and labour
Supplied by	Ken Ives Ltd., 220 Loughborough Road, Leicester.	NVT Motorcycles Ltd, Lynn Lane, Shenstone, Staffs.

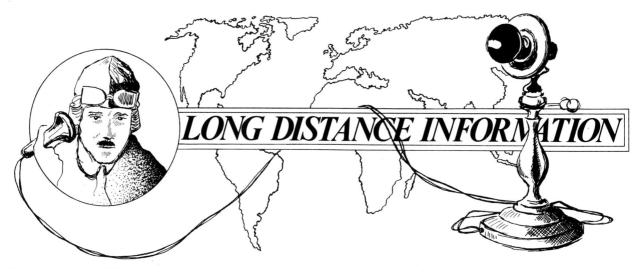

☐ My Commando VCT 2IK was bought from Grantham dealers A&A Cox Motorcycles on December 8 1971 for the "on the road" price of £585. A Tower rack, still on the bike, was fitted before delivery.

Careful running-in followed throughout the winter of 1971-72 and all warranty servicing was done by A&A Cox. Although I noticed a gearbox whine in third when pulling from about 40mph, I never bothered to complain and over the years the whine has gradually decreased, though never quite disappeared. It's just one of those little things that makes a bike your own!

Very few problems occurred during the bike's early life and only a few claims were necessary. They included a new fork leg to replace the original which had a broken lug, an exhaust pipe due to poor chrome and a rear sprocket because a tooth had sheared off the old one. The replacement sprocket is still fitted and has plenty of life left in it despite its having survived nearly thirteen years.

After running-in, the bike was used in the way you would expect of a twenty-year-old rider on a sporting roadster; although not mindlessly thrashed, it was certainly ridden in the fashion I believed it was meant to be. Had I wanted to ride everywhere at 50mph on square tyres I would have bought something smaller. Although experience has taught me to choose the appropriate time and place, the bike is used regularly to this day for hard, fast, bend-swinging riding. This is what the Norton Commando is all about.

The first modification I made was a simple one – to block off the rear chain oiler. The pipe to the oiler was removed and a self-tapping screw soldered into the feeding unit outlet on the oil tank. I refuse to believe in pouring oil on the chain to lubricate it, any more than I believe in pouring oil over the engine for the same purpose! Throughout the life of the bike, successive chains have been removed and boiled in chain lubricant.

At 6,000 miles the main bearings failed and on examination I noted that, when the engine was built, the crank had been left with nearly 0.040in end float. The pins holding the steel cages together

DAVE CHARITY recalls 13 happy years with a Norton Commando.

had fallen out and the balls were free to clatter about in the races. These rather nasty bearings were replaced with brass caged roller bearings (of course, Superblends were not available in those days) and the engine was rebuilt with about 0.008in crank end float. Except for grinding-in of the valves, no other part of the engine needed attention.

Japanese indicators from a Honda 750/4 were fitted in 1972 and the reason for this is still a source of amusement. A friend who was broke and having difficulty with meeting his HP payments decided to make ends meet by selling various bits. I bought the indicators and although a number of spills over the years have claimed the original units, I have never had to replace all four in one go. This means that each replacement had to match the existing ones and consequently they have never been changed for Lucas units. Apart from that I prefer them to the Lucas components.

In the summer of that second year of ownership, I took the bike to Paris for

four days. On the way there it rained persistently but no electrical faults or misfiring of the engine occurred. On the return journey I noticed a tinkling noise coming from the head in the region of the left hand exhaust port and a small stream of oil which was seeping past the exhaust ring and over the head fins. A strip down revealed a loose valve guide; a new one was bought and after sizing it and the hole, I had 0.002in of copper plating deposited on the outer diameter of the guide. This was fitted in the head using Loctite and has been no trouble since, though the guides now need replacing and this winter will see some careful work done on the head.

A useful birthday present was a steering damper which I fitted with homemade brackets. It made the bike more stable at speed, compensated for the unsuitably wide roadster bars and helped reduce the Commando's tendency to weave when crossing white lines and tar ridges in the road. Other minor mods included the fitting of a small magnet to the dipstick on the oil filler cap, a sealed beam headlight to replace the old bulb and reflector and the fitting of sealed bearings in the rear wheel. The original rear wheel bearings were the type which have to be packed with grease, which was fine. Not so good were the felt seals used to keep the grease in, and the dirt and water out. Because I wash the bike often, water would eventually pass the felt seals and wash away the grease. The bike had two sets of this unsealed type in its first year but since then it has run on just one set of the sealed replacements.

The frame was re-stove enamelled because the quality of the original paint was very poor. I removed the engine and gearbox as one piece and therefore did not need to disturb them. At the same time I had several items, e.g. the swinging arm and centre stand chrome-plated. I consider the plating of these two items to be of practical use as well as making them aesthetically pleasing; both are otherwise vulnerable to chipping and scratching.

The following year the ungainly socket placed on the air filter box was replaced with a neater jack socket mounted in the

It still looks quite standard, but much has been improved.

Norton steering is good, but a damper adds stability, especially with high bars.

A sump guard protects the engine and lower frame from flying crud.

Auxiliary jack socket was moved from the air filter into the side panel.

top forward corner of the oil tank cover. It provides power for lead lights and the like when camping. If electronic ignition is fitted, as on my bike, and lead lights are used for long periods the bike may not restart if the battery is low.

To prevent the bottom of the engine and frame tubes being blasted with stones, a guard was fitted by mounting it on the frame tubes. This simply consists of a piece of alloy sheet and four plastic pipe clips. The sheet was bent to shape over an oil drum and all four clips secured by 2BA screws. The side-stand boss locates through the guard and prevents movement. The side stand had already been removed the previous year because it was located by a circlip fitted on the boss, and not bolted as on later models. This clip had a habit of peeling out of its groove and I nearly lost the stand on a couple of occasions. Also, being short in the leg, I found it difficult to extend the stand from the rider's seat.

Summer 1973, a bolt broke in the right hand conrod and the resulting blow up meant that a total rebuild of the engine was necessary. Early 850 MK1

crankcases were obtained, new and unstamped, from Andover. That explains why a 20M3S engine number appears on later type crankcases. (Note breather position). Since adopting copper head gaskets in 1973, no further trouble, due to blowing head gaskets, has been experienced. The fitting of AM4 green linings in the front brake by Ferodo at the 1974 TT improved the brake by 100%.

A total overhaul was made during the 1975–76 winter. Four years of hard riding had taken its toll and a lot of annoying little complaints were settled. Modifications were as follows:

Borrani alloy rims replaced the original steel ones, purely for aesthetic reasons.

The original fork stanchions, which were badly worn, were replaced and gaiters fitted over the new stanchions have proved a sure remedy.

The fitting of an Atlas oil feed manifold allowed the oil pipes to run under the gearbox and provide easy access to the primary chain adjusters.

Tapping out the end of the kickstart lever and fitting a screw holding a domed

plate over the rubber was done to prevent the rubber from slipping off when kicking over the engine. (The domed plate came from the inside of a broken lorry mirror and is part of the mounting mechanism).

All the isolastic mountings were overhauled and extra ones were fitted inside the housings by cutting down the spacing tubes. All shims, washers and cups on the isolastics were covered in grease and given minimal clearance (I use .003in to .005in per side; note that clearance must be the same on each side). When set properly, the isolastics give no trouble at all.

Further improvements to the handling included the replacement of the swinging arm bushes and a new pin made from silver steel. Isolastic shims were placed behind the flange on both bushes until they were a firm fit over the gearbox plates. (With the paint removed from the bearing area!) Two extra bolts were fitted to hold the pin firmly in the mounting tube. The original central bolt allows the pin to pivot but makes a good place for filling with oil; I have always used old engine oil. Extra stiffener tubes above and below the swinging arm pivot completed the mods in this area.

Apart from Superblend main bearings, new pistons and light honing of the standard bores, the engine was left alone. All the return springs in the gearbox were changed and a new primary chain was fitted.

A persistent leak from the alternator wire was cured by fitting a waterproof cable gland taken from a military radio: the body of the fitting passes through the chaincase and is secured with a nut and fibre washer, while the cable passes through the fitting and is sealed with a threaded cup and a rubber gland. In all, it's only about 1¼in long and fits inside the chaincase.

The notorious Commando leak behind the clutch was also cured in 1975/76 by cutting a segment from the top of a damper shroud about ¼in high and half

the circumference of the shroud. Fixed with Araldite by its top face to the steel seal holder on the rear chaincase, it sits between the back of the clutch and the chaincase; oil flows round it and into the bottom of the chaincase, rather than along the shaft and out of the seal as it did before. To prevent rotation of the complete seal holder, a segment was removed from the rear of the holder and a flat plate was riveted to the chaincase. This modification effectively prevents the holder from turning and the deflector is always at the top.

No further modifications were done until 1979 when 32mm carbs were fitted. The original ones were getting worn and I came by a pair of 32mm carbs with 32–30mm manifolds at the right price. Being less worn, the 32mm carbs were fitted and acceleration improved slightly.

About this time Boyer-Bransden electronic ignition was fitted, an improvement which made the bike far better in every respect and the most successful modification I have ever made.

A further change was made to the engine in 1983 when I replaced the cam chain tensioner. Never really being convinced of the worth of original plain steel tensioners, I bought a neoprene faced tensioner which proved quite useless as the neoprene was not thick enough. The outer plates soon cut through the material (as they should) and reached the steel backing before the rollers were riding on the neoprene which promptly fell off the tensioner (as it shouldn't). If the neoprene had been just 1/16in thicker, all would have been well. I solved the problem by brazing a narrow strip of steel onto the face of the tensioner and now the rollers roll over the strip, thus avoiding contact between the plates and the tensioner face. It seems to be lasting OK and certainly cannot be any worse than the original idea.

This year new fork springs and damper cups were necessary as the forks had developed a bad sag. A Norvil head steady improved the handling still further, and an 850 Mk III rocker oil feed solved the problem of heat affecting the plastic on the 750 type near the head unions. Many of the bolts have been changed for stainless steel and a few fittings such as coil brackets and chain adjusters, have also been replaced with stainless.

Planned modifications include a halogen headlight and high output alternator, extensive use of stainless steel nuts and bolts and a return to AM4 front brake linings. I have also toyed with the idea of an electric start conversion, although I have never seen one on a 750

Under the finned cover, Dave has fitted Boyer-Bransden electronic ignition – the best mod ever.

An Atlas oil feed manifold allowed the pipes to run under the gearbox.

– still, someone has to be first!

I have ridden the Commando on several continental trips, the longest being to Italy in summer 1981 when the engine torque made the Alps seem like molehills and the bike performed well even at very high altitudes. Being rich at 8,000 feet posed no problems and no re-jetting was done, without ill effect. A round trip of just over 3,000 miles with no mechanical trouble at all, the only attention required was the tightening of the chain and the bolt holding the tax disc! Loaded with camping gear for two made the handling less sure, but by no means bad. I would not hesitate to do a similar journey on the Commando again and hope to make a return trip in 1985.

Summary

Frame: no cracks or failure.
Wheels: hubs no trouble, poor chrome on original rims.
Sprockets: still on warranty replacement. Using 21T gearbox sprocket.
Primary: one chain replaced.
Clutch: one set of plates and diaphragm – can be heavy on cables.
Forks: excellent. One set of springs.

Instruments: on second speedo due to breakage.
Exhausts: silencers tend to become stuck on pipes if not removed for a long time. Keep exhaust rings tightened properly and they will be alright.
Gearbox: spring replaced.
Lubrication: have always run on Castrol GP50 – always will.
Electrical system: no trouble – alternator, rectifier, Zener diode, wiring loom, switches and coil are all original equipment.
Tank (petrol): looks great, but a silly size – holds 2½ gallons.
Tank (oil): in 1976 gave up trying to stop rear upper mounting from breaking, now use two pieces of high-density foam between frame and oil filler cap.
Horn: very sensible size and volume.
Engine: blow up in 1973, reliable before and after. Successful maintenance depends on patience, mechanical understanding and a good tool kit. A torque wrench is essential.
Original finish: could only be described as a joke. Nortons seemed to be having a lot of problems with quality control in the early seventies, and I made my opinions well known to them. The paint on my bike was literally falling off within eight weeks of delivery!
Overall impression: rugged no-nonsense motorcycle with qualities that take time to fully appreciate. Quick and light, the Commando looks, handles, and sounds like a motorbike should.

List of modifications and main replacements:

1971: rack fitted.
1972: chain oiler blocked off, steering damper fitted, sealed wheel bearings fitted, Honda indicators fitted, sealed beam fitted, magnet on dipstick, new mains in engine, frame stove enamelled and parts chromed.
1973: jack socket fitted on oil tank cover, sump guard fitted, engine blow-up, new crankcases, copper head gasket fitted.
1974: AM4 green linings fitted in front brake.
1975/76: Borrani alloy rims replaced steel rims, fork stanchions replaced and gaiters fitted, Atlas oil feed manifold fitted and oil pipes run under gearbox, kickstart rubber retainer fitted, isolastics modified and swinging arm pivot improved, stiffener plates added near swinging arm pivot, centre stand bushed with shouldered bushes, Superblend bearings fitted in engine, pistons removed and bores honed, rocker arms shimmed to reduce noise, oil leaks cured from alternator wire and clutch shaft.
1979: 32mm carbs and 32–30mm manifolds fitted, Boyer-Bransden ignition fitted.
1983: modified cam chain tensioner.
1984: new fork springs and damper cups, Norvil head steady fitted, 850 Mk III rocker feed pipe fitted, many bolts and screws changed for stainless steel.

PHOTOGRAPHY MARTYN BARNWELL

COMMANDING RESPECT

'USER friendly' is a piece of jargon used by computer people to describe an item of equipment that is instantly confidence-inspiring and easy to work with. If you stretch your imagination a little, it is possible to describe some motorcycles as user, or rider, friendly. Ducati's civilised but inspiring 900 GTS tourer from the late seventies is a rider-friendly motorcycle, encouraging the motorcyclist to stretch himself without ever threatening to take him further than he wants to go. Some other machines, like the original Laverda Jota, are best described as user demanding, threatening to overwhelm the rider unless they are mastered by him.

The 850cc Norton Commando on test fits into the latter category. Although at first sight it seems to be just an ordinary, albeit very clean, Mk 111 Commando, Norton fans will quickly spot that the exhaust system and air box are from an earlier model, and the machine is fitted with an after-market steering damper.

But only the most dedicated sprocket-tooth counter will realise that the gearing is much higher than standard, and a Boyer electronic ignition system has been fitted. The result of these modifications to what is one of the biggest parallel twins ever made is a motorcycle that, at first anyway, is very demanding, intimidating even.

Starting from cold is far from easy. The twin carbs should be tickled, but great care must be taken not to over-flood them. Full choke is applied via the hand-lebar-mounted lever, the ignition is switched on and, ignoring the button labelled 'start' (we'll come to that later), the rider swings on the kickstarter.

With luck, or a fair amount of practice, the engine starts with a pleasant bark. Novices may find that they have got the combination of fuel level and choke wrong, and have flooded the motor. Even if they persuade the engine to start, they may promptly stifle it by releasing the choke at the wrong moment.

When this happens, it can be very

850cc Norton Commando Mk III *by Richard Simpson*

Left: handling is dependable, but cornering the Norton fast is hard work.

difficult to get the bike going again. On the first morning of the test, my new neighbour, after watching me struggle for a while, tactfully pointed out the 'electric start' transfers emblazoned on the machine's gleaming flanks and suggested that I press the button instead.

And there's the rub. Anyone who has ever ridden a Mk 111 Commando knows that you stand about as much chance of getting one to fire on the button with a cold engine as you do of revitalising the British motorcycle industry, for the starter motor finds it hard to get one cold piston over compression before it flattens the battery.

This wouldn't be too bad were it not for those side-panel transfers proclaiming the machine's supposed ability to get under way without physical effort on the rider's part. But by 1977 reliable electric starting had been a standard feature on almost all medium-sized and large motorcycles, including NVT's own Triumph Trident, for long enough for it to be a totally unremarkable item in a machine's specification. That Norton should see fit to advertise such a feature, especially when it was so poor that even factory personnel referred to it as an 'electrical starting assister', is a sad indication of the state that the NVT group was in by that stage.

Once the machine has been ridden about twenty miles, however, and the engine-oil is thoroughly warm, the starter works quite well.

The high gearing of the test machine dominates initial riding impressions. A healthy handful of revs and plenty of clutch-slip are necessary to get the bike under way, and although the seat height, at 31 inches, is not excessive, its width and the positioning of the non-folding footrests can make pulling away a shin-banging experience at first.

The brakes also take some getting used to. For anyone accustomed to twin discs, handlebar lever pressure appears to be very high, and at first I thought the front brake was really poor. However, if the lever is given a hard squeeze, the single Norton-Lockheed caliper is capable of producing a reasonable amount of braking effort, but I understand now why Norton racers are so keen to fork out for Norvil brake kits.

A similar unit on the rear wheel is much more effective, and the rider can give the pedal a healty press with the right foot, so the high working pressure is not so noticeable. The discs themselves have had their original coating of flash chroming skimmed off, which helps both wet weather performance and pad wear, and the units seem to function better when thoroughly warmed up.

Electric starter (under carbs) can't cope with a cold engine

But the heavy brakes combined with high gearing, limited steering-lock and a 57in wheelbase do make the machine unsuitable for town riding. Add a 5.25-gallon Interstate fuel tank, and the machine's purpose becomes clear — to go 'far, faster', as the Norton advertisements once said.

Indeed, once out of town, the Commando comes into its own. The high gearing that is such a hindrance in traffic gives you four usable ratios for the open road. While I would hesitate to describe the riding position as comfortable — the footrests are too far forward and the bars too high — it is at least possible to live with this arrangement.

The Commando is a demanding but satisfying motorcycle to ride hard. Handling is very good, though it requires far more effort to ride the Norton fast along a twisty road than, say, a Triumph twin. Commandos also do not have a particularly good reputation for handling when compared to their Featherbed-framed predecessors. This is a consequence of the Isolastic engine mounting system which, when adjusted for maximum smoothness, allows some .010in of play at the swinging-arm pivot. The result is a nasty 'hinged in the middle' feeling when shutting-off late in a bend.

However, the test machine has its engine-mountings adjusted to give only .006in of play, a practice followed by most police forces in the days when the Norton Interpol formed the mainstay of their traffic-patrol fleets. Although this results in some engine vibration reaching the rider at low revs, mostly through the footrests, it means that the handling is taut and stable. The steering damper,

Single front disc is puny by modern standards

added by the present owner when he was still running ten thou clearances, is now virtually redundant and remains on its softest setting.

The exhaust system contributes much to the smooth running of the machine. Mk 111 Commandos were originally fitted with very quiet peripheral-discharge silencers which tended to restrict the spread of horsepower. The system fitted to the test machine is that used on the earlier 850, and liberates a lot of extra torque and noise.

It's a sound that will bring back memories. Some will recall the John

Silencers and air filter from an earlier model help the Mk III Commando breathe

Player Norton team of the early seventies, fighting an increasingly desperate battle against Japanese multis. Others will remember the spectacular sight and sound of the Norton Wasp sidecar-cross outfits that dominated the sport for so many years. Although loud, the noise is very pleasant, and some of the most unexpected people commented on what a nice sounding bike the test machine was.

The extra power means that this Norton is well able to exploit its non-standard sky-high top gear, with 90mph being an easy 4,500rpm burble. Geared for a theoretical 140mph at the 7,000rpm redline, in ideal conditions the machine will pull to six thousand, which gives a top speed of 120mph, an increase of five or six miles an hour over the claimed maximum for the standard machine.

Apart from the noise and brakes, the Commando feels very like an 850cc T3 Moto Guzzi. Riding positions are similar, with both machines having large fuel tanks, high and wide handlebars, and forward mounted footrests. There is the same feeling of a smooth and torquey large-displacement twin-cylinder engine pouring out power, and what the Commando loses by having only four gears and chain drive, it makes up for by not being plagued by torque-reaction and a clonky gear-change.

The high gearing destroys fuel economy round town, with figures as low as 40mpg being returned. Long journeys and higher speeds see it improve to as much as 60mpg, which combined with the large fuel tank provides a good range for touring. The engine does like a good supply of fuel though, as it starts spluttering and running roughly quite soon after going onto reserve.

Had time not caught up with the Commando when it did — this example is one of the last built — fuel economy would have been improved by the substitution of a single SU carb for the twin Amal instruments fitted to all production versions. However, the final models did incorporate several very useful modifications, showing that contrary to common belief, the British factories sometimes listened to constructive criticism.

For example, adjustment of the Isolastic engine mountings, initially by shim, was changed to a vernier system that is much easier to use. Early Commandos had a terrible reputation for poor finish and mechanical unreliability, although both were vastly improved by the time that the final batch was built in Wolverhampton.

But by 1977, the Commando was an almost prehistoric bike. Its non-unit construction, four-speed gearbox and traditional styling combined with the stifling effect of noise and pollution regulations on a design that could trace its roots back to 1947, to make the Norton a poor buy. The British bike must have appeared very unattractive, given that the Japanese were starting to produce big bikes with acceptable handling, and Italian machines in a similar mould to the Norton were becoming available at sensible prices.

However, the passing years have been kind to the Commando. Spares availability seems to be almost as good as ever, and the bike's rugged simplicity looks more and more appealing as the Italians follow the Japanese down the blind alley of 'designer' styling and 16in front wheels. The Commando's faults are well known, which is more than you can say

Specification

ENGINE
Type	ohv twin
Bore x stroke	77 x 89mm
Capacity	828cc
Compression ratio	8.5:1
Carburation	2 x 32mm Amal
Output	60bhp @ 5,900rpm

TRANSMISSION
Primary drive	triplex chain
Clutch	diaphragm, multi-plate
Gearbox	four-speed

CYCLE PARTS
Frame	tubular
Suspension	
(front)	telescopic fork
(rear)	swinging arm
Wheels	
(front)	4.10 x 19
(rear)	4.10 x 19
Brakes	
(front)	10.7in disc
(rear)	10.7in disc
Wheelbase	57in
Seat height	31in
Ground clearance	6in
Dry weight	466lb
Fuel capacity	5¼gal

PERFORMANCE
Top speed	120mph
0-60mph	4.5sec
Fuel consumption	50mpg

OWNER .... Rodger Feneley, Sleaford, Lincs

for next year's Hondas, and a careful blending of parts from various models can produce a very practical machine, as this example demonstrates. To anyone prepared to cope with its idiosyncracies, the Norton Commando has a lot to offer.

SUPERBRITS!

PHOTOGRAPHY MARTYN BARNWELL

750cc Norton Commando Roadster and Triumph Trident T150V by Peter Watson

Classic TEST

Classic TEST

BIKE British. You've arrived. Remember those NVT advertisements for the Trident and Commando in the mid-seventies? This test turns back the clock to a time when you could still buy a brand-new British superbike. All you had to do was choose between Triumph's smooth triple and Norton's hairy-chested twin. . .

Thundering twin

SOME motorcycles can't fail to bring out the hooligan lurking inside even the most sober-sided citizen. However much you fight it, Roy Horne's 1973 Commando 750 keeps you coming back for more. That's more throttle, more revs, more surging acceleration, more speed and lots more of the gorgeous sound pouring out of those upswept peashooter silencers. I was hopelessly addicted within 50 miles.

In fact I've rarely sampled such a crisp big British twin. Set up for both road and racetrack use, the 750's performance has been liberated by taking advantage of tuning parts and services available to anyone at affordable prices. This is definitely the authentic Norton Commando – strong and super-torquey low down, but with lots left to give in the upper reaches of its rev range.

Performance modifications to the engine are very far from exotic. There are 10.25:1 Powermax pistons (£60, but act now as Hepolite has discontinued its Norton range), standard 32mm Amal Concentric Mk I carburettors equipped with ram stacks and flexibly mounted, Boyer Bransden electronic ignition (£32), a 4S camshaft (£48.30) and an FBS Motor Cycles gasflow job on the cylinder head (from £55). These improvements probably boost power to at least the Combat-spec figure of 65bhp.

Despite the high-compression pistons, this engine kicks over easily and fires up instantly if you've tickled the carbs. Tickover is regular and reliable, with no hint of the 'half race' cam there or when tooling around town. Although there's power available from the moment you twist the grip, the motor really starts to fly beyond 4500rpm. Its mid-range poke left our completely standard Trident trailing.

Suspended in large rubber mounts, the engine still manages to transmit some vibration to the rider in the 2500-3000rpm rev range. And that's not some barely notice-

Below: Isolastic engine mountings insulate the rider from the worst of the Commando's vibes
Right: Norvil disc front brake on Commando needs a lot of lever pressure

able tingling felt through the high, wide bars but the genuine article. The answer to this problem is to keep the engine spinning freely in every gear. Commandos are never completely smooth: there's always the feeling that, somewhere between your knees, there's a whole lotta shakin' goin' on.

So the Commando never manages to feel as sophisticated as the lower-slung triple. The overall age of the basic design is sometimes very obvious. That separate Norton-AMC gearbox – with its one-up, three-down pattern – may have a smooth action, but lever travel feels as if it might be feet compared to the Triumph's inches. Horne has fitted threaded adjusters on both sides of the gearbox to ensure perfect alignment for primary and final-drive chain lines.

On the Trident, I'd felt reasonably comfortable until the harsh suspension and the riding position numbed my rear. In comparison, I felt perched up on top of the world upon the Norton. Its seat is ludicrously far from terra firma and its handlebars are not

designed for over 90mph motorcycling.

The racing rear-sets are quite an improvement over the position of the standard pegs, but they provided an unexpected problem. Swinging my leg over the Commando, I neatly swiped the ignition key protruding from the left-hand side panel clean in two. The switch is in an even dafter position than the Trident's, but the Norton is even easier to hot-wire.

Against all Roy Horne's advice, I'd opted for the tiny black and gold Roadster fuel tank instead of a proffered 5.5 gallon Interstate item. There's something far more attractive about the peanut-sized 2.5 gallon Roadster tank, intended primarly for the US market where the Hi-rider Commando carried a bare two gallons of fuel. But it gives a mere 100 miles between fuel stops and virtually no reserve.

I was unsurprised to discover the twin's thirst for fresh lubricant, about 500ml every 250 miles. Roy Horne has had to modify the bike's double-gear oil pump – narrowing the

feed gears to Dominator width – because of a bad idea Norton Villiers had for '72-'73 production. This was to delete the sump filter in the base of the crankcase and add a remote cartridge filter in the return line. Over-oiling is the result unless you reduce the feed, for far more lubricant is reaching the sump than is being returned to the tank.

The Norton may be too tall, but it's also a good 100lb lighter than the Triumph and gives a much better ride. At the rear there's a pair of Koni units that ably complement the Roadholder fork. Nor did I approach left or right-handed turns fearing that I might soon be ploughing up tarmac with the Commando's centre stand.

Dunlop Arrowmax tyres of ample section bulge out of the alloy rims. Although these provide good-sized contact patches, the Norton's braking equipment is disappointing. At the rear, the racing-type lever is too short to exert sufficient leverage, and ventilating the 7in drum via the brake plate is a bit of a joke. Up front, the Norvil disc conversion calls for a lot of pressure before it begins to deliver the goods. Exploiting all of the Commando's performance, I found myself yearing for an extra disc brake.

You pay for this sort of street racing with fuel consumption plummetting to 40mpg. However, some might consider this money

Below: the Trident offers precise steering and handling, but cornering clearance is limited
Left: though lacking feel, the Trident's single disc works well

well spent, considering how many owners of Japanese models you will have sent scurrying back to their dealers with vociferous complaints.

High-speed cruising is limited only by the Norton's handlebars – like so much of its equipment, reproduced in stainless steel – while the engine is virtually ambling along at the legal maximum. Despite its non-standard appearance, the Commando drew admiring glances and comments wherever we went.

Roy Horne's bike reintroduces the rider to all the big-twin virtues – instant poke, low weight and sharp handling – while demonstrating a sensible limit to hot-rodding an engine design that dates back to the late forties. It's interesting that the hemi-head twin would pink only under severe provocation, despite those 10.25:1 pistons.

There's just one question you're left to ponder after another satisfyingly exhilarating ride. If someone could carry on making the 750cc Triumph Bonneville into the late eighties, why did the Commando have to die?

Triple treat

THE only way to overcome temptation is to succumb to it. As the series of bends came into view, snaking across prime Essex countryside, I mentally changed gear. Seconds later I'd slipped from fifth to third, wound the Trident wide open and was moving over towards the verge to get on line for the opening right-hander.

Classic TEST

It's difficult to explain to an outsider what bends mean to a motorcyclist. Car drivers who travel with you on the road will occasionally enquire – in the slightly strained manner appropriate to interviewing a potential suicide – why we tend to speed up for bends instead of slowing down.

Since cornering hard on four wheels feels positively tame to anyone who's done it on two, it's difficult not to sound patronising in response. Mental challenge and physical sensation become compressed into the simple notion that it's just *fun*, yes, *fun*. No wonder they think we're inarticulate lunatics.

Back in rural Essex, I approached a tight left turn with barely controlled elation. There aren't many – some would say *any* – British production machines that steer and handle with the precision and security of a Triumph triple. So you tend to make the most of any example that comes your way.

Chopping the Triumph over fast and late, I smacked something hard and metallic-sounding into the wounded tarmac below. The sidestand! How one earth could I have forgotten that blasted sidestand?

I used to wonder who it was at Meriden who so disliked left-hand bends. For the 750cc Triumph twin is also partially crippled – by the loop of metal protruding leftwards from its centre stand. On the triple, it's the sidestand that mars your pleasure, for static ground clearance here is a bare six inches. Examination revealed that the stand was deeply scarred already.

Such a deficiency calls into question BSA-Triumph's translation of the triple's basic design philosophy – smoother than a twin, narrower than a four. It's certainly smooth, with its 120° crankshaft layout eventually adopted by Laverda. Yet it retains a certain raw edge that is far more addictive than the blandness of a four.

Vibration reaches you through the footpegs and seat base, especially if you rev the engine beyond 6000rpm. Big fat handlebar grips insulate your hands, but you tend to notice the seat fairly early on in a journey. The footrests are too far forward for good balance, thrusting all your weight down on to the foam: numbness sets in rapidly.

The T150V represents a half-way house in Trident styling. Those ray-gun silencers from '69 are gone, but the slab-sided fuel tank – quickly dropped on US export models – remains. It's a handsome looking machine, yet the final, electric-start T160 is the most appealing triple.

The owner of the test bike, Malcolm Avery, didn't like the standard 1974 livery of a black tank with yellow panels, and resprayed his machine with the next season's Cherokee red. He was exceptionally lucky to pick up his bike for just £1700: it had a mere 2600 miles on its bores, having formed part of the Amal carburettor company's test fleet.

I found it a little odd that he's opted to fit a new fork slider with provision for an extra disc, while retaining the Trident's worst feature, its triple contact breaker set. Expensive to replace, and prone to horrifyingly rapid wear, this is best jettisoned for Lucas RITA electronic ignition from Mistral Engineering at £70.

Incorrect ignition advance probably explained the bike's poor starting from cold and a tendency to pink alarmingly at high speed. This cut my cruising speed and produced a flattering average fuel consumption of 44mpg, where 35-37mpg is the norm. Oil consumption over 300 miles was 500ml; nothing out of the ordinary for a triple.

Given the 750's relatively buzzy nature, it's surprising that it was ever built with a four-speed gearbox. The five-speed unit arrived in 1972, and it enables you to make the most of the triple's dramatic acceleration. Rejoining a motorway after a fuel stop, I was able to scorch up to 80mph in a couple of hundred yards.

The gearbox proved to be delightful. Lever action is positive and short-throw, but the clutch was a disappointment. This is a Borg & Beck car-type diaphragm spring unit which required a lot of effort at the lever and took up with a rather nasty noise. That heavy clutch spoiled my enjoyment of the Trident around town. With three carburettors, the throttle action is also slow, if less painful.

At night, the Lucas headlamp puts out a lot of light. However, the main beam has a diffuse pattern; dip fails to illuminate the margin of your carriageway adequately. Both speedometer and revcounter are ill-lit, and one indicator proved lazy. The switch-gear is confusing at first, while the position of the ignition lock – in the left-hand headlamp mount – is typical of scrappy '70s styling.

I was lucky with the weather over a couple of days, because it's always pleasant to ride a Trident in the wet. With a brand-new Dunlop TT100 cover on the rear wheel, the T150 felt typically secure. Mud,

Smooth and powerful, the triple's engine needs to be revved. Fuel consumption can be worse than 40mpg

Of relatively crude design, the 750cc Norton engine offers exciting acceleration. This example is mildly tuned

Classic TEST

gravel and damp leaves all failed to faze the Triumph.

It's difficult to identify the source of this security, although admirable weight distribution must play a large part in the equation. After all, the Trident was never light for a 750, but it feels remarkably lithe on the road.

Both machines have extra-thick barrelled hand grips and Lucas switchgear. Modern mirrors have been added on the Triumph, while the Norton has no indicators.

specification

750 NORTON COMMANDO ROADSTER

ENGINE
Type: ohv parallel twin. **Bore x stroke:** 73 x 89mm. **Capacity:** 745cc. **Compression ratio:** 10.25:1. **Carburation:** 2 x 32mm Amal. **Output:** 65bhp @ 6500rpm (see test). **Electrical:** 110W alternator, 12v battery, Boyer-Bransden electronic ignition.

TRANSMISSION
Primary drive: triplex chain. **Clutch:** multi-plate, dry. **Gearbox:** 4-speed.

CYCLE PARTS
Frame: duplex cradle spine type, with rubber engine/gearbox mounts. **Suspension (front):** telescopic fork; **(rear):** swinging arm. **Tyres (front):** 100/90 x 19in Dunlop Arrowmax; **(rear):** 120/80 x 18in Dunlop Arrowmax. **Brakes (front):** 11.5in Norvil disc; **(rear):** 7in drum. **Wheelbase:** 58in. **Seat height:** 33in. **Ground clearance:** 7½in. **Kerb weight:** 420lb. **Fuel capacity:** 2.5gal.

PERFORMANCE
Top speed: 120mph (est). **Standing start ¼-mile:** 13sec (est). **Fuel consumption:** 40-45mpg.

FOR: fairly smooth, surging acceleration, wide torque spread.

AGAINST: high seat and bars, limited fuel capacity.

750 TRIUMPH TRIDENT T150V

ENGINE
Type: ohv triple. **Bore x stroke:** 67 x 70mm. **Capacity:** 740cc. **Compression ratio:** 8.25:1. **Carburation:** 3 x 27mm Amal. **Output:** 58bhp @ 7250rpm. **Electrical:** 120W alternator, 12v battery, coil ignition.

TRANSMISSION
Primary drive: triplex chain. **Clutch:** single plate, dry. **Gearbox:** 5-speed.

CYCLE PARTS
Frame: full cradle, single downtube. **Suspension (front):** telescopic fork; **(rear):** swinging arm. **Tyres:** 4.10 x 19in Dunlop TT100 K181. **Brakes (front):** 10in disc; **(rear):** 7in drum. **Wheelbase:** 58in. **Seat height:** 31in. **Ground clearance:** 6in. **Kerb weight:** 525lb. **Fuel capacity:** 4.5gal.

PERFORMANCE
Top speed: 120mph (est). **Standing start ¼-mile:** 13.6sec (est). **Fuel consumption:** 43-45mpg.

FOR: superb handling, good turn of speed, fairly smooth.

AGAINST: choppy ride, poor ground clearance, heavy clutch.

Where it begins to show its age is in terms of suspension. At both the front and the rear the ride can become very choppy, which is just what you'd expect from a firmly-sprung British sporting motorcycle. Yet although noticeable, this behaviour never gets out of hand. The Trident flatters any rider, since its abilities make you think the more of your own.

With a 10in Lockheed disc at the front and a 7in drum brake inside the conical hub at the rear, there's more than enough stopping power to hand. By today's standards the disc brake lacks feel, but it works very well.

At an indicated 70mph, the revcounter needle holds steady on 4500rpm and the ride is smooth and relaxed. But riders raised on Triumph twins, with all that low-down grunt, tend to find the Trident's top gear roll-on acceleration flat and uninspiring. You need to work the gearbox and twistgrip hard in unison to get the best from this engine.

A few dribbles of oil around the top end of the engine spoiled an otherwise clean record. Lubricant had been escaping up the cylinder studs, offering a reminder of this model's reputation for variable build quality. Indeed it used to be said that the only problem with the Trident was the fact that it was built by Triumph.

A strange quip, given the fact that the triple engines were always produced by BSA. The Meriden workers' blockade forced NVT to re-tool for complete Trident production to recommence at Small Heath in 1974.

On the road, the Trident must rate as one of the most enjoyable machines ever made in this country for it combines power, acceleration and handling in an almost irresitable package. In all, about 60,000 BSA-Triumph triples were built. The vast majority were T150 models: 45,000 from '69 to '75. This helps to explain the relative rarity of BSA Rocket IIIs and the final T160 Trident.

So if the Trident was the best of British, is this the finest example of the breed? The disc brake and five-speed gearbox of the T150V mean that it can be made to give of its very best. Yet I've always found the looks and riding position of the short-lived T160 an improvement, while others value its electric start.

The tragedy of the Trident was played out in several acts. Launched too late, and often poorly manufactured, it was finally killed off before its true potential had been realised.

But if I was asked to advise an aspiring manufacturer of British motorcycles on the format of a new 750 model, I wouldn't need to think twice. It'd have to be a three for me.

Conclusion

BOTH of these 750s offer an exciting ride in the best British tradition. Twin or triple? It's a tough decision. On performance there's virtually nothing in it, although maintaining a Trident in good heart probably calls for more skill and more time in the workshop. But both Triumph and Norton have the support of a whole raft of companies dedicated to proving that it's still fun to bike British □

COLQUHOUN'S
COMMANDO

A TOP NVT EXECUTIVE IS REUNITED WITH A BEAUTIFUL EXAMPLE OF (ARGUABLY) THE BEST PARALLEL TWIN. STEVE WILSON RIDES BILL COLQUHOUN'S 1970 NORTON COMMANDO 750 FASTBACK

Bill Colquhoun was part of the fabric of the Norton Commando story.

From his early job with Norton Villiers 'assault party' on Plumstead after their take-over of the AJS/Matchless factory there, to 'the best time of them all' in the early Seventies selling Commandos in California, to a job in charge of Norton Villiers Europe, Colquhoun's life has been intertwined with the not always happy tale of the Commando. (For the full story, see *CBG* 71)

Bill is now at the far end of a career which sees him still managing the small BSA subsidiary in Blockley, Gloucestershire, on the same rural industrial estate which houses Watsonian-Squire, the current importers of Enfield Bullets. So it was natural that his thoughts bike-wise should turn to acquiring a really nice example of the big Norton twin. Bill's good friend and former business partner, ex-NVT super-salesman Mike Jackson, located one for him Stateside and had it brought home. And top spannerman Mike Guildford sorted the bike out for him.

Guildford's credentials are impeccable. In the mid-Sixties he was British sidecar scrambling champion on a 650 Triumph Wasp outfit; he subsequently contested the sidecar-cross GPs on 750 Norton Wasp machinery, and was regularly to be seen on the winners' rostrum. After putting in his time as workshop foreman for the legendary Syd Lawton, he went to work briefly for the John Player Norton team, and then for Robin Rhynd-Tutt's Wasp company, so he clearly knows his way around Commando engines.

The front stopper looks well, and sometimes performs adequately, but is overshadowed by the performance of the torque-laden twin.
The early Commando's Atlas ancestry is plain (if you know where to look!)

Now he's in business on his own. Such is his reputation that he's never had to advertise, but if you want top class work on Commando or pre-'65 moto-cross machinery, his number is 01794-301456.

FAST TRACK FASTBACK

Colquhoun's choice was a fairly early Mk II Fastback 750 from 1970. Many people, including the excellent former classic journo Peter Watson, have rated the Fastback, one of half a dozen variations on the 750 theme, as the best looking Commando of the lot. Personally I've never agreed, being mid-Atlantic enough to have always thought that the 750 Roadster, particularly in gold-lined black, was the quintessential Commando roadburner. Mike Jackson

has confirmed that it was certainly the best seller in the States, where the Fastback's more restrained European styling never really caught on, despite its fibreglass tail end's echo of the Mk III Rickman moto-crosser's seat/tail unit, as well as of contemporary road racers.

Bill's example had less than 15,000 recorded miles on the clock when he got it, and while contemplating it didn't quite change my mind about the Roadster, it certainly was one good-looking machine. Particularly in the absolutely classic and utterly appropriate British Racing Green finish found here, set off by the smart, chromed Roadholder forks. It's hard to imagine or recall, but 1970 Fastbacks were also offered in metalflake Fireglo Red or Pacific Shimmer Blue!

The Fastback's good looks centre on the pleasing way in which the horizontal lines of the tank base, tail unit, and even the Norton name cast horizontally on the timing cover and repeated by the tank transfer, echo each other and are at the same time held in tension to the tilt of the cylinders, the curve of the export handlebars, the kicked-up seat tail and the upswept exhaust pipes which, along with the points moved to a housing in the timing chest, identify the April 1970-on Mk IIs. Non-standard on this bike were the silencers, not the 'peashooter' reverse cone megas fitted as stock, but early, surprisingly slim Interstate mufflers. These look much better tilted on the rising

up in the air as the kickstart refused to budge an inch. O my God – no longer man enough to kick a Commando over! Was this a Combat engine, which had been optional since mid-1970? The next few efforts were more successful (and revealed that the kickstart was fouling the exhaust pipe), but they didn't start the bike, and the kickstart still hung up, intermittently and unpredictably, contributing to a badly accelerated heart rate and a beet-red face.

Finally I remembered advice that if the bike proved hard to start, I should try changing the plugs. Hunting out a pair of NGK BP7ES sparklers from a previous

exhaust than they did on the kinked Interstate pipes, from which they had run horizontally, to allow panniers to be fitted. They also proved less raucous than the crackling 'peashooters'. They were fitted to the bike as found, and retained because Bill liked them.

That was enough ogling, it was time to fire up the brute, which had arrived at Schloss Wilson by trailer. Mike Guildford had fitted new Concentric carburettors and these featured no chokes. He had also advised that the juice in the 3.25 gallon fibreglass tank was high octane unleaded. As an ex-750 Commando owner I knew that the standard 9:1 compression engines, let alone the 10:1 Combat versions, required a healthy kick. But even after clearing the clutch, my first efforts had me suspended awkwardly

Commando incarnation, I set to again. After a few frustrating preliminary burps and barks, the Fastback beast eventually burst into life – and belched out thick, copious clouds of black smoke, particularly from its right hand pipe (and the right plug had also been ultra-sooty). It was only later that I discovered that since Bill had put in his first 300 miles or so on it during an outing in Scotland with The Club, the industry insiders' organisation, the bike had been standing for three months... After its throat had been cleared, the Fastback started 2nd or 3rd kick every time.

The Norton settled down quickly, and after checking that the 20/50 was up to level and circulating healthily, we moved on out. The diaphragm clutch

Although these silencers were never fitted to Fastback Commandos, you have to wonder why not. They do indeed add to the already rakish looks.

IT'S HARD TO IMAGINE OR RECALL, BUT 1970 FASTBACKS WERE ALSO OFFERED IN METALFLAKE FIREGLO RED OR PACIFIC SHIMMER BLUE!

The styling of the original Commando was a little controversial when it first appeared, but it has aged well. Fastback tanks are built from fibreglass — some concerns have been expressed over their resistance to attack by Lead Replacement Petrol...

engaged early and was an On/Off device which once or twice nearly got me into trouble down-shifting on loose gravel, until I had learned it. But the gearbox was beautifully set up and changes were never less than smooth, with neutral always easy to snick into, even at rest.

Out in the lanes the very first impression was of the likeably solid handling, winding through the bends at low and medium speeds. Good suspension, good tyres, plus the Isolastic-induced smoothness, all contributed. The unique engine/gearbox/swinging-arm rubber-mounting system killed vibration for the rider from as low as 1500rpm, unlike the later 850s where it only cut in as high as 3000rpm. It was great to be back aboard the one parallel twin where the white-knuckle element should come from speed rather than shakes.

But it wasn't all slickness and light. Disguise it as they might, the Commando was a big, beefy motor-cycle, on which the rider sat quite high up, on a frame originally designed for a taller engine. The initial feeling was of being perched up on the bike, though one soon became accustomed. Although the design team, to their credit, had kept catalogued dry weight on these early machines to a couple of pounds below their 400lb benchmark (a considerable and significant contrast to the final porky 850 Mk III, at 460lb), it was still a fairly heavy bike.

Back in a Commando's saddle, I felt a bit grim. But the real reservation came when, with the engine

warmed up, I hit a favourite series of long sweepers running beside the railway line, and cranking the throttle on in top failed to produce the expected surge of power, just a gradual, flattish, lumpy increase.

Because despite its firm footprint and thoughtful details, the heart of the matter with the Commando was its free-breathing 60bhp engine, and all did not seem quite right with this one. We rode on, and there was plenty to enjoy, so much so that a preliminary run intended to be five or six miles turned into a twenty-five mile ramble, during which I felt progressively less grim; that's the long-legged Commando character.

The Fastback seat felt firmer and possibly narrower than the later cross-hatched efforts, but it was still comfortable over distance. This rider's knees didn't naturally contact the seat's distinctive 'ears', but that was scarcely a problem. The suspension was firm, but the ride overall pretty forgiving over our bumpy Oxfordshire roads, definitely more so than my Fifties and Sixties BSAs.

And if a bend in the road revealed something needing quick retardation, the drum brakes worked very well together – which was mostly down to the front one, a good-looking 8 inch tls job in polished alloy. Just a touch pulled you down effortlessly to where you wanted to be. I thought the 7 inch rear one was also good – until I tried it on its own and discovered that, like every other example I've sampled, the cable-operated back brake with its flex-prone plate was

TALKING TO THE MAN

So a pleasant enough ride, but once again, getting near home, when I asked the engine a question at an indicated 50 in 3rd, the flatness and lack of response were very noticeable. Even allowing for the fact that the bike had only done 1000 miles since the rebuild, this was disappointing. It was time to get Mike Guildford on the phone.

'We didn't have the engine apart,' Mike told me, 'it was running well. To me it feels like standard com-

Smiths clocks in bright alloy pods; idiot lights and lighting control in the headlamp shell all combine to make the rider's view characteristically Commando.

incapable of stopping the bike on its own, from any speed. This was despite the fact that it had been fitted with a little bracing bracket from the pivot to the spindle, to stop it tipping when the brake was applied. The front stopper too had been fitted with a steel stiffening plate which bridged the pivots, and that had evidently been a very worthwhile mod.

pression – in my experience, with higher compression engines you usually get knocking. In fact it all felt pretty standard, including the gearing. The ignition is still on points, not electronic. If there are any more problems starting it, we may try a grade softer plug. I think the lead replacement chemicals in unleaded petrol coat the plugs with a sticky residue which I find

used to call "Improving 'em worse"!'

There was food for thought here. I had a lively awareness of the unleaded petrol bind many of us now find ourselves in, as even with a lead replacement additive, my A10 Anneka has started giving the occasional hiccup. But the absence of what most people reckon to have been the big leap forward for British twins, namely electronic ignition, also sounded suspicious, especially in view of that overrich right hand cylinder. With the engine's very healthy compression in mind, as an interim measure I added a drop of octane booster, and took the Fastback out again.

There was a definite improvement, though it could have been my own confidence as much as the additive. We ripped back and forwards round the 'railway bends' for Garry the snapper's benefit, and during a prolonged photo session the engine's steady tickover and tireless clutch were very reassuring. The Commando's strength and willingness shone through, never more so than when we hit the steep flanks of White Horse Hill, and the Fastback reminded me how 750 Nortons are the bikes for the mountains.

You can romp up almost any grade in top, or slow and down-change, and then pull away strongly, on any grade, from anywhere in the rev band, in any gear. Finally on a straighter road I wound it up and got to the point around 80 where Commando handling reaches that tip-toe point of slow weaving, not completely precise but not panic-inducing either. At the end of the day, the engine had remained completely oil-tight – except for the rev-counter drive connection, which was so familiar I had to smile.

The more I had ridden the bike, the more I had liked it. If it was mine I would definitely fit electronic ignition, and that plus a little more experimenting with plugs and carburation, plus a few more miles, should release its full potential. Meanwhile this strong, handsome, user-friendly motorcycle had reminded me of all the Commando virtues. The best twin? Maybe, but to me they were definitely the best all-rounder for the road. ∎

While posing with the Norton on White Horse Hill, Steve encountered a passing tourist. Turns out that Tim Shenton contested the 1972 Production TT on a T120 Bonnie (and finished!), and that he started his riding days on a Norton Jubilee. Strange but true!

Ex-British sidecar-cross champion Mike Guildford on Commando engined Wasp. He knows his Nortons.

you can only get off with carb cleaner. I also think people often make the mistake of over-advancing these motors; I've set this one up as a tourer, with 27 degrees of advance, one less than standard, which I think makes for a nicer engine.

'The Isolastics were all clapped out when we got it, so it's been completely re-shimmed. One major job concerned the petrol tank, which looked like new, but leaked. We found it was like Aero chocolate, underneath on the right side. We couldn't get another, I don't think Norvil are making them any more, so I dug that section out, and coated it with Araldite; I think it should be OK.' The repair is well nigh undetectable. 'I was glad it was a 1970 bike,' Mike concluded, 'I think the earlier ones were best. After that, they did what Mike Erskine the speedway mechanic

Continued from page 87

keep the rider comfortable the vibes never reach the seat, tank or handlebars. Even the footpegs and foot brake are mounted on the isolated portion of the machine to this end. How well it works can be seen when the engine is at an idle. The engine is visibly leaping around in the frame but the bars don't even receive a tingle. Once the engine gets up to operating rpm, above 3000, the engine settles down and the only evidence that it's running at all is the sound of the exhaust and the movement of the tachometer needle.

It's a pure joy to ride out on the open highway. The power characteristics of the engine enable it to carry a very high gear ratio and accomplish high cruising speeds with very little rpm. The engine never feels as though it is working, it just loafs along at 70-plus and yet has much more on hand. This low revving feature contributes to the high average of 42 miles per gallon of our over 2000-mile test. With the Interstate tank holding a full 6 gallons, that means a range of over 230 miles before switching to reserve. On one particular section we managed almost 250 miles before the switch was necessary, and

upon filling up the tank would only take 5.6 gallons. With many of the other superbikes running dry at around the 100-mile mark, the Interstate's touring capabilities get a big boost.

Though the large tank certainly doesn't look as large as it might thanks to the styling department, it is a little wide at the back for the average rider. A slight indentation around the knee area would aid the comfort without sacrificing much capacity. The other comforts are acceptable. The seat is well shaped and soft, but can be removed by loosening the two large knurled nuts at the top of the shock units. That's handy to get to the oil filler but doesn't provide much security should some other Norton owner need a new seat. And the oil filler is all that's there. Access to the battery and the tool kit is provided through the left side cover. Also, the rear of the seat is unsupported and since it provides a convenient grab handle when placing the machine on the center stand, it is prone to rider-inflicted damage.

However, the list of grievances is short when compared to the list of niceties. The riding position is suitable to most riders, short or tall, although the shorter ones will have difficulty retracting the side stand from a seated position. It is just a little too far forward for anyone 5'7" or smaller. Handlebar location is right on for the average and all the controls and levers are right there where you can get at them.

To our way of thinking one of the biggest features of the Interstate is the fact that it is a muscle-bike that isn't muscle-bound. It has all the hotty features and yet weighs in with many of the middle weights. With a full six-gallon load of fuel it tips the scales at 460 pounds, over 40 of which is gasoline. This low weight contributes to that feeling of confidence, as does the Lockheed front disc brake. The compact caliper is hidden behind the right fork leg and the master cylinder is a small unit that includes the brake lever itself. The reason for mounting the caliper behind the fork leg instead of in front as is the practice with everyone else is another attempt at good handling. With the caliper weight behind the axle it falls almost directly in line with the steering axis of the front forks and provides lighter steering. When mounted out front it acts somewhat like a pendulum when the forks are turned, requiring a little more effort to control the direction of the front wheel.

The Interstate is a true all-arounder. You can play the stoplight Grand Prix game or set off on a 1000-mile trip with the same assurance that the machine is up to the job. There are more exotic machines; there are less expensive machines; but we doubt that there is a better machine made anywhere. •

NORTON 850 JPS
Continued from page 143

loosened up, confirmed again the Norton gearbox reputation. It's notchy enough so that you never have to struggle to find neutral, but the lever never resists the foot. Its throw is both short and positive. The Norton gear changer, like Italian ones, retains mechanical feel. You know upshifts and downshifts are mechanically actuated. But most Italian bikes have longer throws than the Norton. Japanese changers have short throws; though compared to the Norton, Japanese levers generally have a hydraulic feel. In its first thousand miles, the Norton belied its reputation in one respect. Thrashing the bike down a winding road, the gearbox would momentarily get lost in the four-three downchange. The shift would go through, but it was still disconcerting.

Our test machine was built before September 1, 1974, so right-side shifting was retained. In compliance with U.S. requirements, machines built after September 1, 1974 for sale in the United States must have left-side shifting and right-side braking. We hope the Norton gearbox loses none of its shifting feel and crispness in the changeover.

The rear brake has little to lose in the change. Thanks to the leverages, there's not much braking force available at your left foot. Enough perhaps to keep the bike steady, but that's about all. Shoes and

boots kept knocking the lead wires out of the stoplight switch terminals. The footwear would scuff on the exposed switch, and this, together with engine vibration, was enough to disconnect the leads. JPS owners should wrap the switch securely in black electrical tape.

The *Cycle* staffers (and hangers-on) divided on the Player's appearance. One allowed that the bike looked like a frog which had been tire-creased on a Texas highway. Others thought the JPS looked fabulous from certain angles, but lumpy from others. Still others saw the JPS as a bold departure from normal inbred cafe-racer patterns. Everyone agreed that the JPS was an eye-catcher—and an expensive one at that.

Whether a factory does the building, or some small constructor or the individual enthusiast, specials by their nature are expensive. The JPS wears a POE price of $2995. A standard Commando retails POE for $2500. Some might consider building their own Norton cafe-racer; those enthusiasts can fashion a bike to their own individual tastes, though it's still going to be expensive (these days alloy tanks cost $175 a copy). A lavish project could swallow $500 easily.

What about other factory-built caferacers? In California the BMW R90S comes in at $3400-plus; Ducati Super Sports fetch $3500, and that figure won't touch a Laverda 1000 ($3900). The Norton

is a $400 notch away from these heavy-spender specials, and that price differential is significant. There are two clip-on sports bikes which share roughly the same price slot as the John Player Special: the Ducati Sport ($2600) and the Moto Guzzi 750 Sport ($2750). Both these machines represent more modern engineering than the Norton. Nevertheless, outside the engine bays, neither Italian bike can match the Norton network for parts and service. Here in the United States, there's just a greater body of knowledge about Nortons, their care, tuning, and idiosyncracies.

Remember that *Cycle* does not consider any cafe racer–British, Italian, German or whatever–a "best buy." Even those who are looking for purely good dollar buys should skip over cafe racers, and leave the clip-on runners to someone else.

And leave the JPS for someone who knows how to light off a cold 850 twin with one sure kick . . . who loves an interested and appreciative audience . . . who complains about scraping pipes and stands with transparent satisfaction . . . who points smugly to his feathered-in TT100s . . . who believes that the Norton engine never gets old, just better . . . who doesn't give a damn about little oil leaks . . . who will testify that brute horsepower alone makes good brutes and poor motorcycles . . . and who looks at his JPS and sees Peter Williams in full flight down Bray Hill on a fine June day in 1973. ⊛

NORTON COMMANDO
Continued from page 35

those brought up on a diet of pushrod twins . . . don't hesitate, but don't try a Commando unless you can afford to buy one. Looking to the future, the main limiting factor on the Commando, as it stands, is the cylinder head: when Norton Villiers get round to designing a new casting we can expect some remarkable improvements in performance. There is a lot of leg room left in the Commando engine yet, and most of the machines on British roads seem to be lasting well.

Norton Villiers cannot at present meet the demand for Commandos, but as production builds up at Andover the hungry markets all over the world are waiting. **M. R. W.**

The
Knowledge

Norton Commando

The Commando is an exuberant performer, but if adjustment of the Isolastics is neglected it will wallow like a hippo in a hollow...

All you ever need to know about the best British twin of them all

1966 ASSOCIATED MOTORCYCLES LIMITED, MANUFACTURERS OF MANY FAMOUS BRITISH NAMES, LIKE AJS, MATCHLESS AND NORTON, AS WELL AS UK IMPORTERS FOR SUZUKI, WENT POP AFTER SEVERAL YEARS OF STRUGGLE. The battered remnants were acquired by Manganese Bronze Holdings, and rationalised. It became clear that the company, restructured or not, needed a new flagship motorcycle if it was going to have a future. In the meantime, sales of several of the existing range continued, while the prototype great white hope, the Norton P10, was evaluated. It was soon understood that the dohc parallel twin P10 had fundamental

flaws and that further development would be both lengthy and costly. Great deliberations ensue.

Meanwhile, the company continued to sell Norton Atlas-based machines in various forms, badged variously.

This was a stop-gap measure, and an enduring irony is that the bikes produced as Norton, Matchless and AJS N15, G15 and Model 33 respectively are now highly sought after.

Not least because... after due ›〉

The Knowledge The Knowledge The Knowledge The Knowledge The Knowledge The Knowledge
Norton Commando Norton Commando Norton Commando Norton Commando Norton Commando

The 850 is the One To Have, says Retro's Bendy expert

Look Out! For...

Commandos, especially 750 Commandos, are exuberant performers. Sadly, to maintain this exuberance they require a lot more TLC than more modern (or even contemporary) oriental machines.

Regular lube changes are essential – every 1000 miles is good – and fitting an oil filter to any bike which didn't have one from new is obligatory. And although the Isolastic system keeps the engine's vibration away from the rider,

the engine is still vibrating – a point often forgotten by late-comers and nostalgics. This means that it will shake its fasteners loose as rapidly as that old Ariel Huntmaster, and a weekly walk-around with the tightening spanners is a great idea. Especially if

you are not a fan of oil leaks.

If adjustment of the Isolastics is neglected, a Commando will wallow like a hippo in a hollow, and even if the mounts are correctly adjusted, long sweeping curves are usually characterised by a long sweeping weave.

Nothing dangerous; amuse your friends, but don't take your hands from the bars. Some riders reckon that a steering damper is obligatory, but others (like your author) don't.

However, replacing the Lucas Variable Inaccuracy Points Ignition System with something solid

850
COMMANDO
ELECTRIC START

Norton

Norton

« They used
to call them
Bendies, you
know, because
they were like
that in the
1970s...

The Knowledge

Norton Commando

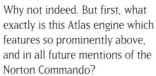

They created a legend, a motorcycle which won Machine of the Year from the readers of MCN for five years on the trot

deliberation in no-doubt smoke-filled rooms, the new management of Norton-Matchless (as the new company was known for a while, at the start of a lengthy series of confusing name changes) realised that they had neither the time nor the moolah to turn the rattly, leaky bag of bolts which was the P10 engine into a shining vision of the future. A lack of the same resources also meant that there was no hope of developing a new powerplant for the new motorcycle. If you add to these small enlightenments the fact that a developed and slightly re-worked version of the Atlas engine could reliably develop as much power as the prototype P10, then a route away from disaster starts to appear. The answer? Why not use that developed version of the Atlas in the smart new bicycle intended for the Great White Hope?

Why not indeed. But first, what exactly is this Atlas engine which features so prominently above, and in all future mentions of the Norton Commando?

History. In the late 1940s, Norton joined the rest of the UK's bike builders in bringing a twin to market. Theirs was soon monickered as the Dominator, and was slightly unusual in trad Brit engineering terms in that its single camshaft was driven by a chain, not a gear train, and the rockerbox was cast integrally with the cylinder head. Otherwise, it was a worthy, but unremarkable Brit 500 twin. This grew, as was the way with Brits of olde England, first to a 600, then to a 650, and finally to a 750. That was the Atlas engine, and by this stage, although the fundamentals of the engine's design were as they had been twenty years earlier, the whole thing was fairly modern, in Brit bike terms anyway. Well, it had twin carbs and an alloy head; what more would you expect from two decades of development?

But it had a flaw. The trad Brit twin flaw, in fact. Bluntly put, if a rider endeavoured to use all the 750's considerable performance, the resultant vibration was likely to be punishing, to both man and machine.

1967
THE ANSWER? THE CUNNING 'ISOLASTIC' ENGINE MOUNTING SYSTEM. This is the secret of the Commando. The engine, gearbox and final drive —

including the swinging arm, were isolated from the main frame (and thus from the rider) by a simple rubber bushing system, which absorbed the engine's primary vibration, protecting man and machine from its effects. Rubber mounting was not a new idea, but the Isolastic system's secret was that two of the three mounting points were adjustable in compression, allowing a careful compromise between steering finesse and smooth riding.

Stir in some swoopy 'Fastback' styling, and you have the first Commando. The greatest achievement was getting it on sale before the supposedly more sophisticated triple from BSA/ Triumph and the actually more sophisticated four from Honda. But they did it, creating a legend, a motorcycle which won Machine Of The Year from the readers of MCN for five years on the trot.

1968
THE COMMANDO BOUNDS ONTO THE UK'S ROADS, AND THE LONG PROCESS OF DEVELOPMENT AND IMPROVEMENT BEGINS. This year sees the first acknowledgement that the (old, inherited from AMC, 4-speed) gearbox was struggling with Commando power; the factory modify tooth forms.

The Knowledge The Knowledge The Knowledge The Knowledge The Knowledge The Knowled
Norton Commando Norton Commando Norton Commando Norton Commando Norton Comman

Classic clox: clearly capable!

state and electronic is a fine idea, if you intend to ride the thing, that is. There are a few available, and they are all a lot better than the original. Likewise, some replace the original twin Amal Concentric carbs with either a single Amal or an SU. Total heathens

recommend Mikunis, but then...

The vernier adjustment system for the Isolastics, which appeared on the MkIII 850, is retro-fittable, and should be done, taking advantage of the opportunity to replace all the associated steel gubbins with stainless

components while you're at it. This is one of the great joys of the Norton Commando: parts availability in Y2K is better than it was in 1975, and most of the parts are in fact better than original.

Buying

There are several

schools of thought about which is The One To Have – and they are all of them correct. The earliest 750 Fastbacks, with their peppy engines, brilliant styling and 2ls brakes are possibly the purest form, it being one of life's little ironies that as the Commando developed

so it became every more traditional in appearance. Others recommend the 850 MkIIA, with its civilised intake and exhaust, preferring to retain the Olde Brit right-foot gearshift and drum rear brake. Yet others suggest that the best is also the last, and that the

1969

THE FASTBACK MKI BECOMES THE FASTBACK MK II, AND IS JOINED BY THE 750 'S' TYPE AND ROADSTER MK I. The 'S' featured US street scrambler styling, with a QD headlamp assembly, and with both exhausts swung up to one side, exiting by the rear number plate, in a glorious and distinctive sweep of chrome and noise. The Roadster was similarly styled, but carried a less flamboyant exhaust system and a conventional headlamp. So there are now three versions of the Commando available. Clever marketing, and with only minor mechanical differences to interrupt the production flow.

1970

NORTON ACCEPT THAT ALTHOUGH THE TRICK FRAME WAS BRILLIANT, IT HAD A FLAW. Early frames, christened 'the widowmaker' by US pundits could bend or even break under extreme loads. Improved triangulation and bracing fixes that. A first attempt at fitting a starter motor fails...

1971

THE NEW YEAR SEES THE NOTIONAL 'MK III' MODELS. Norton's Commando numbering and pedantically accurate identification is too complicated for this piece, so we'll ease up on the 'Mk' designations and concentrate on major changes. The process of development at Norton was ongoing, as we say...

New fork yokes appear, still mounting a modernised and up-dated version of the old 'Roadholder' fork legs, which had been in production since the late 1940s, allowing the fitting of more modern rubber. This is either Avon or Dunlop, each using the same 4.10 x 19 rubber at each end of the bike. Arguments ensue among owners about which was better.

A considerable improvement is the adoption of a disc brake for the front wheel to replace the original twin leading shoe device. The latter was effective if set up properly, but doing that was not too easy.

Another model also joins the Commando squad in the form of the wholly remarkable Hi-Rider, possibly the first-ever factory custom. These are very tacky, very rare, and supposedly a response to customer demand in the wake of the Easy Rider film phenomenon. The basic good looks of the Commando were disguised by a small tank, insanely high handlebars and little else. Apart from the silliest seat in the history of motorcycling.

1972

MEANWHILE, WHILE NORTON FANCIERS THE WORLD OVER WERE BASKING IN THE APPARENT SUCCESS OF THEIR BIG TWIN (and let us not forget that the Commando was intended as a stop-gap model, supposed to stay in production only until The New Engine became available), the Japanese had unsportingly been moving the goalposts. 750cc twins were increasingly seen as being outmoded; multis were the way forward. Norton respond by developing a high performance version of the Commando twin engine; the Combat engine, introducing riders everywhere to The Curse Of The Flying Combat (sorry).

The sad fact is that the hi-spec Combat engine was a lot faster than the stock 750, delivering explosive world-beating acceleration times along with a thunderous roar and great mechanical clangor. It was also explosive in the disintegration sense, boasting an enviable ability to wreck itself in very short order if worked hard. In the Great British way, production and sales continue while factory engineers search ≫

⌃ **Get your leg over a Commando and you too could be a very happy chappy**

final development, the electric-booted MkIII is the least flawed of them all. That's my own preference, and the household boasts a pair of them.

When buying a bike that is at least two decades old, examine the owner while examining the bike. Does he/she know what they're about? Have they maintained the bike? Have they serviced it? Can they start it easily? Are they members of the Norton Owners Club, and have they understood The True Way? All of these things are important.

Ride it. Oil leaks are bad. It should not leak oil, and if it does that oil should be golden and clear, like that in the tank. Filthy slime in the oil tank filler is indicative of short journeys and poor maintenance. The exhaust pipe locking rings have a notorious tendency to loosen themselves, then chatter about in the exhaust port, mashing thread – the wise buyer checks here for signs of bodged repairs.

If the bike wanders about or feel mushy, its Isolastics are goosed – no big deal, but a good bargaining point. Does third gear howl like a banshee? The Commando – especially those ridden by the police or hooligans (ahem) – can chew up third with a vengeance.

The front disc is up-gradeable; there are several excellent kits about which will the anchoring up to modern standards without looking ghastly, and all of the bits

The 750, for purists and the strong of leg!

The

Knowledge

Norton Commando

for a solution. This arrives later in the year, when a better type of main bearing is introduced, and the Combat engine's 10:1 compression ratio lowered. Sighs of relief all round. Now the Combat engine is little faster than the original one, but at least it explodes less often.

This is all a bit sad, as the Combat engine had been introduced for the last major new variant on the Commando theme; the Interstate. The Interstate was in fact to mature into a fine motorcycle indeed, with its 5-gallon petrol tank and trad Brit tourer riding position.

The starter is worthy of an article on its own and soon developed a rep for being an electric non-starter. But the thought was there!

1973

THE 'MK' NUMBERING SYSTEM HAS NOW REACHED MkV, AND WE HAVE REACHED THE END OF 750 COMMANDO PRODUCTION. Make way for the new, improved ... 850 Commando. Hurrah! Basically a boring job, taking the engine's capacity out to 828cc from its original 745cc, Norton's revised engine wisely develops no more power than its smaller predecessor. Instead, much work has gone into making it develop more bottom end grunt and be stronger mechanically.

New bearings go into the bottom end (again), the swinging arm is beefed up and the performance claims are muted, in favour of an emphasis on sophistication, stamina and general bulldog spirit.

1974

MOST DEVELOPMENT WORK IS GOING INTO THE FINAL VERSION, BUT THIS YEAR SEES THE ARRIVAL OF THE MkIIA 850, FOR MANY RIDERS THE BEST OF ALL COMMANDOS. This sports much intake and exhaust silencing for the ever-tightening US restrictions, and the overall gearing is raised, making the whole thing more relaxed to ride at speed.

1975-78

THE FINAL VERSIONS OF THE COMMANDO ARRIVE. Norton have tackled the US insistence on a left-foot gearshift by redesigning the whole power train surprisingly thoroughly. Previously, as in all non-unit designs (where engine and gearbox are entirely separate entities), primary chain tension was adjusted by moving the gearbox away from the engine. Crude, but effective and simple. The switch to a left-foot shift means that the gearbox had to be fixed in position, and Norton take the opportunity to design a new primary chaincase incorporating an electric starter! It is only 1975, after all. The starter is worthy of an article on its own, and soon developed a rep for being an electric non-starter. But the thought was there.

At the same time, the rear wheel grows a disc brake of its own to match the front one, and the Isolastic mounting system is improved by introducing vernier adjustment, in place of the original shimming approach. Ironically, the 1967 prototypes had just such a system, but it was left off early models for cost reasons.

Production dribbles on until 1978, but then the company founders. A legend had been made. ∎

The Knowledge The Knowledge The Knowledge The Knowledge The Knowledge The Knowled
Norton Commando Norton Commando Norton Commando Norton Commando Norton Commando Norton Comma

Norvil's Commando: handbuilt to your spec

which can rust or corrode are replaceable with stainless. And there are some excellent parts suppliers, a fine Owners' Club (with an excellent, informative and entertaining emailing list) and lots of bikes about.

Or of course, you could buy a brand new one. The Norvil Motorcycle Co will build you a Commando to your own spec, and they are very good!

RetroReading

A couple of good books: **British Motorcycles Since 1950, Vol 3,** by Steve Wilson, is excellent on Commandos, and

Norton, by Mick Woollett, is also interesting on the subject. Most other Norton volumes are race-obsessed...

Clubs

The Norton Owners' Club is very good, and strong on Commandos, publishing the invaluable Norton Commando Service Notes, without which life would be so much more of a challenge. Contact them: **c/o Colin Coleman, 110 Skekby Road, Annesley, Woodhouse, Notts NG17 9FF, or at www.noc.co.uk**

Specialists
The Norvil Motorcycle Co; Tel: 01543 278008

Burton Bike Bits; Tel: 01283 534130

Mick Hemmings; Tel: 01604 638505

RGM Motors; Tel: 01946 841517 ∎